Whether you are still in the process of deciding on a therapy, about to begin treatment, or already on it, it is important to remember that many people before you have gone through chemo, that they did manage to cope, and that there are ways that have been developed to help you get through it, too. The same strength that stems from the will to live and enables people to make the tough decision to undergo chemo continues to stand them in good stead during the actual treatment. So do a positive attitude, a good doctor-patient relationship, and a realistic picture of what to expect in the way of results and side effects.

We all learn to cope because we have to—the alternative is much worse. We choose chemotherapy because no matter what the price we pay—in time, money, side effects, and emotional energy—the benefits are greater than being without it. Ultimately it is something within ourselves that allows us to make the extra effort to tough it out.

COPING
WITH
CHEMOTHERAPY

Revised Edition

Nancy Bruning

BALLANTINE BOOKS • NEW YORK

*I would like to dedicate this book to my husband,
my oncologist, my mother, and my friends—
all of whom, in their own ways,
helped me find the strength to cope with chemotherapy.
And to you, the chemotherapy patient,
who helped me find the strength to write it.*

Contents

Acknowledgments

There are so many people who believed in this book and helped me in so many ways that I scarcely know where to begin to offer my appreciation.

Perhaps at the beginning, to the editor of the original Doubleday edition, Fran McCullough, and my agent, Susan Protter, whose encouragement and guidance were instrumental in its inception and indispensable to its completion. To the editor of this edition, Robert Wyatt. Also to my husband, Michael Gross, and to my good friend Kathleen O'Reilly, who read the manuscript, understood the magnitude of the task, and offered valuable support and suggestions when I needed them most.

To the cancer patients who shared with me their experiences with chemotherapy in the hope that others might benefit from them.

My thanks—and admiration—to the oncologists and other cancer care professionals who graciously took time from their busy schedules to answer my questions, in some cases for both the original and revised editions.

From Memorial Sloan-Kettering Cancer Center: Grace Christ, former director of the Department of Social Work; Dr. Thomas Fahey, deputy physician-in-chief; Dr. Richard Gralla, former associate attending physician; Dr. Thomas Hakes, associate attending physician; Patricia Henry, former oncology nurse; Jimmie Holland, M.D., chief of psychiatry; Linda James, former planning analyst of the Department of Strategic Planning; Matthew Loscalzo, assistant director of social service; Donna Park, former assistant director of nursing, ambulatory care; and Sister Rosemary Moynihan, former assistant director of social service and current coordinator of the HIV Mental Health Project at St. Joseph's Hospital and Medical Center, Paterson, N.J.

Pam Felling, staff physical therapist; M. L. Frohling, biofeedback technician; Lisa Logan, clinical dietician; and Regina Schmidt, oncology nurse/team coordinator, all formerly at the Denver Presbyterian Medical Center.

From the University of Texas M.D. Anderson Cancer Center: Katherine Crosson, former director of patient education; Dr. Gabriel Hortobagyi, head of Medical Oncology Breast Service; Mary Hughes, psychiatric clinical nurse specialist; Dr. Irwin Krakoff, head of Division of Medicine; Dr. Peter McLaughlin, associate professor, Department of Hematology; Dr. James A. Niedhart, former chairman of the Department of Medical Oncology; and Dr. Karen Ritchie, chief of psychiatry.

From St. Vincent's Hospital and Medical Center: Dr. Judith Bukberg, clinical associate professor and associate attending physician in psychiatry; and Dr. William Grace, chief of oncology.

Special thanks to New York oncologists Dr. Ward F. Cunningham-Rundles and Dr. Ronald Bash, Los Angeles oncologist Dr. Michael Van Scoy-Mosher, and Dr. Richard Cohen, clinical professor of medicine, University of California—all extraordinary oncologists and remarkable human beings.

I would also like to thank the following: Barbara Blumberg, Linda Anderson, and Betty MacVicar from the National Cancer Institute; Diane Blum, executive director of Cancer Care, Inc.; Dr. Micheal Schachter; Dr. Philip Schulman, associate professor of clinical medicine at North Shore University Hospital; Patricia Fobaire, radiation social worker at Stanford University Medical Center; Dr. Maryl Winningham, exercise physiologist; Dr. Charles Vogel, director of the Comprehensive Cancer Center for the State of Florida; Lari Wenzel, medical psychologist of the Memorial Cancer Institute at Long Beach Memorial Medical Center; Sylvia Weissman, former associate director of social services at Cancer Care, Inc.; Shari Lieberman, New York dietician and nutritionist; Lin Perkin, Denver exercise physiologist; Mr. Nicholas, wig stylist for the Kenneth Beauty Salon of New York; Joseph Rodriguez, general manager of the Vidal Sassoon Salon in New York; Edith Imre, proprietor of Edith Imre Hair Fashions, Inc.; Evelyn Ricki Dienst, professor of psychology at the California School of Professional Psychology; Michael Lerner, president of Commonweal; Susan Liroff, director of the Women's Cancer Center; Barbara Carter, R.N., D.N.Sc.; Mary Wieneke, R.N., M.S.; and Peggy Knight.

Finally, I would like to extend very, very special thanks to Victoria Wells, cofounder and director of the Cancer Support

Community in San Francisco, my new home—I only wish she had been in my life when I was going through chemo in 1980; and to the late Rose Kushner and Elenore Pred, who continue to serve as an inspiration to me and countless other activists who are working to improve the state of cancer care: wish you were here.

Introduction

In 1980, at the age of thirty-one, I discovered I had breast cancer. A biopsy had revealed that the lump that had grown alarmingly large over the last few months was not a cyst—it was a malignancy. In order to save my life—so my surgeon said—I had to have the standard surgical procedure, a modified radical mastectomy, the very next day. Although this removed all the visible tumor, unfortunately some lymph nodes were involved, and this meant that the cancer might have spread to other parts of my body. The only way to kill those stray cancer cells was with chemotherapy, which I was advised to have "just in case."

Without a doubt, I found the idea of chemotherapy more frightening than the surgery I had just been through. The fact was that in spite of major, mutilating, and supposedly life-saving surgery, my surgeon might not have "gotten it all." It wasn't over yet: Cancer might still be somewhere in my body, and I was now being offered a treatment about which I knew very little, and what little I did know was all bad. I had allowed my surgeon to lop off my breast without investigating my options, and, by his own admission, it hadn't worked. I felt betrayed and, mistrustful of medical advice, was not about to be rushed into something else I didn't know a lot about.

So I went to a chemotherapist other than the one recommended by my surgeon. Through sheer luck—referral from a friend of a friend who also had cancer—I found a capable, compassionate cancer specialist whom I liked, respected, and trusted immediately. (And during the course of treatment I grew to like, respect, and trust him even more.) He explained the statistics: Without chemotherapy my chances of remaining disease-free for ten years would be about 15 percent; according to the latest scientific study, published in 1979, the best standard chemotherapy increased my chances to about 70 percent—at least for the next eight years. He described the course of therapy—the scheduling of the drugs and their likely side effects—and then assured me he would do everything he knew, nutritionally and otherwise, to help minimize the side effects. Clearly, 70 percent was better than 15 percent; a quick assessment of the unorthodox therapies revealed no comparative figures, which made those therapies more frightening than chemo. Under the circumstances, I agreed to the plan. I wanted to live, and chemo seemed the best chance there was.

Were I in a position to have to do it all over again, I would. Looking back, chemotherapy was not as bad as I had thought it would be. I continued to work and enjoy most of my usual activities, even though I didn't feel exactly wonderful. I had a relatively hopeful prognosis, I got low-dose chemo under the care of a good physician, and I was surrounded by people who cared. Everyone thought I coped amazingly well, and I suppose I did. But I know I would have coped even better if I had done some things a little differently.

It wasn't until about two years after my treatment was over and life had settled down to a semblance of normality that I could begin to look back at my experience with a critical eye.

I realized after the fact what I couldn't see while I was busy grappling with the awful, earth-shattering possibility of my own death: I realized that I should have been better informed about my disease and its treatment, that I should have been better prepared to deal with some of the side effects, especially the complete hair loss. I realized that I would have coped better if I had had more support than my doctor, family, and friends could give me and that I did not have to suffer alone in my feelings of depression, anxiety, doubt, fear, anger, confusion, sadness, ignorance, and isolation.

I realized, too, that a book about chemotherapy—one that really talked about what it's like, what I might expect, and what could be done to make the experience more bearable—would have been a great comfort to me. As a journalist, I naturally thought that maybe I should be the one to fill this information gap.

Although there were by then several excellent books on cancer and its treatment, there was still nothing for the general audience—patients and their families—that focused solely on chemotherapy. No books were around that helped answer the questions foremost on people's minds: Should I have chemotherapy? And if I do have chemo, how on earth am I going to get through it?

And so the idea and the conviction to write a book on coping with chemotherapy came about, a book based in part on the methods that I found successful and in part on the experiences of others.

Throughout my research—as I absorbed (or tried to absorb) the medical literature and spoke with over fifty cancer specialists, social workers, nurses, and cancer patients all over the country—I learned that chemotherapy is a highly individual matter. There are hundreds of different chemotherapy treatments, and people's diseases, personalities, life circumstances, prognoses, levels of tolerance, and reactions to the drugs can and do vary. So do the will to live and the ability to fight.

Chemotherapy is clearly not for everyone, but anyone who is faced with its mixed blessings should be fully informed before making any decisions about it. No one should accept or refuse, or continue or stop, chemotherapy out of ignorance or fear. The cruel facts are that there are patients who might be helped by chemotherapy but who are not getting it, that there are those who might be better helped by it, and that there are some who are harmed rather than helped by chemotherapy and who shouldn't be getting it at all.

The chemotherapy experience can fall short of what it might be—how it can be used, how it can benefit, and the degree of comfort the patient maintains while undergoing it—because chemotherapy patients suddenly find themselves plunged into a maze without a map. Cancer care for most people is completely foreign territory—full of half-truths, myths, and misconceptions, of personal issues and dilemmas, of complicated new words and procedures, of hot and cold running hope and fear.

But chemotherapy is not what it used to be. If it is given wisely and well to informed patients, chemo can cure some people and extend the comfortable productive life spans of many others.

Since the first Ballantine edition of *Coping with Chemotherapy* was published in 1986, there have been a number of improvements in chemotherapy, making it more beneficial for some people and more tolerable, too. Although these developments are small, incremental steps, there have been enough of them to make a difference and to require a new, updated edition of this book.

For one thing, there are new chemotherapy drugs and new ways of administering them. For another, the cancer profession is finally recognizing the extent of the physical and psychological burdens experienced by patients and their families and acknowledging that these burdens must be considered when treatment choices are made. The realization that in addition to improving the effects of chemo on the cancer they must work harder to reduce the emotional and physical side effects means they are more likely to offer support therapies. Nutrition, exercise, mind-body therapies, and emotional support are becoming much more accepted as adjuncts to chemotherapy drugs. Also, there are several new drugs used along with chemo to reduce the distressing side effects, particularly nausea and vomiting. The new ways of administering the drugs make them not only more effective but less toxic, too.

This information is gradually trickling into the world of chemotherapy, thanks in large part to patients becoming more active in their own care. More and more are asking how the coping process can be made easier, swifter, and better. More and more patients are taking it upon themselves to make sure they are getting the best chemo regimen available and asking their doctors and nurses for help in getting through it as easily as possible. More and more are investigating and taking advantage of ways and people to make their treatment less formidable, to help them, their families, and their friends meet new challenges from a position of strength rather than weakness.

As a chemotherapy patient, you are in dire need of *information* in order to be able to weigh your options sensibly. You need *guidance* so you can help your cancer specialist help you. You need *practical suggestions* to make living under chemotherapy more comfortable. Most of all you need to be *reassured* that others have entered the special world of chemotherapy, have come out the other end, and are managing to adapt to the new life the experience has presented to them. This is what I hope this book will provide.

Ideally, *Coping with Chemotherapy* should be read from beginning to end. But this is a less than ideal world, and you're probably not too interested in the history of chemotherapy if your hair has just begun to fall out in handfuls.

Although I have had many, many patients, family members, nurses, doctors, and other health professionals thank me for writing this book, I have also heard from a few that the book is too frightening. The last thing I want to do is frighten people unnecessarily, but getting a diagnosis of cancer is frightening, too. Yet few people today would say, ''It's best not to tell her.'' Gone are the days when doctors and families felt they needed to protect the poor passive patient, to keep her in the dark about her disease. Why should it be any different when discussing the treatment for the disease?

There's no getting around the fact that chemotherapy can be a highly toxic therapy; not knowing this will not make it less dangerous—only more. This isn't to say that people don't vary in the amount of information they need and want, and it isn't to say that you need to absorb all this information at one time. Too much information, for certain people or at certain times, does not help them cope better—they cope worse.

So, a few words of advice: Be aware that you may not be ready to learn certain details now but may welcome them later. At times you may feel overwhelmed by it all, overloaded with information. If you sense this is happening to you, back off for a while. You don't need to know everything at once—it's not likely you'll be able to process it. But when you *do* need to know, I have tried my best to provide it. I hope you will be able to take from this book what you need, when you need it. Remember that chemotherapy is a young, evolving field, so this book is by no means the final word on this treatment. Nor can it take the place of a qualified physician or other health care professional.

Coping with Chemotherapy is a supplement to your doctor's care and a resource for the many other aspects of cancer in which you may be interested. The book necessarily concentrates on the aspects that are most directly related to the issue at hand— chemotherapy. But where does cancer end and chemotherapy begin? Chemotherapy does not exist in a vacuum: A chemo patient is, after all, a cancer patient. I have touched briefly upon many areas that concern all cancer patients in the hope that this will pique further interest and self-education in this endlessly fascinating subject that will on some level be of concern for the rest of our lives. Volumes have been written about areas I have kept brief, for example, about other forms of therapy and psychosocial concerns. I have also stayed away from childhood cancer, because that is a whole other world that could not have been treated adequately here. Many sources of information about these and related subjects are listed in the Appendices, to which you may want to refer.

Anyone facing chemotherapy surely has a big job ahead. The physical and psychological changes and challenges in your life begin at the time of diagnosis; they may come to a peak sometime during the treatment; and they can continue for long afterward. It is not an easy road you travel, and it may often be a lonely one. *Coping with Chemotherapy* was written for you to turn to again and again, whenever you need information, inspiration, or simply a hand to hold. I hope you will be able to draw strength, comfort, courage, assurance, and wisdom from these pages and the people who have given of themselves in order to help others who are going through a similar difficult time. But no matter how much help you have, it is still up to you and your own strength and determination to make it as you pick your own way along the path to coping with chemotherapy.

Should You Have Chemotherapy?

Coping with chemotherapy begins with the decision to undergo it. This decision is not an easy one, but then, important decisions rarely are. Though you may rely on others for information and advice, ultimately the choice is up to you.

However, whether you are on the threshold of chemotherapy or already well into it, the choice to begin and/or the choice to continue can be made much more wisely and responsibly.

Many patients and cancer care professionals find, for instance, that learning something about cancer is the first step in a sound decision-making process. An understanding of what chemotherapy is, how it works, and its advantages and shortcomings is also essential, as is a realistic picture of its goals, your prognosis, your alternatives, and how chemotherapy fits in with and compares to other forms of treatment. You also need to find a competent, caring cancer specialist (oncologist) who will be responsive to your needs and who will give you the most effective treatment with the fewest possible side effects. Access to the many methods used to support chemotherapy patients is also paramount.

Admittedly, some of these factors carry more weight than others, depending on the individual. But all contribute to your making informed, intelligent choices throughout your therapy, to a basic conviction that you are doing the right thing, and to your having a feeling of control over your life. These are all fundamental to accepting treatment and learning to live with it.

Understanding Cancer

When I was diagnosed with cancer, I knew very little about the disease. That probably put me at a disadvantage. Most cancer patients are in the same position.

No one can expect to become a cancer specialist overnight, but acquiring a basic understanding of your disease is worth the effort and is a necessary preliminary to understanding all cancer therapies. Dr. Richard Gralla, an oncologist, says:

"People try to understand cancer without understanding very much about biology in general. I think people do not understand their disease because they don't understand a little of the basic science that goes into it. And yet you hear people complain that when your doctor tells you something, you have no choice; you have to listen to him. What choice do you have if you don't know very much about these things in general?"

CELL BIOLOGY

Your body is made up of many different types of tissue—skin, muscle, bone, blood, glands, and other organs. The tissues in turn are made up of tiny specialized cells that perform specific functions. Within each cell is a *nucleus* that contains *chromosomes*: There are twenty-three sets of "regular chromosomes" and one set of "sex chromosomes." Each chromosome can contain up to several thousand genes. The genes in turn are made up of *deoxyribonucleic acid* (DNA), which takes the form of two spiraling strands. The DNA can be likened to a foreman who controls the cell's activities; it is the DNA that ultimately makes up the genetic program of each cell.

One of the activities the DNA oversees is that of reproduc-

3

tion. Cells reproduce themselves in order to replace those which have become damaged or have died or if more cells are needed for some special reason. Some cells, like those making up the blood, are replaced more often then others are. For example, the white blood cells are replaced completely every six hours, a rate of production that is stepped up during infection, when a greater than normal quantity of them is needed.

Cells reproduce by division—one cell splits in half to produce a "daughter" cell. There is a time in every cell's life when it reproduces; there is a time when it is "fertile" and a time when it is not. Cells go through four phases during each of their reproductive cycles in which the DNA makes an exact copy of itself to pass on to the nucleus of the next generation. Some types of cells reproduce within hours; others may take days, weeks, months, or years. After division, the cell begins the next four-phase reproductive cycle, perhaps after first passing through a resting phase.

Normal human cells are obedient and altruistic. They "know" when they should reproduce and when they should not. They stay where they belong. They perform whatever functions they are programmed to perform. Whatever their functions and rates of growth, they are for the good of the entire body. (Cells also respond to other stimuli, such as the commands given by the hormones produced in our endocrine glands.)

Cancer cells, however, do not obey the various commands of the body. Unlike normal cells, whose motto might be "One for all and all for one," cancer cells behave as if it were every man for himself. They reproduce wildly, more often than the normal cells that surround them. They are usually unable to perform any useful function for the good of the entire body. On the contrary, they are *malignant*, meaning they invade and injure vital organs of the body, thus interfering with those organs' ability to perform needed functions. In advanced stages of cancer, these cells spread and grow in other parts of the body to wreak havoc there, too.

Though they arise from normal cells, cancer cells usually don't look exactly like the other cells in the tissue of origin. They may be oddly misshapen, have a strange membrane or nucleus, or contain the wrong number of chromosomes.

CAUSES OF CANCER

It is believed that cancer cells arise from normal cells that have undergone a change called *carcinogenesis*. Throughout history there have been various theories as to how the original cancer cell is produced. Recently, researchers have identified and isolated single genes in several types of human cancer called *oncogenes* ("onco" comes from the Greek word *onkos*, meaning "mass" or "tumor"). Many scientists believe that oncogenes are commonly present in our cells but remain dormant unless "turned on" by carcinogens.

It is natural to wonder why such troublemakers exist in the first place. Scientists believe that oncogenes are somehow involved in normal growth and may be needed at some point in human development—before birth, during childhood, or during the healing process—and then are "switched off" when they are no longer needed. Oncogenes, it is believed, become troublemakers only when they are activated by an inherited defect or exposure to an outside agent called a carcinogen. Oncogenes are normally suppressed by "suppressor" genes; in some cases these controlling genes may be missing. Once we know what turns an oncogene on, perhaps we will learn what turns it off. This would open up a whole new area of research that could ultimately lead to a cure for cancer.

The current view also includes the theory that cancer is a two-step process of *initiation* and *promotion*. According to this theory, the initiators prime the cell and so set the stage for cancer development. Initiators include viruses, radiation, and chemicals such as those contained in cigarette tobacco, toxic waste, or food. But these initiated cells are harmless and behave normally and eventually die—they may even be repaired or normalized by the body—unless promoters are also present. Promoters include anything that enhances the effect of an initiator, such as diet, hormones, chemicals, environmental conditions, and an inherited predisposition.

Current theory holds that cells usually require a number of "hits" to switch on the cancer process. This theory looks promising and would help to explain why everyone who smokes doesn't get lung cancer, why all X-ray technicians don't get leukemia, and why a diet of junk food doesn't guarantee the development of gastrointestinal cancer.

HOW CANCER GROWS AND SPREADS

Cancer, as we now understand it, consists of well over a hundred different diseases. These, however, fall into four main categories: carcinomas, lymphomas, leukemias, and sarcomas. *Carcinomas* are the most common—between 85 and 90 percent of all cancers are of this type. They are solid tumors or "lumps" originating in the lining (epithelium) of the organ. Examples are carcinoma of the breast, lung, uterus, intestines, esophagus, stomach, and kidney. *Lymphomas*, cancers of the lymphatic system, cause the spleen and lymph nodes to produce abnormal cells. Lymphomas can cause solid tumors to grow in various parts of the body. *Leukemias* are disseminated (circulating) tumors that involve bone marrow, which is the blood-forming system, where they cause abnormal white blood cells to be produced. *Sarcomas*, the rarest form of the four, are solid tumors that develop on the connective tissue of the muscles, bones, nerves, and other organs.

The carcinomas share a common pattern of growth and spread. Cancer of this type begins as a single abnormal cell, which reproduces itself over and over again until it becomes a mass, or a tumor, at which point it can begin to cause problems for the host. If the cancer has spread to other, distant parts of the body, more problems can arise. Nonmalignant tumors are also sometimes called cancers, though they do not spread unless they become malignant. These tumors are not treated with chemotherapy. The medical profession calls all abnormal growths *lesions* or *neoplasms* and calls precancerous conditions *dysplasia*. The earliest cancer is called *in situ* or *preinvasive cancer*. At this point the cancer is still *localized* and highly curable.

If early cancer goes untreated, it begins to invade the surrounding tissue. Though it is still considered localized and the cure rates are high, *invasive cancer* is a serious condition. The tumor may grow so large that it crowds out the healthy cells, destroys them, and reduces their functions; forms an obstruction in a vital pathway of the body; or exerts dangerous pressure on nearby vital organs. Surgical removal of the tumor is usually still possible as a cure, though some or all of the cancerous organ being invaded may be removed as well.

But cancer is not content to grow and grow in one place; at some point during the growth of a tumor, cancer cells begin to break off. They hitch a ride from the bloodstream or the lymphatic system and circulate freely throughout the body like seeds on the wind. This tendency to spread (metastasize) is perhaps cancer's most frightening and deadliest characteristic. When metastatic or advanced cancer has spread to vital organs such as the brain, bones, liver, or lungs, it cuts off the organ's blood supply or crowds the organ and crushes it. Either way, the organ is no longer able to perform its function. It is not uncommon, for instance, for a woman with metastatic breast cancer to die of liver failure caused by her cancer spreading to that organ. (Even though the cancer is in the liver, it is still breast cancer.)

In general, the longer a tumor exists, the greater the likelihood that it has shed cells and the greater the number of those cells there will be. It is thought that our immune system plays a large role in defending our bodies from cancer, just as it protects us against undesirable creatures such as bacteria and viruses. It is widely believed that the immune system controls early cancer cells routinely, before they reproduce to the point where the cancer is large enough to be detected. The immune system may also be able to control advanced cancer, which would explain how the rare but documented "spontaneous remissions" can happen.

But sometimes the immune system slips up, even at the early stage. There are many reasons why it may not successfully destroy the abnormal cells our bodies are constantly churning out, but they all boil down either to a system that is too weak or to cancer cells that are too clever. The immune system may be weak because of age, stress, overwhelming systemic infection, factors in the environment, or nutritional deficiencies. Cancer itself may suppress the immune response. There may be a constitutional deficiency. Cancer cells have the unique ability to produce a protective coating that fools the immune system into ignoring them. Unfortunately, surgery, radiation, and chemotherapy—three major conventional treatments now used against cancer—can also suppress our natural immunity. (The fourth major form of treatment—immunologic therapy—seeks to do just the opposite and so holds great promise.)

Although our immune system may still battle valiantly against proliferating cancer cells, there may eventually be too many of them and our natural defenses may become overwhelmed. Our immune system has fumbled the ball, so to speak, and outside treatment now may be called upon to try to save the game.

How Cancer Is Treated

In the relatively young field of effective cancer therapy, chemotherapy is still in its infancy. Since no one cancer treatment has proved to be perfect from the standpoint of either effectiveness or undesirable side effects, chemotherapy is rarely offered as the only treatment. The trend more and more is toward using combined modality therapy—chemo in combination with one or more other forms of therapy, usually the conventional therapies of surgery and radiation but sometimes along with the more investigational therapies such as immunotherapy. Recently, aspects of unconventional cancer therapies have come to be taken seriously and integrated into the overall treatment plan.

Though this is a very complex subject when looked at in detail, the fundamentals of chemotherapy are not beyond the grasp of the average person, nor is an understanding of other therapies and how they relate to chemo.

SURGERY

Surgery is the primary treatment for most of the major forms of cancer. However, it is effective alone as a cure only in early, localized solid-tumor cancer. In such cases, the object of the surgery is to physically remove all traces of the malignancy—to "get it all." When, as in my case, there is evidence or good reason to believe that the cancer has spread to distant parts of the body, the object of surgery is to remove as much of the tumor as possible so that additional treatment—radiation, chemotherapy, or immunotherapy—is better able to control or destroy the remaining cells that have escaped the scalpel. Some experts believe, however, that a tumor begins to shed cells from the very beginning of its growth, and so even in "early cancer" there is

8

the possibility of spread. Surgery may cure cancer in these cases because few enough cells were shed for the immune system to handle. Surgery may also be used to remove metastases in some types of cancer and for palliation of symptoms such as blockage or pain. Surgical procedures are used to implant radioactive "seeds" and to implant catheters, ports, and pumps used to administer chemotherapy and other drugs.

A certain percentage of patients do not survive cancer surgery, and pain is frequently present after the extensive surgery that cancer often requires. But perhaps most distressing of all results is the change in body image that surgery leaves in its wake. Many patients say they feel mutilated or somehow "not whole" afterward, especially if the affected area is highly visible, useful, or symbolic. As is the case with chemotherapy, advances in surgery have improved safety and reduced the suffering patients experience after surgery.

RADIATION THERAPY

Radiation therapy, or radiotherapy, is the recommended primary treatment of choice for some forms of cancer, such as early Hodgkin's disease, some lung cancers, and head and neck cancers. It may be used alone for cure, but it is often used in conjunction with surgery or chemotherapy. Radiation is also effective as palliation to relieve symptoms of cancer.

The radiotherapy may be administered from outside the body via machines whose radiation penetrates deep inside the body, avoiding healthy tissue as much as possible. Or it may be internal—a radioactive isotope encapsulated in a container such as a needle, tube, or seed is implanted in the body, either directly into the cancer or nearby. Radioisotopes may also be injected into an organ or into the bloodstream, where they go directly to the tumor.

Radiation therapy changes cancer cells' chemistry with rays or charged particles. When the radiation reaches the tumor cells, it either kills the cells directly or damages the DNA and makes it impossible for the present cells or the next generation of cells to reproduce. In effect, the tumor becomes "sterile."

Radiation has its own set of advantages and drawbacks. Like surgery, this treatment is most effective when it can be used locally. Unlike surgery, it can destroy a tumor without grossly disfiguring the patient; it leaves vital structures intact. It does not work on widely spread metastases unless wide-field radiation is used, but this technique has serious side effects on healthy tissue. Cancers vary greatly in their "radiosensitivity": Radiation is highly effective for certain types of cancers, somewhat effective for some, and not at all effective for others. The tumor must be in a location where the radiation can reach it.

Even with improved technology, some normal tissue does get damaged from radiation. This includes a wide spectrum of side effects that depend upon the area being irradiated, the dose, and your individual constitution. Patients may experience skin reactions such as dryness, itchiness, and burns; loss of hair; lowered energy and appetite; constipation or diarrhea; sore mouth or throat; changes in taste perception; tooth and ear problems; and nausea and vomiting. In addition, radiation has been shown to have the ability to cause leukemia, fertility problems, and birth defects.

CHEMOTHERAPY

You will find a more detailed picture of chemotherapy later in this book, but for now this quick sketch will help you understand where chemo fits in with the other therapies used to treat cancer.

Chemotherapy literally means the treatment of disease with chemicals, or drugs. Usually, though, the term is understood to mean treatment with anticancer drugs. The post–World War II era is generally considered the beginning of its development. Now dozens of drugs are in standard use alone or in many different combinations. In addition, new drugs and new combinations of drugs are constantly being investigated and evaluated and are available to patients participating in clinical trials, and in some cases outside of the trials.

Chemotherapy is unique among the major conventional approaches to cancer treatment because chemicals have the ability to circulate throughout the body. Only chemicals can reach cancer cells that have broken off solid tumors and spread to distant sites and that may be undetectable and/or untouchable by local treatments; only chemicals are useful in treating disseminated tumors of the blood and lymph. Chemotherapy works because it is *cytotoxic*—it poisons the cells, especially those that reproduce rapidly, as cancer cells do. But as with other therapies, chemo doesn't always work. And because normal cells are also vulnerable to varying degrees, there are also many potential side effects, the most common of which are loss of energy, loss of hair, nausea and vomiting, and susceptibility to infection.

Originally, chemotherapy was used only as a last resort after all else had failed. This tactic has changed drastically. Using chemotherapy as a second line of defense, after a recurrence has already happened, is an approach that has failed to improve the survival of many patients with the most common solid tumors. Chemotherapy is being given earlier and earlier during the course of the disease because, as with the other modalities, that is when it works the best. Today chemotherapy may be the treatment of choice to actually cure certain cancers. But a newer strategy is to use chemotherapy as *adjuvant therapy* as soon as possible right after surgery or radiation has "debulked" a tumor or "reduced the tumor burden." It is hoped that when used this way, chemo will prevent or postpone suspected micrometastases from causing a recurrence. Chemotherapy is also being used after surgery to shrink already evident nonoperable metastases. It is sometimes used before surgery to reduce the size of a tumor and make it more operable ("neoadjuvant" chemotherapy) or along with radiation to make a tumor more susceptible. Chemotherapy cures only a few types of cancers; however, even when a cure is not achieved, chemo is enabling people to control their cancer for many years and allowing them to live longer than they would have without it. Though inroads are being made in minimizing the side effects, they are still a problem for many people, and whether the risk is worth the benefit is always an individual choice.

HORMONE THERAPY

Hormones are substances that are naturally produced by our endocrine glands; their job is to stimulate other organs. If a cancer begins in tissues that are affected by hormones, usually the tumor will be affected by them, too. Such tumors are called hormone-sensitive or hormone-dependent; by changing the hormonal environment, we can affect a tumor's growth.

Originally, hormone therapy consisted of the surgical removal of the glands that produced the hormones (ablative surgery). This method is still used. But in addition, synthetic hormones or hormone suppressants are often given alone or along with other anticancer drugs for certain types of cancer, including cancer of the breast, uterus, prostate, thyroid, and kidney and lymphomas, leukemias, and myelomas. Even though their action is very different from that of the other drugs, hormone therapy is a type of chemotherapy. At this time it is not completely understood how hormones or hormone-blocking drugs work. This field is considered experimental, but it is in fact incorporated into many standard treatments. Cancer specialists are beginning to use hormone therapy much more often than in the past, particularly to treat breast cancer. Now tumor cells are routinely tested for hormone sensitivity (hormone receptor assays). These assays help identify women who have tumors that are highly dependent on estrogen or progesterone and so are most likely to benefit from hormone therapy. According to San Francisco's Dr. Richard Cohen, tamoxifen, which blocks estrogen in breast cells, is now the agent of choice for women with positive estrogen receptors, even when they have no lymph node involvement. In postmenopausal women there is evidence that tamoxifen's benefits go beyond controlling the diagnosed cancer and include lowering the risk of cardiovascular disease, osteoporosis, and cancer in the opposite breast. In fact, scientists are so excited by tamoxifen that it is being tested to see if it can prevent breast cancer in healthy women who are at high risk for developing it.

Unlike the other drugs used in chemotherapy, hormone therapy is not cytotoxic to cells—it does not kill them directly. These drugs don't cure, but they may cause long-term remissions or enhance the effect of cytotoxic drugs. Their side effects are usually mild compared with those of their more toxic cousins. In addition to their antitumor activity, hormones may be used to reduce certain side effects of chemotherapy, including loss of appetite, and to increase a sense of well-being.

Though hormone therapy is used for several kinds of cancer because of its relatively few and mild side effects, in this book "chemotherapy" and "anticancer drugs" will refer to the cytotoxic group of drugs, except when hormones are specifically mentioned.

IMMUNOTHERAPY OR BIOLOGICAL THERAPY

Another approach to treating cancer that shows promise is immunotherapy. Immunotherapy is based on the widely held belief that our immune systems, which can recognize and eliminate foreign substances such as bacteria and viruses, also can destroy cancer cells.

Our immune system consists of a complex interplay among many different kinds of cells. These cells have different roles to play and communicate with each other by means of various proteins. Immunotherapy utilizes a number of natural and synthetic substances called biological response modifiers (BRMs) or biologicals, which are known to boost, direct, or restore the body's normal immune system defense mechanisms. Some BRMs themselves have antitumor properties.

This new approach to cancer treatment is appealing because it appears to be more "natural"—its goal is to harness and enhance the body's own ability to take care of itself. The side effects are dissimilar to those of surgery, radiation, and chemotherapy. But immunologic substances have their own set of possible disturbing side effects, including flulike symptoms of chills, fever, nausea, general malaise, and body aches, as well as seizures, ulcers and scarring at the injection site, and even death.

In spite of the brouhaha with which immunology was originally greeted, this approach has not lived up to expectations. Although biological therapy is accepted as treatment for a few cancers, in most instances it is considered to be experimental. Biologicals are most often used along with standard therapy, such as chemotherapy, to help the body recover from the damage done by these treatments and perhaps to prolong a remission and increase survival time.

We are still struggling to understand exactly how BRMs work and why they don't have the dramatic effect that they should in theory. Perhaps the immune system as we understand it doesn't play as large a role in cancer control as we think. There may be other defense mechanisms that also play significant but as yet unrecognized roles. Or perhaps the problem is that the immune system needs more help in recognizing cancer cells, which, after all, are not obviously foreign like viruses or bacteria but are just slightly different from our normal cells.

The main biological therapies being used and investigated are interleukins, interferon, tumor necrosis factor, colony-stimulating factors, and monoclonal antibodies. These therapies are described in the Guide to Anticancer Drugs in the Appendices.

UNCONVENTIONAL THERAPIES

Thus far I have discussed only conventional cancer therapies that are offered by mainstream American medicine. Although some of these therapies are still experimental, the basic approach is "accepted" and they are being investigated under the auspices of major cancer institutions and the National Cancer Institute.

However, there is increasing interest in approaches that fall outside the mainstream. These unconventional cancer therapies are also known as nontraditional, alternative, unorthodox, unproven, alternative, or nontoxic therapies.

In contrast to surgery, radiation, chemotherapy, and current immunologic approaches, which have side effects because they harm normal tissue, alternative therapies are usually nontoxic and noninvasive and do not endanger normal tissue. This, combined with their strong holistic philosophy, makes this approach immensely appealing.

The overwhelming problem with unorthodox therapies is that we are not sure about the possibility of benefit because they have not undergone the kind of scientific support and testing that the standard and experimental mainstream-endorsed therapies have received. Unfortunately, almost all the evidence about their effectiveness is anecdotal or testimonial in nature or remains unpublished by accepted medical journals. The medical mainstream says this lack of concrete proof of efficacy is why it does not recommend these treatments to its cancer patients as primary treatments. Although the direct risk is attractively low, many doctors feel they are indirectly harmful because patients who go for alternative therapy are lured away from effective traditional treatment and possibly a cure.

Patients who are attracted to alternative therapies have nowhere to turn for concrete information about their safety or effectiveness. Until recently the cancer establishment had lumped all these therapies together, branded them as quackery, and dismissed them as totally worthless. Recently, the Office of Technology Assessment, a research arm of the U.S. Congress, commissioned the evaluation of unconventional cancer treatments. The resulting book has been published and is listed along with other sources of information about unconventional therapies in the Resources section of this book. We still don't have scientifically conducted studies on which to base an informed decision, but at least these books shed some light and provide more evenhanded discussions. You will find clear descriptions of the most widely used therapies—what they involve, what they claim, where they are offered, whom to call, and how much they cost. You will also get guidelines for evaluating the treatment as best you can, and you will be able to get a clearer understanding of the history and current state of the field.

Dr. Michael Van Scoy-Mosher says that when patients come to him to discuss unconventional treatments,

"I don't belittle their beliefs—people who explore these therapies tend to be intelligent. If a person wants to do it instead of conventional treatment, but conventional treatment has a lot to offer, I would try to talk her out of it. If conventional treatment has little to offer, I wouldn't take much of a stand. However, I do feel I owe people my honest opinion about these treatments. If she wants to do it in addition to conventional treatment, I would tend to support that because these treatments are relatively nontoxic and if a person believes in it, it helps increase their sense of empowerment and to that extent they are useful."

Still, many people find it a tough decision to make. Michael Lerner, Ph.D., has studied unconventional cancer treatments since 1981, when his father was diagnosed with a life-threatening cancer. He subsequently served as special consultant for the OTA report *Unconventional Cancer Treatments*, and is widely regarded as one of the leading authorities on the objective evaluation of these therapies.

"People ask me, as someone who has studied unconventional cancer therapies, what to do. First, I never recommend therapies to anyone because I am not a physician. Second, the question is very difficult to answer even at a general level because there are so few scientific studies available assessing most of these unconventional therapies. Third, as a general rule, I believe that the open and intrinsically health-promoting spiritual, psychological, nutritional, and physical therapies, undertaken in a balanced way with appropriate professional guidance, can be sensible adjuncts to appropriate mainstream therapies in enhancing health and quality of life. On the other hand, my father never used any of the unconventional therapies that I researched, and he has done exceptionally well with mainstream therapies alone.

"What my whole experience has taught me is that unconventional therapies are not appropriate for everybody with cancer. In fact, I think they are really appropriate only for a minority. Unconventional cancer therapies can be considered most appropriate for cancer patients who are strongly drawn to them, who are inclined to believe in them, who want to be engaged actively in their own treatment, and who have the good sense to integrate the best of these therapies with the best mainstream medicine. At the same time, I usually suggest that cancer patients who are not drawn to unconventional treatments can comfortably put them aside. Until there is robust scientific evidence of real benefit from any therapy, alternative or mainstream, no patient should be pushed in the direction of therapies that have not proved themselves."

You may find it helpful to discuss the issue with a knowledgeable professional. For example, Michael Lerner is the president of an organization called Commonweal, a health and environmental research institute. Located in California, Commonweal offers weeklong retreats designed especially to help people with cancer think through treatment options and make informed, considered decisions. However, it is to be hoped that you will find guidance closer at hand. Even if your oncologist doesn't "believe" in alternative therapies, he or she should at least try to answer any questions you may have and be willing to discuss the issue calmly. Your oncology nurse, the social service department, and the dietary department of your hospital are other potential sources for information. Though it is a subject that is being brought up more and more frequently, some patients may still be afraid to bring up unorthodox therapies to their orthodox health practitioners. It is, however, part of their jobs to be informed and to help you become informed in order to make an intelligent decision—one that is right for you. And it is your right and responsibility to still any doubts you might have about your therapy.

COMBINING THERAPIES

In modern cancer care it is becoming rare to use only one type, or modality, of treatment. Today a combination of two or more is increasingly favored, because one enhances the effect of another or supplies a therapeutic strength where the others are weak. Though the conventional therapies—surgery, radiation, chemotherapy, and immunotherapy—are the most often combined, cancer care providers and their patients are dipping also into the unconventional therapies with greater frequency, enabling them to enjoy the benefits of both and sparing them the agony of making an either/or decision.

It is becoming clear that all nontraditional therapies cannot forever be dismissed as completely worthless in light of continuing revelations about the interrelationship of the immune system, the mind, nutrition, and cancer. As a result, some practicing oncologists are beginning to suggest—or at least not object to—a more "holistic" approach for their patients undergoing traditional therapies.

Although most are still skeptical of claims that these therapies have any anticancer effect, many are increasingly comfortable with the idea that alternative therapies can make chemotherapy an easier treatment to take. Although not all alternative therapies are compatible with chemotherapy, in general this seems to be a reasonable road to take, at least until we have more evidence that any of these alternative therapies alone can help control the disease.

The elements of the alternative approach—emotional support, stress management and reduction, nutrition, and exercise—that are most commonly accepted as useful adjuncts are treated more fully in later sections. When the first edition of this book was published, there was only common sense and a few tantalizing bits of evidence that patients were helped when these therapies were integrated with chemotherapy. But evidence continues to accumulate, and additional studies are ongoing.

For example, a study by Stanford University's David Spiegel, M.D., and colleagues looked at the effect of psychotherapy on survival time and quality of life. Patients who attended support groups lived twice as long as did those who did not. Another example exists in the growing evidence of links between cancer and nutrition and an appreciation of dietary support during chemotherapy. The National Cancer Institute is conducting major studies of the role that nutrients such as specific vitamins and minerals, fiber, and fat play in preventing, inhibiting, or developing cancer.

In China, traditional Chinese medicine (TCM), which consists of acupuncture and herbs, is commonly combined with Western cancer treatments such as chemotherapy. Studies of TCM show that it can improve the immune response; reduce side effects such as nausea, vomiting, and fatigue; and increase the effectiveness of chemotherapy. Many of these studies have been published in English, for example, in the *Chinese Journal of Integrated Traditional and Western Medicine*. The author of the definitive textbook on the subject (see the Resources section) writes: "Chinese medicine [can] minimize or control the side effects caused by radiation and chemotherapy, thus enabling the patient to complete their course of treatment more smoothly." Although knowledgeable practitioners are scarce in the West, there are indications that this is changing.

In addition, some alternative practitioners are softening their stances and adding either chemotherapy or other traditional treatments to their nontoxic programs or referring their patients to mainstream doctors for conventional treatment. Clearly, there is as yet no single "magic bullet" against cancer, and the best approach seems to be an eclectic one.

Perhaps the most persuasive argument for opening up the traditional treatment plan to some elements of the alternative therapies does not rest directly on any claims about their possible anticancer abilities. It lies rather in the fact that some of these practices do foster better overall health, help minimize the side effects of cancer and chemotherapy, and allow patients to participate more actively in their treatment and assume some control over some aspects of their lives. In a medical world that consists largely of our passively waiting around for people in white coats to pump us full of toxic chemicals, doing health-building things for ourselves, preferably under the guidance of a qualified but accessible professional, is a welcome change. (See Chapters 7–9.)

In the June 17, 1982, issue of the *New England Journal of Medicine*, Barrie R. Cassileth, Ph.D., of the University of Pennsylvania Cancer Center, addressed her colleagues:

> "The anti-medicine, pro–self-help bias of the new alternative treatments arises in the context of increasing mistrust and dissatisfaction with the standard healthcare system and with researchers' failure to cure malignant disease. Traditional multimodality care of cancer, often fragmented and associated with a passive role for the patient, contrasts starkly with the active, personalized, nontoxic, home-based alternatives. . . . There is something to be learned from the seductive draw of alternative remedies. We may not wish to recommend wheatgrass therapy or spiritual healing in lieu of chemotherapy, but we might well consider the merits of patients' needs for involvement in their own care, their interest in helping themselves through attention to diet, their requirements for personalized attention to self as opposed to disease."

Understanding Chemotherapy

HOW CHEMOTHERAPY BEGAN

Cancer chemotherapy is part of a long medical tradition of using chemical compounds to treat disease. From natural herbs to sophisticated synthetic substances, effective medicines were usually discovered accidentally, and chemo is no exception.

The lucky accident that made modern cancer chemotherapy possible occurred in 1942, ironically as a result of a war in which millions of people were killed. In that year a U.S. naval vessel sank while in the Naples harbor. When the mustard gas it was carrying exploded, the casualties who had been exposed to the poisonous gas were examined and it was found that large numbers of the cells in their bone marrow had disappeared and that their lymphatic systems had atrophied. The significance of this was not lost on C. P. "Dusty" Rhodes, the chief of the biological branch of the U.S. Army Chemical Warfare Service, who was on leave from Memorial Hospital Cancer Center, where he was the director. He began large-scale testing on animals of hundreds of drugs similar to the poisonous gas that went down with the ship. These drugs were found to inhibit lymphoid tumors in the animals. The drugs were tested on humans with Hodgkin's disease in 1943, and the subjects experienced temporary remissions.

Around the same time that the beneficial effects of nitrogen mustard (mustard gas) were so serendipitously discovered, scientists began to realize they had reached an impasse in cancer treatment. Surgery and radiation were local treatments, inappropriate for systemic, disseminated cancers of and by the blood and lymph systems and ineffective once solid tumors had visibly spread. But more frustrating was the fact that these treatments

19

didn't always cure what appeared to be localized cancer. Scientists theorized, and proved in experiments, that even one or a few surviving cancer cells could result in a recurrence.

Because the preliminary results of the early cancer drugs were so promising, a large-scale search for other drugs that were effective against cancer was begun. In 1955 the National Cancer Institute, an arm of the National Institutes of Health, directed a mammoth screening program. Investigators in England, continental Europe, and Japan participated. Hundreds of thousands of drugs were tested, with forty thousand as the all-time high in 1975. This screening continues today, albeit on a more organized, and smaller, scale. (See pp. 314–319.)

HOW CHEMOTHERAPY WORKS

Chemotherapy is the only scientifically proven method we have that can reach virtually every part of the body to seek and destroy cancer cells that surgery and radiation can't reach and that even sensitive instruments can't see. It is able to penetrate every nook and cranny because it circulates throughout the body just the way the cancer cells do, by flowing through the bloodstream. Once the drug meets up with a cancer cell, it wreaks havoc in a number of ways, which are only partly understood.

Chemotherapy affects the course of cancer by taking advantage of the cancer cell's penchant for constant reproduction. Almost all the drugs used in chemotherapy suppress cancer by somehow altering the cells' DNA and thus their ability to reproduce. Since DNA is most vulnerable to drug interference during the reproductive phases of the life cycle, cancer cells are more likely to be affected than are the bulk of the body's normal cells, which reproduce at a much more relaxed pace. Thus, the very characteristic that makes cancer so dangerous has proved to contribute to its undoing. In scientific terminology, chemotherapy drugs are either "cell-cycle-specific" (lethal to cells only during a specific reproductive phase) or "cell-cycle-nonspecific" (able to sabotage the cells no matter what phase they are in). Dr. Ronald Bash, a New York oncologist, explains it this way: "In a sense, the inner workings of cells (cancerous and otherwise) are like gearboxes; what chemotherapy does is to throw a biochemical monkey wrench into the gearbox causing the machine to grind to a halt—causing the cells to stop working, to die."

WHEN CHEMOTHERAPY DOESN'T WORK

If chemotherapy works at all, you might wonder why it doesn't work all the time. No medicines, not even those for minor ailments, work all the time. Though cancer is admittedly far more complex than athlete's foot, pimples, and headaches, it may be a bit unrealistic to expect a science that has failed to produce surefire cures for these relatively simple conditions to be able consistently to crack a sophisticated disease like cancer. Since cancer is not a foreign invader like bacteria but an aberration of the body's own cells, it is in fact amazing that anticancer drugs work at all.

The reasons chemotherapy may fail are legion. First of all, there may simply be too many cancer cells, growing too rapidly, for the drugs to wipe out or even keep at bay. If the goal is to cure, every single cancer cell must die. If even one cell is left behind and manages to proliferate, the cancer will recur.

Chemotherapy may fail because it works best when there are (1) small numbers of cancer cells that are (2) actively dividing. These conditions are not always present when chemotherapy is given. In "cell kinetics" experiments it has been shown that drugs destroy a constant fraction or percentage of cells, not a constant number. So if there are 10 trillion cancer cells and 99 percent are killed, 100 billion are still left after the first treatment! After the second treatment, 1 billion cells are left, and after the third 10 million remain. The proportion of cells killed is the same, but each time a smaller number of cells is killed. The cells that are resting rather than actively reproducing escape the drugs' killing effects. In between treatments, when it is safe, the resting cells resume production and replace the ones that have been killed. Chemotherapy under the best of conditions is a matter of taking two steps forward and one step back, and it is very difficult to make enough progress to kill off every single cell.

Kinetic studies have also shown that as the cancer increases in size—the more cells it contains—the number of actively reproducing cells (the "growth fraction") decreases. The higher the number you start with, the harder and longer you have to work at getting the cell population down, because not only are there more cells to kill, there are more cells that are not vulnerable.

In addition, the tumor may not be getting enough of the drug to affect it. Once a drug is injected or ingested, it becomes extremely diluted and weak because it is distributed throughout the bloodstream and the tissues of the body. Many tumors do not have a robust blood supply, so drugs may not reach them. In addition, it has been problematic getting drugs at all to the brain and central nervous system because there is a natural protective mechanism called the blood-brain barrier, which prevents drugs from passing through, though there are now ways of getting around this.

Time works against chemotherapy. The body quickly begins to break down toxic substances such as chemotherapy drugs into less harmful substances—another protective mechanism—and then excretes them. Cancer cells and normal cells alike can therefore be exposed to the drugs for just a minimum amount of time—minutes. Since many drugs work on cells only during a specific phase of the reproductive cycle, only cells that happen to be in the vulnerable phase will be affected during the few minutes that the drug is viable. Cells in other cycles escape unscathed.

Because the drugs are also highly toxic to normal cells, we are limited in the amounts of the drugs we can tolerate, and it is said that chemotherapy drugs have a low "therapeutic index." The difference in the amount needed to kill more cancer cells than healthy cells is low; sometimes it is zero. Many promising drugs never get off the drawing board because the amount that would totally wipe out a tumor would also kill the patient.

Third, there is the possibility of drug resistance. A single tumor is usually heterogeneous (composed of a mixture of different cells). Each type of cell varies in its ability to metastasize, its susceptibility to drugs, and its other properties. It is thought that the older a tumor is, the more likely it is to be heterogeneous, thus increasing the probability that some of the cells will be resistant to drugs. In addition, resistance develops as the treatment progresses—just as insects, bacteria, and other unwanted creatures adapt and become less sensitive to pesticides and antibiotics. Eventually all the sensitive cells may be killed, but the sturdy ones remain and continue to grow. There is chilling evidence that indicates that the very things that kill most patients—metastases—do not arise from the random survival of cells released from the primary tumor, as was previously thought. Rather, they are growths of special tumor cells that are particularly heterogeneous, clever, and resistant to the body's own defenses as well as to drugs. It is as if the parent tumor sent its brightest, most athletic children out into the world of the cancer patient's body.

These are the main reasons why chemotherapy is more effective the earlier it is used and after the bulk of the tumor has been reduced by surgery or radiation. They help explain why chemotherapy doesn't always work and why it sometimes works only a little bit, for a little while.

GETTING CHEMOTHERAPY TO WORK BETTER

However, researchers have been experimenting with ways to get around these roadblocks and make chemo more effective. Of course, new drugs are always being developed and tested, but drugs already in use could be used differently to squeeze out additional benefit. Dr. Richard Cohen explains that there are two basic approaches: to enhance the effectiveness of the drugs and to "rescue" the patient after high-dose chemo.

One trend is to give more intense doses, but over a shorter period of time. This may prove to be at least as effective as conventional doses and scheduling but less toxic to the patient as well as less life-disrupting because of the shortened duration of the therapy.

Another technique is to infuse the chemo continuously over a long period of time. With the development of portable pumps, chemo can be administered round the clock, maintaining effective levels of the drug in the blood. This approach offers the possibility that more cancer cells will be killed while reducing the toxicity and avoiding the necessity of long stays in the hospital.

A related approach is based on the principle of *chronobiology*, the study of body cycles that govern our susceptibility to disease and our response to medications. According to oncologist Dr. William Hrushesky, a major proponent and researcher of this approach to cancer treatment, studies have shown that the toxicity and effectiveness of many chemotherapy drugs depend on the time of administration. This effect has been documented for twenty anticancer drugs in animals and for five or six in humans. With the advent of the portable, programmable drug pump, "chronotherapeutics" is becoming a more practical option for delivering drugs. (This principle may also change the way surgery is done: A well-publicized study found that premenopausal women who received mastectomies around the time of menstruation had four times the risk of recurrence and death compared with women who were operated on during the middle of the menstrual cycle. Another study found that survival increased from 54 percent to 84 percent when surgery was timed according to the menstrual cycle.)

As a result of the principle that if a little bit of a drug is good, then more is better, researchers are pushing the doses of anticancer drugs as close to the edge as possible. They then "rescue" the patient from potentially fatal side effects by either bringing back injured cells or stopping the side effect from happening. For example, Leucovorin is a drug used to block the toxicity of high-dose methotrexate. An exciting development in colorectal cancer is the discovery that immune-stimulating drug levamisole increases the effect of the anticancer drug 5-FU.

The bone marrow, where blood cells are made, is usually the organ that is most sensitive to chemo. Damaged bone marrow leaves the patient susceptible to infections, which can be fatal. This limits the doses that can be given and therefore has been a major obstacle to administering high-dose chemo. However, there are now substances that help counteract bone marrow damage. Colony-stimulating factors (CSFs) are biological material that can rescue the individual from low white cell counts and perhaps prevent these counts from dipping too low in the first place. Erythropoietin is another biological material that is helpful in treating low red blood cell counts.

Bone marrow transplantation illustrates another dramatic avenue for pushing the dose very high (ten to twenty times higher than conventional doses) and then rescuing the patient. After chemo, the wiped-out bone marrow is replaced with marrow that has been harvested from either the patient or a donor. As a result, the immune system cells have a chance to regenerate, and the very high risk of a potentially fatal infection is lowered. This procedure is discussed more fully in the Appendices.

Other research involves drug resistance. Although we don't yet understand all the mechanisms behind drug resistance, one mechanism is that of the molecular "pump." Cancer cells have a protein on their surface that ejects chemo drugs out of a cell before the drug can damage it. We are at the point where we can measure the amount of the protein pump a cancer has, and researchers are trying to devise ways to overcome it. For example, cyclosporins bind to the protein and prevent the drugs from being pumped out of the cancer cells.

Hyperthermia is an approach that is based on the theory that fever is a key element in our biological defense against disease. Laboratory tests have shown that heat can stimulate the white blood cells in the immune system to attack cancer cells, but hyperthermia has been disappointing when used alone.

However, it seems that heat also sensitizes cancer cells and makes them more vulnerable to radiation and some forms of chemotherapy, so combining it with these therapies may increase their effectiveness without increasing toxicity. Research is ongoing using hyperthermia devices that heat just the tumor, the region of the body in which the tumor exists, and the whole body.

Another use of heat combined with chemotherapy is called hyperthermic perfusion. It involves isolating an arm or a leg from the circulatory system and infusing the limb with a heated chemotherapy solution. Much higher doses of cancer-killing drugs can be given this way, directly to the tumor and to sites where the cancer is most likely to spread, without exposing the rest of the body to the toxic effects of the drug.

Other methods being used experimentally include instilling drugs into specific body cavities where tumors occur and "chemoembolization," which enables the drug to be delivered directly to the tumor and block the tumor's blood supply at the same time.

Researchers have also been experimenting with ways to tailor chemotherapy treatments to each individual tumor rather than relying on the drugs' past performance with other people's tumors. For example, drugs may be pretested on a cancer outside the patient's body. A sample of the cancer is taken, and the cells are grown in test tubes. Several anticancer drugs are applied to the different groups of cells. The drugs that are more effective against the samples are used on the patient. It is hoped that tailoring techniques will take some of the guesswork out of chemotherapy, thus saving valuable time and needless wear and tear on the patient. Tailoring techniques suffer, however, from great expense, and it should be added that responses in test tubes do not necessarily correlate well with responses in humans.

Dr. Richard Cohen adds that the tests currently available take more time than most patients can wait to start treatment. He feels that tailoring the treatment this way is best saved for people who have had chemo and want to know what other drugs might be useful if the tumor recurs or breaks through in the future.

Getting the Best Care

It is the rare cancer patient who doesn't get thrown into a panic after the initial diagnosis, who can think clearly and doesn't feel rushed into treatment, who feels well enough to be able to explore treatment possibilities. It is natural to feel overwhelmed and to want to trust and rely on the first doctor you see. But in most cases of cancer it is not dangerous to take a few weeks to digest the new earth-shattering information. On the contrary, since the quality of chemotherapy varies so greatly, it is wise to take steps to see that you get the correct diagnosis and the best treatment. The quality and quantity of your life depend on it. A little effort now can make a big difference later on.

The single most important step you can take is to see at least one qualified cancer specialist. Only then is it possible to get a firm, detailed diagnosis and a clear picture of your options. The final steps are to evaluate the doctor(s) and treatment(s) and choose whichever suit you individually.

WHY A CANCER SPECIALIST (ONCOLOGIST)?

Most often, suspicion of cancer or the initial diagnosis comes from a family doctor or a specialist in the area in which symptoms are first noted, such as a gynecologist for a breast lump or a urologist for a testicular or prostate problem. These physicians may be very qualified in their particular fields and may have treated cancer years ago. However, in most cases they are not the best qualified to treat cancer today. Because cancer diagnosis and treatment have become so complex, a special branch of medicine called *oncology* has evolved. Oncology (from the Greek *onkos* meaning "lump" and *logos* meaning "study") is a branch of medicine that deals specifically with the study of tumors. A doctor who is specially trained in this field is called an *oncologist*.

Today there are surgical oncologists, radiation oncologists, and medical oncologists (chemotherapists), any and all of whom may be on your treatment team and involved in your overall treatment plan. Oncologists usually refer patients to their colleagues in the other subspecialities when they feel a multidisciplinary approach would be beneficial. For instance, a surgical oncologist may refer a patient to a medical oncologist for chemotherapy. My own experience followed this familiar pattern: My gynecologist examined my breast lump and sent me to a surgical oncologist who specialized in treating breast disease; my surgeon then suggested that I see a medical oncologist for further treatment.

Whereas your primary concern is your chemotherapist, it is to your advantage if all the members of your treatment team are well qualified. The best oncologists are usually board-eligible or board-certified, meaning they have been formally trained in this subspeciality and, if certified, have passed an exam.

Your surgeon, therefore, should be board-certified and should specialize in your type of cancer. If radiotherapy is on the agenda, you should go to a board-certified radiation oncologist rather than to a radiologist whose training is mostly in diagnosis.

And anyone who has been told that he or she needs chemotherapy should be seen by a board-certified or board-eligible medical oncologist who has received two years of formal training in the use of chemotherapeutic drugs.

Hematologists—internists with special training in the area of blood—were the first to use chemotherapy because the earliest cancers treated with drugs were the "blood cancers." Board-certified or board-eligible hematologists with training and experience in cancer still treat the disease. Though they may continue to confine themselves to blood cancers (leukemias, lymphomas, and myelomas), many also treat other cancers. More recently, board-certified internists who are not hematologists have begun specializing in chemotherapy.

The importance of being seen by at least one qualified medical oncologist cannot be overemphasized. Dr. Ronald Bash, a hematologist/oncologist in New York, says: "There are a lot of people giving chemotherapy who probably shouldn't. Some surgeons, for example, particularly for colon and breast cancer."

Chemotherapeutic drugs are highly toxic, and the treatment can be very complex. Their use changes rapidly, and the prescribing doctor not only must know of their availability but must know how to use them and how to monitor the patient properly to achieve the ultimate therapeutic effect without severe toxicity. Only a physician who specializes in the use of these drugs is qualified to evaluate a cancer, to choose a chemotherapy protocol, and in most cases to administer or supervise the administration of the drugs. If you like, you can still be seen by your primary physician during your cancer treatment and sometimes even receive some portion of your treatment from him, provided that it is under the guidance of an oncologist.

WHERE TO FIND AN ONCOLOGIST

Comprehensive cancer centers, university hospitals, large medical centers, clinics, community hospitals, and oncologists in private practice all offer chemotherapy. If your primary physician has not referred you to an oncologist, ask him or her for a recommendation or locate a cancer specialist through another doctor you know, your friends or relatives, your local county medical society, the nursing department at a local teaching hospital, the National Cancer Institute (NCI), or the American Cancer Society. You can also contact a hospital directly.

In deciding which of these facilities is best for you, getting the best *treatment* should not be confused with getting the best overall *care*; it is possible to get the most effective, up-to-date technical treatment while other needs go unheeded or unfulfilled. For example, some believe a big cancer center is the place for the seriously ill, but others argue eloquently that these are the very people who should stay closer to home and family. Factors you will need to consider are medical (Which offers the most effective program?), practical (How far am I willing to travel for treatment? How much can I pay?), and personal (Do I like the environment? Do I have a good relationship with the doctor?). The effectiveness of the treatments, the personalities of the doctors, the surroundings in which the treatment is administered, and the cost can and do vary greatly. So does the distance you can travel—be it within your own town, to the next city, or all the way to another state. Fortunately, most chemotherapy is given on an outpatient basis—only the heaviest doses of the most toxic drugs and some highly experimental treatments require hospitalization.

It is a common prejudice that the best place to go for cancer treatment is a big cancer center or university hospital. That is where the famous cancer specialists are, where the most modern technology is available, and where the latest experimental therapies are developed and administered. Yet few people understand what they are or what they have to offer. "Comprehensive cancer center" is a special designation given by the National Cancer Institute to cancer centers that have met certain strict, specific criteria. "Clinical cancer centers" are similar to comprehensive cancer centers in many ways, but they do not have the same status.

At one time, cancer centers *did* offer the very best cancer treatment across the board. However, this is no longer necessarily true. Most cancer patients can get just as good chemotherapy—even investigational drugs—much closer to home. The comprehensive cancer centers are the first to admit this.

One of the staff members at Memorial Sloan-Kettering, one of the best-known cancer centers, notes that

> "Hundreds of physicians pass through cancer centers like Memorial each year to train in oncology and then go out all over the country. We screen patients who call to determine whether they really need to come here or can be diagnosed and treated closer to home. Patients may come in for a diagnosis and we may develop and assign a chemotherapy protocol, but then we try to make every effort to locate local physicians and facilities where they can get high-quality treatment."

A physician at Memorial says, "People who should come into a cancer center are people with unusual diseases, or people who need a treatment that cannot be offered at another facility."

Cancer centers have physicians and teams who subspecialize in particular cancers. In certain cases it may be wise for you to contact a cancer center to confirm a complicated diagnosis or to get a second opinion about the treatment of choice.

It might also be advantageous for you to begin your treatment at a cancer center, particularly if you require specialized surgery, radiation, or treatment with technical equipment not available at your local hospital. If you are a patient who has an unusual or difficult cancer and for whom the standard or the locally available investigational treatment leaves much to be desired, it may definitely be worthwhile for you to travel to see highly experienced specialists.

Dr. Thomas Fahey of Memorial Sloan-Kettering in New York City uses breast cancer as an example. The consensus recommendation from the NCI is that patients with positive lymph nodes and most patients with negative lymph nodes should receive adjuvant chemo. But only 30 percent of node-negative women will relapse. What's needed is to determine who that 30 percent will be. Some factors, such as the size and location of a tumor in the breast, can be assessed anywhere. But, he says, "There are biochemical and molecular biological factors that may further identify the high-risk women." And for that you probably need to go to a comprehensive cancer center or major university hospital that has a breast cancer center for a detailed workup of the characteristics of your tumor.

Another valid reason for seeking treatment at a cancer center is when it is the only source for a particular experimental program that might help you. You or your local physician can easily find this out through a computerized cancer information service called Physicians' Data Query (PDQ), which is available through MEDLARS, the National Library of Medicine's data base subscribed to by hospitals, cancer centers, and medical libraries. This program provides physicians and patients in communities all over the United States with access to the most up-to-date information about your type of cancer, standard and experimental treatment, the prognosis for survival, and physicians who offer state-of-the-art treatment. In some geographic areas with multiethnic populations, information is available in languages other than English.

Many Cancer Information Service offices (1-800-4-CANCER) provide PDQ searches and will send you a computer printout, or you can ask them to explain how to obtain direct computer access to the data base. Through PDQ you can get descriptions of current NCI-supported clinical trials (studies) that are accepting patients, including information about the objectives of the study, medical eligibility requirements, details of the treatment program, and the names and addresses of the physicians and facilities conducting the study.

Although PDQ is available to the general public, in order to get the most out of this service you must be prepared with detailed information about your diagnosis (such as stage and cell type). In addition, the printout is written in technical terms.

Therefore, it is helpful if you and your doctor go over it together and discuss your treatment options.

Cancer centers are not the only source for all investigational protocols—just for the newest and most experimental ones. The NCI and the cancer centers are trying very hard to see that the public has greater access to the clinical research advances possible only through participating in investigational trials. Regional cooperative oncology groups and the Community Clinical Oncology Program (CCOP), established in 1983, allow more patients to enter clinical studies in their own communities.

There are no studies that compare the quality of chemotherapy treatments across the board between cancer centers and local facilities. But there was a reassuring study that compared the results of the Eastern Cooperative Oncology Group consisting of university hospitals or major treatment centers with 100 affiliates consisting of small community hospitals and private-practice groups of physicians. The study involved ninety-seven randomized trials and 4,506 patients. The authors of the report of the study, published in the May 6, 1982, issue of the *New England Journal of Medicine*, wrote that "over a wide spectrum of studies and sites, the survival, response, toxicity, and data quality were the same in affiliates as in major treatment centers."

University hospitals and large medical centers can offer the same advantages as comprehensive cancer centers: up-to-date experimental treatment by highly experienced cancer specialists and a full range of on-site support services such as blood transfusions, laboratory testing, and social services. They also have many of the same disadvantages of being treated away from home and all that that entails: commuting long distances, which is disruptive and lonely and possibly uncomfortable and depressing; the hassle and expense of making travel arrangements and perhaps accommodations for outpatients and/or accompanying family members; and surroundings that are strange and frightening.

Finally, some patients in large facilities complain that the surroundings are too cold and clinical, that the care is on the impersonal side, that they feel like cancer case #342, with outpatients being seen more by the nurses than by the doctors and inpatients being seen by a number of different doctors, including experienced residents, interns, and students. Dr. Thomas Fahey comments on this. "To me, when you talk about support for the chemotherapy patient, it begins when you give the treatment. The environment is important."

Community hospitals often supply excellent care for the average cancer patient. The faces seem friendlier, the care more personalized. Some people are more secure being treated at smaller hospitals where they feel there is more compassion, more respect for their wishes, and less risk of becoming guinea pigs or being lost in the shuffle. However, some feel that small hospitals are more likely to have limited or substandard services. They may not offer the treatment plan you need, although they can often follow through with a chemotherapy protocol that has been established by more experienced specialists at larger hospitals, medical centers, or cancer centers. In most cases adults can be treated in an accredited community hospital under experienced direction.

Medical oncologists in private practice can give you highly personalized care in relatively small, unthreatening, comfortable surroundings. Sometimes they can be more than comfortable. My oncologist had his practice in a lovely brick town house. The office was furnished just like a real home—carpet, wallpaper, sofas, chairs, even chamber music tapes that played continually—and had a lovely garden I could gaze upon before and during my treatment. It was very comfortable, and that made me feel more at ease than a run-of-the-mill doctor's office would have.

Dr. Michael Van Scoy-Mosher, an oncologist at Cedars-Sinai Medical Center in Los Angeles, says:

"I personally think that the most personalized care is in a private office. I may be prejudiced, but I've spent six years at three different cancer centers, so I do have a basis for comparison. A patient may be sent to a center for a consultation, but he may be seen and evaluated by an intern. At the very end, the attending physician may only briefly see the patient. What value is that? Mostly there's a difference in orientation. The private practitioner should be concerned only with the patient sitting in the room with him. In a cancer center, there is concern for today's patient, but there is just as much concern with the research that will help the patient who will show up five or six years later. That's fine, but I don't want to be that patient sitting in the room today. It's not the way I would want to be treated, and it's not the way I'd want my mother to be treated. However, certain patients really feel confident only if they are treated in a 'Cancer Center.' If I perceive this to be the case, I will recommend a referral there.''

Some physicians have a private practice in a hospital and full and immediate access to backup services. Some patients feel safer with physicians in a group practice or in a hospital because this means they are subject to constant review by their peers. At any rate, an oncologist should be affiliated with an accredited hospital in case a patient needs to be admitted. One who was trained at a cancer center and retains his or her ties is more likely to provide up-to-date treatment; private physicians often consult with their fellow specialists at a cancer center and follow through on a treatment program initiated there.

It makes very little sense, then, for the majority of cancer patients to travel very far from home for their chemotherapy treatments. Community facilities do not necessarily provide treatment that is inferior to the treatment you would receive at a large cancer center. And you have the advantage of keeping the disruption of your life to a minimum. (As one health professional asserted, ''Patients will do anything to be able to go home at night.'') It cannot be stressed enough, however, that you should be treated by a competent medical oncologist, not a local physician who does not specialize in this field.

YOUR RELATIONSHIP WITH YOUR ONCOLOGIST

Cancer is a frightening disease that may require treatment or monitoring for the rest of your life. The kind of relationship you have with your oncologist can have a great influence on the way you feel about your disease and its treatment. I was very resistant to the idea of having chemotherapy at first. But I found a wonderful oncologist who trained at a comprehensive cancer center and who was kind, was open to questions, spoke regular English (not medicalese), and even had a sense of humor. I trusted and liked him, and that made the therapy less scary to start and more bearable as it wore on.

The ideal is to find a crackerjack oncologist who really knows his stuff *and* who treats you like a human being. It is advisable to ask yourself whether your doctor has the unique combination of good credentials, a compatible personality and approach, and the willingness to answer questions. Is he or she a doctor you will be able to stand seeing every week, or every two weeks, or every month for the duration of your therapy? A doctor you will be able to forgive for making you so miserable with such regularity? Good credentials are no guarantee that the doctor will treat the person as well as the disease, that you will get the best treatment and overall care.

In his book *The Facts about Cancer*, Charles F. McKhann describes the special relationship a cancer patient has with the oncologist:

> "It is a long-term association that should sustain you through good and bad, through the uncertainties of the disease, the triumphs of success, or the disappointment of unsuccessful treatment, possibly to the very end of life. A doctor in whom you have real confidence can make everything more tolerable. Your doctor should be compassionate, understanding, and interested in you as a person as well as a patient. If honesty is important to you, insist that you discuss your disease and its treatment openly. For many, however, it is more important to know that the lines of communication are open and that your questions will be answered than to ask actual questions at the time. While it is not essential for good care, it helps a lot to have a doctor whom you really like."

Other pluses to look for are a cheerful pleasant office, twenty-four-hour phone accessibility, and laboratory diagnostic tools such as X rays and blood testing nearby or in the office.

Most patients would agree with this portrait of the ideal doctor-patient relationship. I know that the relationship I had with my oncologist shaped my attitude and ability to cope. While I was researching this book, my heart went out to patients who said their oncologists fell far short of the mark. Many complained about a coldness, a lack of communication and information, and a lack of respect and concern, about doctors who seem too busy, use technical language, or keep patients waiting very long times without apology or explanation. These failings add insult to injury; chemotherapy is enough of a strain without oncologists adding to their patients' difficulties, as these patients attest:

> "I have a theory that all oncologists are Serbo-Croatian terrorists-in-training just waiting to get their terrorist licenses and practicing medicine in the meantime. They are so single-

minded in their ruthless pursuit of knowledge; they strike me more as scientists doing battle than as caring professionals.''

"I hate the patronizing attitude doctors have toward women. I wonder how much oncologists really listen to their patients.''

"The man had no bedside manner. There was only one reason I stayed with him: I had been told he was a big man in his field and the best in the city.''

Although an overly technical approach and lack of human warmth has been a charge leveled at the medical profession in general, there seems to be widespread agreement among patients and doctors alike that there is a unique ''oncology personality.''

Dr. William Grace, chief of oncology at St. Vincent's Hospital in New York City, says:

"Oncologists can be a funny breed. Many can be highly intellectual, cold, and terribly austere. They can be rather abrasive and not quite so personable. This may be due to the fact that they are involved in an emotionally stressful field for a long period of time.''

Dr. Ronald Bash adds:

"Communicating with patients is an art, and some oncologists can't do it. Sometimes it's a question of doctors lapsing into medical jargon. Most patients don't understand it, and it builds a little barrier between them and their doctors, of which most doctors are unaware.

"If you don't talk to your patients, you can insulate yourself from their pain. But I think part of the 'territory' is accepting the fact that a number of your patients are going to suffer. You have to learn to endure it, too. The justification that some physicians make for their distant attitude is that if you don't achieve that distance, you end up getting very nuts. That's only partly true at best.''

My oncologist says he feels ''a tremendous outrage'' on the behalf of cancer patients:

"It's a chilling disease. Almost all individuals who have it are inclined to feel shut out from the rest of the world, and to a large extent they are. And because of its nature, taking care of dying patients tends to have a chilling effect on the doctor. It is very easy to be very cold and unable to hear about the aspects of life that are difficult. It's extremely important for the oncologist to be available and willing to hear about that aspect of human existence. There are other people to whom the patient can talk, but it's difficult if the doctor is just writing the prescription and coldly looking at the size of the tumor."

Cancer Care, Inc., a New York–based social service agency, recommends that in addition to his or her medical competence, you look for the following professional and personal qualities in a doctor:

- Has twenty-four-hour telephone accessibility (including coverage for weekends, vacations, emergencies)
- Allows enough time for you to explain and discuss issues
- Has reasonable fees and will discuss them with you
- Keeps a careful record system and a smooth appointment schedule
- Takes a detailed history
- Clearly and openly explains your diagnosis, treatment, and condition (if that's what you want)
- Answers your questions in person and on the telephone
- Does not use medical jargon when speaking to you
- Is someone you feel you can trust
- Occasionally indicates that he or she does not know something but suggests referrals to specialists or a consultation with another physician if necessary

Many experienced patients and professionals point out the importance of entering into a partnership with your oncologist in which you regard each other as equals. They also believe that being reasonably knowledgeable about cancer and its treatment is an intrinsic part of coping. It is our right and responsibility to be active, informed participants in the vital decisions affecting our bodies. The more we know, the less of the unknown there is to fear and the better partners we make in the treatment process, because we meet our doctors on more equal footing. And as our understanding about the potentials and limitations of oncology improves, so will our relations with our doctors improve.

Diane Blum, executive director of Cancer Care, Inc., points out that any relationship is a two-way street, that a patient has to have some responsibility, too. "You have to know how to work with the doctor—when to ask questions, how to ask, how to use his or her time well," she says. "Doctors are people like everybody else. We try to teach patients how to work with them in a cooperative way—it doesn't help anybody to be adversarial."

A satisfactory relationship between you and your oncologist can make any chemotherapy plan go more easily and the continual follow-up more pleasant. Honesty, compatibility, mutual respect, an openness and willingness to communicate, trust, confidence—these are the characteristics of any good relationship. They are difficult but not impossible to attain, provided that both parties are aware of their importance and are willing to encourage each other to cultivate them.

The Oncology Nurse

Oncology nurses are becoming more and more involved in all aspects of the care of cancer patients, and many patients will have a nurse or nurses as part of their treatment team. Oncology nurses have specialized training in giving chemotherapy, managing the side effects, controlling pain, and providing emotional support and education to cancer patients and their families. Nurses are often involved in the initial planning of a chemo plan, such as choosing the anticancer drugs and antinausea medications. Since they provide direct care, they are often aware of changes and information that can affect your treatment.

Oncology nurses have become such an integral part of the treatment team that patients may see them more often and for longer periods of time than they see their doctors. Many patients find their nurse to be a valuable ally, a crucial source of strength and support as well as a link with their doctor. Oncology nurses can sometimes provide you with a humanizing touch that might otherwise be missing in an oncology practice and so make up for a doctor who doesn't provide you with everything you need.

IS CHEMOTHERAPY FOR YOU?

Patients usually regard undertaking chemotherapy with *at least* some ambivalence and fear. Having a clear, realistic picture of its goals, the costs versus the benefits, and your alternatives will help you avoid either a distortedly negative picture that may lead to a refusal of beneficial treatment or an overly optimistic or naive one that may lead you to accept a treatment you decide is ultimately not worth it to you and may lead to disappointment and resentment.

Dr. Michael Van Scoy-Mosher emphasizes:

"Chemotherapy is a true cooperative venture. The physician gives the drugs, but the real work is done by the patient. As much as I might sympathize, it is the patient who undergoes the unpleasant therapy. I think whatever it takes—seeing five different doctors, reading in libraries, talking to other people—it's very important that they become convinced that they have made the right decision.

"A lot of the bad things you hear about chemotherapy occur because of the ways it's been misused, such as giving chemotherapy to people whom there's no chance in the world that chemotherapy is going to help—give them chemotherapy for a couple of months, make them bald, make them sicker, and they die anyway. You know what the family of the patient says later? 'That chemotherapy—it's the worst thing in the world. It killed my brother—he was bald, he was sick.' It's hard to separate out the effects of the cancer from those of chemotherapy anyway, but the next time someone in that family gets cancer, they say they will never take chemotherapy. So I have to undo all of that if they've had a previous experience."

These patients bear him out:

"I had a fear of chemo. I knew people who had had it, and I had seen the horrors of chemo. They just faded away, they became skeletons. But now I realize that there's chemo, and then there's chemo. I just thought everybody got the same thing and reacted the same way."

"I didn't like the idea that they were going to be putting poison in my system. I was upset about losing my hair—all my life it's been my pride. I had already had gum problems and now they were telling me I might have mouth sores. As soon as the doctor left the room, I had this terrific outburst of crying. I cried and cried and really got it out of my system. And then I started to get hold of myself. If I didn't have it, and God forbid something happens a few years from now, I'm going to say to myself, 'You know you had a shot at this and you didn't take it.' It took me forty-five minutes to decide that I was going to take the best shot I had.''

Others accept the doctor's advice without question, without finding out what they are getting into:

"My regular medical GP, the surgeon, and the oncologist had a conference and decided I should have chemo. I was kind of stupid in a way. When they suggested I have it, I said, 'Oh sure,' not knowing what chemo was like. I knew nothing about it. I figured if other people have gone through it, it can't be that bad.''

The decision to undergo chemotherapy cannot be made intelligently, confidently, and wholeheartedly unless you have gathered enough pertinent information to allow you to assess the risks versus the benefits for *you*, in your particular circumstances. Your doctor is your *primary* source for medical information and advice. But it should not be left up to him to make the final decision—or to provide all the information you might need in order to make the choice. Dr. Van Scoy-Mosher, for instance, finds that

"In very controversial uses of chemotherapy some patients want me to make the decision for them. Much as they try to pin me down, I won't do it. All I can do is spell out the arguments for and against a treatment. Often they'll leave the office more anxious than when they came in; but the important issue to me is that they've made their own decisions. And in the long run, patients who have made their own decisions do quite well with those decisions. I know that a year or two from then, they'll feel good about it.''

Dr. Richard Gralla says:

"For me, I have to talk to my patients a little bit to find out what their outlook is. I have to tell them what we have available and what their alternatives are. I can give my advice, what I would do if I were they. But ultimately the choice comes to them. Some people say, 'I want this treatment if it's a one in a thousand chance.' Some people say that a three out of four chance of benefit is not good enough. But that's their individual philosophy. I can just tell them their alternatives and help them make that decision.

"What's really important is that people have to understand that when a cure is not possible, then improvement of quality of life becomes a major goal. Some people say they want their quality of life, not their length of life necessarily, to be improved. Usually the two go hand in hand. It is rare to get one without the other, and I think a lot of people don't realize that. If you have improvement in time, usually you have improvement in quality of life during that time."

THE GOALS OF CHEMOTHERAPY

In the early days chemotherapy was considered a last resort to be used only in terminal cases when all else had failed to cure a cancer. When it was used so late in the disease, there was every reason for pessimism, for the chances were indeed slim that drugs—or anything—could save anyone at the eleventh hour. Chemotherapy then was highly experimental, and there were relatively few drugs to experiment with. No wonder it usually failed to perform the hoped-for miracles that surgery and radiation had also failed to perform, and it was said that the treatment was worse than the disease.

Although, as my oncologist admits, "Chemotherapy is still in the Stone Age," new drugs have been introduced and we are learning more and more about these drugs and the diseases they treat. We know more about how and when to administer them, how much of them to give in what combinations and for how long, what side effects to expect and what to do about them, and what kind of response to expect. For instance, we now know that chemotherapy works best when used as early as possible, when the tumor burden is small. The increasing success of chemotherapy is due in large part to the big push toward giving it much sooner than was previously thought advisable, even when there is no detectable spread. However, there are also drugs that are effective even in the more advanced, metastatic cancers.

Today chemotherapy is being used to achieve goals that are

both more optimistic and realistic than those in the past. It is being used to

- Cure some cancers outright
- Induce long-term remissions in others
- Decrease the likelihood of a recurrence or spread after surgery or radiation (adjuvant chemotherapy) in potentially curable cancers
- Slow the growth and alleviate symptoms such as pain (palliation) in incurable or recurrent cancers
- Shrink large tumors to operable size
- Make radiation more effective

According to the National Cancer Institute, the overall cancer survival rate for "serious" forms of cancer is approximately 50 percent. The survival rate used is the "relative survival rate"—the percentage of people who can expect to reach the five-year mark or are curable. This rate has been adjusted to take normal life expectancy into consideration and to factor in deaths from other causes, such as heart disease and accidents. "Nonserious" cancers—nonmelanoma skin cancer and in situ cervical cancer—are highly curable and are not included.

Since this is a book about coping with chemotherapy, I would be remiss if I didn't include a discussion of the uncertainties and controversies surrounding the treatment. It's no secret that chemo has had it critics, and not just among the proponents of alternative therapies. Many mainstream scientists disagree with the National Cancer Institute's estimate that conventional treatments now cure half of U.S. patients and that this figure continues to rise thanks to advances in treatment.

For example, in 1986 a report coauthored by John C. Bailar III, a biostatician and epidemiologist who worked for twenty years at the NCI, was published in the *New England Journal of Medicine*. The authors found that mortality rates hadn't improved since the 1950s; that statistical improvements in the number of "cured" patients were largely due to earlier diagnosis, not treatment advances; and that the most significant advances have occurred only in relatively rare forms of cancer. The report concluded that "some thirty-five years of intense effort focused largely on improving treatment must be considered a failure."

In 1987 the U.S. Congress's General Accounting Office (GAO) released a study of the years 1950 to 1982 that basically confirmed Bailar's conclusions. "Progress has been made," the report said, "but not as great as that reported." The GAO did not challenge the data on survival rates but did question their interpretation; it cited earlier detection as a factor, plus changes in the way data were compiled as reasons why the amount of "true" progress appeared inflated.

Dr. Vincent DeVita, Jr., who was director of NCI at the time, replied that the figures did not reflect recent treatment advances that would become evident in the future. Chemotherapy has certainly had stunning results in some cancers, such as Hodgkin's disease and childhood and testicular cancer.

In 1990 a West German biostatician named Ulrich Abel, who had worked for ten years helping cancer doctors conduct research, evaluated chemotherapy studies published all over the world. He found that overall there is no conclusive scientific evidence that chemotherapy appreciably extends the lives of patients suffering from the most common cancers. Another of his findings relates to the definition of success. In most clinical trials, it is defined in terms of the "response rate." Most patients interpret this as a "survival rate" when it actually means that the tumor has shrunk partly or completely, which doesn't necessarily correlate with a longer survival time.

Shortly after Abel's report was published, a prominent West German oncologist, Dr. Kurt Hossfeld, was interviewed in *Der Spiegel.* During the interview he admitted that in chemotherapy, "[T]here is no black and white. It is largely a gray area. For those who understand chemotherapy, the decision to use it, or not use it, is an insanely difficult one."

If you, like me, find these criticisms and issues disturbing, I encourage you to discuss them with your oncologist in relation to your individual disease and prognosis. In the meantime, here's a closer look at the goals of chemotherapy.

To Cure Cancer

In cancer treatment, no word is more controversial than the word "cure." This is so because in the first place it is difficult to cure cancer and in the second it is difficult to know when it has been cured. Even when doctors are reasonably sure that a cure has been accomplished, the nature of the disease makes it difficult to confirm this with the certainty with which one can proclaim, for instance, that a case of bronchitis has been cured. With cancer—a varied, capricious, tenacious disease—it's not quite so simple.

Part of the problem is that cancers grow at different rates.

Their progress is unpredictable. They may grow back slowly or astoundingly fast after a seemingly successful course of treatment has been completed. Take, for example, the frequently heard term "five-year survival," which is often equated with a cure. Some patients believe once they have passed the five-year mark, they are cured once and for all. Others are under the impression that even though they have been disease-free all that time, their disease will reoccur after five years are up.

In actuality, once some cancer patients pass this benchmark and are without symptoms, they *can* breathe more easily because the chances for a recurrence are sharply diminished. However, while this is true for *some* cancers, it is by no means true for *all*. With some, it takes less time to start talking about a cure.

In the case of some cancers, such as leukemia, Burkitt's lymphoma, and testicular cancer, two years is enough time to pronounce a cure. With others, such as breast, thyroid, and bladder cancer, and with melanoma, eight to ten or more years must pass before we can begin to entertain thoughts of a cure. However, even with these stubborn types, the chance of a recurrence decreases with each passing year. Statistically, patients who survive for five years after diagnosis have, on the average, an 85 percent chance of surviving for twenty years. Five-year survival rates, then, have some meaning for some cancers and are useful when one is talking in terms of general averages. It is not an arbitrary cutoff date, but neither is it some universal magic number.

Compounding the growth-rate problem is the newness of much of the treatment. How do you know if someone is cured if the therapy is only five years old? If even a single cancer cell escapes treatment, it may reproduce and form a recurrence somewhere—perhaps twenty years down the line. Modern organized, scientifically controlled chemotherapy is just twenty years old; some forms are only a few years old when they reach patients, and newer experimental therapies have even less of a track record.

Therefore, doctors would much rather stick to terms such as "no evidence of disease" (NED) and "remission." NED or full remission means that the patient has no cancer that is detectable using the techniques that are currently available. Since a person can be alive after five (or ten) years and still have (undetected or detected) cancer, these are much more cautious, though more accurate and realistic, terms that are usually used for several years after treatment.

Most chemotherapy given with an intent to cure widespread cancer is aggressive, high-dose, and highly toxic. The side effects can be severe, and complications requiring hospitalization are more common. However, because the chances are so good for a cure, most people feel the risks are worth it. For them, the time lost to chemotherapy—usually a year or less—is a reasonable price to pay for the chance of living out a normal life span.

To Prevent or Delay a Recurrence or Spread (Adjuvant Chemotherapy)

Chemotherapy is being given earlier and earlier in some types of cancers, before metastases are detectable. When the drugs are administered soon after surgery or radiotherapy has eradicated the bulk of the tumor, the chances are high that the drugs will be able to mop up the microscopic stragglers left behind. The goal is to wipe out the small numbers of circulating cells before they have time to mature and grow into secondary tumors. Thus, a recurrence is at least delayed; time may prove it to be prevented altogether and the patient cured.

The concept of adjuvant chemotherapy began to be tested only in the early 1970s. But since then evidence has been accumulating to show that it does work in several cancers—mostly children's cancers such as Wilms' tumor and osteogenic carcinoma. Many women have also responded to adjuvant chemotherapy for breast cancer. As of this writing, adjuvant chemotherapy for colon cancer also shows promise.

Adjuvant chemotherapy should be given only to people whose disease has been carefully diagnosed and who have a high risk of recurrence, and only when there are drugs available that have been proved effective against their type of cancer. This is the case with breast cancer when there are more than four positive lymph nodes—a woman has a 75 percent chance of a recurrence within ten years even though a mastectomy or lumpectomy plus radiation removed all detectable traces of cancer—and in osteogenic sarcoma, which has an 80 percent chance of recurring with lung metastases within a year after surgery. However, the encouraging results of adjuvant chemo studies with these cancers suggest that other cancers may respond as well because it is now suspected that microscopic colonies of cancer cells are present in the majority of cancer patients with solid tumors.

Historically, in breast cancer, adjuvant chemotherapy has

been given to women who are at high risk for recurrence because the cancer has entered their lymph nodes. But 30 percent of women who have no lymph node involvement will also have a recurrence, and recent studies show that some of these women may also benefit from adjuvant chemotherapy. But it makes little sense to treat every breast cancer patient so that a few may gain. Although some tests do exist, we need to develop better ways to determine who among these groups has the highest risk of a recurrence and therefore the greatest chance of benefit.

Adjuvant chemo is being given in an increasing number of cases, but the practice is controversial because we can't say with certainty who will benefit and because it may prove to be more harmful than beneficial: In some cancers patients have actually done worse, and the cancer recurs earlier and with greater frequency than in patients who have not had the drugs. (No one knows why, but perhaps it is because the drugs weaken the body too much.)

The decision to undergo adjuvant chemotherapy is in some ways harder to make than that for other types of chemo. The chances are overwhelming that the micrometastases are there, but there's always a chance that there is no spread or that the body will be able to control the remaining cancer cells naturally. This is chemotherapy as an insurance policy, and it is difficult to justify at the time because there's no concrete proof, except for past experience and statistical probability, that cancer is still there. The patient feels well, there is no discernible disease, and he or she may undergo all those side effects for nothing. Dr. Van Scoy-Mosher's concern that his patients understand adjuvant chemotherapy led him to write a booklet for his breast cancer patients who receive this type of therapy. He is aware that it presents quite unique and troublesome issues:

"I find adjuvant chemotherapy for breast cancer is one of the most interesting and challenging things in the world to give. Because the questions that come up all the time are: How do you know it's needed? How do you know it's working? The only news in adjuvant chemotherapy is bad news. As long as I find nothing, that's good news.

"I make it clear to patients that I don't know if they need it—there's no way of knowing because the surgery might have cured them to start with. And as years go by and the patient remains fine, I'll never know whether that's because of the therapy or whether she would have been fine anyway.

And if that bothers me, I can imagine how it would make the patient crazy: The therapy's a drag, you get sick, maybe you didn't need it. At some level, you're going to have to take this on faith: that my educated guess is the right one."

Lari Wenzel, Ph.D., medical psychologist at Long Beach Memorial Medical Center, thinks:

"People who undergo this type of therapy have a great will to live. They also have some advantages. They know that they will not be on these drugs forever: It is not an infinite process. They know that their disease is fairly local or in an early stage. I think it really helps to tackle something like chemotherapy knowing that your chances of getting well are so great. The decision to choose chemotherapy is much different for people with advanced disease. They must hope for disease control and palliation."

To Control Cancer

Even when a cancer isn't cured, it may be controlled for a time by chemotherapy. The goals here are to stop or slow down the growth of a tumor or shrink it at least partially (partial remission) and to alleviate any pain, bleeding, obstruction, or other symptoms of the cancer (palliation). As a result, some patients feel better and live longer.

Although, as we have seen, cancer can be a curable disease, the idea of controlling cancer so people can still live with it reflects one current medical view of cancer as a chronic disease. By definition, a chronic disease is not curable; however, it is treatable, and people don't usually die from it right away. Dr. Charles Vogel of the University of Miami's Comprehensive Cancer Center explains:

"When one speaks about incurable cancer, as in the case of some metastatic disease, that's a chronic disease. But even with people who have had a recurrence, though we usually can't cure them, we can maintain these people's normal lifestyles, without hospitalization, for three, four, five, eight, or ten years. This isn't commonly realized even by my medical colleagues. There is a gestalt that equates cancer with imminent death. When we talk about chronic disease, we talk about people with arthritis, congestive heart failure, emphysema, multiple sclerosis. You can't cure these, but you can give people drugs and keep them functioning. Many types of cancer fit into that category."

When chemotherapy for palliation is offered, it is crucial to weigh the severity of the symptoms against the toxicity of the drug and the expected response rate to the drug. Also considered are the patient's age and general health, the cost of treatment, and where it will be given. When cure is not a realistic hope, the minuses may outweigh the pluses. It may not be worthwhile to begin or continue treatment if a few extra months of life are spent feeling nauseated, vomiting, and being away from family and friends.

Cure, preventing or delaying recurrence, and palliation—these are the main goals of chemotherapy, and it is important that you understand the difference. As Dr. Thomas Hakes, a physician at Memorial Sloan-Kettering in New York, says, "When you're trying to decide whether to go on chemotherapy or not, you should have a clear understanding of what you are trying to accomplish. People often have unrealistic expectations."

According to a 1989 issue of the *Medical Letter on Drugs and Therapeutics*, chemotherapy (which may include hormone therapy) has *major activity* in these types of cancer: acute lymphocytic leukemia (ALL), acute myelogenous leukemia (AML), breast cancer, choriocarcinoma, embryonal rhabdomyosarcoma, Ewing's sarcoma, hairy-cell leukemia, Hodgkin's disease, small-cell (oat-cell) lung cancer, and non-Hodgkin's lymphoma—Burkitt's lymphoma, diffuse large-cell lymphoma, osteogenic sarcoma, testicular cancer, and Wilms's tumor. Diseases in which chemotherapy has *moderate activity* are adrenocortical carcinoma, bladder cancer, brain cancer, cervical cancer, chronic lymphocytic leukemia, chronic myelogenous leukemia (CML), endometrial cancer, gastric cancer, head and neck cancer (squamous cell), islet-cell carcinoma, Kaposi's sarcoma (AIDS-related), mycosis fungoides, myeloma, neuroblastoma, and non-Hodgkin's lymphoma—follicular lymphoma, ovarian cancer, prostate cancer, retinoblastoma, and soft tissue sarcomas in adults. Diseases in which chemo has *minor activity* are colorectal cancer (however, as of this writing, a new combination chemotherapy is having a much better response than earlier chemo regimens), liver cancer, lung cancer (non-small-cell), melanoma, pancreatic cancer, and kidney cancer.

After asking your oncologist what the goal is in your case, you can also ask what the likelihood is of achieving that goal.

The response rate varies from treatment to treatment; the average rate at which patients respond to a specific treatment is based on a statistical analysis of past experience, and this rate differs in different treatments. For example, the cure rate may be 50 percent or more, as in Hodgkin's disease or metastatic testicular cancer; or there may be a 15 percent chance of temporary improvement, as with metastatic melanoma. Awareness of such response rates and of what is meant by "response" can be useful when one is deciding upon a treatment.

But beware of the doctor who tells you how long you have to live; even though the doctor may be correct statistically, patients and their cancers are highly individual. Statistics are based on average figures for a group of patients with the same type and stage of cancer who get the same treatment. To get this average number, patients who lived much shorter periods of time and those who lived much longer were included. While statistical comparisons are valuable for comparing overall results of treatments, no one can ever say with certainty at which end of the spectrum any one particular patient will fall. Dr. Philip Schulman, an oncologist at North Shore University Hospital in New York, feels that "percentages simply don't mean anything. Each individual is either 100 percent or zero percent. Nobody wants to gamble with his or her life, and that's what percentages are."

OTHER FACTORS

Whether you're a gambler or not, percentages are not the only issue. Dr. Van Scoy-Mosher enumerates some of the many other factors that influence patients' decisions to have chemotherapy or not:

"You have to consider the cancer and the stage, the symptoms or problems with cancer they are having, what kind of longevity they are likely to have, the question of them getting much sicker from the cancer—these are medical issues.

"There's a real dilemma in evaluating the cost-benefit ratio: What's the realistic goal of this therapy—what am I likely to do *for* the patient as opposed to what am I likely to do *to* the patient? How do you balance those two things? Is a little longer life, but a sicker one, worth it? Or is just the chance of a longer life worth the certainty of a lot of side effects?

"Then there is a whole set of issues related to the individual person—age, psychology, expectations, family structure, which is something very important—some are under a lot of pressure from their family to take chemo. You have to blend all these.

"It's a complex decision to make in some patients; other situations are fairly clear-cut to me. If a person has advanced Hodgkin's disease, I know realistically I can probably cure him with chemicals. Assuming he wants to live, I don't see a big dilemma there. If there's a person with breast cancer with positive nodes, I am quite convinced that chemotherapy is a good idea and will recommend it very strongly. Then there are the marginal situations where chemotherapy may or may not help for a short period of time. Here's when you have to consider the other factors. Then there are other situations where I think chemotherapy is far more likely to make someone worse than better. The decision not to give chemotherapy is easy in those patients. What's harder is telling them."

Chemotherapy, for instance, is not for anyone whose diagnosis has not been confirmed via biopsy, whose tumor has not been staged and graded via X rays, scans, and other diagnostic tests. In addition, chemo may be too much of a strain on you physically and mentally if your general health is weak. Poor nutritional status or digestion, liver or kidney problems, infection, and other conditions may preclude, postpone, or modify the treatment with chemotherapy.

Dr. Gralla thinks this is a "very important point." He says:

"Chemotherapy works best in people who are not greatly disabled by the cancer. There's a certain point beyond which I don't believe chemotherapy is a good choice for a patient. If there's a chance that it will do more harm than good, I try to talk with the patients and their families and explain the situation. If they insist—'I really want the treatment'—I can say, 'We can try to get you up to the point where you're strong enough for chemo—use antibiotics, nutrition, pain medicine. Then maybe yes. But I'm not comfortable giving you this, I don't think it's a good idea.'

"Sometimes I'm criticized by my colleagues outside this hospital because in general I will not treat people's lung cancer with drugs unless they are capable of being an outpatient. If somebody's bedridden, then they're usually too sick for drug therapy for lung cancer. This is not the case with some other cancers such as leukemia or lymphoma. But you have to know the patient and find out what his or her philosophy is. Everybody's different, both in terms of outlook and physical condition at the time of presentation."

To help you make this all-important decision, you can refer to any one of several comprehensive books on cancer care. These include Malin Dollinger and Ernest Rosenbaum, *Everyone's Guide to Cancer Therapy*, and Marion Morra and Eve Potts, *Choices*. They contain individual chapters on specific cancers and their treatments and are excellent sources of information about the many aspects of cancer. (These and other books are listed in the Bibliography.) You may also find it helpful to go to a medical library and read articles about your cancer that have been published in professional journals within the last three years. These may be difficult for the average person to understand, but they will provide the names of doctors and institutions that specialize in your type of cancer and that you can contact for advice.

Ideally, the therapy and its ramifications should be discussed with one or more people who are close to you and who will be involved in your life while you undergo the treatment. They are the ones who can help support you during treatment if and when you need it. Together with a few health professionals whose judgment you trust—nurses, social workers, your family doctor—they can form a network of helpers who can offer to gather facts about alternative therapies, including alternative chemo protocols, support services, side effects, and economics. They can also help sort out conflicting information, evaluate and "translate" technical information, and participate in your making decisions based on that information.

I decided to have chemo because it seemed to be my best chance to continue to live and be well, to be cured. Even though I knew that there would be side effects and that chemo was no guarantee, it was still the lesser of two evils. People decide to have chemo because they believe it will give them something they need and want. What it gives in return might be a cure, it might be a few extra years of life or a more comfortable life, it might only be hope that makes life bearable. Whatever the reason, it is a positive choice, a vote for life, which seems more precious because it is being threatened, and a vow to fight to the best of your ability to enjoy your life for as long as you can.

Many people are alive today because they decided the risk of chemotherapy was worth taking. Many others have lived beyond expectation, long enough to accomplish important goals such as completing the writing of a book, seeing a daughter graduate from college, or enjoying the birth of a grandson. Even those who were not cured were able to share a few more precious moments with people close to them, buy extra time to come to grips with their illness, take care of business, say good-bye.

Elenore Pred is a prime example. Seven years after an initial diagnosis of breast cancer, she suffered a recurrence. Chemotherapy kept her alive far longer than expected—over three years. It allowed her extra time with her grandchildren and time to become an advocate for breast cancer patients. She founded Breast Cancer Action, an education and advocacy organization. In a little over one year Elenore and her organization became nationally prominent in the effort to get medical policymakers to pay more attention to the disease. Although toward the end, as toxicity took its toll, Elenore felt that three years on chemo was "a hell of a way to live," she also realized that it allowed her to make a difference and leave behind a powerful legacy.

Barbara Blumberg, formerly a public health educator with the National Cancer Institute's Cancer Information Service, sums up her attitude this way:

> "In the past few years there have been a lot of different things done to help patients get through the drugs, from new anti-emetic [antinausea] drugs to people recognizing that some of the nonmedical methods to help people relax are really useful.
>
> "We know so little, but we do know there are a lot of treatments that do a lot of good for a lot of people with cancer. If I had cancer and could have chemotherapy, those are the statistics I would go by. I know I'm a person, not a statistic, but look at all the people who have done well."

Questions to Ask about Your Chemotherapy Program

This checklist of questions is based in part on suggestions from the National Cancer Institute. The questions are a good starting point; you may have others of your own.

- Why do I need chemotherapy?
- What are the pros and cons (benefits and risks)?
- How successful is this treatment for the type of cancer I have?
- Are there other treatments for my type of cancer?
- When will my chemotherapy begin?

- Who will be giving me the treatments?
- Where will I receive my treatments?
- How long will I need chemotherapy?
- What drug or drugs will I be taking?
- How will they be given?
- Will I be able to work while I have chemotherapy?
- What kinds of tests will I need?
- What are the possible side effects?
- Are there any long-term side effects?
- What should I do if I have side effects?
- Are there any side effects I should report right away?
- May I take other medicines while I'm having chemotherapy?
- May I drink alcohol, such as wine, beer, or cocktails?
- Are there any foods I should avoid?
- Is there anything I should not try to do during treatment?
- How much will the treatment cost? How will payment be handled?

IS STANDARD OR INVESTIGATIONAL CHEMOTHERAPY FOR YOU?

Standard Chemotherapy

It has been estimated by the National Cancer Institute and others that 250,000 to 400,000 people receive chemotherapy each year. Most of them receive the standard therapy for their particular form of cancer: the drug or combination of drugs that has been proved to be the best treatment available "off the shelf." All drugs used in standard treatment have been tested to the satisfaction of the Food and Drug Administration and approved for use. The medical profession is confident that it knows enough about the side effects so that these drugs pose an acceptable amount of risk in relation to the benefits they offer. No formal consent form needs to be signed for standard therapy; the physician simply tells the patient what the known possible risks and benefits are, and if the patient accepts the treatment, it is begun soon afterward.

However, standard therapy does not work for every cancer patient or may have only a minimal effect; in some cancers, no effective standard therapy exists. These patients are usually offered new experimental chemotherapy that may be more effective.

Experimental or Investigational Chemotherapy

Each year approximately 30,000 patients receive experimental, or investigational, treatments. Formal experiments are called clinical trials; in effect, they put new, promising treatments on trial. If one proves itself to be more effective than any standard treatment, it, too, becomes standard. And if a treatment is at least equal to other established treatments but is toxic in a different way, it becomes an alternative standard therapy useful for some patients.

There are many kinds of clinical trials. They range from studies of ways to prevent, detect and diagnose, control, and treat cancer to studies of the psychological impact of the disease and ways to improve the patient's comfort and quality of life (including pain control). There are also studies of support therapies, such as the impact of support groups. However, most trials evaluate innovations in treatment: surgery, radiation, chemotherapy, and immunotherapy either alone or in combination.

In chemotherapy, studies are needed to test each new drug individually, to test drugs in new combinations, to test using standard drugs in new ways, and to directly compare two types of treatments, each of which is known to be effective. The development and widespread use of a new drug is a long, complex, expensive process involving testing cancer in test tubes, laboratory animals, and humans. Human testing itself goes through three phases. Occasionally, experimental cancer drugs are available outside clinical trials. For more details about the approval process and outside trials, see pp. 314–319.

Since less is known about the new drugs being tested than about the old standard drugs, it is difficult, if not impossible to come up with a realistic cost-benefit ratio. Because of this, some people derisively call those who participate in trials "guinea pigs." In some small sense, they are. But real guinea pigs are not asked to sign consent forms; they are not given any options in their treatments. People are. It is true that human subjects are taking a gamble, but it should be their informed decision to do so. Participating in an investigational trial gives patients an opportunity to receive state-of-the-art treatment—imperfections and all—that would not otherwise be available and that can make a vast difference in their prognoses. Though these studies can vary tremendously in their risk to the patient, there is always an implied double benefit: Both the patient and the discipline of medical oncology can gain. In addition, some feel that a patient gets better all-around treatment in a clinical trial because there are strict criteria for control. The diagnosis must be specific and confirmed, the staging complete, and the required laboratory tests done. Patients are thoroughly monitored during and after treatment. This is true even if a patient is randomized—assigned by chance—to a standard therapy.

As a result of investigational chemotherapy, some people are helped, some are cured, but many are not. Some get sicker because of the drugs, and some even die because of them. (However, patient deaths are still more frequently caused by the cancer than by the investigational drug.)

Experimental chemotherapy is given by "investigators"—physicians who are usually highly trained and qualified to specialize in cancer care and who conduct studies. They must have access to laboratory and hospital support facilities. If the therapy is very new and highly experimental, it may be given only at comprehensive cancer centers or university hospitals. Recently more and more investigational therapies have become available from physicians at community hospitals or physicians in private practice. These physicians usually would not normally have enough patients of their own to complete a study. To overcome this deficit, cooperative oncology groups have been established. Doctors who are members participate in cooperative studies that include patients in other cities with similar cancers. A program called CCOP (Community Clinical Oncology Program) has been instituted to involve more local physicians. Cooperative group studies and their affiliated CCOP-member studies help ensure that enough patients will be found to complete the study and to make experimental treatment available to a larger segment of the population. There are also minority-based community programs in a dozen states. Your local physician can make arrangements for you to be included in a study.

Costs are a major concern of patients and their families. In some cases patients undergoing investigational therapies are treated without charge. However, different arrangements and policies exist at different institutions, and of course, insurance coverage varies. Patients should freely discuss what costs are involved in their cases ahead of time. Not everyone who applies will be accepted. You must fit the eligibility criteria as to type and stage of cancer, general condition, and previous treatment.

Federally funded and federally regulated clinical trials must first be approved by an institutional review board (IRB) at the institution where the study is to take place. IRBs, designed to protect patients, are made up of scientists, doctors, clergy, and other people from the local community. An IRB reviews a study to see that it is well designed with safeguards for patients and that the risks are reasonable in relation to the potential benefits.

Anyone who enters an investigational study must sign an "informed consent" form. These vary from institution to institution and from group to group, but in general the form tells the patient the known possible side effects and the possible benefits to be expected from the treatment.

Informed consent forms are written by the institution or group conducting the study. To ensure adequacy and accuracy, each form is reviewed and approved by the institution's own IRB and then by the NCI. Thus, many experts have examined it before the patient is asked to sign and the study can proceed.

If you are contemplating investigational therapy, the informed consent form should be only a jumping-off point for healthy discussions between you and your doctor. Study it carefully. It may not contain all the information you need to make your decision. If you want to know more, ask your doctor. He or she should be willing to explain the treatment thoroughly and honestly tell you what benefits you might derive. In all cases, be sure there is no alternative therapy that you might prefer. Ask about what is already known about the drug—whether it has worked for other cancer patients and what the rare side effects might be. Find out how many people with your type of cancer have received the therapy and how many have responded. Knowing that others were helped by this treatment might influence your decision, no matter what the risks. Remember, you have the right to refuse this treatment or to discontinue it at any time.

You might want to consider experimental therapy simply because it's better than doing nothing. If you are the type of person who refuses to give up, who will try anything to live longer, investigational therapy may provide you with more than a physical therapy—it can help you psychologically. Some patients' motivation is the emotional satisfaction they derive from knowing that they are helping others who might benefit from the therapy in the future.

Dr. Thomas Hakes explains:

"A person who gets an investigational drug is someone for whom we have exhausted all standard therapy or for whom standard therapy is ineffective. At this point we can only treat the patients symptomatically to try and make them comfortable and allow them to go about their business as best they can. Or we can try investigational drugs, which we certainly cannot guarantee are going to help. By their very nature they're not likely to help because we go through ten or fifteen investigational drugs for every one that turns out to be useful. A lot of people don't want them, but a surprising number of people do.''

In general, the further along the investigation is, the higher the likelihood that you will benefit. In phase I, the chances are small. Usually very little is known about the drug. Therapeutic effect may be seen in phase I, but since doses may be below the ideal therapeutic range, positive results often do not occur even with drugs that later prove to be effective. An estimated 10 percent of patients respond to phase I drugs.

A doctor who offers a patient a phase I investigational drug is saying in effect: ''We know of nothing that will help you. But we have a new drug that might. It might also make you worse, and you might die sooner than you would without it. But if you take it, I will be watching you very carefully to try to prevent anything really bad from happening.'' Some of these adverse reactions may not be predictable from the animal studies—mice, rats, dogs, and apes do not react exactly like human beings. These preclinical studies usually do reveal liver and kidney toxicity, but they may not alert investigators to possible damage to the central nervous system, heart, lungs, and skin in humans.

Toward the end of a phase I trial some encouraging data might have come in about the drug, and you might be able to find out if the drug has helped anyone else, particularly with your type of cancer. In addition, more will be known about the range of therapeutic dosage. This bit of knowledge can significantly shift the odds in your favor.

Since there is no accepted form of effective treatment for people who are offered phase I drugs, some may prefer to have no therapeutic treatment. They may prefer to let the disease run its course without the additional discomfort that chemotherapy can bring.

It is a bold, brave soul who accepts phase I treatment. In their book *Cancer Care*, Drs. Harold Glucksberg and Jack W. Singer write:

''We urge that you carefully consider whether you want to enter a phase I trial. We definitely do not feel it is worthwhile for you to travel to a medical center not in your community to receive a phase I drug. If the drug is available in your community, there are only two reasons for trying it: It offers hope and it may help others with cancer."

For phase II subjects, the outlook is better. At least most of the side effects and dose limitations are known. Still, it is usually uncertain whether the drug is effective in human cancers, let alone which types are most likely to respond. So the chances that you will benefit are still rather small. However, it is possible that someone with your type of cancer did respond to this drug. In the early stages of a phase II study there may be some positive data from phase I, and in the later stages of a phase II there may be some good news from the previous studies done in this phase. So ask your doctor—if you happen along at the end of a phase II that has shown good responses to your type of cancer, it could mean a dramatic difference in your prognosis.

A doctor who offers a patient a phase II drug is saying: "We have very little standard therapy that can help you. We think we have a drug that might work in your type of cancer; we're pretty sure it won't harm you severely, and we have a very good idea of what to watch out for."

Phase III trials are usually the safest of all. By the time a drug reaches this point, it has gone through enough testing so that doctors know which cancers respond to it, how much they respond, and what the side effects are. You are offered this treatment only if it has already been proved effective in your type of cancer.

If you are offered phase III treatment, your doctor is saying: "We have standard drugs that we know will help you. But we think we have something that may be even better. The investigational arm of the study consists of a recipe (protocol) that we have a tremendous amount of confidence is just as good as the conventional arm and that we think is better. This study compares the two treatments and we think will prove that the new is better." So with phase III the patient is not taking much more of a gamble than if he or she took conventional therapy.

Questions to Ask about a Clinical Trial

If you are thinking about taking part in a clinical trial, the National Cancer Institute recommends that you ask these important questions:

- What is the purpose of the study?
- What does the study involve? What kinds of tests and treatments will be given? (Find out what is done and how it is done.)
- What is likely to happen in my case with or without this new research treatment? (What may the cancer do, and what may this treatment do?)
- What are the other choices and their advantages and disadvantages? (Are there standard treatments for my case, and how does the study compare with them?)
- How could the study affect my daily life?
- What side effects could I expect from the study? (There can also be side effects from standard treatments and from the disease itself.)
- How long will the study last? (Will it require an extra time commitment on my part?)
- Will I have to be hospitalized? If so, how often and for how long?
- Will I have any costs? Will any of the treatment be free?
- If I am harmed as a result of the research, what treatment would I be entitled to?
- What type of long-term follow-up care is part of the study?

GETTING A SECOND OPINION

As cancer care has improved, it has gotten more complex and sophisticated. If you have any lingering doubts about your diagnosis or the recommended treatment, you should definitely consider getting a second, and perhaps even a third, opinion by consulting with another expert in the field. (Be sure to find out from your oncologist how much time you have to decide—some cancers do not require immediate treatment, but a delay in others could alter your prognosis dramatically.)

Consultations are especially important at the time of diagnosis, and many oncologists routinely send biopsy slides to a second pathologist. You can ask whether this has been done—biopsies examined in small communities by a lone pathologist are prime candidates for second opinions at larger institutions such as cancer centers, major medical centers, and university medical centers. The finer points of a diagnosis can dictate crucial differences in your prognosis and treatment. Being dissatisfied with the therapeutic effects of your treatment, the side effects and the way they are handled, and an irreconcilable doctor-patient personality conflict are other possible motivating factors for getting a second opinion.

Training, capabilities, and philosophies vary greatly; no one can expect every doctor to have learned everything in his field, even if he is a specialist. Some stay more up-to-date than others by attending seminars and conventions and reading many journals; some have a more aggressive approach to disease than others. Some have sub-subspecialties, such as bone cancer, breast cancer, or lung cancer. None of the conventional or investigational treatments is fun. You want to be sure to get the maximum return on whatever effects you suffer, and a consultation helps you do that. Remember to ask your insurance company if they pay for second opinions—many of them do.

Often a situation is not clear-cut, or new therapies are being developed. Dr. Thomas Hakes specializes in treating breast cancer at Memorial Sloan-Kettering and gives a lot of second opinions. "Often there are no real right answers or best answers," he says. "Rather, there are several possibilities." How often does he disagree with the first opinion? "I'd say 40 to 50 percent of the time I agree exactly; about 25 percent of the time it's not exactly what I would do, but it's still acceptable; and 25 percent of the time I disagree completely."

Going for a consult also gives you time to think, reflect, and digest—time that is invaluable for the coping process. Many health care professionals, including oncologists themselves, recognize the advantages of hearing someone else's views at any point during treatment.

Though justifiable, asking for a second opinion is not always easy. An oncology nurse at New York's Memorial Sloan-Kettering points out that "there's a certain gut feeling you have about a doctor. If you like him and trust him, you may be reluctant to see someone else. It's hard to break in a new doctor." For some patients, such as this one, the idea never occurs. "This whole thing was rather new to me—though I suppose it is to everybody. I never thought about my alternatives. I just trusted my doctors and did what they told me."

Other cancer patients, no matter how they long for a confirmation or consultation, are timid about suggesting it. "I don't want to hurt my doctor's feelings," they say, or "I'm afraid my doctor won't treat me if I go see someone else." This lung cancer patient, for example, was very unhappy with the treatment her oncologist, who was affiliated with a top cancer center, was giving her:

"I was so violently ill—I thought dying couldn't be worse. So I went to the Cancer Management Center in Kansas City for another opinion. My doctor was very angry with me. But I said, 'Doctor, I *need* this.' Finally he agreed to forward my records. The panel at Kansas City told me the way I was being treated was *the way*, if I was to survive this. That put my mind at ease; it was the best five hundred dollars I ever spent."

Most oncologists, however, encourage their patients to tap another expert's thoughts. Dr. Michael Van Scoy-Mosher is one:

"I might want to hear what another doctor has to say. Somewhere early on, I bring it up with the patients, just so they don't view it as an insult to my ego. I really like my patients to know that they can do that. The other thing I do is ask that they let me guide them a little bit about where to get that second opinion. I want to be sure it's from a reputable, well-respected oncologist. They also must understand that when you seek another opinion, you risk actually *getting* another opinion—and that you will then have to reconcile the conflict."

Though you may find a good oncologist locally, he may not have access to all the benefits of the explosion of knowledge in the cancer field. He should, however, make sure that somehow *you* do have access. Most smaller local hospitals have tie-ins with nearby larger centers. The key is for you to be able to discuss the need for expert consultation with your doctor and have his willingness to cooperate.

If you do go for a second opinion, the names of consulting physicians may be obtained and their credentials and affiliations checked out by using the same channels and methods suggested for finding a first physician. In addition, your first physician may be more than happy to recommend other specialists. Many people also find that participants in a support group can recommend good physicians.

In their book *Choices: Realistic Alternatives in Cancer Treatment*, Marion Morra and Eve Potts suggest that if you are hesitant about broaching the subject with your doctor, enlist the aid of a relative or friend. They can supply moral support or courage when you explain your need to your physician or perhaps do the explaining for you. The authors point out that a concurring second opinion will strengthen your physician's conclusions and make you feel more secure, confident, and at ease with the treatment. Belief in the treatment seems to have a strong effect on how well a patient does with chemotherapy. If your doctor is offended at the suggestion to get another opinion, Morra and Potts suggest that you get another doctor.

I remember when my oncologist outlined the course of the chemo he planned for me. The next week, when I came back to start the treatment, he told me he'd found that an older protocol for adjuvant breast cancer chemotherapy was more effective than the one currently in vogue. It called for slightly different drugs and a different schedule, and it lasted nine months rather than the twelve months the other therapy stipulated. I was glad about the relative brevity of the plan, but I also felt a vague uneasiness about the therapy. I wondered: Is there yet another therapy that's even more effective? In spite of this, I never went for a second opinion. It wasn't until I researched this book that I inadvertently got a belated "second opinion" from one of the oncologists I interviewed: He confirmed that my oncologist "knew what he was doing," and I breathed a huge sigh of relief. Three years is a long time to wait for that kind of reassurance, no matter how slight your doubt.

When calling for an appointment, make it clear that you are interested in a consultation; arrangements will have to be made for your records and test results to be forwarded. Although the consulting physician could end up treating you if you prefer, you are not obligated to stay with the last doctor you see.

What if you receive two differing opinions about the diagnosis or treatment plan? You could consider breaking the tie by getting a third opinion and going along with the majority opinion. Another alternative is to ask the two differing doctors to discuss your case and perhaps come up with a solution they both agree on.

Should You Change Doctors?

Cancer Care, Inc., suggests that you consider changing to another doctor if

- You are not satisfied with the care you are getting
- Your doctor repeatedly does not listen to you or answer your questions in a way you can understand

- Your doctor or the staff members treat you with a lack of respect or don't take your concerns seriously
- Your phone calls are not returned or the doctor is never available to talk

Help for the Mind, Body, and Spirit

Coping with Chemotherapy

Whether you are still in the process of deciding on a therapy, about to begin treatment, or already on it, it is important to remember that many people before you have gone through chemo, that they did manage to cope, and that there are ways that have been developed to help you get through it, too. The same strength that stems from the will to live and enables people to make the tough decision to undergo chemo continues to stand them in good stead during the actual treatment. So do a positive attitude, a good doctor-patient relationship, a strong and reliable support system, and a realistic picture of what to expect in the way of results and side effects.

Dr. Michael Van Scoy-Mosher, an oncologist at Cedars-Sinai Medical Center in Los Angeles, believes that "it's very important for most patients to have an understanding of what the therapy is all about, what its purpose is, what its goals are—and to have a certain attitude about it that the therapy is more an ally than an enemy. It is the disease that is the enemy."

Barbara Blumberg, formerly a public health educator at the National Cancer Institute, thinks it's important for people to keep in mind the reason why they're doing the chemotherapy—that it's for the ultimate good. "You have to be goal-oriented because the way to that goal is not that wonderful."

Psychologist Lari Wenzel says:

"People who want to know as much as possible about their disease and treatment, why they are experiencing side effects and that these side effects can be controlled—those people tend to do well because their attitude and approach allow them an active role in fighting their disease. People should try to retain their life-styles as much as possible so that they

65

are not identifying themselves only as cancer patients under-going chemotherapy, but rather thinking that this is one event among many that is taking place in their lives. People who are able to work, even part-time—if they can retain their work identity and family identity—tend to cope better."

Patients have their own theories about coping, too:

"When you're so very sick, you go through all these emotions. You're angry and sorry for yourself at first. And then you say, 'Hey, I'm not going to let this get me down.' I just made up my mind I wasn't going to have to worry about who was going to raise my daughter. I was going to do it myself."

"I guess everybody handles it in his or her own way. There's no set answer. If you're religious, you pray. If you're not, you turn to an inner strength. But behind all of us, there has to be some stirring, some push. Because we're all afraid. When you're told you're going to die, you'll put yourself through anything to be able to live."

"It wasn't easy, but you learn. Friends would pitch in when my wife wasn't there to help me. We all worked together. Somehow, you just *do* it."

"The mind has to really take over the body. If you let what they are doing to your body really sink in and go to your head—chances are you won't make it. I just stopped thinking about my body being systematically poisoned, the fact that I was agreeing to it, paying for it, and even putting some of it in my mouth myself."

In a study of the effects of coping style on anxiety, depression, and nausea caused by chemotherapy, researchers found that there are differences among people with different coping styles. The "monitors" tend to want information when under stress, and the "blunters" tend to distract themselves when faced with stress. Interestingly, the blunters came out ahead in the study—they reported less anxiety, depression, and nausea.

Obviously, people seldom fall into only one of these two categories—usually they're a blend. At first I was much more of a blunter. But this style backfired later, when I was stuck without the information I needed to allay my fears. Now that my chemo is well behind me, I'm still under stress (from the possibility of recurrence). But now my style is more that of a monitor (some of my friends would say "obsessor")—perhaps because this is stress of a different kind or perhaps because I was always a monitor but was too much of a wimp during chemo to go out and get the information I needed.

With the admirable resilience, adaptability, and ingenuity that characterize the human race, most patients do manage to adjust to living in what has been called chemotherapy's "twilight world" of not being really sick but not being really well, either. In spite of the side effects great and small, physical and emotional, many people find that they are able to live fairly normal, satisfying lives while on chemotherapy. They continue to work, play, eat, socialize, go to school, take care of their households and families, and even travel pretty much as usual, at least most of the time.

In most cases chemotherapy is only a temporary way of life, but it is still a life that must be lived. Regardless of your prognosis, you can have a rich and rewarding life if you make every moment count. There is no reason to deprive yourself unnecessarily. Every avenue should be explored that will help you live fully within your real—and not your imagined—limitations. It may take some extra effort and planning by you and those who care about you; adjustments and perhaps some substitutions may have to be made. You may need to set up new priorities. But there is usually some way to do the things that are most important to you. There *is* more to life than cancer and chemotherapy.

If you find you are particularly bothered or concerned about a side effect, refer to the individual chapters on side effects (Chapters 10–15) and the chapters on support services (Chapters 6–9). Be sure to report your side effects to your doctor, who should have some suggestions that may help. For example, it's quite common to have a few days after a treatment when you feel more or less out of commission and simply have to take it easy. No one should expect to maintain a full schedule of activities when saddled with nausea, vomiting, or just plain overwhelming weakness. Eventually, a certain rhythm will take hold; you may learn to dread this part of the cycle or actually welcome, in some strange way, the quiet days. Should your life be too disrupted, nutritional support, household help, physical activity, or psychosocial counseling can often help alleviate your troubles. Remember that schedules can be adjusted so your worst days coincide with the times you least mind having to take it easy, be it weekends or workdays, and most dosages and drugs can be adjusted, too.

My ability to cope was certainly helped by a relatively good prognosis, a supportive husband-to-be, a compassionate and optimistic oncologist who added nutritional therapy and encouraged me to exercise, the ability to continue to work and keep my sense of humor, and the means to escape reality for a few moments by focusing on something other than chemotherapy.

We all learn to cope because we have to—the alternative is much worse. We choose chemotherapy because no matter what the price we pay—in time, money, side effects, and emotional energy—the benefits are greater than without it. Whether chemo gives us a cure, a few extra years, or only hope, our will to live is what gives us the wherewithal to find and utilize whatever inner and outer help is available. Outside support makes it easier and removes some of the strain, but nothing can make chemo go away completely. The stubborn daily reality of chemo always remains.

I knew I was going to be on chemo for a specific period of time, that it would at some point be over. Like other people in this situation, I needed to figure out how to just "get through" this period on drugs even if I hated the treatment. For those who will be on chemo for an undetermined length of time, perhaps for the rest of their lives, the task is different. They must somehow integrate chemo into their lives, learn to live with it, to not only "tolerate" it but "embrace" it, as one counselor put it.

Making peace with chemo is no easy task, although it is easier for some than for others. It probably doesn't help to hate chemo, to think of it as the enemy. The experiences of two different women, each with advanced breast cancer, illustrate this point. Both were on long-term chemo with a drug whose color was bright blue. One of them had many clothes and home furnishings in the same bright blue because it had been her favorite color. But while on chemo, she began to associate the color with chemo and the side effects it caused. She began to enjoy the color less and less, even hate it, because she hated chemo. All the blue things in her life were negative reminders. The other woman associated the blue with chemo, too, but in a positive way. She knew the drug was keeping her alive and well. She went out of her way to surround herself with clothes and household things in bright blue to serve as a reinforcement, a positive reminder that the drug was doing her good.

Ultimately it is something within ourselves that allows us to make that extra effort to forge a certain relationship with chemo. Chemo for me seemed very much like life itself, only more so: a great challenge and a great adventure. I had my ups and downs, but I learned to take one day at a time. I tried not to expect the worst, not to think too much about the bad things that might happen—only the good ones.

GETTING INFORMATION

Being well informed is widely recognized as essential to the coping process. Most people fear the unknown more than anything; the fantasies they conjure up are often far worse than the real thing. A reasonable amount of information can put anxieties to rest or at least into perspective. Since your oncologist knows the most about your particular case—your disease and its treatment—he or she should ideally be your primary source of information. Yet what patients want to know and what their doctors think they want to know rarely coincide.

Dr. Michael Van Scoy-Mosher thinks that as a general rule doctors tend to underestimate their patients' needs for information and understanding of their disease and its treatment. He feels they don't supply patients with nearly enough information and hesitate to bring up touchy issues on their own.

It's up to the patient to ask if more information is wanted. Patients are often hesitant to pose additional questions once the initial explanation has been provided or as the therapy wears on. Patients have many reasons for this: They say they are still in shock from the diagnosis, or they don't know what questions to ask, or they forget to ask, or they feel too shy and intimidated, or they don't want to look like fools, or they don't want to "waste" time asking silly questions of a busy doctor. Faced with an authority figure who knows more about us than we know about him, who has the power to cure, to heal, to relieve us of our pain, or to make us feel sicker, we can feel as though we were children who should be "seen but not heard."

Patients should not feel guilty about taking up a lot of the doctor's time—that's what the doctors are there for. Taking up time *unnecessarily* is another matter, so it is best to come prepared. When you are asking questions, there are several procedures you can follow so that your queries are more effective. You can educate yourself by reading up on your disease and its treatment (your doctor can refer you to specific volumes and periodicals, or your librarian can). You can contact local branches of national cancer organizations such as the American Cancer Society and the National Cancer Institute's Cancer Information Service. They will give you information over the phone and send you booklets and articles pertinent to your disease. It is difficult to retain huge amounts of new information; at a time when your mind is under a lot of pressure, it is impossible. You can overcome this problem during visits to your doctor by bringing a pad and pencil and jotting down notes, or you can bring along a small cassette recorder and tape the whole conversation. Bringing a friend or family member with you is another possibility. They can remember things you don't, act as your health advocate by thinking up questions that you might not have, and pose questions you may not have the nerve to ask.

Many cancer patients and professionals suggest that you write down your questions as you think of them during the visit or during the time between visits. Some suggest you send a copy to your doctor ahead of your next visit so he or she can be prepared, and your concerns can be kept as part of your records.

I didn't start writing down questions until well into the therapy for fear of feeling foolish. Finally, I decided it was more foolish not to. When I whipped out my list, my doctor just quipped, "Oh, a shopping list," and didn't bat an eyelash.

YOUR CHEMOTHERAPY PLAN

The chemotherapy plan (also referred to as a protocol, program, or regimen) is like a cooking recipe that specifies the drugs, the baseline doses of the drugs, and the scheduling of the treatments. Cancers as well as people vary in their responses to different plans, so in choosing a protocol, the oncologist tries to match your disease and general condition with the possible effectiveness and side effects of the thousands of available protocols. The plan he or she chooses and how it is implemented play a crucial role in how well you cope.

As you have seen, your chemotherapy may be standard or investigational; in addition, it may be a single drug (single-agent chemotherapy), or your cancer might respond best to a multitude of drugs given simultaneously or sequentially (combination chemotherapy). You may be getting high-dose chemo, which is generally reserved for systemic cancers such as leukemias and lymphoma or for metastatic disease that has a good chance for a cure or remission. Or the chemo may be conventional-dose or low-dose, which are used for adjuvant chemo and for palliation. The actual dose you get is usually calculated according to a formula based on body weight or total body surface area. Using the body surface area is more reliable because it tends to fluctuate less than body weight.

HOW MUCH LEEWAY?

Every effort is made to adhere to the established program as closely as is feasible because past experience shows that the treatment works best that way. An investigational protocol must be followed to the letter because it is a test, or else the results of the trial will be inaccurate. (However, a patient may be taken off a study and still receive some type of chemotherapy.)

But chemotherapy is not an all-or-nothing proposition. The goal in chemotherapy is to administer the "maximum tolerated dosage." This is the delicately balanced point at which as many cancer cells as possible are being killed without sacrificing too many normal cells. Too little of the drug, and too few cancer cells are killed; too much of it, and too many normal cells are killed. When too many normal cells are affected, the therapy becomes too toxic and side effects become intolerable and possibly dangerous.

Everyone comes to chemotherapy with a different set of physical characteristics, and everyone reacts in a unique way. The art and science of giving chemotherapy well in part consist of knowing when and how to change a protocol so the patient is getting the best care. An oncologist will make changes in your treatment if the side effects are too debilitating or the drugs are not working well. Initially, a set protocol may be used intact, or drugs may be dropped and/or added. For instance, certain drugs may be toxic for a patient when a key organ is weak or malfunctioning. The anticancer drugs are processed and excreted by the liver and kidneys, so those organs are particularly stressed. But problems with other organs may mean that your doctor will have to give you less of a drug than it is standard practice to give, drop it from the plan entirely, or simply keep a very close watch on organs that he or she suspects may be dangerously affected.

Chemotherapy is commonly begun within a month after diagnosis since it is in part a race against time. Thereafter, the treatments are paced carefully. They must be given intermittently, in cycles, with enough time between treatments so that normal cells can reproduce and replace their lost sister cells in sufficient numbers to maintain an acceptable level of function. However, there must not be so much time between treatments that the cancer cells can recoup their losses.

Consequently, patients should try to make their treatments as scheduled, if possible on the exact day stipulated by their protocol, and to continue it for as long as the oncologist recommends. As with the drugs themselves, the timing and length of the therapy may be fine-tuned according to your response, your side effects, the goals of the treatment, and the availability of alternative treatments.

Chemotherapy protocols given with an intent to cure or bring about complete remission usually have a predetermined end date. They can last three months, six months, nine months, one year, two years, or three years. Experience has shown that on the average this is the minimum amount of time required to get the sought-after results, with acceptable side effects, in the greatest number of people.

Where the goal is partial remission or when the protocol is investigational, the therapy is more open-ended. Chemotherapy may be relatively brief, a long constant haul, or an on-again, off-again proposition for the remainder of the patient's life. Drugs, doses, and schedules may be switched regularly in an attempt to prolong comfortable, productive life.

In cases of discernible disease, chemotherapy is given for as long as the drugs can be seen to be affecting the tumor and the patient is not suffering from severe side effects. The way the patient feels and various tests tell the doctor how well the drugs are working: Is the tumor still growing; if so, how fast? Has it stopped growing? Is it shrinking? Is it gone?

If your tumor continues to grow or "progress," most oncologists will take you off chemotherapy or switch to a different group of drugs no matter how well you tolerate the first group. They feel that if it continues to grow despite various different drugs or combinations of them, chemotherapy is probably doing more harm than good; you are probably wasting your time, energy, and whatever health you have left. In some cases a tumor whose growth has slowed down is an acceptable response and you may continue to be treated with chemotherapy, provided that the side effects are tolerable. In others a stable tumor (one that has stopped growing but is not shrinking) may be the criterion for continuing.

If the tumor responds so well that it actually shrinks (partial remission), chemotherapy may be continued until the tumor either no longer responds (i.e., shrinks) or begins to grow again; at this point other drugs are given, if possible, to which the tumor is not resistant. If the patient is in full remission with no detectable disease, chemotherapy may be continued on a maintenance basis or stopped—it depends on the cancer. Long-term remission can indicate a cure, but many remissions do not last forever; when the disease recurs, chemotherapy may be started again with the same or new drugs.

Doctors use only very rough guidelines as to how much time the drugs should be given to work. As Dr. Richard Gralla, formerly of New York's Memorial Sloan-Kettering, points out, it may depend on many factors:

"For the most part, as least in the disease that I treat, which is lung cancer, you usually can tell within six to ten weeks whether a treatment is working.

"In breast cancer, though, it may be several months before you know whether hormone therapy is definitely helping. With most chemotherapy drugs—be they standard or investigational—the general range is four to ten weeks. With some people it's very easy to see if their tumors are getting bigger or smaller and if they're feeling better or not feeling better. For others it's not so easy to tell because you can't measure the disease very well and their symptoms may be complicated."

How much leeway to take in a chemotherapy regimen is one of the greatest dilemmas facing the oncologist and one a cancer patient faces, too, if he or she is an informed partner in the decisions concerning the treatment. Doctors often treat patients who are vomiting, who feel sick, whose blood counts are slipping, who are on the edge of developing any number of possibly serious additional ailments. How much toxicity is too much? At what point do you reduce, postpone, alter, or stop treatment even though you know it probably lessens the chance for a cure or a remission? A heart-to-heart discussion with your doctor should enable both of you to plan a treatment program you are comfortable with. Together you must take personal factors into consideration, such as whether you need to keep on working or keep your household together.

In these cases it is not advisable for your doctor to prescribe drugs that would knock you off your feet. You have to balance your emotional need to stay alert, capable, and "up" with the physical need to take strong chemotherapy to treat your cancer. There usually are a few choices to make.

If you suffer from immediate debilitating side effects and need to stay well and alert because you are continuing to work, you can often schedule your appointments for late on a weekday or for a Friday. If weekends are important to you, you can have your treatments early in the week. Both these strategies will usually allow time for the worst of the immediate side effects to wear off in time for you to live your life pretty much as planned. Because work was important to me, I got my treatments on Friday. That way I could moan and mope over the weekend, when the side effects were the worst. By Monday I'd be ready to face the world again.

Itinerant chemotherapy patients can stay on schedule, too, with a little ingenuity. When I took a trip related to my work, I didn't miss a shot (much as I would have liked to). I told my oncologist my itinerary, and he located a lab in one city and an oncologist in another and gave me my drugs to tote along. I had two blood tests and one treatment away from home under his long-distance guidance. Two weeks later I got off the plane and had my next treatment, right on schedule.

THE METHODS

Chemotherapeutic drugs may be given in any of several different ways, depending on the dose, the preferences of the doctor and the patient, and the type of cancer. The drugs may be introduced into the body in the following ways:

Orally (PO)—pills, capsules, or liquids taken by mouth
Intravenously (IV)—injected into a vein, either fast (IV push) or slow (IV drip or infusion)
Intramuscularly (IM)—injected into a muscle
Subcutaneously (SQ)—injected underneath the skin
Intraarterially (IA)—injected into an artery
Intrathecally (IT)—injected into the spinal fluid
Intracavitarily (IC)—injected into the pleural cavity of the chest or into the abdomen
Topically—applied directly to the skin, in the mouth, or into the vagina

Most chemotherapy is given either orally or intravenously; many protocols combine both methods. When given orally, it enters your bloodstream via the digestive system; intravenous medication enters the blood directly via a vein. Once in the bloodstream, the drug diffuses throughout the body and goes to every cell of every organ supplied with blood by the capillaries. The other methods are generally reserved for special conditions to increase the drugs' effectiveness, reduce the side effects, or both. For instance, a great deal of effort has been made to give drugs intraarterially, by *regional perfusion*. This method allows spot treatment of tumors in which very high concentrations of drugs circulate only in the region of the tumor. When it is used in cases such as arm, leg, neck, or head tumors or liver metastases, the results of this method compare favorably with those of intravenous administration, with fewer side effects to the rest of the body. Intrathecal injections directly into the spinal fluid are another example. They are an attempt to overcome the blood-brain barrier and are often used in cancers, such as leukemia, that tend to spread to the central nervous system.

Oral Chemotherapy

Some cancers are treated solely with oral chemotherapy. In many other protocols oral drugs are used in addition to the injections. Your plan may call for you to take oral medication a few days every month or every day throughout the therapy. Since the pills, capsules, or liquid can be taken over the course of the day, oral administration allows a steadier supply of the drug to be circulating in the body.

Oral chemotherapy is particularly useful for patients who have "bad veins" and for whom IV chemotherapy is difficult, very painful, or impossible. However, it leaves the accuracy of the dosing up to the patient, and the pills themselves can have a horrible taste that stubbornly refuses to be disguised. One patient comments:

"I took six pills a day, and they tasted so bitter. I can still taste them now, five years later. My oncologist suggested putting them in applesauce, but I don't like applesauce. I tried jelly, but that didn't work. I knew that people wrap pills for animals in chopped meat or bread, so I tried that for me, but they stuck in my throat. I'll never forget the taste."

Following these simple procedures will make pill taking easier. It is better to stand rather than to sit. Take a sip of water or another liquid to lubricate the throat to prevent the tablet from getting stuck. Then take a sip of liquid along with the pill and tilt the head back to swallow. Wash the pill down with a hefty chaser. It is important to remember to lubricate the throat first. In the October 1982 issue of the *Journal of Nuclear Medicine*, a study by R.S. Fisher used X rays to reveal that medications stick in dry throats despite up to forty swallows and additional gulps of water. If you still have trouble, you might try coating the pills with a bit of margarine or butter before taking them. This reportedly makes the pills slippery for easier swallowing and eliminates any bitter aftertaste.

If you are taking oral medication, it helps to establish a schedule that has some relation to your other activities. For instance, coordinate your pill taking with certain meals or with a favorite TV or radio show. Or a family member or neighbor may be able to remind you. Ask your doctor, nurse, or pharmacist to help you set up a workable schedule. Some drugs are best taken on an empty stomach, others on a full one. Some should not be taken just before bedtime. If you are taking a number of drugs by mouth, take care not to mix them up and to take each one at the proper time. If you are following a very complicated schedule, it may help to set out your medication for one day in a special container or to keep a written record of your tablets. Another aid is to hang a large calendar near the location of your pills and mark large X's on the dates you are to take your pills. If you are taking several pills, use a different color pen to mark each medication.

If you miss a dose, check with your doctor about how to proceed. Sometimes you should take a missed dose as soon as possible; sometimes you should not take the missed dose or double up on the next dose to make it up but continue as usual with the next scheduled dose.

Even though you may experience side effects from oral chemotherapy, you should not stop taking it or reduce the dosage on your own. Check with your doctor. He may prescribe different drugs, reduce the dose of your present drugs, prescribe additional drugs, or make suggestions that will alleviate the side effects.

Chemotherapy pills are very strong medications. As with all drugs, keep your chemotherapy pills out of the reach of children and do not transfer them to another drug container that might cause confusion and accidental dosing.

Intravenous Chemotherapy

For many drugs, IV injections are the preferred—or only—way for the drugs to enter your body. Drugs are usually given IV because they reach more parts of the body that way or because they are easier or cheaper to manufacture in that form. Some drugs are absorbed only when they are given by injection. Some may be too irritating or unstable to be used in oral form.

Chemotherapy is most often injected into veins in the lower arm or hand because they are usually the most accessible and convenient. Sometimes veins in other areas of the body are called upon when these are not usable.

If you don't have any good, accessible veins or if your good veins have been "used up," there are ways of avoiding the need to stick those veins again and again. A catheter, a port, or sometimes a pump may be surgically implanted, usually under local anesthesia.

An indwelling catheter is a thin plastic tube that is temporarily implanted under the skin and extends into a vein in the neck, chest, or abdomen. The catheter provides access for injections or slow drip infusions. Catheters are also used to administer other drugs, such as antibiotics, antinausea medicines, antipain medicines, or nutritional formulas. With proper maintenance and cleaning, catheters can stay in place for weeks or months.

A port is a small disk-shaped chamber placed under the skin. Most often it is implanted in an area on the upper chest, near the shoulder. The port is attached to a catheter that is placed in a vein or artery. Drugs are then simply injected through the skin into the port, which then empties into the blood via the catheter.

There are also ambulatory pumps, which may be internal or external (worn inside or outside the body). The pump is filled with a drug or drugs, which are then slowly and steadily infused into the body. Pumps are becoming quite sophisticated, and some can be programmed to deliver several different drugs in a specific sequence. Dr. Richard Cohen has seen how portable pumps are "changing people's lives—they don't have to go to the hospital and treatment is less costly. In addition, now we can control certain cancers that couldn't be controlled at all, with less side effects."

There are two methods of giving an intravenous injection of chemotherapy drugs: push and drip (infusion). The push is the fastest and simplest, but the method used for specific drugs on specific people depends on which works best and which is least painful. Drugs given by the drip method are usually those that are deactivated very quickly; to increase the number of cells killed, the drip method is used to maintain a certain level of the drugs for a long time. Sometimes a drug must be given slowly, in a diluted form, because it hurts the patient or results in adverse effects when it is given quickly.

An IV push takes five to fifteen minutes, depending on the number of drugs, the size of the needle, and the ease with which the needle can be inserted into the vein. If you are getting combination chemotherapy, your doctor or nurse will insert a single needle into a vein and one by one feed a succession of drugs through the same needle to spare the vein from repeated piercings.

An IV drip takes longer—up to twelve hours for a single drug. For this technique, a bottle of the drug hangs from a pole. A thin tube connects the bottle to the needle and allows the drug to drip slowly at a steady rate into the vein. Patients who are on a protocol involving several drugs given by slow IV drip stay in the hospital for several days, and the IV needle remains in the vein for the duration of the treatment, with each drug administered in succession. Thanks to the aforementioned pump, more and more IV drip chemotherapy is being given on an outpatient basis.

The sensations felt during the actual chemotherapy injection depend on the skill of the oncologist or oncology nurse who administers the injection, the nature of the drugs, and the size and condition of the vein. A psychological component enters into it, too—in some people fear and apprehension can make an unpleasant sensation feel worse.

Knowing this, I tried to relax as much as possible when the moment came. Eventually the treatments became less painful, less shocking, almost routine and normal. My oncologist had a skillful, gentle technique and used a tiny needle; still, a needle is a needle, and I never got used to it completely. I looked away when he made the injection, especially when he was having trouble. Even though the pain was minimal compared to the surgery I'd been through, I couldn't stop a few tears from forming just the same—at that moment I'd feel sorry for myself all over again, and I'd think, "Isn't it bad enough? I don't *need* this."

Some fortunate patients are endowed with huge, ropy veins, close to the surface of the skin. They never realize how lucky they are until chemotherapy enters their lives—"God may have given me cancer, but at least He gave me good veins.'' At the other end of the spectrum are the unfortunate ones with truly ''bad veins''—small, thin-walled or tough-walled, or buried below the surface. If your veins are in this category, you will probably be advised to have an indwelling catheter or port implanted surgically.

A good oncology nurse or doctor will do everything possible to make a vein more accessible to treatment and spare the patient discomfort. They may use ultrasmall needles and look for veins in odd places. Some try wrapping the arm with warm towels or running warm water over the area to get the veins to come closer to the surface. Dr. Ronald Bash recommends that his patients exercise, since this pumps up the veins: ''It makes a modest difference, but that's often enough. This is especially so in women undergoing chemotherapy for breast cancer, and who are getting injections in only one arm.'' My oncologist specifically recommended that I squeeze a rubber ball as often as possible to ''pump up'' the veins, but any exercise helps.

The drugs themselves—and the imagination and sensitivities of the patient—also impart unique sensations at injection time. A lot of the sensations are minor, localized, and temporary. Some patients say they feel a burning at the injection site; others feel a coldness or a warmth that spreads throughout the body and lasts for several minutes or more. Others feel an overall tingling, a chill, or a kind of ''high.'' Some say they can ''taste'' their drugs within a few seconds of the beginning of the injection. I'd joke around and say, ''Mmm—strawberry,'' and name another flavor every time. For other patients, the taste is no joke. For example: ''That metallic taste would hit my mouth shortly after the infusion began. If I live to be a million I will never forget it. It's just bad. We tried using mints, which were somewhat effective, but not really. And it was one of those long-lasting things.''

Some of these reactions are predictable, but others are not. Always tell your chemotherapist or nurse of any sensations, no matter how silly they seem to you at the time. Occasionally the drug may leak into the surrounding tissue; this can be a serious side effect of chemotherapy and is called *extravasation*. (See Chapter 12.)

THE FIRST TREATMENT

Some patients look forward to their first treatment because it signifies help for their disease. They are relieved that something can be and is being done. Some experience an element of curiosity or excitement; many, however, approach their first "shot" with a good deal of anxiety and fear.

My doctor had warned me about vomiting and tiredness after a treatment and had told me that my hair might fall out later. These were only possibilities; I had no idea whether I would have them, and this uncertainty was kind of exciting and horrifying at the same time. When the treatment was over, my husband and I rode the bus home. The anticipation was excruciating, but as the hours passed I only began to feel a little queasy and spaced-out, a little tired. That was all! Hardly the vision I had had of hanging out over the toilet bowl for hours. The next day I still felt crummy, tired, and cranky.

Many people experience minimal side effects as I did, but the initial experiences vary, just as the overall experiences do:

"I was petrified to go for my first treatment. My doctor gave me the injection and had me lie down. Five minutes later he came back and asked, 'How are you feeling?' I felt fine and went home by subway alone, having sent my future husband, Larry back to work. I thought if this is the way it's going to be, what's the big deal? About three hours later, I felt every ounce of energy drain from my body. Larry helped me get into bed, and from that moment on I proceeded to throw up for four days."

"They started me on my first round of chemo while I was still in the hospital recovering from surgery. The resident on the case came in trundling a whole sack of little chemicals. Vile yellow colors, an ugly brown thing . . . some of them were so-called antinausea drugs which knocked me out for the better part of the first day. That first day . . . it was miserable. Feeling totally out of it, weak from the surgery, vomiting in spite of the antinausea drugs, my wife sort of floating in and out of my consciousness. My surgeon recommended that I hire a private duty nurse, and I thank God we had a health plan that allowed it—having someone there around the clock that first day really made a great deal of difference in my case."

"I thought: 'I'm going to go into this office and I'm going to see all these awful-looking people sitting around with all white faces.' I thought they would all be dying of cancer, and it would be depressing seeing all those people. But it didn't turn out like that at all."

"My doctor didn't tell me much about the side effects. So I wasn't terribly nervous—I didn't have that fear. When I started throwing up violently that night, I was frightened to death. I called him on the phone and said, 'If this is the way it's going to be every time, I can't go through with it!' It wasn't, though."

Since there's no way for you to know exactly what the initial chemo treatment is going to be like for you, the best course is to be as generally prepared as possible for every eventuality. Your preparation should include a basic grasp of what is going to happen before and during the injection, what will be expected of you, what the surroundings will be like, how long the injection will take, and what the immediate side effects might be. There is some dissension among the ranks as to how much detail a doctor should go into when describing the possible side effects of a particular set of drugs.

But if you are being treated as an outpatient, you should at least find out whether the side effects might affect your ability to get back home and function for the rest of the day. It is probably unwise in most cases to plan to put in a full day's—or evening's—activities after your injection. Though most drugs don't cause vomiting until hours after administration and you may not feel any immediate effects at all, it is better to be safe than to be caught by surprise feeling sick in the middle of Main Street. In addition, you should be able to contact your doctor or a knowledgeable nurse in case anything occurs that you might need help with (as should be the case throughout your therapy).

Dr. Van Scoy-Mosher acknowledges that anxiety is a problem with some patients:

"What I've seen to be useful is for patients who are feeling particularly anxious to talk with another patient who had the same therapy. Patients can ask their doctors—I often arrange for this. Even if the patient had gotten sick with it—just to talk to somebody who had it a while ago or is having it and is still functioning, is doing okay, can relieve a lot of anxiety.''

Many hospitals have instituted—or are in the throes of instituting—some kind of group orientation meetings or workshops to deal with the ins and outs of chemotherapy. While these can prepare you generally, they usually include a large variety of patients, cancers, and treatments and so may not be specific enough. Your doctor or nurse is still the best source for nitty-gritty information about your chemotherapy plan. In addition, a patient volunteer—someone who has been through it—can share valuable firsthand experience. Your doctor, nurse, or hospital may also give you drug information cards that list the side effects and remedies or other printed matter such as booklets to reinforce whatever you have been told.

An oncology nurse at a large cancer center says:

"Patients should have some knowledge, something in their hands, because they forget by the time they get home. They get bombarded with so much, and by the time they come for chemotherapy here, they're tired, they've been waiting for the doctor, the doctor has seen them, they may not like what was said to them or the way it was said to them, they may have gotten bad news, they may be worrying about the kids coming home from school, or feeling angry . . . they're just not concentrating. They should have some form of written instruction.''

Most oncologists advise against the patient's going alone for any treatment, but this is especially important for the first treatment, when the immediate side effects are more up in the air than at any time during treatment. A familiar presence—a spouse, parent, son or daughter, friend or neighbor—can allay a lot of anxiety. He or she can also run interference, help deal with red tape, ask questions for you, and perhaps retain more information than you can at this time. From a purely practical standpoint, another person can keep you company during long waiting periods and accompany you home or take over any driving that is necessary.

HANDLING THE SIDE EFFECTS

Without a doubt it is the side effects that have given chemotherapy a bad name and worry people the most. Dr. Richard Gralla feels that the media help paint an unfair view of them. "People are misinformed, and some extra anxiety has been built up because of that. A magazine article once said that the cancer patient had to face the 'twin horrors' of cancer and chemotherapy. That doesn't help people. A lot of things have been done, especially in the last few years, to make the side effects easier to take. Response to treatment can greatly reduce the symptoms of cancer and bolster a person both physically and emotionally."

On the other hand, playing down the side effects or sugarcoating the experience paints a false picture that can be just as harmful. A women's magazine quoted a noted breast cancer specialist as saying, "The vast majority of patients should experience chemotherapy as no more than an inconvenience in their lives. . . ." Although some women do breeze through, this is patently untrue of the "vast majority," and it does these women a vast disservice to tell them that this is so far from the norm.

To a certain degree your side effects can depend on you—your attitude and overall health—and on your doctor. A positive attitude, full of hope and confidence, can make side effects less noticeable and more tolerable. A strong, healthy young body may withstand the rigors of some drugs better than a weakened or older one. A good doctor-patient relationship can make a contribution, too: Sometimes it seems that the way a patient feels about the oncologist has a great deal to do with the severity of the side effects and how well the patient can cope with them. In the hands of a competent, caring physician or health care team, and with the judicious use of the support services and therapies, the side effects picture is much better than it used to be. Today the side effects of chemotherapy are preventable or treatable or have the potential to be made more bearable.

Coping with side effects begins with an understanding of what they are, which ones you can reasonably expect to get, which ones are serious, and what you can do about them. Ideally, your oncologist will be able to help you in all these areas.

Some physicians and nurses feel that giving patients information about side effects increases the likelihood that the patients will develop the side effects or will increase their severity. However, there have been several studies conducted by Marilyn

Dodd, an oncology nurse and the author of *Managing the Side Effects of Chemotherapy and Radiation*, that have shown that this is not the case. She found that patients who were fully informed did not report more side effects and that they were more active in taking care of themselves than were patients who were not well informed.

The science and art of medical oncology consist of treating the patient's cancer and treating the side effects caused by the treatment. Doing both well takes a lot of time and skill, as Dr. William Grace, chief of oncology at St. Vincent's Hospital in New York, explains:

> "Good care of patients is attention to detail. It's like anything else: If you are concerned about your patients, you make every effort to assure that they don't get too sick from the disease or the therapy. Good care is labor-intensive, feeling compassion, having good ideas, and common sense. It means you have to do a lot of fine-tuning. When the doctor-patient exchange is fruitful, medication can be given carefully and effectively in high doses without unacceptable toxicity."

No two people are exactly the same, and no two will react exactly the same to the same drugs, just as no two tumors will. The side effects that can be caused by the specific drugs in your chemotherapy plan are listed in the section that begins on page 296. A glance at this list can be terrifying and misleading unless you remember this very important point: These are the side effects that *might* occur; they are not the ones that necessarily *will* occur. And as you will see, there are many ways that you, your doctor, and your support system can work to prevent or alleviate those which do occur.

A few of the side effects listed for the drugs in your chemotherapy plan are very common and happen to some degree to nearly everyone who takes them; others are less common; and still others are quite rare. Side effects can sometimes occur in only a fraction of a percentage point of the total number of people who take the drugs. Some side effects may be only temporary or intermittent, or they may persist for the duration of the treatment, linger after treatment is just a memory, or never go away completely. They may be severe or slight, serious or minor, annoying or devastating. Sometimes there is confusion about whether a condition is actually the result of chemotherapy. Oncologists are therefore put in a very tough position when their patients ask about side effects. People want to know what side effects they are going to get; they want to know what they can expect. Dr. Thomas Fahey of Memorial Sloan-Kettering in New York expresses the frustration of all oncologists when he says:

"One of the things that's so frightening about it is that you can't sit down with a patient beforehand and say, 'Look, this is exactly what you can expect. And since this is what you can expect, this is what we're going to do about it.' It's so variable. I think it's probably not a good idea to present all the possible terrible things that can happen to people before they get chemotherapy because they may not get any of them. The patients should know, however, that certain side effects of chemotherapy are experienced to some degree by most patients who receive these treatments, and although they are variable, they are not unexpected. These could include stomach upset, hair loss, loss of energy, and blood count depression.

"You don't dwell on what the side effects are but say that if there are side effects, we can anticipate them, and there are methods we can use to make them minimal. For example, now you can really reassure people that you can virtually stop nausea and vomiting. The newer antinausea drugs are very effective."

In addition, it is usually impossible to say exactly when side effects will occur and how long they will last. Some may occur within a few minutes or hours after the treatment. These include nausea and vomiting, extreme tiredness or weakness, dizziness, diarrhea, and constipation. These typically last a few hours to a few days and then, like a bad dream, are over. In some cases these side effects can plague the patient in milder form for some time. Sometimes a patient experiences a severe reaction with the very first treatment. At other times it can take many treatments until toxicity has built up. Reactions may be more severe after some treatments, almost negligible after others. Emotional states, too, can vary, with some reactions not taking hold for months until the reality and drudgery of chemotherapy set in.

Dr. Fahey says:

"For some patients the hair loss is the worst possible thing that could ever be inflicted on them. Others, that doesn't bother at all. . . . It's the fact that they have to keep coming back to an institution or an office and being reminded that they have cancer. The chemotherapy is a continual reminder of the disease, the treatment must be given on a certain schedule, and their lives become so ordered around the schedule that that's the worst part of it. Then there are others who say they just feel crummy, that it makes them feel sick, nauseous. Some describe it as depression; I'm not sure it is a psychological depression, I think it's a physical depression. Chemotherapy depresses the whole body, and that's the most disturbing thing to them."

Sister Rosemary Moynihan, former assistant director of social service at Memorial Sloan-Kettering, says, "I find what really upsets people is prolonged nausea and vomiting, and weakness. Feeling tired, unattractive, not yourself, having no interest in anything. Even supermarket tabloids can look too detailed or half-hour sitcoms can be too long for concentration."

For others, just the idea of chemotherapy is harder to cope with than the physical side effects. Sister Rosemary continues:

"Chemotherapy is not like other medicine. It has a mystique built up around it, and people have all sorts of fears about what will happen. They have a lot riding on this, but there are so many uncertainties and ambiguities. Most people feel anxious about receiving chemotherapy. What will it feel like? Will I be able to tolerate it? How will I cope? Will it work? They expect to feel bad, but if they don't, does that mean it's not working? It's important for people to talk about these feelings, clarify misconceptions, and find someone to walk them through that initial treatment."

Your oncologist will be giving you tests and physical exams regularly to keep tabs on your condition. These tests, though bothersome, reveal valuable clues about what is going on inside your body and are an integral part of the chemotherapy treatment. Many of these tests—scans, X rays, lab tests—are also used during the initial diagnosis; during chemo, tests involving the blood are used with the greatest frequency and regularity.

Some of these tests reveal how well the drugs are working; others indicate how much damage is being done to normal cells (toxicity). Using the results of the tests, the oncologist decides whether to switch drugs, increase the dosage, decrease the dosage, change the schedule, or continue the therapy at all.

COMPLETE BLOOD COUNTS

Blood counts are the bread-and-butter tests of chemotherapy. The blood is composed of various types of cells that are produced in the bone marrow, spleen, and lymph glands. Both cancer and chemo can affect the composition of cells in your blood. A complete blood count (CBC) shows how your blood compares with the normal amounts of these cells and blood substances. Below are the normal amounts.

White blood cells fight infection (4,500–10,500).
Red blood cells, or erythrocytes, carry oxygen and waste (4.5–5 million).
Platelets, or thrombocytes, help clot the blood (200–350,000).
Hemoglobin is contained in the red cells and is responsible for carrying oxygen (13–16 g/100 ml).
Hematocrit is the percentage of red blood cells (38–46 percent).
Differential is the ratio of mature cells to immature cells (100).

Your oncologist will order a CBC for you at least every time you are due for a treatment. Many oncologists feel that weekly tests are best even if you don't have weekly treatments because real trends are more easily discernible the more data there are to go on and because a low count may require attention immediately. Very low counts may require transfusions of blood products. If your count drops too low, your oncologist will hold back on your treatment, usually by reducing the dosage or postponing the treatment.

Blood tests may be performed in your oncologist's office if there is a lab on the premises or at a hospital, clinic, or independent laboratory. Blood may be drawn from a vein separately or through the intravenous needle or catheter used to administer chemotherapy if you are getting an IV drip and/or are being admitted as an inpatient to a hospital. Blood may also be taken from a finger prick—to spare veins for chemotherapy injections, oncologists sometimes order blood to be drawn only by this method.

After some time on chemo I became adept at guessing when my blood count was down. I'd be feeling pretty down—tired, with no pep and a gray face—and sure enough, it was down. So my doctor would pull back a bit on the drugs, and I'd start to feel better. My count would creep up, and he'd be able to blast away again. I think I found the blood tests more loathsome than the chemo injections. My technician had to use the finger prick each time because I had only one good vein in one good arm— the other arm was off limits because of the mastectomy. She'd say "Ready?" and then make a quick jab and then squeeze and squeeze. I'd scrunch up my face each time; that somehow made it more tolerable. Between the blood tests every week and the chemo every other week, I felt like a pincushion. Over nine months of therapy I was stuck a total of at least sixty times. In spite of all the jabbing, some patients manage to keep their senses of humor, as did this one who told me, "Every Wednesday I had a blood test for lunch. I called the nurse my little vampire."

BIOCHEMISTRIES AND OTHER TESTS

The bulk of chemotherapy's side effects is due to toxicity to the rapidly reproducing cells in organs such as the blood-producing bone marrow. But as Dr. Richard Gralla points out, "When you look closely at a variety of drugs, it's not the bone marrow that is the major limitation, it's other organs." This second group of vital organs includes the lungs, heart, liver, kidney, bladder, and nerves. Damage to these organs may be quick, dramatic, and difficult to predict or slow, insidious, and easy to miss. Sometimes these organs need to be pushed only a little before the damage becomes irreversible. The danger to these organs may be great or small, depending on the drugs, the doses, and the health of the organs to begin with. New drugs and high doses pose especially high risks. Your oncologist will order tests to monitor the condition of these organs if you fall into the high-risk category.

With adriamycin, for example, the dose-limiting toxicity (the side effect that limits the amount of drug that can be safely given) occurs to the heart; with cisplatin, the kidneys and auditory nerves are in jeopardy; with the nitrosoureas, the kidneys and lungs may be damaged; high doses of Cytoxan can affect the bladder. The danger of harming these organs is why it is necessary to give tests such as an ECG or echocardiogram for the heart, hearing tests, blood chemistry tests, liver function tests, and pulmonary functions tests periodically and sometimes daily for a period of time.

BIOLOGICAL MARKERS

Biological markers (also called tumor markers) are substances that either are contained within cancer cells or are released by them into the bloodstream. Some of these are chemicals that normally occur in the body but whose levels are higher when cancer is present. A few of these tests have become fairly standard. Many more have recently been developed and are being tested. So far, none of these tests is perfect. They are not foolproof in detecting all types of cancer with 100 percent accuracy. Though they are not the last word, they are useful tools in monitoring and detecting cancer growth and regression, especially in the early detection of recurrences or metastases. Among the alphabet soup of biological markers for which your blood may be tested are CEA for colorectal cancer, CA 15-3 for breast cancer, and CA125 for ovarian cancer.

But lab tests and physical exams are only one component of the ongoing monitoring process. It also consists of the feedback you give your oncologist. Doctors and their nurses should be accessible and willing and able to give you the time you need, but they are not mind readers.

When your doctor asks you how you feel, be honest. You may fib to your friends and family if you feel it's necessary to put up a good front, but you should never lie to your oncologist about your condition. Don't say you feel fine when you feel lousy. It is not your responsibility to make him or her feel good and be pleased with your condition. It is your responsibility to do all in your power to help your oncologist help you; help cannot be forthcoming if he or she hasn't a clue. Bravery can make you very sick, so don't tell your doctor what you think your doctor wants to hear—tell what he or she needs to hear.

The sooner you report a side effect, the sooner it can be treated. Even if it's not "serious," there's no reason you should suffer even the slightest unnecessary discomfort, worry, or danger. In addition, what seems unimportant or insignificant to you could lead to something serious or be an indication of other already serious troubles.

Dr. Michael Van Scoy-Mosher says:

"There's no question that patients are very symptom-conscious. I think one thing the physician can do is make the patients feel welcome to call with what they know are often minor complaints. One minute on the phone can sometimes head off two weeks of anxiety.

"Sometimes when patients call up with certain complaints, I try to explain to them why I don't think that's important. I don't just say, 'Don't worry about it.' It depends upon the patient—for instance, if he or she has a backache today, and tomorrow the shoulder aches a little bit, and next week the rib aches, that's not something to worry about."

Many side effects can indeed wait until you see your doctor or nurse during your next scheduled treatment. Some, however, may indicate that you are seriously ill and should be treated right away.

I have included a list of possible signs of side effects that can be serious enough to require immediate treatment. If you are unsure or worried, speak up instantly. Speak to the doctor or nurse on the phone; your problem may be able to be settled right then and there. If not, your doctor might want you to make an appointment or admit you to a hospital. If you cannot reach your doctor, you can get in touch with the physician who is covering for him or her. As a last resort, you can go to the emergency room of the nearest hospital to which your doctor has admitting privileges or to the hospital at which you are receiving treatment as an outpatient. Not all cancer centers have emergency rooms, and clinics do not have inpatients at all. If you do go to a hospital with which your oncologist is not affiliated, he cannot treat you while you are there; you will be treated by a staff or house physician.

SIDE EFFECTS THAT SHOULD BE REPORTED IMMEDIATELY

- Fever over 100 degrees Fahrenheit
- Bleeding or bruising
- Rash or other allergic reaction (swollen eyelids, hands, feet)
- Shaking and chills
- Pain at the injection site
- Unusual pain anywhere, including headaches and joint pain
- Shortness of breath
- Severe diarrhea or constipation
- Bloody urine

Your oncologist has several approaches available to alleviate the side effects you may develop. One is to change the timing or the way chemo is given—this works for a few side effects, such as nausea, tiredness, phlebitis, and heart toxicity. A recent study showed that there was much less toxicity when cisplatin was given in the evening rather than the morning and when adriamycin was given in the morning rather than the evening. Another option might be to suggest nondrug therapies such as nutrition, exercise, and psychological therapy or counseling. (See Chapters 8, 9, and 15.) A third approach is to reduce the dosage or frequency of treatment. This course is usually taken only if the side effect is serious—that is, life-threatening—such as a low blood count as opposed to nausea, and if no other effective method exists to relieve it. The last tactic, to prescribe additional symptom-relieving medication, is sometimes preferred when the other methods are ineffective or because reducing the chemo drugs reduces the drugs' effectiveness to too great a degree. (Doctors may, of course, use any combination of these methods.) Fortunately, medication usually works just as well on conditions caused by chemo as on those due to some other reason.

Medication is useful, for instance, in controlling pain that might otherwise ruin your sleep, your appetite, and your social life. If you are nauseous and vomiting, an antinausea drug may help you maintain a better nutritional status and boost your morale. Insomnia can wear you out, but the short-term use of sleeping pills will help you get the rest you need to face the next day and help your body replace the tissue being damaged by chemotherapy. If you are anxious or depressed about your disease and its treatment, a tranquilizer or antidepressant can help restore your sense of well-being and relieve stress that may be detrimental to your prognosis and your quality of life.

Drugs such as these can bring welcome relief, but they can also impose their own set of distressing side effects. They may not, but if they do, these in turn can be treated. For instance, narcotics used to control pain often cause constipation, which in turn can be alleviated by laxatives, enemas, stool softeners, and a change in diet. Antinausea medication is usually sedative, but this can be dealt with by changing the schedule of medication.

Though it is generally wise to keep any additional drugs to a minimum and though some people may prefer to try nondrug methods first, drugs do have their uses. Just as strong drugs are needed to fight cancer, other drugs may at some point be justified to keep us going. When symptoms are severe or acute or don't respond well enough to nondrug measures, the stress and discomfort caused by the unrelieved symptom may be more harmful than the drug that relieves them. It is reasonable to be concerned about drugs you don't need, but drastic times call for drastic measures, and you shouldn't hesitate to call upon modern medicine for help. Part of living with cancer entails living in the here and now—and not being overly concerned with what a drug might do in some undefined future. The benefits of taking additional medication, especially if it's temporary, may far outweigh the risks.

I had a prescription for Compazine, but I never took it. My nausea wasn't bad, and I figured that since I was being pumped up with all those other drugs, why take more unless I really had to? I did eventually take something for a week or so to help me get to sleep. And then I also took an antidepressant for about a month. But it made me feel dizzy, so I stopped. By that time I was over the big depression, anyway. As my doctor said, "We have to use whatever we need to get you through this."

Dr. William Grace believes that you should "use whatever pharmacology you have to so a patient may lead as normal a life as possible." He notes that some of his patients have discovered that Dexatrim counteracts some of the fatigue related to chemo; some doctors even prescribe Dexedrine for this same purpose in selected patients. He says:

"You have to remember that in small, careful doses, it's safe, and that chemotherapy patients are not drug abusers—they are quite normal people for whom a little bit of Dexedrine goes a long way. These people don't easily become drug-dependent. When they finish the chemotherapy course, they don't want any more Dexedrine or other medicines that made the therapy more tolerable."

You should be aware that both over-the-counter (OTC) and prescription drugs can affect you more than usual or interact dangerously with chemotherapy drugs. Common aspirin, for example, can compound the problem of slow blood clotting. Chemotherapy patients are usually advised to switch to aspirin-free analgesics and to learn to read labels carefully since many

OTC products contain aspirin. Even diuretics and antibiotics can interact with your chemotherapy regimen.

Always inform your chemotherapist about any drugs you may be taking and keep him up-to-date on any changes. Other drugs that may interfere with chemotherapy include anticoagulants, blood pressure drugs, anticonvulsants, barbiturates, cough medicines, sleeping pills, tranquilizers, and birth control pills.

Alcohol is not usually thought of as a drug, but it *is* one, so some thought should be given to its use during chemotherapy. Usually, the chemotherapy patient is able to drink some alcohol—one or two glasses of wine or beer a day. Occasionally, however, no alcohol is allowed because it can aggravate the side effects of some drugs. In addition, consumption of huge amounts of alcohol can cause liver damage and vitamin deficiencies. Not only can chemotherapy cause the same thing to happen, but a well-functioning liver is crucial in detoxifying the anticancer drugs, so be sure to ask your doctor about alcohol consumption. I'm not exactly a lush, but I do like wine when I go out. When I asked if wine was permissible, my doctor said, "Sure, go ahead, have some fun." But I began to notice that even a glass or two made me more tired the next day. I was feeling tired enough from my chemo, so I stopped the booze altogether. Later, my surgeon told me this was quite common. (Still later, a study showed that alcohol can increase the risk of breast cancer.)

Other common medical measures that may be called upon to support the chemotherapy patient and limit the short- and long-term effects include the various blood products. When the blood count falls too low, transfusions of red cells, platelets, or leukocytes may be required together or individually. Some new therapies are adding substances that stimulate blood cell growth such as colony-stimulating factors. Bone marrow transplants, though still considered experimental for many cancers, are coming into use. Leucovorin rescue is a procedure that enables patients to withstand huge doses of methotrexate without harming the healthy cells. In this technique, the methotrexate is followed by another drug—Leucovorin—which protects or "rescues" normal cells from the methotrexate's life-threatening toxic effects.

TREATING THE WHOLE PERSON

There is more to progressive, caring chemotherapy than simply giving a passive patient the right anticancer drugs in the right amounts, and there is more to minimizing side effects than supplying patients with yet more drugs. Though a sound, disease-oriented treatment is paramount and symptom-relieving drugs have their place, a disease cannot be treated completely and humanely in isolated technological splendor. It is becoming increasingly obvious that since the chemo patient is affected totally, he or she needs to be treated as a whole person. Medicine, in the narrow sense of using drugs to treat disease, cannot begin to determine and fulfill the patient's physical, psychological, social and spiritual needs, but broadening its scope to include nondrug support therapies can. "Good medicine" can help you keep your life at the highest quality possible by taking care of the rest of you while the chemo takes care of the cancer.

The next few chapters include suggestions for a wide variety of steps you can take and methods you can utilize to get through chemotherapy as unscathed as possible. They include emotional help from family, friends, and professionals; stress management and reduction; diet and nutrition; and exercise. Which ones you choose, to what degree you utilize them, where you find them, and how they fit in with your chemotherapy program depend on your individual reactions to chemotherapy, your needs, your style, and your own resources. For some patients these therapies play a major and integral part in keeping body and soul together.

My oncologist, who looks to both traditional and nontraditional sources of support for his cancer patients, believes:

"The most important thing in medicine is to individualize. Each person needs something slightly different. You can't just use the cookie cutter system. An oncologist has to use the very finest that is available at the present time. That includes a continuing search for protocols that have been demonstrated to be of validity in doses that have been shown to be valuable; it includes very careful attention to the known side effects and known toxic effects of the medication; and it includes their application in a program that involves a certain amount of building and strengthening of the body as well as simply destroying."

Through all your emotional and physical experiences, your oncologist is the central figure around whom everything else seems to revolve. Your doctor, then, is the most natural person to whom you turn for support. In an ideal world, he or she would be able to treat all your related needs or recommend people who can. In reality, doctors are somewhat limited in their methods and patients often look elsewhere for help—to a primary-care physician or nurse or to someone outside the medical mainstream. It's best to inform your oncologist of any additional therapies you are undertaking. Make it clear at the outset that they are being used as supplementary therapies to, not in place of, chemotherapy. Even if your oncologist does not endorse a particular therapy (chances are getting better that he or she will), it is important to reveal everything there is to know about your health practices. Some—such as the more extreme diets—may actually do more harm than good. But if a therapy does do good, your doctor may pass the information on to other patients.

When used as supplements to chemotherapy, support therapies can be thought of as a form of "insurance" and a means of improving the quality of life that is being eroded by the drugs. In addition, these therapies can help fill the gap between the cold technical approach sometimes offered to the patient and the warm, human approach the patient really needs. Perhaps their greatest value, however, lies in the way they enable you to play a more active role in your treatment, to feel a sense of control rather than playing the part of a passive patient leaving your life totally in the hands of the doctor and the drugs. Chemotherapy need not be a spectator sport. Dr. Ernest Rosenbaum writes in the introduction of his book *A Comprehensive Guide for Cancer Patients and Their Families*:

"When you are an active participant in your medical care and rehabilitation, you can maintain a sense of control over your disease and your therapy. Only you can take responsibility for your state of mind, nutritional status, and physical fitness. The act of taking responsibility is in itself an important factor in maintaining self-esteem, a feeling of independence, and faith in your ability to cope. It is a critical part of therapy."

Emotional Support

Beginning with the diagnosis and continuing throughout and after treatment, cancer patients need to make many psychological adjustments. Your new life has brought with it both intangible emotional reactions and concrete problems. Though many patients (and their families) manage somehow to cope well enough on their own, there is no reason not to call upon the many services and therapies that have been designed to make the coping process easier.

Ordinary life certainly has its stresses, and cancer and its treatment add more stress to the brew. Getting emotional support is one important way to deal with chemo-related stress. Some people believe that anything that helps reduce stress may also extend the life of a cancer patient. While this specific effect has not been proved, studies have suggested that stress can affect the immune system and thus perhaps can influence the course of a disease such as cancer. (The next chapter discusses this and the many concrete benefits of specific stress reduction-relaxation techniques.)

Like the other support services for cancer patients, the field of *psychosocial oncology*, which deals with the way the patient and family react to the disease and its treatment, is fairly new. Grace Christ, the former director of social work at New York's Memorial Sloan-Kettering and editor of the *Journal of Psychosocial Oncology*, says, "It's taken time for people to appreciate some of the psychosocial consequences of cancer and its treatments. But as cancer patients live longer and the disease becomes long-term or chronic, or one from which people are cured, the social and emotional effects become much more visible."

FAMILY AND FRIENDS AS SUPPORT

Today, few of us have families in the traditional sense of blood relatives. Our "family" may, instead, be or include a circle of close friends.

Studies have shown that people who have strong relationships or support systems—whether family or friends—usually do better than those who go through it alone.

In his book *Living with Cancer*, Dr. Ernest Rosenbaum points out that as the traditional concept of the passive patient is becoming old hat, so is the idea that the family is an outside element. Both patient and family or close friends are able to contribute immeasurably to cancer care. He writes: "Having the family 'wait outside' wastes a great deal of valuable energy that could be available as additional 'people power' to facilitate a patient's recovery. Also, many family members need to do something to actively contribute to the patient's getting-well process."

How the family handles the crisis of cancer and chemotherapy usually depends on how well the family has functioned in the past. Good relationships often get even better, many cancer patients report a learning, growing experience that brings them closer to their spouses, other family members, and friends.

You can let your friends and family know when their help is welcome in practical matters such as child care, cooking, shopping, phone calls, housework, and other errands and domestic chores. They can encourage healthful activities and low-key diversions such as taking a walk; going for a drive; taking in a movie, museum, or play; and visiting others or—keeping your physical limitations in mind—more strenuous activities such as swimming or bike riding. They can improve your sense of well-being through massage. They can act as researchers—by asking questions, writing letters, or going to the library—if you want additional information about your disease and its treatment.

Loved and loving family members often provide moral support and the motivation to continue treatment when one's own will falters:

"Sometimes I didn't want to go for the chemo. Just as I was getting my system back together, it was time to go back for another treatment. My twenty-one-year-old daughter was with me through it all. When I got a little weak and didn't want to go, that little stinker said, 'You'd better go and have those treatments because if I ever got breast cancer and I needed chemo, I'd go. But if you don't finish your treatments, Mom, I'm not going either.' Blackmail! But she kept me going."

"I don't know how many nights I spent sitting on the floor in the bathroom, my head bent over the toilet bowl, my husband patting my head, and my saying to him, 'I'm quitting it. I've had enough. I don't need it. I don't want it.' I might have quit, too, if I didn't have someone there stroking me saying, 'You're going to be okay. You're going to see this through. You know you can. You know you have to.' "

Family members can help by accompanying you to the facility when you go for a checkup or a treatment. Having someone come along during a question-and-answer session or during a treatment is a simple yet important step in their understanding the treatment and lending their support.

Sometimes I'd feel so alone and vulnerable sitting in my doctor's waiting room and later on the bus ride home that I'd ask Michael to come with me. It wasn't that I felt sick after my shot or that I couldn't get home on my own. Sometimes I was just frightened and it felt good just having him there, holding my hand, or just reading magazines together while we waited. Once a friend asked me if I wanted her to go with me. I knew she was torn up over my having cancer and hated the fact that she couldn't do anything about it. I think she was just plain curious about the chemo, too. So even though it didn't make the cancer or the chemo go away, she came along. She felt better, and so did I.

And yet obstacles often prevent family and friends from living up to their full potential as helpers—the patient won't let them, or they don't know how, or they are having too much trouble coping themselves to help the patient cope. There may be some difficulty in discussing the illness, the treatment, and the prognosis. There may be a reluctance to face the unpleasant or a desire to protect each other. (Cancer patients have said that a lack of communication within the family is one of the major problems they face in coping with their disease and its treatment.) Cancer and its treatment cause massive shifts in responsibilities, roles, and life patterns in addition to emotional upheavals. It is tempting for the family to focus exclusively on the patient's disease, so that friendships fade away and hobbies and interests fall by the wayside. Or people may feel that since the patient is in the hands of the doctors, there is nothing they can do. Patients may have trouble balancing the desire to assert their independence with the real need for help and the desire to let others feel useful.

Mimi Greenberg, a psychologist who specializes in counseling women with breast cancer, has written a book called *Invisible Scars*. In it, she advises that you ask yourself these key questions before reaching out to a family member:

1. What has my history been with this person? (Has my husband, wife, mother, father, sister, or brother been able to support me emotionally during other times of crisis?)
2. Are my expectations of the person realistic? (Am I asking too much or not enough?)
3. Is this person "cancerphobic"? (And likely to hurt me by running away or being distant?)
4. How does this person react to stress? (Will he or she be calm and reassuring or add to the stress and calamity?)
5. Does this person encourage me to do the talking while he or she listens empathetically without interrupting or giving advice?
6. When asked, will this person provide objective, sound advice?
7. Will this person maintain my confidences and refrain from discussing my problems with others?

SUPPORT OUTSIDE THE FAMILY

Some families are able to solve their own problems and adapt to the new situation easily. But many others could benefit from some kind of assistance in adjusting to the new reality before they can effectively help each other. If help is not offered and you feel you and your family could use some assistance in getting back on the right track, ask for it. Meeting with your oncologist, oncology nurse, a social worker, a family therapist, or a family-oriented support group can make great strides in educating your family unit, helping its members communicate and sort out their feelings and realize they are normal, and encouraging them to develop their own coping strategies.

The idea of emotional counseling for the cancer patient and family has met with resistance from professionals and patients alike. On the patient's side, old taboos die hard: There is still some stigma attached to admitting that you might need a little help with your emotional problems. A social worker told me:

"People tend, in our culture especially, to underappreciate the impact of the disease and the treatment. We tend to be a bit stoical in general and don't really understand how much we're being affected. Talking to someone, or using some outside help, doesn't mean we're weak, it doesn't mean we're coping poorly. It means we'd like to cope better, and this is one way to do that. Most people manage to cope reasonably well. But sometimes you can cope better and your whole experience can be of a different quality."

Lari Wenzel, medical psychologist at The Long Beach Memorial Medical Center, says:

"It is not unusual for people to have a need for support services during a time that is particularly stressful, regardless of what that stress is. Cancer as a chronic disease introduces particular stressors to the individual's life. Even people who normally handle stress well can use a little help with problems that may arise as a result of this diagnosis."

The whys and hows of getting information are discussed more fully elsewhere in this book. But this approach bears mentioning here because we have an emotional as well as practical need for information. Don't be afraid to ask questions of your health care team. Some people find that using books and the information they contain helps them cope; in fact, the term "bibliotherapy" was coined to describe this option.

It's a good sign that community hospitals, agencies, and large medical centers are sponsoring more and more educational conferences and workshops geared specifically to the cancer patient and the family. I have been a presenter at several and have found them to be excellent sources of information as well as an opportunity to meet other people who are going though similar experiences. There are also an increasing number of individual classes and lectures that your health care team or a community agency should be able to refer you to.

Your oncologist, family doctor, or nurse may be able to help you and your family get over some of the emotional hurdles you will face and perhaps all of them. However, physicians are often unaware of their patients' need for emotional support; as patients, we want our doctors to be more "human," but we are often reluctant to tell doctors about our emotional needs. We may try to look like exceptional copers, afraid doctors will think our emotions are too trivial. In addition, most doctors and nurses are not trained as counselors or therapists. You may find yourself turning elsewhere for additional emotional support.

When shopping around for emotional assistance, be as choosy as when looking for medical help. Some professionals are more skilled or have had more experience with cancer patients than others, and some approaches may be more comfortable for you than others.

One bad or unproductive experience should not discourage you or prevent you from seeking another more understanding or suitable source of therapy, as happened in my case.

The only person I spoke to about my cancer was the Reach to Recovery lady who just popped into my hospital room a few days after the mastectomy. She was so stiff and formal, I couldn't identify with her at all. She just left me a ball, a booklet, a bra, and a boob made out of polyester. Sure, she wore a tight sweater to let me know that it is possible to look "normal" after a mastectomy. But she came before I was really ready to see anyone; I was still too shocked to think straight and ask questions. When I visited the Reach to Recovery office to look at prostheses, they were so grim about the whole thing . . . maybe I'm nuts, but I saw some humor in opening up a whole filing cabinet drawer full of breasts. I wanted to talk to someone, but I knew I didn't want to talk to *them*.

I've since talked to many women who have had much more positive experiences with Reach to Recovery volunteers. Sometimes a successful match depends on location (as in any field, American Cancer Society chapters vary in style), or it could depend on timing and individual "chemistry."

Reach to Recovery did refer me to a prosthesis shop whose manager and salesperson had both had mastectomies many years earlier. Although neither had had chemo, both were wonderful women with whom I had an instant rapport. I and the friend who had accompanied me ended up spending hours there, having a terrific time, gabbing and laughing and trying on bras and breasts.

Grace Christ feels that "people should not hesitate to seek help. I think it can't hurt, even if it is just to stabilize yourself. But it's not always as accessible as it should be." Part of the problem, she feels, is that in the past people tended to think that support for cancer patients was either straight education—giving information—or intensive psychotherapy. Though it can include both of these, today psychosocial support comes in a wide variety of flavors (or "interventions"). Whatever your tastes and your needs, there is something for you, be it talking to your family and friends, reaching out to another patient, going to cancer-related talks and workshops, participating in a self-help or support group, or engaging in some form of individual counseling or psychotherapy. Sometimes one or two sessions with a social worker or psychiatric nurse will point the way for your problem solving, or a chat with a patient volunteer will help to put things in perspective and set your mind at ease.

Reputable sources for emotional support include your physician, nurses, hospital social workers, psychologists, psychiatrists, county health departments, neighborhood mental health clinics, and the various national, regional, and local cancer support organizations listed in the back of the book, such as the American Cancer Society and the Cancer Information Service.

SOCIAL WORKERS

Social workers serve a wide variety of functions in our society but unfortunately are usually thought of in terms of the welfare system. Medical social workers, however, are the mainstay of the medical system in helping cancer patients and their families find ways to get through it all. In their basic roles of troubleshooters/problem solvers, social workers can help you grasp the realities of living on chemotherapy and work to improve those areas over which you have some control. To that end, they will familiarize themselves with your problems and concerns and work with you to take care of them, be they medical, financial, emotional, religious, or related to your family or employment situation. Social workers can help you communicate with the medical system, help you slice through red tape, and help you and your family work together to detect and meet any emotional or practical needs. They can provide or help find useful items like wheelchairs, prostheses, bedpans, bandages, and financial assistance if you need them. Social workers can help you fill out forms, organize your time around your treatment schedule, and arrange for housekeepers, child care, housing, or hospice service. Psychiatric social workers who are specially trained in this field can provide psychotherapy when emotional problems appear to keep you from functioning as well as you might.

Social workers often engage in individual counseling with patients alone, with patients and their families, or with families alone. They also either run support groups or can put you in touch with support groups near your home. Every hospital has social workers, but their availability and usefulness vary. If you need help, a good way to start is to contact a staff social worker at your community hospital or the hospital where you are being treated and see to what extent that person meets your needs. If their time is limited (which is often the case), they are also a good source of information about other professionals who can offer ongoing treatment.

PEER AND GROUP SUPPORT

Support groups have an overwhelming advantage over other forms of support in that they consist of your peers—other people like you who have cancer. Because of this common bond, many people feel more relaxed and find it easier to communicate with other cancer patients than with their families, friends, doctors, or nurses. "Because it reduces anxiety," says Ms. Christ, "this kind of group is often the kind of forum in which people hear most easily." Many patients and professionals agree that a group is an ideal environment to exchange experiences and methods of dealing with both the practical and emotional issues surrounding cancer and its treatment.

Ricki Dienst, Ph.D., is a cancer patient herself as well as consulting psychologist for the Cancer Support Community, an organization that provides psychological and educational support for cancer patients and their families in San Francisco. She states:

"People don't have to feel they are handling things poorly to join a support group. Many participants find their groups provide both social support and coping assistance. A group can be a good source of information and a place to talk about the experience with others who are interested and understand. It's especially good for those who find it awkward to talk much to family and friends. Often there can be a very useful lighter side to the group, and it can even be a humorous and uplifting experience . . . even if the sense of humor that develops might seem a bit strange to people without cancer. And, of course, participants often gain a great deal through what they are able to offer others in the group."

A social worker and support group leader points out:

"Groups help patients to make the decision to accept therapy, to continue it, to change it, to stop it. They help patients fill in gaps in their information or correct misinformation. We often try to help patients clarify their thoughts when they may be having trouble putting them into words."

However, another social worker observes: "Many people are shy of groups and given an option would avoid them. But once they get started, they find it's something that's very useful." Dienst adds that men are often particularly reluctant to go to groups because they are afraid they will be too emotional. But when they go, they find them helpful. People who participate in support groups say they sleep better, are less depressed, and feel more comfortable talking about their illness. For example:

"The night after the first meeting, I went home and slept like a baby—fourteen, fifteen hours—better than I'd slept in a long time. I'd talked to people who understood. At first I thought it would be a waste of time, but it was very comforting. Now that I belong to a group, I can let out my feelings without burdening my friends with my concerns. I wish I had joined one earlier—I was one and a half years into cancer. I went through all those things you go through alone."

"I think it's better to talk to other people who are having chemo because the doctor doesn't know how you feel. If you talk to patients, they have the same problems as you."

"It's so good to talk to somebody who's been through it and is living a normal life again. I was so afraid of losing my hair, losing too much weight, not being able to take care of my children."

Support groups can help you keep or regain your self-esteem, your balance, and your self-worth. A good support group is made up of people who believe in each other, who offer each other optimistic, realistic help, encouragement, stimulation, meaningful advice, and valuable connections. When you belong to a group, you get help and give it, too.

Today, thank goodness, there are many more support groups, and many more types of them, than when I was undergoing chemo. Each has its own characteristics, its own pluses and minuses, so you are much more likely to find something that suits your needs and personality.

There are self-help groups that are organized and run by cancer patients themselves; some are local chapters of national organizations. Sister Rosemary feels there's a great value in self-help groups, especially for people who are less vulnerable emotionally, such as those who are completing treatment and cancer survivors.

Support groups, by contrast, are generally led by specially trained individuals—social workers, psychotherapists, nurses, members of the clergy, and sometimes doctors or patient volunteers. Sister Rosemary recommends this form to people who are actively dealing with their disease or treatment because there's a resource person to see that the information being relayed is appropriate and correct so that people aren't more upset by receiving confusing information. The leader helps keep the discussion going and protects people who might be more emotionally vulnerable.

As we gain in experience and as demand goes up, support groups are becoming more finely tuned and specialized. Support groups for patients may be heterogeneous and consist of people with a variety of cancers and prognoses and of people of different sexes and ages. Or they may be more specialized as to the type and stage of cancer. The more specific the group, the more individualized the support because the participants have more in common and can more closely compare experiences and share information and understanding.

According to Dr. Jimmie Holland, chief of psychiatry, Memorial Sloan-Kettering has one of the few groups in the country focusing specifically on support before and during chemotherapy. To help people control their anxiety, "We're doing pre-chemo counseling, educating patients about what they can anticipate in terms of side effects and about relaxation, stress control, diet and nutrition, exercise, and anticipating what it will be like when the treatment is over."

Where a specific disease is concerned, breast cancer groups are becoming subspecialized, perhaps because the incidence is so high and because there are so many treatment-related and other issues involved. For example, the Cancer Support Community in San Francisco has groups for newly diagnosed women, women with metastatic disease, and women who have completed treatment. They also run groups for men whose partners have cancer. The M.D. Anderson Comprehensive Cancer Center has a group for single women who are newly diagnosed because, according to Mary Hughes, a psychiatric clinical nurse specialist, "it's hard enough to start a relationship these days without wrestling with 'whom to tell' and 'how to tell' a prospective partner."

Vital Options, based in southern California, was formed by and for young adults with cancer. Support groups for spouses, children, and family members are becoming more available, as are survivors groups and bereavement groups.

Within these variations there are more variations. Groups may meet once a week or once a month. Some are ongoing, but most are time-limited, such as the American Cancer Society programs and many Cancer Care programs, to eight to twelve weeks. These groups are generally "closed"; that is, they accept only a certain number of participants, who must preregister and are expected to attend as regularly as their disease and treatment permit. The director of Cancer Care, Diane Blum, believes that "a lot of people are more willing to join a group if it is time-limited rather than something that stretches on. Everyone's energy stays higher when it's got a start and a finish."

There also are "open" or drop-in groups with no registration or commitment. For some people this is the perfect interim support until a more formal group opens up. Others may actually prefer the flexibility inherent in the drop-in arrangement; perhaps one or two visits to such a group may be all a person needs.

Or you may want to look into special workshops and retreats for cancer patients and their families, such as those offered by Commonweal and Exceptional Cancer Patients.

Support groups are being recognized as an integral part of the cancer patient's total medical care. Many people have learned firsthand that they can improve their quality of life by supplanting fear, anguish, alienation, helplessness, and hopelessness with hope, strength, productive activity, and a sense of community. As if this weren't enough, new evidence suggests that they can prolong life as well.

A study that stunned the cancer care field was published in 1990 by David Spiegel and his colleagues at Stanford University and the University of California, San Francisco. The study involved two groups of women with advanced breast cancer. The group that received medical care and went to a support group lived twice as long as did the group that received medical care only.

How group support had this effect is not known and awaits follow-up studies. But it is likely that these groups helped their members gain more time by encouraging them to be more active in their care, helping them tolerate and stick with their treatment, and allowing them to take better care of themselves generally.

With all these options, it makes sense to shop around for the type of group that's right for you. The quality of the groups and the degree to which you find them helpful will vary. It depends in part on the experience and capabilities of the leader, so ask about their credentials and training. Try to find someone who has been in the group and ask what that person liked and didn't like. Individual personalities, input, and group dynamics enter into the equation, too. These elements, of course, can't be completely assessed beforehand, but you can learn what the screening process is and whether the group is mixed or more specific as to cancer type, stage, and so on. Some groups focus on information or are action-oriented and focus on practical issues. Others are more introspective and may even incorporate music, poetry, or role playing to help participants explore their feelings. Is the group time-limited or ongoing? Does it include families as well as patients?

Most groups do not subscribe to a specific philosophy or belief system. But some do, and this may or may not appeal to you personally. As psychologist Ricki Dienst points out, Spiegel's study notwithstanding, "there is little evidence that groups have a direct biological effect on the immune system or cancer cells. Some groups talk about the 'healing' properties of group support and positive attitudes. Patients often take this to mean physical healing, but many therapists really are talking about emotional healing." So make sure you understand the attitude and philosophy espoused by the sponsoring organization.

However, the whole idea of baring your innermost thoughts in front of a group of people may not be your style, or it may not be helpful. And it may be difficult to find the right group, as this patient comments:

"The doctor got four of us together. It was nice in a way because I walked in feeling I was the only person in the world who had to wear a wig, and here were these two other girls in wigs looking perfectly normal. But part of it was depressing. One of them was only twenty-one years old, and I found it difficult to deal with somebody that young going through this. She was getting a more difficult chemo than I was—it really broke my heart; I really felt for her.''

Dr. Ward F. Cunningham-Rundles, an oncologist at Memorial Sloan-Kettering in New York, finds that groups may not be the answer for everyone:

"One certainly has to have some kind of personal interaction; if people don't mesh, then they don't mesh. They have to be the *right* people, too. If you're in a protocol that causes you to be affected in a different way from the others in the group— if there are other patients with a very poor prognosis and one by one they do poorly, that can be difficult to take."

One-on-one peer support is an alternative to support groups that might suit your needs better. These are trained volunteers whom you can meet with personally or are just a phone call away. Your hospital or physician or community cancer organization can put you in touch with a trained volunteer, or you have access to an empathetic ear via the cancer hot lines scattered across the country, as this patient did:

"Unless you have gone through the same type of situation, or are very close to someone who has, you just don't have the empathy, you don't understand. We have nobody to talk to. The day I called the Kansas City Hotline, I was crying, I was feeling so sorry for myself. But the woman I spoke to was so warm—and she was a living statistic. It made me feel so good. It cost me twelve dollars—we talked a long time—but it was worth every dime of it.''

I wish I had been as smart as this patient. I think if I had just talked to even one other person who had had or who was having chemotherapy, I wouldn't have felt as terrified or as alone as I did at times. I wish that I had thought of it or that my oncologist had suggested it instead of mentioning psychiatrists, but we didn't.

If you don't have access to peer support or support groups in your geographic location, consider starting one. M.D. Anderson has established a toll-free 800 number for people to call a network of patients who have returned home and are doing just this in "their own backyards." There are many other hot lines across the country.

COUNSELING AND PSYCHOTHERAPY

Sometimes it is helpful to explore your emotions more deeply with a person who is knowledgeable about cancer and experienced in helping others work out their feelings. Therapy goes beyond supporting the patient and family emotionally, beyond dealing with the common elements of the disease and its treatment, beyond encouraging you to talk about your feelings. Therapy looks into why you are feeling the way you do.

Dienst describes psychotherapy as dealing with the unique issues that individual patients bring to the cancer experience and that may cause unique difficulties in facing common problems. Therapy is a more intense experience, as it explores "old" issues that cancer has resurrected, such as self-esteem, self-worth, and relationships to parents. However, successful therapy frees patients from the burden of psychological ghosts that impose special meaning on cancer (such as thinking of cancer as some sort of punishment) so they can face the difficulties of cancer (which is tough enough) without this excess baggage. A therapist helps you understand feelings of guilt, resentment, and intense anger in a nonjudgmental way and helps you channel them more constructively.

Since cancer and its treatment affect the whole family, some families benefit from family counseling. Family counseling helps soften the shock and stresses of living with cancer; it opens up the lines of communication among family members, allowing participants to express the negative emotions and easing any resentment that may be part of the cancer package.

Therapy can be long-term or short-term; it may be one-on-one or take place in a group setting. Crisis intervention is short-term therapy specifically designed to get you through a tough time. Unlike support groups, which may be free or relatively inexpensive, there is generally a substantial fee for therapy. (However, many therapists will charge on a sliding scale, according to one's ability to pay.)

RELIGION AND THE CLERGY

In times of trouble, religion is a refuge for many, be it drawn upon privately in the form of meditation and prayer or more publicly in the form of support and guidance from the clergy and/or fellow members of the congregation. A strong belief system can be a source of hope and comfort to a person who is undergoing treatment for cancer, as this patient explains: "I had a lot of help because I have a lot of faith. There's a psalm that goes 'Lift up your eyes into the hills from whence cometh my help. My help cometh from the Lord.' And oh, that verse really took me through it."

Severe stress may lead some people to revert to discarded religious beliefs. Even when patients no longer have any religious affiliation or are not about to return to the fold, a member of the clergy—of no matter what faith—can still be a welcome, sympathetic figure. It is part of the clergy's job and training to comfort the sick and troubled, to encourage people to unburden their souls. However, you should be aware that there are increasing numbers of clergy who are specially trained to counsel people with cancer and their families. If yours isn't one of them, you can ask to be referred to one who is. Members of the clergy can be very good listeners, and the trappings of religion aside, just having someone who is interested, who understands, and who has time for you can be very good for the soul.

YOUR CHANGING NEEDS

Whichever type of emotional support appeals to you, remember that you may need different approaches at different stages of the disease and treatment. What works for you now may not work two months from now, and what you would never consider now may start looking good in a year or so. Lari Wenzel advises that ultimately you need to know yourself well enough to know what is beneficial. Ask yourself whether this form of support is meeting your needs. Do you want immediate support or long-term reworking of the psyche? Is your anxiety increasing or decreasing? If it's increasing, why? Is it because you're dealing with a difficult issue on a particular day?

As Dienst points out, after treatment is over, patients sometimes want more intensive work that reexamines life issues because they want to make changes in how they live their lives, to live more satisfying, less conflicted lives.

Stress Management and Reduction

Whether stress plays a role in the development or growth of cancer is still an unanswered question. What is certain is that stress can affect your quality of life as well as the success you have in coping with cancer and its treatment. Many studies show that stress may affect our immune systems, but we don't know what effect this in turn may have on cancer. A strong immune system plays a role in controlling infections and perhaps cancer, but chemotherapy weakens our immune systems. While evidence is mounting that reducing stress may help bolster immunity, the evidence is far stronger that it may also help us tolerate the emotional and physical side effects of chemotherapy. Logic dictates, then, that we would be wise to pay attention to the negative stresses in our lives and learn techniques designed to reduce or manage stress.

But what is stress? And how can it have these effects on our well-being?

Stress can be positive or negative. Positive stress makes life interesting—it stimulates our minds and bodies to act purposefully in response to it. Positive stress occurs, we deal with it, and then it's over and we can relax and recover. Negative stress, however, increases our fears and makes us feel helpless and unable to function purposefully. Since we don't "take care of it," it's never-ending and we never relax or get the chance to recover.

As Lenore Dollinger explains in her book *Everyone's Guide to Cancer Therapy*, people with cancer suffer negative stress from many sources. These include fear of dying, loss of the ability to work, pain, changes in appearance, changes in relationships, the need to make life-or-death decisions, and anxiety about the effects of cancer and chemo, such as fatigue, vomiting, and hair loss. Such stresses tend to be ongoing, and it's this unremitting negative stress that has been shown to affect many body systems, including our immune systems.

Recently a new field has emerged that studies some of the links between mind and body. This field of study is called psychoneuroimmunology (PNI), and it is dedicated to unraveling how the nervous system and the immune system communicate back and forth. While the interactions are mind-bogglingly complex, one key mechanism seems to be hormonal in nature. Studies have shown that the body releases ''stress hormones,'' which in turn affect immune system responses. Hormones, for example, appear to reduce the ability of our body's natural killer cells to destroy cancer cells and control life-threatening infections. Other studies have shown that depression and anxiety make outbreaks of herpes more frequent and painful and that highly stressed people are more likely to get colds. Another well-known body-mind phenomenon is the ''placebo effect''—about 25 percent of patients respond to ''sugar pills'' simply because they believe that they will work.

In one of his movies Woody Allen said, ''I can't express anger. That's one of the problems I have. I grow a tumor instead.'' While the neurotic character was joking (I think) and few scientists would subscribe to such a direct connection, fewer still would insist that the mind doesn't exert any influence on the body. Stress is widely acknowledged to contribute to many illnesses; estimates indicate that from 50 to 80 percent of illnesses are linked to stress. Fortunately, there are many stress reduction techniques that have proven track records and are being used with increasing frequency by people undergoing chemotherapy.

WHAT YOU CAN DO ABOUT STRESS

Basically there are two things you can do to relieve stress. First, you can try to remove as much stress as possible. Second, you can try to learn how to deal with the necessary stress in a positive way. In order to accomplish either of these tasks, you must first be able to discern exactly what it is that is creating the stress. Sometimes just becoming aware of stress can begin to help; then you take it seriously and figure out ways to deal with it. Saying you are afraid of ''cancer'' or ''chemotherapy'' is not specific enough. For instance, if you are concerned about your prognosis, speak to your doctor, who may be able to help get your concerns more in line with reality so the unknown becomes known as much as possible. If you are afraid of being alone during treatments or afterward, ask a family member or close friend to stay with you. If you feel uncomfortable because you've lost all your hair, make the effort to find a natural-looking wig.

Emotional counseling, discussed in the previous chapter, is another avenue to explore. With professional guidance, you can begin to fight back. Instead of bottling up frustrations and tensions and leaving them to bubble up inside, letting them out and letting go can reduce the harm that chronic tension can do. Feelings that are repressed or denied during treatment often crop up later as posttreatment depression. And you can help your body withstand stress better by maintaining general health—getting adequate nutrition, avoiding cigarettes, limiting your intake of coffee and alcohol and other drugs, and getting enough rest and exercise.

Another way to cope with stress is through specific stress management/reduction techniques. Eastern medicine and philosophy have long recognized that the mind and the body are one and that people have the potential to control their minds and, through them, their bodies. This interrelationship between mind and body and the techniques used to exploit it have only recently begun to be appreciated by Western medicine. Though these techniques can be used by anyone, many of them are now being developed specifically and used as adjuvant treatments to relieve the physical and emotional side effects of cancer and chemotherapy.

These techniques, which range from simple relaxation methods to more advanced "mind-control" practices, include biofeedback, meditation, controlled deep breathing, progressive muscle relaxation, self-hypnosis, and creative imagery or visualization. Therapists usually combine two or more into a unique package, in accordance with their style, training, and preferences and the requirements and abilities of the patient. Often the simpler techniques serve as stepping-stones for the more advanced methods. (In addition, there may be a psychotherapeutic element involved.)

Matthew Loscalzo, a social worker at Memorial Sloan-Kettering in New York who is trained in these techniques, stresses the importance of using an integrated approach:

"Some people feel that self-hypnosis is a strong enough tool to use by itself to reach many goals. I do not share that view.

I never do only one thing: Hypnotherapy is only part of my overall treatment plan. The issues going on are much too important and complex. We need to carefully tailor our treatments to meet the specific needs of our patients and their significant others."

Regardless of the name or level, such techniques are all based on the ability of the mind to directly control many of the bodily processes that the Western way of thinking has traditionally thought to be involuntary. For example, athletes and soldiers are often able to ignore or tolerate an incredible amount of pain during a competition or battle. Traditional medical doctors tend to have trouble with this concept, even those who accept the results of studies that show that placebos (sugar pills) work 20 to 40 percent of the time. If a placebo works because the mind, which believes in the medicine, actually brings about the expected effect, why can't these techniques work this way, too?

These techniques take time to learn, to use, and to show results. We don't know exactly why or how they work; they do not work for everyone or always work to the same extent. But in many cases where drugs have failed to work their magic, and without adding any harmful side effects of their own, these techniques are achieving results in reducing stress and controlling the symptoms and side effects of cancer and chemotherapy. They have successfully reduced or eliminated anxiety, tension, insomnia, nausea, vomiting, diarrhea, lethargy, depression, feelings of helplessness and hopelessness, and pain in chemotherapy patients. They have increased patients' feelings of well-being, relaxation, and control over their lives.

Biofeedback

When you are under stress, your body reacts in several ways—muscles tense up, blood vessels constrict, blood pressure goes up, hand temperature goes down, and so on. Biofeedback (short for biological feedback) is a way of measuring and monitoring these bodily processes and feeding this information back to you visually or aurally so you can see or hear it. But having a direct line to your physiological responses is only a beginning. While you are hooked up to the machinery, the idea is to learn how to follow its signals and thus voluntarily change them.

Unless you know specific relaxation techniques to effect these changes, you learn to relax by trial and error, a process that takes considerable time, effort, and patience. In many cases biofeedback is the first step in a total therapeutic package that utilizes a combination of several techniques.

Meditation

Meditation is an integral part of life in Asian cultures, whence it sprang and where it is tied up with a view of the world and with spiritualism. Western science has shown that meditation has deep and measurable relaxing effects that are inherently pleasant and useful. Although here transcendental meditation (TM) has gotten the most publicity, there are many schools of meditation. So whether or not you revere a maharishi for spiritual reasons or for his business acumen, you may be able to turn to some type of meditation to your advantage.

All schools of meditation aim to focus your attention inward by concentrating on (meditating upon) the steady rhythm of your breathing or on a single object, thought, word, or sound such as the mantra "om." When you focus your concentration so intently, your mind becomes empty of all distracting thoughts.

Deep Breathing

This is a simple technique that you can do on your own, after checking with your doctor. It actually relaxes your muscles and can slow down your heartbeat, lower your blood pressure, and increase blood flow to your hands and feet. Matthew Loscalzo, who lectures and trains others in hypnosis, feels that slow or rhythmic breathing is especially helpful when you need to gain a sense of self-control quickly:

> "An example is with uncontrollable crying. It's amazing. The tears actually do stop flowing. The person will still feel the appropriate feelings of fear or sadness but will experience a greater sense of self-control and will stop crying. This in turn has an effect on one's self-esteem. All people need to feel they can maintain self-control, not just cancer patients. This in no way means that people should not cry, which is a healthy and desirable human response, but rather that there are times when people need to control their emotions."

Such a time may be during a meeting with your doctor, when you need to ask specific questions and listen to the answers. You can't do this if you're crying. Another example might be during a diagnostic test. I remember that during my bone scan I was sobbing so uncontrollably that it was interfering with the imaging. Perhaps if I had done deep rhythmic breathing, I could have controlled myself long enough to complete the test rather than coming back again later in the day. Still another instance might be during a counseling session. As Loscalzo points out, "Sometimes these are the only times that people can cry, and we encourage them to do that. But if they can only cry, they can't get to what their fears and sadnesses are about."

Sitting or lying in a comfortable position, close your eyes and try to empty your mind of all thoughts. Place your hand over your abdomen and inhale through the nose, slowly, to the count of four, while puffing up your stomach and letting your diaphragm expand and the air travel up to the chest, back, and shoulders, and imagining it filling your entire body. When you feel as full of air as you can be, hold it a second. Then slowly, to the count of four, exhale through the mouth and feel the tension drain out of you along with the air. Repeat this, gradually slowing down the inhalation and exhalation to a count of ten and holding it for ten.

Loscalzo warns patients that if this is done incorrectly, there is the possibility of hyperventilating: "Breathing too fast can make a person scare themselves more." He emphasizes that "the breathing needs to be slow and rhythmic so the brain gets the message that it's safe."

Progressive Relaxation (Muscle Tensing and Relaxing)

This technique has been around since the 1930s, when Dr. Edmund Jacobson, a psychophysiologist, developed it. Since then many variations have evolved, but they are all basically a way of systematically relaxing the body by alternately tensing and relaxing individual parts of it. It is easier to relax something that has been made very tense first: Using the principle of extremes, you first get to know how it feels to be really tense, then let go completely and thus get to know how it feels to be really relaxed. Here is an abbreviated form of progressive muscle relaxation you might want to try.

In quiet surroundings, lie or sit down (lying is best) in a comfortable position, wearing comfortable, loosened clothing. Close your eyes and become aware of your body and your breath. You should breathe deeply, easily, and rhythmically throughout the exercise. Focus on your right foot and flex your toes back really hard; hold it this way for a few seconds and then let it go completely limp and relaxed. Work up your right leg by tensing each muscle group and then letting it go completely, making note

of and enjoying the difference between the two sensations. Then
do your left foot and leg. Then the hips, waist, back, chest,
hands and arms, shoulders, neck, and scalp. Move to your face,
open your mouth wide, raise your eyebrows, stare with wide
open eyes. Next, scrunch your face and purse your lips as if you
had just tasted something sour—and then completely relax those
muscles. Stretch your arms overhead, point your toes, and stretch
and tense every single muscle in your body at one time. Then
relax. Return your focus to your breathing, gradually open your
eyes, and bring your awareness back to your surroundings.

Hypnosis and Self-hypnosis

Sleeping and daydreaming are two altered states of consciousness; we enter these naturally and frequently. Hypnosis is
thought to be an altered state, too—one that has been used in
some form for many years. Lately, it has been increasingly used
by the medical profession and related professions for a number
of reasons, often to relax patients before anxiety-producing procedures, as drugless anesthesia, and as a means of controlling
acute and chronic pain and discomfort.

Loscalzo feels that though "this technique is becoming increasingly utilized, a lot of people still have a lot of ignorance
and misconceptions about hypnosis. People fear that the hypnotist has power over the patient, rather than it being an exten-
sion of some everyday normal processes, such as daydreaming
or fantasy. There is always a part of the self which is observing
and protecting, regardless of the depth of the trance."

A hypnotist helps us enter the trance and may then go on to
train us in self-hypnosis so we are no longer so dependent on
the skills and time of another person. The hypnotic state has
been compared to a meditative trance—both are valuable sources
of relaxation and lead to a sense of well-being. But hypnosis is
more than entering a relaxed state—it is a goal-oriented technique used to focus on specific problems that are usually stress-
related. Self-hypnosis increases self-control. It is generally
agreed that when a person is in a deeply relaxed state, he or she
is more open to "suggestion"—the introduction of a believable
idea, thought, or image into a person's mind. As Loscalzo continues:

"Hypnosis is somewhat like a meditation technique. If people already know how to meditate, my work is half-done. I
ask them to put themselves into a meditative trance, and we

do the work in that state. But a trance itself doesn't do the work. It does nothing but put you in a relaxed state, which creates a medium for communication. Being in a relaxed state is not necessarily therapeutic in itself. It's a technique or a tool, or a way of thinking about treatment, it's not therapy.''

Hypnosis and related techniques such as relaxation and desensitization help some patients cope with some of the side effects of chemotherapy and with some of the medical procedures that usually go along with it. Hypnosis can counteract conditioned aversions (such as anticipatory vomiting, which occurs before a chemotherapy treatment), posttreatment nausea and vomiting, phobic reactions (such as fear of a hypodermic or intravenous needle), acute or chronic anxiety (such as that surrounding a treatment or procedure or surrounding the diagnosis of cancer), and some types of acute and chronic pain. It can also be used to relieve depression by overcoming the "learned helplessness" common to many patients and imparting a generalized sense of self-control.

VISUALIZATION/CREATIVE IMAGING

Various forms of visualization have been used for many years in conjunction with hypnosis and relaxation to treat many ailments, complaints, and undesirable habits—pain, fears, overeating, and smoking. During visualization, people first enter a deeply relaxed state and then create a mental picture of a desired goal or outcome. Overweight people, for example, picture themselves as thin. When cancer patients use visualization, they often imagine their cancer cells as weak and confused, their treatment and white blood cells as destroying the cancer cells, and their bodies as recovering and being healthy.

Medical doctors, nurses, psychiatrists, psychologists, and social workers use visualization, usually after other relaxation techniques have been firmly established with their patients. A biofeedback technician told me that she begins with an education component. She explains to patients that chemotherapy is a stressful situation and helps them understand the way they are perceiving and reacting physically to the treatment. She uses biofeedback to measure the physical effects and point them out to the patient. Then she teaches them breathing and progressive relaxation, which they practice at home three times a day. "Once I see a patient is doing a lot of home practice and can really relax the body, I add visualization.'' She then uses visualization three ways:

"I use it for rehearsal. The patients envision themselves getting the therapy, it coming into their bodies and killing the cancer cells. I have them picture themselves going through the treatment, feeling good, calm, relaxed, and in control. They feel themselves participating in their treatment process, seeing themselves healthy. We can start this a few days before the therapy is administered and then do it during the chemotherapy treatment itself, actually visualizing the drugs killing the confused cancer cells.

"I also use it for manipulation, for pain reduction. I teach them how to manipulate pain by using some kind of symbol. For instance, they may assign a color and shape to areas of the body that are feeling pain; then the pain-free parts are assigned a light blue soothing color that gradually creeps into the colors where they feel the pain, slowly shrinking and easing the pain.

"Finally, I use visualization as a minivacation. They visualize a safe, comfortable place that they enjoy going to and can relax in. Taking a vacation away from where you're at will create a relaxation response.''

One patient describes her experiences with these techniques that she became interested in because of her anxiety and nausea:

"I felt kind of silly at first. It's a crazy thing to imagine your own cancer cells and create your own army of white cells to fight them. But believe it or not, you *are* able to visualize these things. As we get older, maybe we're stupid not to do things that are silly. Maybe we become too realistic.

"The self-hypnosis helped me stop the anticipatory anxiety and vomiting; it also eliminated the metallic taste in my mouth from the drugs. The doctor tried to help me control the nausea after the chemotherapy, but that he couldn't do. I think that's because I didn't believe in it as much as I should have.

"I think the thing with this is it gives you a sense of control of yourself. It's like your own personal chemotherapy. It's something you can do for yourself. I think it is also a way of letting out hostilities. It takes me twenty-five minutes every day and it's hard to find the time to do it, but it's very relaxing and I feel such a sense of well-being. Even though I'm off chemo now, I'm continuing to do it."

Some proponents of visualization believe that the mind can actually control the cancer. There is no real proof of this in the form of the controlled studies that scientists have been trained to go by; there are only anecdotal material and uncontrolled studies. While the thought that we have the power within us to control our own minds and bodies to such an extent as to influence the course of our illness is an exhilarating one, it can also be frightening in its implications.

Critics of this view say it implies we somehow caused the disease in the first place. As Susan Sontag writes in *Illness as Metaphor*, it manages to "put the onus of the disease on the patient." This is "preposterous," she says; it is a punishment, a moralistic view of the disease. It seems to me that once you become sold on the idea that you have caused and can therefore "uncause" your cancer, you become solely responsible for your disease. Under these conditions, it may be more devastating when there is a setback. If the cancer is not controlled, it follows that *you* alone are guilty of failure, or weakness, of a lack of faith, of having the "wrong" feelings, of wanting to die no matter how much you really want to live—a tremendously unfair additional burden for a cancer patient to have to bear.

Matthew Loscalzo says, "I do visualization and all that stuff. The literature shows that white blood cell counts can be raised through these techniques, and I'm comfortable with that. But I'm very skeptical of people who take people's money and say they are curing cancer."

Of the many therapists who are trained in these techniques, few would go so far as to say that visualization alone can control cancer. Most use it in conjunction with other therapies, including conventional therapies such as chemotherapy, because it helps their patients feel more in control over their lives and because it helps them tolerate the therapy better and come to have faith in it as a friend, not an enemy.

Relaxation Tapes

There are now many different audiocassette tapes designed specifically to help you relax. They may contain specific instructions for entering a relaxed state, usually some variation of progressive relaxation or visualization. Some, rather than being formal "relaxation tapes," are just recordings of pleasant music, natural sounds such as the ocean or rain or birds, or a combination of both.

"People use tapes for running and working out but don't think of using them for chemotherapy," says Moynihan. "Yet developing a reverie from sound can be very helpful to people. It can help you center yourself, relax, sleep." You can try using tapes during the actual chemo treatment, during a hospital stay, or in the privacy of your own home.

Most experts feel it's ideal to have a tape individually made for you by a therapist. The images and sounds will be those you associate with feeling safe and comfortable, and the voice will belong to someone you have met. But this isn't always possible. Ready-made tapes are available from some cancer support organizations, through mail order, and at music stores, yoga schools, health food stores, bookstores, drugstores, and libraries.

OTHER THERAPIES

There are many other therapies, disciplines, and practices that cancer patients have found help them cope with the mental and physical stresses of chemotherapy. Body work such as yoga, exercise, and massage therapies are one type. These are discussed in Chapter 9. Creative or expressive therapies such as dance therapy, music therapy, and art therapy are another— these enable people to be expressive in nonverbal ways. "People can be inhibited verbally—they can't talk about what's going on inside them," says M. L. Frohling. "But they can feel it. They might be able to move or draw and express it that way. When they do express it in some form, there is a sense of completeness and relaxation."

Music can be quite therapeutic, and is being offered as an option to cancer patients at a growing number of medical facilities all over the country. Soothing classical and/or harp music is often used in conjunction with the relaxation techniques described earlier to make chemotherapy treatments more bearable, to help patients sleep, or to ease anxiety in general. A lung cancer patient who discovered music early during the course of her very difficult therapy said using her small cassette player and earphones during and after each treatment got her over the roughest spots.

Music has indeed been shown to have direct effects on the mind and body, although we're not yet sure exactly how. Music can generate feelings of serenity and relaxation, cheerfulness and excitement, or gloom and melancholy; it can conjure up all sorts of mental images; it can affect our blood volume, our heart rate, and our blood pressure. Because it can affect us so powerfully, choose your playlist carefully. You may want to follow the advice of most music therapists, who recommend that people with medical problems work with professionals who will teach you how to use music specifically to reduce your perception of discomfort and create a positive state of mind.

Laughter therapy is a new addition to the menu of stress-reducing techniques. The idea may make you laugh, but laughter is one of the best coping mechanisms there is. Norman Cousins put laughter therapy on the map with his well-known book *Anatomy of an Illness*, which chronicles his use of humorous books, old episodes of "Candid Camera," and old Marx Brothers movies to help him recover from a crippling degenerative disease. (The Alan Funt Fund is a nonprofit corporation that lends "Candid Camera" videotapes: the address is P.O. Box 827, Monterey, CA 93942.)

There's nothing funny about having cancer, but we can still laugh at the world. Sometimes we can even laugh at ourselves or appreciate the absurdities involved with our disease and our treatment. It's hard to imagine laughing when you've been throwing up for three hours straight and know you'll be doing the same thing every two weeks for the next year, when you're so weak that you can barely drag yourself out of bed, when you're so pale and bald that even *you* don't want to be seen with you. And yet patients do find it within themselves to laugh. These things are so awful that people need to laugh—as an escape, a defense, and as a release of tension. Patients often joke about looking like Kojak or majoring in advanced toilet bowl or how they might get arrested because their arms look like a junkie's. As one patient says, "It doesn't seem so awful when you laugh about it."

Your oncologist's attitude can encourage or discourage a healthy sense of humor about your situation. I sometimes spent more time joking and laughing than being treated. My doctor said I had the same type of humor you usually find in an oncologist. Dr. Charles Vogel of the Comprehensive Cancer Center for the state of Florida likens the atmosphere on some oncology services to that of the M*A*S*H unit of film and TV fame. Los Angeles oncologist Dr. Michael Van Scoy-Mosher is a firm believer in the value of laughter for his patients:

"I think humor can be used—not that this isn't serious—but I found there's a real place for seeing it in an almost absurdist way. This view can be very useful. I remember, for example, I was treating a guy with a real sickening therapy for Hodgkin's disease. He happened to see me one day out in a store. The moment he saw me and his eyes met mine, he threw up. We both understood, but of course, nobody else in the store understood—they just saw this weird guy come in, throw up, and leave. We had a good laugh about it later."

Scientists actually have an explanation as to why laughter does us so much good. When you laugh, many parts of your body contract—your chest, abdominal muscles, diaphragm, and lungs. Your systolic blood pressure soars, your pulse rate can double, adrenaline is pumped into your blood, and endorphin (the body's natural painkiller) may be released. A good belly laugh is like a miniworkout, an internal jogging. Afterward, everything goes back to normal or slightly below, which results in a release of tension and an all-around feeling of well-being.

Pure Pleasure

Feeling pleasure is an important part of life, especially when you're undergoing chemotherapy. Yet it's easy to forget about pursuing pleasure when you're caught up in the whirlwind of treatments and side effects. It may seem frivolous at a serious time. But experiencing pleasure helps restore a much-needed balance to your life and offers a well-needed break from chemo-related routines and stresses.

As Robert Ornstein and David Sobel show in their book *Healthy Pleasures*, feeling good not only enriches our lives, it can extend them. "The human desire for enjoyment evolved to enhance our survival," they write. "What better way to assume that healthy, life-saving behaviors occur than to make them pleasurable?" The book then goes on to document how small, simple pleasures and "stolen moments" help absorb the everyday stresses of life, making them easier to bear. So go ahead and enjoy such healthy pleasures as a walk in the park, a hug, tasty food, a movie or a play, a good book, a fun game, collecting, creating, and immersing yourself in a favorite hobby.

A positive attitude, a will to live, optimism, and a fighting spirit are crucial elements in your treatment. Even though the part they play in actually fighting cancer may be relatively minor, the part they play in your desire and ability to tolerate debilitating treatment may be major. A positive outlook that makes you feel more relaxed and in control will improve the quality of your life no matter how much time you have left. How much better it is to face everything with hope and equanimity than with helplessness and despair.

Diet and Nutrition

While good nutrition is important for everyone, no one really knows *exactly* what good nutrition is for the average healthy human being, let alone what is needed by the chemotherapy patient. Two facts have emerged from recent research, however. First of all: Diet and nutrition are an important source of support for those who are living under the special conditions and stresses that cancer and chemotherapy impose. And second: Nutrition is probably compromised to some degree in every person who undergoes chemotherapy.

HOW YOUR DIET AND NUTRITIONAL STATUS ARE AFFECTED

The chemicals used in cancer chemotherapy affect your mind and body and thus your diet in many ways. They cause a loss of appetite, a change in your ability to taste foods, nausea and vomiting, and changes in the mucosal lining of the mouth, esophagus, stomach, and intestines. All this can lead to alterations in the kinds and amounts of food you eat as well as your body's ability to absorb and utilize what you do eat. Some drugs can themselves chemically deplete or destroy nutrients in the body. As a result, chemotherapy alone can cause multiple obvious and not so obvious nutritional deficiencies.

In addition, the cancer patient is exposed to many other factors and conditions that deplete the body's supply of nutrients and/or increase its demand for them. Physical and psychological stress such as the diagnosis of cancer itself, surgery, and radiation have well-documented deleterious effects on nutritional status. The mere fact of being hospitalized—the physical and psychological stress of the treatments and the poor diet—has been shown to cause nutritional deficiencies. Other deficiencies or imbalances might be present as a result of the cancer itself or as carryovers from dietary conditions that contributed to the development of cancer in the first place.

My oncologist says:

"It's well understood now that many patients who have gone through surgical operations and who are in the process of receiving toxic medications have serious nutritional deficiencies. One of the most serious forms of malnourishment that occurs anywhere on earth occurs in the modern hospital. A person is thought to be okay because he is on intravenous feeding. The fact of the matter is that the total amount of nutrition he receives over the course of twenty-four hours is about the same as a couple of Coca-Colas."

There is an appalling lack of knowledge about the changes in one's dietary needs during chemotherapy. Therefore, as the authors of *Nutrition for the Chemotherapy Patient* write, "In clinical practice, nutrition is often neglected. The assessment of nutritional status . . . is generally quite casual" and is based on a "quick glance" and a "mental estimate" of how much body fat you have. Unfortunately, you can look well developed and well nourished, but underneath the layer of fat you may have lost significant lean body mass (muscle). "Further, where there are no overt signs of vitamin deficiency . . . the physician usually assumes the vitamin status to be normal. In fact the patient's vitamin status . . . is often marginal at best."

Dr. Samuel Dreizer and colleagues at the M.D. Anderson Cancer Center have been treating chemo patients for twenty years and find that the nutritional status of most of these patients ranges from the "subnormal to the extremely precarious." It's not uncommon for patients to have severe deficiencies in vitamin B_1 vitamin B_2, vitamin K, folic acid, niacin, and thiamine and the symptoms of sore, cracked lips and mouth, skin rashes, and bleeding. They have reversed these deficiencies and others with oral or IV supplements.

Chemotherapy patients often lose weight (although some actually gain it), become deficient in many vitamins and minerals, lose energy, and generally fall into a malnourished, unhealthy state at the very time they need to remain as strong and healthy as possible to fight the cancer, repair the damage done by the disease, and withstand the side effects of therapy. This not only lessens their quality of life while on chemotherapy, it could be setting them up for problems in the future.

WHERE TO GET HELP

The ways in which nutrition, diet, cancer, and chemotherapy interrelate is a frustratingly complicated field of study. Much more work needs to be done. Yet evidence is accumulating, and you can put it to work for your benefit. As D. M. Hegsted, professor of nutrition at the Harvard School of Public Health, declares in "Optimal Nutrition," an article published in the May 1979 supplement of *Cancer*: "The fact that we do not know the optimal solution cannot and does not prevent us from using whatever relevant evidence is available to make the best judgment possible. If we wait until we know everything we need to know, we will wait forever." He is addressing the problem of nutritional links with the onset of cancer, but the same arguments are being made for treatment, too.

Self-education is the first step toward making that judgment. What follows is a brief outline of the various types of thinking on the subject, from the most conservative through the moderate and up to the more progressive. Findings are often contradictory or inconclusive. Because the issue is so complex and important, only a qualified dietitian, nutritionist, or nutrition-oriented physician can intelligently advise you about making any drastic changes in your diet or taking large doses of vitamins, minerals, or other nutritional supplements. Although you should let your oncologist know if you are concerned about nutrition, you shouldn't expect your oncologist to dispense nutritional advice—most traditional doctors are lamentably ignorant about nutrition: Some are downright hostile toward the nutritional approach to anything, perhaps because nutrition has been overhyped, perhaps because they fear patients will forgo conventional cancer treatment and do only nutrition instead.

This problem is well recognized by experts in the nutrition field, be they of a conservative or a progressive bent. However, this state of affairs is gradually improving; imagine my own surprise when my surgeon, who had always seemed very traditionally minded, started asking me whether I take vitamins B,

C, and E and selenium! Lisa Logan, former nutrition support clinical dietitian at Presbyterian Denver Hospital, says:

"Many oncology patients have very complex medical problems, and frequently nutrition may be the last problem addressed. The current literature, which supports early nutrition intervention to lessen complications and improve tolerance to therapy, can no longer be ignored. So I have seen a gradual improvement in the awareness of physicians I work with. Also, many hospital outpatient clinics have nutritionists that deal specifically with oncology patients. Physicians concerned with the importance of nutrition will refer their patients for more extensive nutrition assessment and intervention."

Shari Lieberman, a nutritionist and registered dietitian in private practice, speaks from her own experience:

"The problem with conventional doctors is not that they don't believe in nutrition but that they are uneducated in that area. They don't admit this to their patients, but they admit it to me. They tell me to do what I think is best and to let them know what I'm doing. The added need for nutrients during chemotherapy is well documented, particularly as it relates to physical and physiological stress. So doctors that argue about this are just not reading. Maybe there's a little bit of tunnel vision.

"Dietitians are trained in food service science and have a minimum of an undergraduate course in nutrition. Although some hospital dietitians are doing progressive work, generally they are conservative. Nutritionists have a minimum of a master's degree in the nutritional sciences, which allows them to understand the subtleties of nutrition and the therapeutic nature of the components of food. Not all nutritionists are progressive. Ask your health food store to make a recommendation, or someone in your support group. Then make sure to ask where they got their training and education—some people call themselves nutritionists but aren't."

Dr. Michael Schachter is a physician in private practice who combines nutrition and holistic health with mainstream medicine. He treats many cancer patients who are on chemotherapy with other physicians, and he thinks oncologists tend to resist the idea of nutritional therapy as an adjunct to chemotherapy for several reasons:

"In some respects the two approaches are antagonistic—one tends to break down the body, the other tends to build it up. Or it may be related to the old expression, 'If you're not up on something, you're down on it.' They may think if there's some value to nutrition, then they should be doing it, too—but they're not doing it. So to protect themselves they have a very strong negative feeling about it.

"The position of many oncologists is they say the nutritional approach has not been sufficiently proved. But studies relating nutritional factors to cancer may take many years to complete, and cancer patients can't wait for these to be finished before taking action to help themselves. Some chemotherapy patients feel pretty terrible, and clinically they feel a lot better when they undertake a nutritionally supportive program along with their chemotherapy.

"We are happy to work with oncologists, if they are willing to work with us. Frequently oncologists do not support their patients being on a nutritional program, but patients are convinced that it will help. Consequently, patients surreptitiously undertake nutritional programs. We often get feedback from the patient that his oncologist is extremely pleased at how well he is doing, that the patient is zipping through the therapy with a minimum of side effects. I can also say that more and more oncologists, though skeptical of nutritional therapeutic approaches doing much good, are not taking as hard a line as they did previously. They say to go ahead and do it if you want to, as long as you take the chemotherapy, too."

My oncologist, who stresses the importance of individualizing all aspects of cancer treatment, sometimes suggests adding nutritional therapy to the chemotherapy regimen despite its "unproven" nature:

"My approach is that there are many things we don't know in medicine. But there are substances which are of use in assisting people to be able to perform better and do better which have negligible side effects. These can be useful in improving the strength of a person who is receiving therapy for malignancy. So I have tried to bring in elements that might be of benefit in terms of improving the body's strength. I have had to look at many sources, both traditional and nontraditional. Traditional approaches tend to look at data more critically and use double-blind testing to validate the doses of substances that are required. The nontraditional ones tend to say, 'Why don't we just try this and see what happens.' That latter approach has also produced some interesting effects. So I am in the position at this point in time of having to take somewhat sketchy, experimental data and apply it, perhaps in advance of its complete understanding.

"My basic point of view is that you keep your eyes open. You keep trying to apply as many things that may help as you can get your hands on, without being kooky. One has to be modest but listen to everything. I feel that as an internist I have to be well versed in everything that happens."

WHAT GOOD NUTRITION CAN DO FOR YOU

Whether you follow the conservative, moderate, or progressive approach, proper nutrition can help you in four important ways.

Improves Tolerance of Therapy

A well-nourished body is stronger and more resilient than a poorly nourished one. Studies have shown that nutrition can decrease the severity and duration of side effects such as vomiting, nausea, weakness, lowered immunity, and susceptibility to infection. There may be other special side effects that we do not know about yet, but in general people who eat well while on chemotherapy tend to feel better and stay more physically active and more mentally alert.

Increases the Effectiveness of Therapy

When you feed yourself, you also feed your cancer cells. Studies have shown that well-fed cancer cells multiply more readily and so are more susceptible to anticancer drugs than are slow-growing, undernourished cells. In addition, a good nutritional status may allow you to withstand higher doses of drugs and so increase the effectiveness of the therapy in that way as well.

Speeds Recovery From Treatments

Nutrients are the building blocks your body uses to rebuild the normal tissues that have been affected by the chemotherapy. If the proper nutrients in the proper amounts are available, the recovery process takes place much more quickly and efficiently than it does when deficiencies are present.

Regulates Your Weight

Many people lose weight on chemotherapy, but some (notably women on chemotherapy for breast cancer) gain weight. Underweight and overweight are both undesirable for the chemotherapy patient: They can lead to weakness, lethargy, depression, embarrassment, and lack of self-esteem. Being careful about what you eat will help control both these extremes.

THE BASIC FOUR + ONE

All approaches to nutritional support for the chemotherapy patient are grounded in the concept of a well-balanced diet. Simply stated, a balanced diet contains a variety of foods that will give you the vitamins, minerals, protein, carbohydrates, fats, and water needed to keep your body working normally. In order to help people get the variety of foods in the right amounts, the basic four food groups were established. Adhering to this basic plan is good practice for everyone, chemotherapy patients included. Since some anticancer drugs can affect the bladder or kidneys, it is important for you to include a fifth group: liquids (water, juices, tea, broth, soup). Every day's menu should include:

Fruit and vegetables: four servings (two of each)
Meat, fish, poultry, eggs, cheese: three servings
Grains: four servings
Milk and milk products: two servings
Liquids: eight to twelve glasses.

It is likely that you will need more protein and calories than usual after surgery to help you heal, and during chemotherapy to help your body replace lost healthy cells and keep up your weight, fat stores, and lean muscle mass. Even though you may not be feeling well or don't feel like eating these particular foods, it is important to eat well. If side effects make it difficult for you to eat according to this plan or if you have lost or are losing weight, turn to the chapter on gastrointestinal side effects for tips on overcoming your difficulties. Some patients are advised to add liquid nutritional supplements to their diets. Generally, a multivitamin/mineral supplement, which will help make up for the nutrients that your diet is lacking, can be taken safely and is advised. In *A Comprehensive Guide for Cancer Patients and Their Families*, Dr. Ernest Rosenbaum writes:

> "In some cases vitamin and mineral supplements may be needed because of the side effects of certain types of cancer or of therapy, which may result in vitamin or mineral losses or increased requirements. Vitamin and mineral supplements may also be needed by patients who are unable to eat a balanced diet, or who have loss of appetite, malabsorption or weight loss, or who drink or smoke excessively."

The majority of chemotherapy patients fit into at least one of these categories. Remember, too, not to rely solely on supplements—real foods contain nutritional elements that supplements don't, perhaps some we don't even know exist. (In extreme cases of advanced cancer or severe weight loss, an oncologist or dietitian may put patients on supplemental tube feedings—either through tubes inserted into the stomach or small intestine or through intravenous feedings.)

THE NEW GUIDELINES: IMPROVING UPON THE BASIC FOUR

The advantage of the basic four food groups model is that it is fairly easy for the average person to follow: The typical American diet can easily satisfy its requirements, so no major changes are needed in the way we're used to eating. This is in some ways a disadvantage because it has been discovered that as a population we are not eating as well as we thought we were, and we should make changes. It's possible to appear to be following the basic four and still get too little of some nutrients and too much of others. For example, you may not accept the concept of catsup as a vegetable but readily accept canned string beans or French fries, which are also fairly low in the hierarchy of wholesome food.

There is so much evidence that the typical American diet is a contributing factor to many diseases—cancer being one of them—that even conservative government agencies (such as the

Department of Agriculture, the National Cancer Institute, the Senate Select Committee of Nutrition and Human Needs, the Department of Health and Human Services, and the National Academy of Sciences) have released very similar dietary guidelines urging Americans to change their eating habits. The National Academy of Sciences surveyed the scientific literature and concluded that cancers of most major sites are influenced by dietary patterns. Based on animal studies and observation of many human populations, it has found that we eat too much fat, too much salt, too much sugar, too much cholesterol, and too much food in general. And our health is suffering because of our indulgence. If you want to take further steps to safeguard your health, use these guidelines when choosing from the basic four food groups.

Easy on the Fat

Several studies show that people who consume greater quantities of fat have a higher incidence of cancers of the breast, bowel, and prostate. Americans should reduce the current level of their fat intake by more than one-fourth so it accounts for 30 percent or less of their total calories rather than the usual 40 percent. To do this, we should eat less beef and other fatty meats, reduce our consumption of cheese and other whole-milk, full-fat dairy products, and avoid fried foods.

As a result of consumer demand, low-fat beef is readily available. If you want to avoid added antibiotics, hormones, and pesticide residues, you can buy organic beef and free-range chickens in many supermarkets, butcher shops, and health food stores. And there are loads of vegetarian and low-fat diet books and cookbooks on the market to make low-fat meal preparation easier.

Vegetables, Fruits, and Whole Grains

There is evidence that vitamin C and beta carotene, which is converted to vitamin A in the body, protect against the development of cancer. Oranges, grapefruit, apricots, cantaloupes, peaches, strawberries, dark leafy green vegetables, carrots, winter squash, tomatoes, green peppers, and sweet potatoes—all are high in one or both of vitamins A and C. Cruciferous vegetables (broccoli, brussels sprouts, cabbage, and cauliflower) contain these vitamins plus certain compounds called indoles that research indicates can increase the body's capacity to convert carcinogens into harmless substances.

Fruits and vegetables are also high in fiber, as are whole grains such as whole wheat bread and bran cereal. Lower fiber consumption has been implicated in bowel and breast cancer, and the National Cancer Institute recommends that we increase our intake.

There is so much interest in food and cancer that the National Cancer Institute recently launched a five-year program to follow up on promising studies indicating the cancer-preventing properties of a whole slew of foods, including citrus fruits, garlic, flaxseed, soybeans, umbelliferous vegetables (carrots, parsley, celery, parsnips), cruciferous vegetables, and solanaceous vegetables (tomatoes, peppers, eggplant). At the M.D. Anderson Cancer Center, researchers are studying onions and licorice root.

A chemical called glutathione also deactivates many cancer-causing substances; it is found mostly in avocado, asparagus, watermelon, fresh citrus fruits, strawberries, fresh peaches, okra, white potatoes, squash, cauliflower, broccoli, and tomatoes. Other cancer-preventing substances have been found in bean sprouts, beans, rice, and potatoes; some of these also appear to actually reverse carcinogenesis.

It's no wonder that nutritionists recommend that about half our total calories be derived from these complex carbohydrates and naturally occurring sugars and that our intake of refined and processed carbohydrates be reduced to 10 percent.

Smoked or Cured Foods

Pickled, smoked, and salt-cured foods appear to increase the incidence of cancers of the stomach and esophagus. Japan, Iceland, and China, where these foods are consumed in great quantities, have higher incidences of these cancers. So avoid consuming a lot of hot dogs, bologna, salami and sausages, ham, bacon, and smoked fish; salt should be reduced to five grams per day.

Alcohol

Alcohol, especially when combined with cigarette smoking, has been connected with higher rates of cancer of the breast, mouth, larynx, liver, and lungs. Drinking "in moderation" is advised—probably no more than two drinks per day.

ADDED BENEFITS FROM NUTRITIONAL THERAPY: THE PROGRESSIVE APPROACH

Although these guidelines are a step in the right direction, there are many experts who say they do not go far enough—not for the average population and especially not for the cancer patient who is at high-risk for disease already and who is being further weakened by various therapies.

They point out that first of all, since cancer chemotherapy patients are at a high risk to develop second cancers and other illnesses, they should modify their diets as much as possible to reduce this risk. They feel that the recommended dietary allowances (RDAs) of vitamins and minerals in the so-called balanced diet are hard for anyone—and impossible for the chemotherapy patient—to get every day. They also claim that these RDAs are far too low anyway for optimum health in the average person and do not even begin to answer the needs of the chemotherapy patient. They argue that large doses of vitamins and minerals should be added to the nutritional regimen because they can protect organs from the toxicity of the drugs, counteract the carcinogenic activity of the drugs and other chemicals in the food and the environment, and improve the functioning of the immune system, which plays a role in destroying cancer cells but is being weakened by the therapy.

My oncologist says he is "not a megavitamin person" and thinks it's important to distinguish between megadoses of vitamins and large doses of vitamins. He will sometimes prescribe "large reasonable" doses of vitamins and minerals that might be useful as adjunctives in terms of trying to build the body:

> "Data produced by the National Cancer Institute, for example, have shown that vitamin E is useful as an antioxidant, and it has many other remarkable effects and no negative ones. There's lots of evidence to suggest that zinc is useful in the management of immunodeficiency disease of many origins. There is some data to suggest that selenium is useful under some circumstances. In reasonable doses, vitamin C does tend to promote restoration of normal tissue strength. Vitamin A in reasonable doses has been shown to be an immunostimulant under some circumstances. B vitamins have been shown to be useful during the recovery from many conditions; B vitamins are rapidly used up during cell death and cell restoration. So, for instance, one or two milligrams of vitamin B_1 just isn't enough."

In Dr. Schachter's holistic practice, nutrition is a cornerstone:

"Patients must have appropriate quantities of each of the nutrients in order to optimally support their body defenses. At the same time, nontherapeutic toxic substances should be eliminated as much as possible. We start out by recommending the elimination of junk foods, refined carbohydrates, chemicals, and so on. We emphasize the ingestion of complex carbohydrates—whole grains, vegetables, nuts, and seeds—and that patients try to cut down on their meat and get organic beef if they can. And then we add a nutritional supplementation program—vitamins, minerals, enzymes—as a kind of insurance.

"With regard to cancer, we're especially interested in trying to stimulate the body's defense system. We believe in the surveillance theory that people are developing cancer cells all the time. So we try to supplement liberally with nutrients that are thought to improve the body's defense system. We're also interested in protecting the organs against chemotherapy. One of the things that chemotherapeutic agents can do is form free radicals which damage the cell membranes and lead to carcinogenesis. By taking large (but not toxic) doses of vitamins A, C, and E and selenium, you're nourishing the organs that are being bombarded by toxic substances and protecting them from some of the damage."

Lieberman comments:

"I'm not against chemotherapy per se. It's just that it's done in a very nonthinking way. It's done to people who aren't eating, who aren't taking any supplements, who end up with multiple nutritional deficiencies, which is the last thing you want to do to a cancer patient.

"When people talk about eating a well-balanced, nutritional diet and they say you can get everything you need from food, that is uneducated. In order to get the RDAs of all the nutrients—which as far as I'm concerned are the bare minimum—you have to eat about 2,500 calories a day. That's a lot for the average person, and for people on chemotherapy—forget it.

"The thing that I emphasize for people who are going to take chemotherapy is that they can use nutrition to minimize the risks and negative effects of the chemotherapy. You can take supplements of selenium and vitamin E, which are antioxidants, and of A or beta carotene. Studies have revealed that cancer patients typically have low levels of these nutrients.''

Progressive nutritional therapy for the chemotherapy patient seeks to improve his or her health generally and protect specifically against carcinogens (such as anticancer drugs). It is based on three principles:

1. Avoid foods and nontherapeutic substances that are known to be or are highly suspected of being carcinogenic or that make the body a hospitable place for cancer to develop.
2. Include nutrients that bolster the body's own defenses.
3. Include substances that have the direct or indirect ability to inhibit the formation of cancer in the body.

It sounds simple, but the practice is not without its controversies. We don't know everything about the way the body responds either to chemotherapy or to the various nutrients, let alone about how chemotherapy and nutrients interact in the body. What to take? How much to take? Large doses of zinc, for example, have been shown to inhibit tumor formation in animals, but under other experimental conditions zinc may actually enhance tumor growth. Other equally contradictory findings can be cited for many other nutrients.

For many years these concepts and claims have been lumped with the alternative therapies and dismissed as worthless in the treatment or prevention of cancer. However, aspects of them have recently begun to capture the interest of members of the medical establishment. Most of the evidence so far is based on epidemiological studies that correlate the life-styles of large segments of the population with cancer incidence, on animal studies, and on undocumented human experiments.

Interestingly, M.D. Anderson is the first major cancer research institute to formulate a dietary supplement that contains forty-five vitamins, minerals, and other substances that have been shown in animal studies to inhibit cancer and have other beneficial health effects. The National Cancer Institute is conducting studies of calcium, folic acid, retinal (a form of vitamin A), beta carotene, vitamins C and E, and selenium to see whether they have an impact on cancer risk. Some of the subjects are people at high risk for cancer, including people who have been treated for cancer. The evidence is steadily accumulating that they do affect cancer development, and the case for supplementation, especially for the cancer patient being treated with toxic drugs, is getting stronger every day.

In one intriguing study done at the University of Wisconsin, breast cancer patients with high blood levels of vitamin A responded twice as well to chemotherapy as did women with lower levels. Two theories are being advanced to explain the results: Vitamin A helps protect against toxicity of the drugs, and the vitamin actually interacts with the drug to increase its potency against cancer cells.

In her book *The Real Vitamin and Mineral Book*, Lieberman cites this and other recent research showing that many substances not only possess cancer-inhibiting effects, they may also offer some protection against the negative effects of chemotherapy and environmental toxins and may even make the drugs more effective. For example, vitamin E may enhance the effectiveness of adriamycin; selenium may act additively or synergistically with chemo and radiation; and vitamin E and coenzyme Q prevent cell damage, particularly of the heart, from adriamycin. She feels that "subsequent studies will no doubt reveal other natural substances with similar properties."

Before I began chemotherapy, my oncologist gave me a nutritional evaluation. Based on lab tests and dietary analysis, he suggested a few changes and added nutritional supplements. I took (and still take) doses much higher than the RDAs. Knowing I was doing something that was perhaps protecting me from some of the harmful effects of chemo helped put my mind at ease. It formed an integral part of my overall therapy and ability to tolerate the drugs psychologically and perhaps physically, too. Oncologists say that women on adjuvant chemotherapy for breast cancer typically have minimal side effects, as I did. But I also have met many women who were devastated by it. I have no way of knowing to which of these two groups I would have belonged and whether the handfuls of vitamin pills made any difference. But I think and hope they did; just as I took chemotherapy to help fight my cancer, my nutritional regimen meant I wasn't going to take chemo lying down. It made me feel more confident and secure and less afraid of the therapy and what it was doing to the rest of me while it killed the cancer cells.

Exercise

While many oncologists advise their patients to stay active and try to live as normal a life as possible, few recommend an exercise program as a specific support therapy for those on chemotherapy. This is surprising, since most of us by now know about at least some of the benefits we can derive from exercise. Regular exercise can play an important role in overall health, in our body image, body awareness, self-esteem, and self-sufficiency. It strengthens us and keeps us limber. It is a superb outlet for stress and tension and a proven nondrug antidote to the blues and the blahs. There's evidence that physically fit people have lower death rates from cancer and heart disease.

Linda E. Perkin, a registered physical therapist and exercise physiologist, is the former coordinator of the Oncology Fitness Program at Denver Presbyterian Medical Center. Ms. Perkin worked with cancer patients for six years at Presbyterian and is now in private practice. She says that though more oncologists are recommending that their patients get some exercise, some still think, "Oh don't bother them, just let them lie there. I think perhaps they focus so much on chemotherapy that they don't consider recommending generally healthy things like exercise."

In 1983 the Ohio State University Comprehensive Cancer Center conducted a formal pilot project to study the physical and psychological effects of an exercise program on women with breast cancer. This was the first formal study of this nature ever done and was designed to compare a relatively aggressive rehabilitation program with the standard conservative approach. Dr. James Neidhart, the former deputy director of the cancer center, says: "This project met with a fair amount of resistance from physicians and lay people on our Human Use Committee. They felt that people with this type of cancer on these drugs should not be subjected to exercise, that the drugs are too toxic to allow it.''

The study, which consisted of ten to twelve weeks of a combination of twenty minutes of aerobic training on a stationary bicycle and stretching, demonstrated that some very positive results can be obtained by people receiving chemotherapy. Not only did the subjects not lose any of their fitness, they actually experienced an improvement of 20 percent. This was comparable to the control group of nonchemo subjects and may indicate that at least some chemo patients do not have to "just lie there." Maryl Winningham, exercise physiologist and director of the study, and others are very gratified by the result. In this and subsequent studies, Winningham and colleagues have found that exercise gives a psychological lift, reduces symptoms such as nausea, decreases fatigue, and improves patients' ability to continue normal day-to-day activities. She cites further evidence that the stereotype of the weak, sick cancer chemotherapy patient is not an inevitability. Dr. Winningham placed ads in *Runner's World, Nautilus* magazine, and *Bicycling*, asking that cancer patients who exercised contact Ohio State. She tells of the replies:

"We got over two hundred and fifty responses—all ages, all types of cancers, all stages, from all over the country. These were people who said, 'I am not going to sit down and die. I'm going to stay active as long as I can.' One woman wrote us a letter about her husband, who was a runner. He ran on a Wednesday, entered the hospital on the next Sunday, and died on that Monday. That is not your typical picture of a cancer patient. You can carry on the fight as long as you live."

Ninety-two percent of the respondents claimed that they felt better both physically and emotionally as a result of their activity.

Dr. William Grace, chief of oncology at New York's St. Vincent's Hospital, feels:

"Patients with cancer tend to baby themselves and they tend to get babied. It's good, I think, to emphasize that they remain very active, to emphasize their health rather than their illness. So we recommend a regular exercise program for most patients. There are people who run in races while on chemotherapy. Those high-performance folks do terrifically. People who are physically active seem to tolerate the chemotherapy. They tolerate more drugs, they have fewer side effects, and they often have a longer survival. Nobody knows why. It may be that they got more poison—but they do better.''

These days it is fairly likely that the cancer patient has been on some kind of exercise program before the diagnosis and treatment and would like to continue afterward. Active people want to remain as active as possible but may have questions about whether they should continue, what form of exercise is best, how much to do, whether it will hurt the action of the drugs or deplete the body of the energy it needs to fight the cancer and the side effects of chemotherapy. They—as well as people who have not been particularly active—should be encouraged to exercise because it has been found that many of the common side effects of chemotherapy can be minimized through the intelligent use of exercise.

THE BENEFITS OF EXERCISE

Exercise pays off in these specific ways for the chemotherapy patient.

Increase in Energy

It is well known that rather than making you tired, exercise actually gives you more energy. Your muscles become stronger and more flexible; your body is able to do things with more ease and efficiency. With aerobic exercise especially, the heart and lungs get a workout. As a result, these systems are strengthened; the blood flow increases, as do the number of red blood cells that carry oxygen; and endurance improves. The more you do, the more you can do. Maryl Winningham says: "We think the right kind of exercise helps maintain energy levels. If a person feels tired and just sits around, the enzymes that make energy in the body start going down the toilet—literally. The more you lie around, the worse you feel, and the more you lie around. People are just waiting to feel better, and they don't.''

Psychological Lift

Being physically capable and active is a positive step toward participating in your treatment and your life, especially if you have not been exercising much in the past. Regular exercise gives you a sense of vitality and physical accomplishment at the time you need it the most. It is well accepted that exercise can help you develop a clear, positive outlook.

Dr. Ward F. Cunningham-Rundles, an oncologist at Memorial Sloan-Kettering in New York who encourages many of his cancer patients to exercise regularly, reasons:

> "There's evidence to suggest that exercise tends to release endorphins, and that tends to make one feel better for many elaborate reasons. I also suspect that when a person exercises it tends to increase the amount of circulation to every part of the body, thus encouraging the turnover of end products from the tissues, and that tends to make one feel better."

Endorphins, the morphinelike compounds released by the brain during workouts, produce a "high" and are the body's own painkillers. With endorphins coursing through your bloodstream, you feel a sense of well-being, possibly even euphoria. Exercise can also help reduce anxiety and stress, and it provides a direct physical outlet for whatever frustrations and hostilities you may feel.

"Exercise lets cancer patients feel that they are maintaining control," says Maryl Winningham, pointing out another plus for chemo patients, "and this is of course a critical thing." The increase or maintenance in the level of self-care, independence, and economic productivity provides a real lift. In her survey, cancer patients felt that activity helped them cope with the stress of cancer and its treatment. It has been found that depression, which is one of the most common emotional states in a cancer patient, is relieved by exercise. Some doctors routinely prescribe exercise for depressed patients.

As healthy, attractive changes take place in your body and mind, you realize that your physical limitations are not what you thought they were. In addition, even a few minutes of exercise can be like a short vacation that takes your mind off of cancer, chemotherapy, and how rotten you feel. One patient confesses:

> "I started jogging with a friend just after I stopped the chemo. I decided I had to do something to keep myself from feeling so blah. I just had no energy, and we thought that maybe jogging would help. And it did. I enjoyed it. If you stop thinking about the worst, you can do things that you didn't think you could do before—your job, keeping up with the

other person. Maybe if I used my muscles a little more I wouldn't have felt so blah while I was on the chemo."

And if you indulge in sports it is especially enjoyable because of the company and because it's just plain fun.

I was a fitness nut before I got cancer, and I continued to exercise every chance I got. I wasn't up to running while on chemo, but I could swim and do calisthenics at home and at my gym. No one there except for one instructor knew I was on chemo. It was a great ego boost to see I could do just about everything that "normal" people could and in many cases even more. It made me feel less like a freak, less sorry for myself, and less that my life was a tragedy. I felt proud to be able to do as much as I did and relieved to be able to hold on to that part of the old me.

Physical exercise is an important symbol of health and vitality. If you have been exercising prior to your diagnosis and treatment, keeping physically active is an important affirmation of the continuity of your life and your life-style. In a time when so much may be changing, maintaining your exercise regimen as close to normal as possible assures you that your body and your life will go on and are not falling apart completely. If you can still swim laps, run around the park, dance, touch your toes, things don't seem quite so bad.

Decrease in Nausea and Vomiting

"Exercise seems to cause a decrease in the nausea and vomiting that chemotherapy patients suffer," says Lin Perkin. She continues:

> "We haven't been able to come up with anything scientifically definitive as to the physiological mechanism, but it may be due to the fact that hypermotility in the gastrointestinal tract tends to make people more nauseated. When you exercise, blood is diverted from the digestive system and into the muscles. Since there's less action in the gut and more somewhere else, this could be one of the mechanisms of decreased nausea. Or it may just be part of the proven psychological benefits of exercise—the fact of being active, not sitting around and brooding about the way you feel, or anticipating the way you're going to feel."

Dr. Winningham says that the patients in her studies felt less nauseated within about five minutes of exercising and maintained this for the rest of the day. She suspects the improved circulation, muscle tone, and sense of achievement all play a role and cites the mind-body connection in minimizing physical and psychological stress.

I was plagued by a constant low-level queasiness for most of my time on chemo. Exercise made it better, and swimming made it vanish completely.

Stimulation of the Immune System

There is evidence that vigorous exercise stimulates the immune system, possibly in many ways. This is important for the chemotherapy patient whose immune system is regularly being compromised. Some of the effects may be due to the stress-reducing ability of exercise, but this is not well documented. However, studies have shown that endurance (aerobic) exercise increases the number of circulating white blood cells in the body.

"People who exercise—particularly aerobically—tend to keep their white cells up," says Lin Perkin. "The count still drops, but it stays within a safer range. Not that you produce any more, but the turbulence of your blood brings them out of storage. So patients who have had a drop in their white count from chemotherapy can bring their immune systems back up by being active. This may help keep infections away and increase the effectiveness of chemotherapy by allowing the patient to accept a little more chemo, which might otherwise be held up or held back because of a low white blood cell count."

Although there is general agreement that exercise can have a beneficial effect on the immune system and the white cell count, there is conflicting evidence as to the particulars and some doubt as to the implications. Maryl Winningham, for instance, points out that there is a temporary rise in the white count during and immediately following intense exercise and that patients probably should not exercise vigorously immediately before having a blood test. This could elevate the white blood cell count and result in misleading results of blood tests on which treatments are based. She cautions:

"We are unsure about how chronic exercise affects the white cell count. Our hunch is that it might help stabilize it. Studies by the Russians demonstrate instability of the white count as a result of inactivity—the count fluctuates and the cells break down. We can't say categorically that it improves the count, but we do know that a lack of exercise seems to have a negative effect.''

Dr. Cunningham-Rundles says he has "every reason to believe that patients who exercise do better," but that there's some question as to the amount and duration of the exercise and its beneficial effect on the immune system. He explains:

"The situation is analogous to the relationship between alcohol and hypertension: A little bit will probably relax you a bit, but more will push your blood pressure up. In the same way, moderate exercise will likely improve immune function in many different ways. But if you've ever taken care of marathoners, you'll find they get sick all the time. The stress they put on their bodies is tremendous. It's important to get some exercise, but beyond a certain point, it uses up important body-building blocks.''

Other Benefits

Exercise has many other effects on the body that are of interest to the chemotherapy patient. It helps prevent osteoporosis (weakening of the bones) and coronary-artery disease. It stimulates the process of digestion, absorption, metabolism, and elimination and so can help fight constipation. Recent studies suggest that exercise reduces the risk of breast and colon cancers.

It can help you sleep better on the one hand, and stimulate the brain on the other—endurance exercises may improve memory, mood, and attention span.

In addition, it is an invaluable tool for regulating weight. Many people lose weight while on chemotherapy; exercise can help you gain weight or prevent you from losing it because it can stimulate a waning appetite. Conversely, for people who gain weight from chemotherapy, activity helps prevent weight gain by burning up calories and raising your metabolism so calories are being burned even when you are not exercising. (Incidentally, Dr. Winningham comments on her study of women on chemotherapy for breast cancer: "The group as a whole did not gain any weight." And I didn't gain any weight, either; although I got a little bloated tummy from the prednisone, I actually lost seven pounds during chemo.) Also, exercise gives you a sense of well-being and relieves boredom, which you might otherwise be tempted to alleviate through overeating.

WHAT, WHEN, AND HOW

Your exercise regimen depends on many factors, including your stage and type of cancer, the drugs and your reaction to them, your past and current fitness level, and, of course, your personal preference. No matter how weak and vulnerable you feel, you can do something that will in some way be beneficial. Cancer patients are capable of far more physical activity than most people usually assume. All that's needed sometimes is a little encouragement:

"Before the chemo I used to run up to six miles a day. But while on it I couldn't run for five minutes. My husband encouraged me to try other exercise—he's the type of person who pushes to the limit, and in a lot of respects that paid off for me. I'd say to him, 'What are you doing to me—I can't do this.' But I accomplished a lot more than I would have. He'd say, 'C'mon, you're going to go for a hike in the woods' or something like that. Physically I didn't feel any better after exercising, but psychologically I did."

It's important to rest when you need to, but unnecessary chair and bed rest results in progressive fatigue and weakness. During the first week of bed rest you lose about 3 percent of your strength each day. The longer you remain inactive, the harder it will be for you to regain strength. Even if you have been bedridden or inactive for some time, you should try to become as active as you were before the disease and its treatment took effect.

When lying in a bed, you can wiggle your toes, raise your arms and legs, sit up, do head circles, shrug your shoulders, and inhale and exhale deeply. Try the deep-breathing or the muscle-tensing/relaxing exercises in Chapter 7. Get up and walk around, even if it's just around the room. It's quite common these days to see cancer patients walking up and down hospital halls, IV pole and all. These gentle forms of activity will help you restore and maintain your bodily functions, increase your body awareness, and relax you.

With your doctor's permission, you can begin some form of exercise soon after surgery and continue during chemotherapy. A surgeon might give you recuperative exercises that relate specifically to restoring bodily function after your surgery or refer you to a physical therapist or a rehabilitation program, such as one of the ones offered to postmastectomy women at YMCAs and hospitals and through the American Cancer Society's Reach to Recovery.

If you've been active, you will probably want to resume your regular regimen in some form as soon as possible. But if you're new to exercise, if you've had surgery, or if you have stopped exercising for any reason, many of the guidelines you should follow resemble those applicable to anyone who starts exercising: Start slowly, build up gradually, begin each session with a light warm-up and end with a cool-down, stop when it hurts, and slow down when you become too winded to speak. You'll be amazed at how much you can do if you try.

For some, ordinary activities such as walking, shopping, cleaning, making the bed, climbing stairs, gardening, and playing with children might be enough. Others will want to continue or begin a more serious exercise program. There are many kinds of exercises that can improve your fitness level at all phases of your treatment, and there are dozens of books and classes. (It's wise for rookies to see a professional at first to get the proper technique.)

Experts suggest that you do whatever you like and whatever you can manage. Jogging, alone or combined with walking, fast walking, rebounding on a trampoline, bike riding, climbing stairs, and aerobic dancing are all possibilities.

Winningham especially recommends "rhythmic walking" for cancer patients—walking briskly, arms swinging, so your whole body gets involved. In her book about the technique, she points out that it is inexpensive and requires no special clothes or equipment, except for sturdy, comfortable shoes. When the weather outside is too cold or hot or wet, look for enclosed shopping malls, many of which open early especially for people who want to walk.

The American College of Sports Medicine guidelines recommend weight lifting or resistance training to maintain or enhance muscle strength. But because chemo can affect muscle control, gripping ability, tactile sense, and balance, this should be done using machines rather than free weights to reduce the risk of bruising or bone fractures. In addition, they recommend workouts that use low resistance and high repetition.

Many people find the practice of yoga to be particularly helpful because it systematically reduces stress and increases flexibility, mobility, and strength. There are several styles of yoga, all of which emphasize the benefits of deep breathing and some of which incorporate elements of meditation.

Swimming is also excellent, and many chemotherapy patients report that plunging into the water feels "great." You don't have to know how to swim to reap the benefits of the water's buoyance; water therapy is especially useful after surgery to avoid injury and during chemotherapy, when your muscle strength is diminished. You can still perform movements in water that would be more difficult, and possibly injurious, on dry land. As soon as my surgeon gave me the go-ahead, I was back in the water. I began to do light water exercises and then swam a few laps. I eventually worked up to a mile, and it felt better than it ever had before. The moment I dived into the water, the nausea disappeared, and so did the rest of the world. If it were possible, I would have stayed in the pool the whole nine months of treatment.

In his book *Do Not Go Gentle*, Herb Howe wrote that swimming in particular recharged him: "My pride in pulling against the water and rolling into a flip turn washed away any notions of defeat, dejection, and death." He remembered that Florence Chadwick, the marathon swimmer, had said, "Life in the water is less complicated."

Dr. William Grace says they often recommend the book *Royal Canadian Air Force Exercise Plans for Physical Fitness* at St. Vincent's because "the exercises start off at a very low level and build up gradually. They are also only twelve to fifteen minutes long," he points out, "and it's a very convenient way to judge progress or lack thereof. They're boring exercises, but they are good and they can be done without fancy equipment. A lot of people also walk or jog—and we recommend that."

Special Precautions

Maryl Winningham recommends that patients do not exercise for at least twenty-four hours after having a chemotherapy treatment. "At least nothing that will get the heart rates up. There is a possibility of diverting the chemicals into the muscle cells, which don't normally get a large blood flow, and away from the tumor cells." In addition, some drugs can cause irregularities in heartbeat for hours after the treatment, which could prove dangerous during exercise. Chemo patients should check with their doctors about possible restrictions. For example, a less intensive exercise may be recommended if you are taking drugs that can be toxic to the heart or lungs or if your blood counts fall too low. Platelets below 50,000 increase the risk of bleeding, and hemoglobin below 10 deciliters precludes vigorous exercise. When white cell counts fall below 3,000, avoid crowded facilities, spas, pools, and hot tubs, which can pose a risk of infection.

Dr. Winningham cautions that patients should not exercise if they have recent and/or extreme bone pain, shortness of breath, muscle weakness, or fatigue or if they have recently experienced severe vomiting. It's also unwise to exercise if you have a fever or infection. After surgery or an infection, resist the temptation to begin exercising vigorously until the day *after* the first day you feel better. Perkin also warns against taking dangerous risks involving balance, which may be off because of the drugs. Because I didn't trust my sense of balance, I avoided hopping on my beloved bicycle until after chemo was over. This was not the case with a friend of mine who fell off her bicycle and severely injured her jaw. "What if I had broken my jaw and they had to wire it shut? Can you imagine if the treatment made me throw up?" she wondered with typical chemo-induced black humor.

Both Dr. Winningham and Ms. Perkin warn patients that if there are metastases to the bone, high-concussive types of exercises such as running and jumping are dangerous; they recommend activities that put a minimum amount of force (from the body's own weight) on the skeleton, such as swimming, bicycling, and stretching. They also mention the need to modify the usual formula for obtaining the target heart rate during aerobic exercise in some cases. Ms. Perkin says if patients are very debilitated, she begins with the figure 220, the maximum human heart rate, from which she subtracts the age, then the resting heart rate. She then multiplies by 60 or 70 percent. She finally adds in again the resting heart rate to obtain the target rate. In cardiotoxic therapies, she'll usually have patients use 50 to 60 percent rather than the 60 to 70 percent in the above formula. Finally, certain signs and symptoms mean that you should stop exercising and consult your doctor. These include irregular heartbeat, dizziness or nausea, chest pain, leg pain or cramping, and difficulty breathing.

Exercising for one hour three or four times a week is the goal in most programs, because anything less than that isn't as consistently beneficial. But if you can't attain this all the time, remember that something is better than nothing. Chemotherapy patients often have good days and bad days. When you are having a bad day, says Maryl Winningham, "do something moderate rather than nothing at all. Give your body a break."

If you are uncertain about your level of activity and there is no physical rehabilitation or exercise program at your hospital, a chemo patient's wife offers this tip: Hire a professional trainer to work with you and design two workouts: one higher-intensity workout for the days when you feel best and a second, lower-intensity one for the days when you feel less well. Although personal trainers aren't cheap, only one or two sessions are needed to set up a program, and she feels the money was well worth it.

MASSAGE

A good massage is therapeutic for both the mind and the body. It is relaxing, it stimulates the circulation, it releases the joints, and it soothes away tension accumulated in the muscles. Massage is a particularly useful, though temporary, way of easing the discomfort of a particular physical problem, of physical exercise, or of everyday living. Though massage is not a cure, it can relieve aches and pains and thus reduce or eliminate the need for some medications.

Denver Presbyterian's Pam Felling says, "A lot of people in the cancer ward have a masseuse come in from outside. It is offered to them for relaxation, pain relief, improvement of circulation—all the normal things that massage is good for. They get the same benefits that anyone would—they're not that different."

One possible difference is the danger of massage spreading a cancer, a question that is brought up in massage textbooks. About this possibility, Lin Perkin says, "With really deep massage in the area of a tumor, you can actually physically break off tumor cells into the increased circulation. It used to be thought that the increased circulation itself was carrying off more tumor cells, but now doctors are using hyperthermia in conjunction with chemotherapy and rather than spread the cancer, the increased circulation enchances the effects of the drugs. So it's more the mechanical effects of massage that are dangerous. I don't think a light massage would do any harm; nor would a massage that avoids the area of the tumor or in cases where the tumor has been removed."

Concerned patients should still check with their oncologists to determine whether massage should be light or deep. Massage should not be painful, although in shiatsu the sensation has been described as "a good hurt." Communicate with the masseur or masseuse, too—let the therapist know whether you can tolerate only light stroking or a rubdown or whether you want something with more "oomph."

Your hospital may offer therapeutic touch (TT), as well as traditional forms of massage. Studies have shown that TT can cut the need for painkilling narcotics after surgery, speeds healing, and possibly boosts the immune system. There are now over thirty thousand practitioners in the United States, Canada, and dozens of other countries, and it is taught in more than eighty U.S. universities.

Massage therapy is available from professionals whose skills and manner vary; some states require licensing to ensure a certain level of ability. Your doctor, nurse, or social worker may know of a practitioner or may refer you to a physical therapist who can give you a medical massage. When a massage is given by a family member or friend—no matter how amateur or brief—it can be a reassuring form of physical and emotional communication that closes any gaps between caring and doing. As one patient said, "Massage is one of the nicest things one person can do for another."

Side Effects

Bone Marrow/Blood Effects

The cells of the blood, which are manufactured in the bone marrow, reproduce rapidly and frequently and so are quite vulnerable to chemotherapy drugs. Almost all the drugs used in cancer chemotherapy affect these cells. The drugs that depress, or lower the activity of, the bone marrow are called *myelosuppressive drugs*.

The bone marrow produces three types of cells: the white blood cells, which help fight infections; the platelets, which help clot the blood and control bleeding; and the red blood cells, which carry oxygen to the cells of the body. Low blood counts, therefore, affect you in three main ways: too few white cells (leukopenia) make you more vulnerable to infection; low platelets (thrombocytopenia) mean your blood will have trouble clotting properly; and low red cell counts (anemia) leave you tired, weak, and listless. All three counts can and do drop simultaneously; this is called *pancytopenia*. Blood counts generally are at their lowest level seven to ten days after a treatment, and at this point, called the *nadir*, you are at the greatest risk of developing complications. Low blood counts are expected in most chemotherapies, and your oncologist will periodically order blood tests, called complete blood counts (CBCs), to use as the main guide in determining whether there should be any changes in the dosage and/or scheduling of the drugs. Your body has an enormous capacity to churn out new blood cells but not a great enough one to completely forestall the side effects. As a result, most chemotherapy patients will have blood-related side effects in varying degrees. If the counts dip too low, the treatment will be cut down or held back until the counts return to safer limits. In cases of severe myelosuppression, patients are observed very closely, perhaps in the hospital. In some cases, drugs such as

155

antibiotics, colony stimulating factors (CSF), or transfusions of blood cells may be given. But there are many precautions and special steps that you can take both to minimize the side effects and to prevent complications from setting in.

INFECTION (Low White Cell Count)

Colds and flu are the most common infections that chemotherapy patients have to worry about. These are definitely unwanted additional problems, but they rarely progress beyond the nuisance stage:

"I did get a lot more colds than I usually got. My oncologist gave me a flu shot and ordered me to stay home from work because he was afraid I might get it during the 'High Holy Days' of the flu. He still insists I get a flu shot every year, even though my white blood count has never dropped as low as before and is fine now."

"If anybody came in this house and *sneezed*, I picked the infection up. One weekend I caught a cold from my daughter. The next Monday I was due for a treatment which my doctor wouldn't let me out of. So that day, there I was lying in bed with the shivers, I couldn't breathe, my chest and nose were killing me, and I was throwing up. I was a sight."

But the danger of infection can go beyond these minor respiratory diseases. Infections are the major causes of illness and death in cancer patients. Almost any organ or part of the body can become infected, including most often the mouth, skin, lungs, urinary tract, rectum, and reproductive organs. These infections may be bacterial, viral, fungal, or protozoal in nature; they may be common ones, but a higher than normal proportion are exotic types. Some patients have an episode of shingles from the herpes virus that causes chickenpox. The virus stays dormant in the body until the chemo activates it.

Most are minor and can be treated successfully with antibiotics or other medication. Severe infections require more aggressive therapy, which includes white blood cell transfusions. These transfusions may also be given as a precaution, before infection sets in, when the white blood count dips too dangerously low. In addition, a new biological substance, CSF (colony-stimulating factor), is sometimes used to "rescue" a patient with dangerously low white counts to prevent infection. It may eventually be used to prevent counts from falling in the first place. Infections of the exotic type and infections that are particularly acute can occur in the people with the leukemias, because in these kinds of cancer the chemotherapy is intended to and does greatly reduce the number of white blood cells. Dr. William Grace says:

"People on chemotherapy are going to run a risk of infection. Patients must know the signs of infection, that if they get an infection they can die, and that they should inform the doctor right away if they suspect they might have an infection. Some patients 'don't want to bother the doctor.' They have to learn to bother us. If they have a fever on Monday but don't call the doctor until Wednesday, it may be fatal or it may take them weeks in the hospital to recover from the infection. We now have very good oral antibiotics and can often keep patients out of the hospital if mild infections are detected early."

Symptoms of Infection

There are certain general signs of infection that you should watch out for and immediately report to the oncologist or nurse.

- Temperature of 100° Fahrenheit or higher
- Chills, shivering
- Loose bowels for longer than two days
- Burning sensation during urination
- Coughing, sore throat, chest pain, or shortness of breath
- Unusual discharge or blood from the urinary tract, lungs, rectum, vagina, and so on

In addition, patients should pay attention to the visible, accessible parts of the body that are most prone to infection. Since the immune system is impaired, the usual, normal signs of infection—redness, pus, and swelling—are not present or may not be apparent because they are actually signs of the body trying to fight the infection. In cases of severe immunosuppression or suspected infection, the oncologist may request tests of the urine, sputum, and feces and of nose, ear, and throat secretions.

Infection Preventive Measures

- Maintain a good nutritional status—eat a higher-calorie, high-protein diet. Vitamin/mineral supplements may be advised, especially vitamin C, which many oncologists are prescribing for their patients. Drink two or three quarts of fluid every day.

- Check with your doctor about what foods to eat during your therapy. For example, Dr. Philip Pizzo, chief of pediatric oncology at the National Cancer Institute, suggests that chemo patients check with their doctors about the advisability of eliminating fresh raw fruits and vegetables at certain points in their therapy, such as when the white cell count is particularly low or during a course of antibiotics. These foods may be potential sources for harmful organisms that can migrate from the gastrointestinal tract to other parts of the body and cause serious infection. "Normally these bacteria go in one end and pass uneventfully out the other," he explains, "but in chemo patients this may not be so." Recently, there has been additional concern about salmonella in poultry and eggs, so prepare these items carefully and cook them well.

- Observe good rules of hygiene. Bathe or shower daily if possible; wash the hands before meals and sexual activity and before and after visits to the bathroom. Keep your hands away from your face, and your fingers out of your mouth, nose, and eyes.

- Avoid crowds and particularly people or children with infectious diseases. Avoid exposure to people with herpes, chickenpox, and measles even if you had these infections in the past.

- Avoid exposure to bird and animal excreta—let someone else clean up the mess.

- Stop smoking and avoid smoky rooms. Take deep breaths of clean air occasionally.

- Get some exercise daily (aerobic exercise may help stabilize your immune system) but don't become overly fatigued. Get enough sound sleep and/or rest as needed.

- Avoid bar soaps—they are excellent mediums for the growth of organisms. Use liquid dispenser and/or moisturing soap.

- Keep your skin in good condition—dry thoroughly after washing and moisturize it if it's dry.

- Guard against burns, scrapes, punctures, and cuts; take proper care of them if they do occur. Wear protective gear when gardening, washing, and cooking. Be cautious while shaving—switching to an electric shaver is recommended.

- Maintain cleanliness and proper lubrication during sexual activity. Avoid excessive friction; prevent rectal contamination.

Sometimes antibiotics are used prophylactically. Dr. Grace remarks:

"We identify the people who seem to be at high-risk for infection—either due to their disease or their therapy—and treat them during their low white blood counts with preventive antibiotics that are known to reduce the risk of infections. These are most commonly used in patients with leukemia, but there's no reason not to use them in high-risk patients with other cancers."

Special Precautions for Women

The vaginal infections that plague women can be especially bothersome during chemotherapy, when lowered resistance joins forces with an altered hormonal/vaginal chemistry and less than optimum eating habits. There are several ways you can help protect yourself from these infections.

- When antibiotics are taken for a bacterial infection anywhere in the body, good bacteria are killed along with the bad ones, and in their absence fungus (or yeast) can take hold and flourish. To prevent this, many doctors recommend taking yogurt orally or as a douche to restore healthy bacteria in the body. Liquid acidophilus, available in health food stores, is a more concentrated source of friendly bacteria and may be used instead of yogurt. Using an antifungal (or yeast) vaginal medication may also be advised while you are taking antibiotics.

- Chemicals irritate and inflame delicate tissues and upset the chemical balance of the vagina. Avoid feminine hygiene sprays, commercial douches, and deodorized tampons and napkins.

- Do not use an IUD for birth control; ask your doctor about safer alternatives. Change tampons frequently during menstruation and substitute napkins as often as possible, especially overnight.

- Watching your diet may help you cut down on vaginal infections. Though this has not yet been scientifically proved, many nutritionally oriented health professionals recommend cutting down on sugars and other refined carbohydrates because an overabundance of sugars in the vaginal tract can trigger yeast infections. Fungus-related foods that contain mold or yeast (cheese, beer, wine, vinegar, and breads) should be avoided.

- Your clothes can contribute to a higher incidence of infections. Wear cotton panties or ones with a cotton crotch. Avoid tight pants and prolonged wearing of synthetic exercise clothes or wet bathing suits.

- Maintain scrupulous cleanliness in the genital area. Make sure to wipe from front to back after bowel movements to prevent fecal matter from entering the vagina.

POOR BLOOD CLOTTING
(Low Platelet Count)

When your platelet count drops, the ability of your blood to clot is reduced. Because there are other coagulation factors in the blood, most of them produced by the liver and rarely affected by chemotherapy, the blood will still be able to clot eventually, only the process will take longer than usual.

Your oncologist will know from your blood test whether your platelet count is low. In between blood tests you should watch out for signs yourself: red dots in the skin (*petechiae*), an abundance of black-and-blue marks, unusual bleeding from the nose or gums, or blood in the urine or bowel movements. These symptoms should be brought to the immediate attention of your physician.

When your platelet count is low, you should take precautions to protect yourself from any physical trauma that could cause bleeding. Take it easy and avoid dangerous situations such as contact sports, heavy physical labor, or any violent jarring activity that could cause you to bleed in your joints. Wear protective gear during gardening and cooking and other potentially hazardous activities. Be careful with knives, scissors, and razors. Even blowing your nose forcefully can damage delicate blood vessels and cause bleeding. Doctors advise you not to take aspirin because it further diminishes the blood's ability to clot, so use an aspirin substitute such as Tylenol or Datril. Use a soft-bristled toothbrush and avoid flossing if you find that your gums bleed easily. Sometimes switching from a wet razor to an electric razor is advised.

If you should injure yourself in spite of taking precautions, help the clotting process along by putting a clean cloth or paper towel over the wound and applying pressure for five or ten minutes. Elevate the affected part if possible, and use ice or cold water to constrict the blood vessels. Since a low platelet count is often accompanied by a low white cell count, take careful antiseptic measures to help prevent infection. If the bleeding hasn't stopped after twenty minutes, consult your doctor.

TIREDNESS AND WEAKNESS
(Low Red Cell Count)

For many chemotherapy patients, an ever-present tiredness is the toughest side effect to contend with. Though it tends to come and go in cycles, with the worst days usually occurring right after a treatment, the listless feeling may never really disappear completely. This is how one person describes it:

> "It was like they were shooting an A-bomb into me that blew me away every time. The two weeks I was off chemo I spent getting myself back on my feet again. But I never really had the chance to say, 'Gee I feel great'—by the time I got to feel human again, it was time to go back. It would have been nice to feel what it was like to be normal again just for a minute."

I am normally full of energy, the instigator of escapades (or easily talked into them), but on chemo I did a lot of staying at home. This state of not being quite myself was probably the most demoralizing side effect I had to live with. You think, "Who is this person?" The tiredness of chemo is not an ordinary tiredness and is rather hard to describe. It's more oppressive than coming home from a rough day on the job or staying up all night. I'd hear other people complain, "I'm so tired," and think, "If you only *knew*!"

Sometimes it felt like the day before a cold or the flu arrives: a vague, all-over dragginess, like a car running on the wrong fuel. Mornings were usually the worst; I'm not a morning person to begin with, but some days it was so hard to get started that my husband had to help drag me out of bed even though I knew that I would probably feel better once I was up and about. Other times it seemed I spent whole days sluggishly moving, dreamlike, through air as thick as water, my limbs made of lead, the very cells of my body made of stone. Chemo sometimes deprived me of the energy to walk, to think, to hold a pencil or a conversation, so overpowering was the heaviness in my mind, my bones, my guts, and my soul. The day after a treatment I'd find myself facedown on a friend's couch or under the covers of my bed, unable to do anything but complain.

Eventually, I discovered that on these low days quietly moaning to myself actually helped. It sounds silly, but there was nothing specific I could do to actually change the way I felt, and moaning at least allowed me to express my misery and functioned as some kind of outlet. Who knows? Maybe the inner vibrations became a kind of chant that helped the healing process.

When the weakness was bad, it was very bad; when it wasn't, it was bearable. I did manage to continue to work the whole time I was on chemo—I completed one book in progress, wrote another, and delivered the finished manuscript the same week I wrapped up my chemo. I continued a modified exercise regimen. And I did socialize and have fun—went to dinner, parties, dances, movies, and so on—but I coordinated these outings with my "up" periods, those times when I felt nearly normal, and then I was almost hyperenergetic, as if to make up for lost time.

Though individual, my experience was not unique. "I think the biggest thing that people complain about is being tired," says Donna Park, former assistant director of nursing, ambulatory care, at New York's Memorial Sloan-Kettering. She points out that in spite of the expected tiredness, people, especially women on adjuvant breast chemotherapy, are encouraged to "carry out their current life-styles" while on chemotherapy. However, she adds, "As health professionals we had at first underestimated the impact of this treatment on patients' daily lives."

This feeling of "general malaise," as the textbooks call it, though hardly life-threatening, is the side effect that is nevertheless most likely to turn a cancer patient's life upside down. A constant lack of energy is what keeps people from living more normal lives, from doing all the things that they want or need to do, from feeling like themselves.

Much of the anxiety about the tiredness is related to the issue of working. Showing up at the job every day like everybody else can be a real problem about which not much can be done specifically, unless you have an understanding employer, terrific insurance, and an undemanding job or can make your own hours.

Still, many people who need to continue to work do manage to muster enough strength to get there and get through the work day. So much of our identities and sense of accomplishment are tied up with what we do, and it is this, combined with the necessity of earning a living, that drives us to get up and out in spite of the gargantuan effort it sometimes takes. One patient recounts:

> "I got very tired when my blood count went too low. The lack of energy . . . I'm back to my normal habits now, but it took a while. I'm not one to sleep beyond seven or eight, even on my day off; on chemo I'd stay in bed until ten. Usually I'm at work by seven-thirty every morning; on chemo I got calls at eight-fifteen asking, 'Are you coming to work today?' Twice that happened. Then I got myself two alarm clocks. They were good about it at work, but I was mortified. By three in the afternoon I sat there not moving, thinking, 'I want to go home.' My staff knew it and understood. Usually, I work like a dog."

Sister Rosemary Moynihan, former assistant director of social service at Memorial Sloan-Kettering, tells of an amazing lady with a brain tumor who would call the same taxi every morning to drive her to work. She was very weak and would get dizzy, and she couldn't do too much bookkeeping anymore, but the people at her work were her support system. She would mobilize to go to work every single day until two weeks before she died.

Sister Rosemary believes that the ability to continue to work during chemotherapy can be a major emotional and social support in helping a person cope. She feels it has to do with the opportunity to reach out beyond oneself, to have a broader identity, to feel able to master things. She adds:

> "Of course for a patient who works as an interior designer and has to look good and be on top and be present at odd hours—that's tough turf. People who have jobs where there is physical stress—people who operate heavy machinery or who are in sales and always have to be 'up' and 'on'—and people

in high-powered executive positions find working difficult.
But if you have a job with flexibility, where your appearance
doesn't have primary importance and you can have one day
up and one day down, you do better.''

Overwhelming tiredness affects people's social and home
lives, too. Friends and family members may not realize how
tired and awful you feel; without any outward signs or symptoms, this is a side effect that others easily forget or are skeptical
about. They may mistake your lack of enthusiasm for laziness
or as a sign of depression or unsociability. It is important for
you to make the effort to keep contact with the people you care
about and to continue to do the things you like and need to do.
It should be explained to people that you still want to spend time
with them, but maybe not as often, or for as long, or in doing
the same things you used to. You may need to learn how to get
around the fatigue by, for instance, making some changes, setting priorities, and taking naps. Here is how several patients felt
about this:

"I was exceptionally tired while I was on chemo; I had been
the type of person who took on two jobs and worked sixteen
hours. When I was on chemo, I worked one job and would
come home and have to take a nap if I was going to be able
to cope with the evening's activities."

"I was more tired than usual. In the afternoons I almost always had to lie down and take a nap. Then I was able to get
right back into everything. Right back into my painting, right
back into the choir, right back into the other activities I enjoyed before."

"I used to come home from work and clean—I don't do it
anymore, I have help once a week. Now I clean in the morning when I have most of my strength, because when I come
home in the afternoon I can't do it. I wake up an hour earlier
just to get the house straightened out so at least when I come
home, everything is neat and clean."

At first I'd lie around the apartment in the evenings being so
bored and miserable. I was used to an active life, but I had to
save what energy I had for work during the day. How much can
you read? How much TV can you watch? About three months

into the chemo I decided this would be the perfect time to do something I'd always wanted to do: learn to play a musical instrument. It was just active enough, kept my mind busy, and really gave me a sense of accomplishment.

Fatigue is largely due to anemia, or a lack of oxygen-bearing red blood cells. The cells of your body literally become starved for oxygen and function suboptimally. Feeling dizzy, chilly, short of breath, and having a tendency to become upset more easily than usual are also indications of anemia.

Fatigue may also be caused or contributed to by the accumulation of waste products that are produced when large numbers of cells are killed by chemotherapy, a poor diet, a lack of sleep, and the emotional stress of coping with cancer and chemotherapy. Factors such as boredom, pain, and a lack of exercise may exaggerate the feeling of listlessness. Advanced cancer itself can make you tired.

Marguerite Donoghue and her coauthors list these additional signs of fatigue in *Nutritional Aspects of Cancer Care*: irritability, tearfulness, decreased ability to make decisions, withdrawal, apathy, feelings of hopelessness and helplessness, impaired concentration and memory, psychomotor retardation or agitation, increasing insomnia, lack of appetite, thoughts of suicide. These are all serious impediments to living a full, enjoyable life.

Coping with Fatigue

Researchers hope a substance called erythropoietin will help boost red blood cell counts and thus reduce fatigue. But as an oncology nurse put it, "There's no simple, easy solution to tiredness." However, there are many ways to help you lessen, prevent, and learn to live with it.

- Check your diet to make sure it is nourishing. You may need to increase your intake of protein and carbohydrates or take nutritional supplements. Some doctors may recommend iron or vitamin supplements to help build up your red cell count.

- Make sure to drink plenty of fluids to prevent the accumulation of cellular waste products, the by-products of chemo.

- Plan your days' activities and take advantage of ways to save your energy either by figuring out easier means by which to do them yourself or by getting someone else to do them. Sometimes your family or friends will be glad to pitch in, sometimes not. Outside household helpers can make all the difference during times when you just can't do what's needed—and some social agencies will help pay for this service. Many patients dislike asking for help from anyone, friend or stranger, but sometimes having help is the only way to get things done:

"I didn't do much housework at all. If you could have seen my place, you would have said, 'Oh, I see how she managed.' I didn't do the dishes until hours after dinner was over. My mother was a great deal of help, but the rest of my family did not cooperate in this area. Someone came in to help once in a while."

"I was so debilitated that my husband and daughter were assuming some household responsibilities, and we had someone come in during the weeks I was on chemo. You spend two or three days a week throwing up and it's gonna knock you out."

"The worst part is the lack of energy. Needing the care of other people. It is embarrassing. It makes me feel old. People do things for old people. If you're independent, as I am, you're used to doing things for yourself—and it's hard. I feel guilty when others do the work for me."

- Set reasonable goals and priorities; conserve energy for those tasks you must or prefer to do yourself. Sister Rosemary Moynihan advises patients to "carve out those activities and interests that are most important for you to continue. That may be work, it may be taking care of your children, it may be communicating and socializing with certain friends. Even if you can't do it at your normal level, try to maintain at least some level or one aspect of that activity—it's an important dimension of continuity." Keep safety in mind—accidents tend to happen to those who are tired or weak. Perform as many day-to-day activities as you can. The activity is beneficial and helps you maintain a sense of normality, independence, and self-esteem. Speaking of patients with advanced diseases, an oncology nurse says, "One of my pet things is that when people come into the clinic they're a little bit short of breath and tired. So I say, 'Please use a wheelchair.' For them it's like giving in. And I'll say to them, 'Don't waste your energy here. Save it. Wait till you get home.' "

- Rest when you are tired, especially before and after a chemotherapy treatment. Or avoid trying to do too much after a chemotherapy treatment—pace yourself. No one should expect you to be Superman or Wonder Woman. Many patients find that short naps in the afternoon work wonders.

- Get more sleep—deep, restful, uninterrupted sleep if possible. You may require more hours of sleep than you used to, so don't go by the old days. Go to bed earlier and/or get up later, whichever is more convenient. To help yourself sleep, you may want to take a tranquilizer or a sedative. Alternatively, there are a variety of herbal and homeopathic products on the market that many people find help them relax and fall asleep without adding their own side effects such as daytime fatigue. Many patients also find these tips helpful: Maintain a regular bedtime schedule and ritual; keep your environment quiet and calm, without distractions; use relaxation techniques; and try to find the cause of any sleep-disturbing anxieties and fears and alleviate them. Dr. William Grace of New York City's St. Vincent's Hospital says:

"If the patient is on glucocorticoids [such as prednisone], which will keep some people on a little bit of a high, we recommend that they take this medication in the morning. This way, they don't get the same 'high' and insomnia they usually get if they take it at night. Some patients use Dexatrim to counteract some of the fatigue. There are even some patients for whom we prescribe Dexedrine for chemotherapy-related fatigue. If you give it carefully, in small doses, it is safe, and many patients are able to continue working and lead more normal lives."

- Begin a mild exercise program that may be intensified eventually. Walk, do errands, and do light work around the house. In the right amounts exercise energizes you—it doesn't tire you out.

- Begin or resume a favorite hobby or activity to alleviate boredom. It's best to have some degree of productive work or employment while you are on chemotherapy because it makes life more fun and keeps you from dwelling on cancer, chemotherapy, and how crummy you feel.

Gastrointestinal Effects

The gastrointestinal (GI) system, which includes the mouth and teeth, throat, esophagus, stomach, intestines, and rectum, is lined with cells that reproduce rapidly. These cells are therefore prime targets for anticancer drugs. Chemotherapy drugs also affect other organs that in turn influence the activity of the organs of the gastrointestinal tract. In addition, psychological factors such as fear, anxiety, and depression can affect both the digestive process itself and the way you feel about food, as can disruptions in your life-style and daily routine:

"I still cook for the family, that doesn't bother me. But a lot of times I'd rather not eat at all, just go to bed instead."

"I'd go to the cafeteria for lunch, get a bowl of soup, and think maybe I could eat. Once one of my coworkers came by and said in a friendly way, 'Hello, dear.' I don't remember what was on his tray, but whatever it was, the smell just made me jump up and run out because I thought I was going to vomit. He didn't know I was on chemo, and when I later explained, he said, 'That's all right. It's just that nobody ever turned green in front of me.' "

"I could only eat light breakfasts the days of my treatments. I was so worked up psychologically—knowing what I was going to go through a few hours later—that if I looked at food those mornings it would make me sick."

A change in eating habits and preferences can affect your life in many ways. I think what bothered me most about the change in eating habits was first that I love food and second that eating is such a social event. I had to choose restaurants very carefully and eat differently from usual. Thanksgiving was especially trying, since my mother makes a huge, scrumptious dinner. All that food, that rich food. Friends and relatives eventually understood that I couldn't eat that much and that plain food was the best for me. But it still made me feel guilty and like the odd man out. It was like being on a reducing diet and feeling sick at the same time—it wasn't really by choice that I couldn't join in the gastronomic fun. One of life's greatest pleasures was taken away from me.

Clearly, many of chemotherapy's side effects occur in the gastrointestinal system. The most common are nausea, vomiting, loss of appetite, and weight loss. In addition, chemotherapy can also cause bloating, constipation, dehydration, dental problems, diarrhea, dry mouth, esophagitis (a sore, irritated throat), heartburn, indigestion, milk intolerance, pain, stomatitis (a sore, irritated mouth), swallowing difficulty, taste blindness, and weight gain. In addition, drugs can change the way in which nutrients are absorbed, metabolized, utilized, and excreted.

The side effects can alter both the amounts and types of food eaten as well as the way the body handles the nutrients that are being ingested. Patients on chemotherapy can easily become malnourished to one degree or another. However, a well-nourished patient has been shown to tolerate treatment better, respond to treatment more favorably, recover from individual treatments more rapidly, maintain desirable weight, feel better, and remain more active. (See Chapter 8.) It is ironic that at the very time a patient needs to be highly nourished he or she is undernourished because of the therapy. Sometimes the toxicity to the gastrointestinal system is so severe that the chemotherapy plan will be modified, but since the toxicity is usually not at a life-threatening level, oncologists generally are reluctant to do this. Luckily, there is some headway being made in understanding, alleviating, and preventing many of these side effects through watching what and how the patient eats. Many of the suggestions can be carried out by the patients themselves, their families, and their friends. (A dietitian, nutritionist, or nutrition-oriented physician or nurse can give a nutritional evaluation and more individual advice.)

Living conditions and the presence or absence of friends and relatives can make a big difference in how easily you are able to overcome your side effects and maintain a healthful diet. If you are being treated as a hospital inpatient, you are assured on the one hand of having food of at least a minimum level of quality and quantity. On the other hand, you forfeit a certain amount of control over what and when you eat. Mealtimes can be quite lonely, sterile affairs because most hospitals do not have communal dining areas. Meals are served in large portions, three times a day, but most chemotherapy patients do better with small, frequent meals. Hospital food is notoriously unappetizing, and it may also be of a different type from what you are used to: Very few institutions take into consideration the ethnic backgrounds and cultural preferences of their patients. It is not surprising that malnutrition has been found in 30 to 40 percent of hospital patients and that the percentages are even higher in cancer patients. Friends and relatives can be especially supportive in this area by bringing in some of your favorite foods (after checking with hospital authorities) and by scheduling their visits around mealtimes so you have company while you eat.

If you are being treated as an outpatient or by a physician in private practice, you may be living at home or staying at a hotel, motel, or rented apartment or with friends or relatives. In these cases you should be able to have a certain amount of control over your food and its preparation—possibly over whole meals or parts of them and/or between-meal snacks. It is important to buy and prepare wholesome fresh foods instead of settling for poorly prepared fare such as "fast foods." Friends and family members can help out here, too, whether or not they normally are responsible for preparing the meals in your family.

The National Cancer Institute, among others, has published booklets that deal specifically with gastrointestinal problems that result from cancer and chemotherapy. Many contain additional tips to those suggested here, plus recipes for special diets such as bland diets, blenderized foods, high-protein diets, low-fat or low-fiber diets, and liquid diets. (See the Resources section for a list.)

NAUSEA AND VOMITING

Most chemotherapy drugs cause some degree of nausea and vomiting after injection or administration. Some drugs, however, are notorious for their ability to cause these reactions in a high percentage of patients. Researchers have found that a high potential for nausea and vomiting exists in cisplatin, cyclophosphamide, daunorubicin, doxorubicin, dacarbazine, mechlorethamine, and streptozocin; a moderate potential exists in carboplatin, cytarabine, carmustine, methyl-CCNU, etoposide, ifosfamide, methotrexate (high dose), the mitomycins, lomustine, and procarbazine. The other commonly used drugs have low potential to induce vomiting. We don't know why some drugs in particular cause more vomiting than others—as a group they neither have any other attribute in common nor differ significantly from other chemotherapy drugs that do not cause vomiting.

The intensity, onset, and duration of nausea and vomiting that a patient experiences from a drug depend on the individual patient, his or her nutritional status, the dose of the drug, the rate of administration, and the presence of other drugs. Psychological factors have also been implicated, especially in the case of anticipatory vomiting before the drug is actually given. Basically, patients may experience nausea and vomiting that begin within a few hours after a treatment but are short-lived, nausea and vomiting that last for twelve to twenty-four hours, or a constant, low-level nausea that persists throughout the course of treatment but does not lead to vomiting.

Usually the onset of nausea and vomiting is delayed a few hours—from three to four, possibly up to twelve after administration. In some drugs it is swifter—as soon as a few minutes after injection. Those who experience a constant low-level nausea may find a heightening of this sensation soon after a treatment. Though reactions can vary somewhat from treatment to treatment, a patient's reaction (unless treated) to the same drug is usually fairly consistent. A violent vomiter will not suddenly begin to experience persistent nonproductive nausea or vice versa. Two people describe their usual reactions:

"About four or five hours after my treatment the puke attack would begin. It went like this: The first one usually wasn't so bad because I'd have something in my stomach to throw up. Then I would throw up every twenty minutes for the next hour. Gradually they would get closer and closer together—every fifteen minutes, every ten minutes, every five minutes—by which time it was the dry heaves, pure bile. Then it would gradually slow down to every ten minutes, fifteen, twenty. Then would come the final one—I'd always know it was the final one. I'd put one hand on my forehead, one on my stomach, and breathe a big sigh of relief. Then I'd go to bed and sleep."

"I never threw up, I was just nauseous the five days that I was on the chemo. I'd work all day in the hospital without eating; I couldn't—I didn't want to vomit. Because once I started, I was afraid I wouldn't ever stop. The nausea was even worse when other patients got sick themselves. That was awful."

My own particular reaction was the constant low-level nausea. Though it rarely went away and would heighten at certain periods during my therapy, it was never bad enough to make me throw up—but I seldom throw up anyway and am able to count on the fingers of one hand the number of times in my entire life I've been sick to my stomach.

Because nausea and vomiting are so unpleasant, they are often the side effects that patients most fear. Vomiting can also become one of the most serious from a medical point of view. Deleterious results of prolonged, regular chemotherapy-induced nausea and vomiting include intolerance of the treatment, a generalized weakness, serious weight loss, loss of substances vital to the body such as water and nutrients that lead to malnutrition, dehydration, and an electrolyte imbalance that brings on irritability, lethargy, convulsions, and respiratory and heart problems. Though this is extremely rare, vomiting is sometimes so violent and prolonged that ribs and vertebrae have been fractured and the delicate tissue in the digestive tract has been torn.

Nausea and vomiting, therefore, jeopardize the successful treatment of cancer and reduce the quality of life. A survey of fifty-six oncology centers revealed that up to 10 percent of patients who potentially could have been helped by chemotherapy refused it because of actual or anticipated nausea and vomiting. Dr. Richard Gralla, formerly of Memorial Sloan-Kettering, says:

"If the quality of life is terrible, it makes it that much more difficult to come back for the chemo even though they know it's a good thing to take. Even if you make up your mind to go through with it, it still makes your life miserable."

The Causes of Nausea and Vomiting

Though some drugs may irritate the digestive tract directly, this effect is thought to be only a possible contributing cause of the nausea and vomiting associated with cancer chemotherapy. Rather, the drugs are capable of somehow triggering the parts of the brain that control nausea and vomiting. It may be the drugs themselves that do this, or it may be that the drugs cause a neurotransmitter in the brain to trigger the vomiting.

Nausea is a very common protective mechanism found in many species of animals. When you eat or drink something (the most likely ways for substances to enter the body), it gets into the bloodstream. There are certain receptors in the brain that are constantly sampling the blood. When harmful substances reach a certain level in the blood, it causes nausea. "When you take foreign substances in, there are very few ways you can get rid of them," explains Dr. Gralla. "One of them is by vomiting. Unfortunately, the body doesn't know that you didn't take chemotherapy by mouth but by injection."

Many other factors and conditions can produce nausea and vomiting in cancer patients, such as tumor pressure on the GI tract, metastases in the central nervous system, other drugs being taken, pain, and chemical abnormalities caused by the cancer or the treatment. It is important to determine whether there are any contributing underlying causes of nausea and vomiting because this can influence the measures used to alleviate them.

Using Drugs to Control Nausea and Vomiting

Drugs that cause vomiting are called emetics; the drugs used to control nausea and vomiting are called antiemetics ("emesis" is the medical term for vomit). Until recently, the inability to deliver safe, effective, consistently reliable antiemetics that are inexpensive and easy for outpatients to take has without a doubt been one of the more embarrassing and frustrating failings in the history of the cancer support system. Those most widely used in the past not only have been disappointingly ineffective but have rather undesirable side effects of their own— sedation being the most notable. It has been difficult to find drugs that suppress vomiting, partly because the portion of the brain that controls this function lies so close to the area that controls the heart and lungs. Anything that would interfere with vomiting could affect the functioning of these vital organs as well.

Dr. William Grace, an oncologist at St. Vincent's Hospital in New York, feels that much of the problem lies in the way the available drugs are—and are not—used. Doctors are not well informed and don't sit down and take the time to "fine-tune" their patients' therapies or to explain to them how to take their antinausea medication. "The common perception is that the disease makes you sick, the drugs make you sick, they're all going to be sick people," he says. "But that's not true. A lot of these things can really be done well. A lot of people are getting quite sick because there's not enough attention being paid to detail, to giving chemotherapy well."

Fortunately, there have been a couple of breakthroughs in recent years, and as a result, patients are getting through this particular side effect much more comfortably. This improvement is due to two relatively new drugs—metoclopramide and ondansetron—and the increasingly popular practice of combining different drugs to greater effect.

Classes of Antiemetics

Until recently, a group of drugs called *phenothiazines* has been the mainstay of antiemetic therapy. The drugs in this category are Compazine (prochlorperazine), which may be taken orally, and Trilafon (perphenazine) and Torecan (thiethylperazine), both of which may be taken orally and administered intramuscularly or intravenously. These "old drugs" have not been very beneficial except in cases where the anticancer agents have a low or moderate potential for causing nausea and vomiting. They are being supplanted by other drugs that are probably going to turn out to be much more useful.

The *butyrophenones*, for example, are sometimes effective in patients who do not respond to the phenothiazines. This group of drugs includes Haldol (haloperidol), administered orally or intramuscularly, and Inapsine or Innovar (droperidol), administered intravenously.

A drug called Reglan (metoclopramide) belongs to a group of drugs called *dopamine antagonists*. Metoclopramide had for years been used in relatively low oral doses with little effect. But when it was used in high doses intravenously in experiments by Dr. Gralla and others, it was shown to be highly effective against the side effects of cisplatin, a drug that results in severe nausea and vomiting that had proved unresponsive to the other antiemetics.

A whole new class of drugs—*serotonin receptor blockers* (serotonin is a neurotransmitter)—hold tremendous promise for controlling nausea and vomiting. Ondansetron (Zofran) is the first of this class to be available; for most people it works well even against chemo regimens most notorious for causing severe vomiting. Another advantage is that it doesn't cause the drowsiness that most other antiemetics do.

Corticosteroids, as a class of drugs, have been found to have antiemetic properties, although it is uncertain why. Corticosteroids such as dexamethasone (Decadron) and methylprednisolone in high doses have been found to give good results.

Sedative/hypnotics such as Valium and Dalmane have been used to reduce nausea in patients. Many oncologists are prescribing Ativan, an antinausea medication that also acts as an antidepressant and sleeping pill. One intriguing side effect of this drug, and one that many patients consider a big plus, is that it can also cause amnesia. As a result, it helps dim the memory of any vomiting they experienced that antiemetic drugs failed to control. As Memorial Sloan-Kettering's Dr. Fahey has found, "A lot of patients do better if they are mildly sedated with antianxiety drugs begun before treatment and continued through it, right along with the chemo. With some therapies, you're really better off if you're in kind of a fog, if you just 'lose' that day." Marijuana, a member of this class of drugs, also has been shown to be an effective antiemetic for some chemotherapy patients. In spite of its illegal status as a recreational drug, its therapeutic use for cancer patients has gained broader acceptance and gotten a lot of publicity. As a result, you may be able to get legal "joints" from your oncologist or capsules or suppositories containing THC, the active ingredient in marijuana. However, because of all the red tape involved, it is usually recommended that patients obtain this drug through nonmedical channels; in addition, as one oncologist confessed, "You can get much better grass on the street that you can from the state." My oncologist mentioned marijuana early on in the therapy and said he had no objections if I could get some and use it.

Though it does work for some people, marijuana is no panacea. Its side effects can vary considerably, and they depend on many factors, including the strength of the drug and the patient's expectations and prior experiences. The side effects that might benefit cancer patients include the well-known "high" or sense of well-being, its relaxing and tranquilizing effects, an increase in appetite, and a lessening of pain. Marijuana, however, may also cause undesirable side effects such as paranoia, disorientation, an inability to concentrate, acceleration of the heartbeat, dry mouth, and red eyes. Be sure to check with your physician before taking marijuana if you are obtaining it through nonmedical channels; you may have a physical condition or be taking other drugs on which marijuana might have an adverse effect.

These unpleasant side effects are particularly unacceptable in older patients, and many who have been given THC once have refused to take it again. Research is being conducted to develop synthetic THC that will have fewer side effects than the natural THC found in marijuana.

Patients find that marijuana works best if they begin using it *before* a treatment and continue to use it regularly afterward until the time comes when they would usually stop vomiting. Three to five puffs begin to have effect in a few minutes and last for about two hours. When taken by mouth, in brownies or cookies, or as a capsule, the effect begins in forty-five minutes to two hours and lasts two to six hours. Marijuana is also available as rectal suppositories—when used this way, the effect begins in thirty minutes and lasts up to six hours.

More information may be found in *Using Marijuana in the Reduction of Nausea Associated with Chemotherapy* by Roger A. Rothman, assistant professor of social work at the University of Washington. In this book he describes the psychological and physiological effects of marijuana and how to acquire, prepare, and use it, including recipes for incorporating it in foods.

Antinausea drugs are far from perfect. Not all work as effectively as we'd like; some work better against some emetics than others. The drugs need to be taken hours before chemo is given (some recommend twenty-four hours) and then repeated at two-, three-, or four-hour intervals until the nausea is scheduled to subside. Oral antiemetics have the advantage of being self-administered by the patient, but they may be unreliable and only partially effective against many emetics or, for some drugs, unavailable in this form. Intramuscular or intravenous administration, the most effective mode for some high-dose antiemetics such as metoclopramide or corticosteroids, on the other hand, must be done by a trained professional, is time-consuming, and so is limited to hospital inpatients for the most part. In addition, there is the cost: Oral antiemetics may cost as little as $1 for twenty-four hours worth of treatment, whereas twenty-four hours of a new IV antiemetic given in the hospital can cost over $100— in addition to the other costs of chemotherapy, including the anticancer drugs themselves. None of the antiemetics are without side effects, with sedation being the most prevalent. Marijuana, although it falls somewhere in the medium-price bracket as an antiemetic, in many instances is purchased illegally and so poses its own additional unique disadvantages.

My oncologist gave me a prescription for Compazine when I started the chemo. But my reaction was a slight constant nausea, which heightened in waves without any warning. So I felt I never really needed the Compazine too badly—besides, I would have had to take it every day. I ended up never using it and throwing the pills away. I thought I was putting enough chemicals in my body as it was and decided to grin and bear it. I was one of the more fortunate ones in that I didn't have the severe reaction that necessitates the use of imperfect antiemetics that these patients experienced:

"I spent the year pretty much stoned. I smoked marijuana every time I went for a treatment; I also took Compazine at the same time. I don't know whether there was any effect or not, but I was afraid to try a treatment without that stuff. I had such a terrible time with it, what would I do if it were even worse without it? I didn't want to know."

"You wouldn't believe the drugs they gave me for the nausea. They tried everything on the market. First they tried Compazine. They tried it in different dosages, but that didn't work. They tried it in suppositories, but that didn't work either. Then they tried another drug. That didn't work. Finally they tried a new drug that came in a patch you put behind your ear; I'd start putting that on the night before they gave me the treatment. That didn't work either. They suggested I try marijuana. At first I didn't mind the idea of getting high for medical purposes. But then I thought, 'I've already had one kind of cancer. Now I'm going to start smoking something that might give me lung cancer just so I won't feel the side effects of cancer therapy? What am I, crazy?' "

"One of the amusingly frustrating aspects of my treatment had to do with marijuana. I felt I was cheated—I had heard about using grass to control nausea, and never having smoked controlled substances before, I was looking forward to this opportunity to try it. But they just gave me something through the IV along with the chemo that knocked me out."

The problems with antiemetics are far from completely solved, but there are ways of getting around them and ways to enhance the drugs' effectiveness.

- *Timing:* Dr. Grace says, "You always start antinausea medication before you give the chemo. You've got to put the drug on the emesis center to change the emesis threshold. Once people start to be sick, forget it. It's very hard to stop it. The physician must use antiemetics prophylactically—he must have the pills around, or write the prescription, and explain to the patients how to take it. This is a very labor-intensive field, and doctors must take the time to be compassionate." Dr. Ronald Bash also recommends that his patients begin taking an antiemetic several hours before a treatment. He favors prescribing them in suppository form because many patients tolerate them better than oral medication. In addition, antiemetics should be continued for a day or a day and a half after the treatment, because nausea can persist this long.

Sedation, a common side effect of antiemetic drugs, can limit your mental and physical activities. This disadvantage, too, may be sidestepped by judicious use of timing and may even become an advantage. Patients find it often helps if they can sleep through the hours in which the worst nausea and vomiting are likely to occur. The sedative effects of the antiemetics can help them to do this. In fact, tranquilizers, sedatives, and antihistamines have all been prescribed for their antiemetic effects.

Dr. Gabriel Hortobagyi, a breast cancer specialist at M.D. Anderson Cancer Center, recalls how sedation used to be a problem with younger patients: "They were out of commission for hours. They couldn't drive, take care of their kids, or see a movie." But with ondansetron, the only side effect seems to be a headache, which isn't even experienced by every patient.

Those who are receiving chemotherapy as inpatients are often given an intravenous antiemetic right through the same IV that the chemo goes through. They then spend a whole day and/or night sleeping. Outpatient treatments and antiemetics can also be scheduled so the patients sleep through the worst of it. If you are home, try to have someone check on you periodically because it is possible to vomit in your sleep, inhale it, and suffocate. Elevating the head of the bed with either pillows or a prop under the mattress will help prevent this from occurring.

In addition, oral chemotherapy can all be taken at once, in the evening, instead of throughout the day. If it is taken along with an antiemetic and a sedative, patients sleep through any nausea. Though there is a theoretical possibility that a higher concentration of the drug in the urinary tract could increase the risk of toxicity (cystitis), Dr. Grace doesn't see this effect in his practice: "If patients drink a lot of water at night, they wake up to urinate. The difference is infinitesimal; patients just don't have urinary problems."

- *Type and Dosage:* You may need to experiment with drugs and their amounts in order to hit on the right antiemetic therapy for you. It is odd that the most commonly used agent for antiemesis in chemotherapy is Compazine, which, says Dr. Grace, "is basically a mediocre antiemetic." When one antiemetic doesn't work, you should switch to one of another class, or increase the dosage, or combine drugs of different classes. Chemotherapy appears to stimulate several sites in the nausea-vomiting mechanism, and no single agent blocks all these sites. So, just as combinations of cancer chemotherapy drugs are usually more effective against cancer, combinations of antiemetics work better than single agents do. This approach can also be helpful if an effective antiemetic begins to lose its power. If patients get "breakthrough nausea"—a little more nausea with each cycle because of the accumulative toxicity—"the patient," says Dr. Grace, "might have to escalate the war. You increase the dose or add another antiemetic."

At this moment in the history of chemotherapy, there is no single reliable antiemetic without side effects. In addition, patients and their oncologists must therefore be willing to do a bit of juggling and experimentation. Also, patients must decide which side effects are most acceptable: those from the anticancer drugs or those from the antiemetics. Where effective antiemetics do exist, most patients with severe reactions would rather spend their time sedated instead of vomiting. Where reactions are not so severe, the choice is not so easy. Fortunately, those cases where reactions are severe and the oncologists—for whatever reason—have not found effective antiemetics, are becoming increasingly rare.

Psychology and Vomiting

Nausea and vomiting can have a strong psychological component. The atmosphere and spirit in which chemotherapy is given perhaps can play a role in how nauseated a patient gets, as can the patient's expectations. Dr. William Grace feels strongly about this:

"You can't have cancer patients come in and expect to get sick. From day one we tell them that with the proper anti-emetics the probabilities are very remote. Also, people who get chemotherapy should get it in a private room which is warm and well ventilated so that anybody who is sick in another room is neither heard nor seen by the patient. In some facilities, you sit in a room and everybody watches everybody else getting sick. You get a visual reinforcement that the stuff going in your arm is going to make you sick; there is also auditory and olfactory reinforcement. People like to talk to each other before and after, but getting chemo itself is, I think, a very private thing. I don't think they like to get chemo together, especially if something bad is happening."

In addition, chemotherapy patients can develop conditioned aversions to specific foods. This situation is illustrated by patients who learn to refuse certain foods because they associate them with the treatment and vomiting. There is a well-known study carried out in Seattle in which one group of children were given a particular flavor of ice cream just before a chemotherapy treatment. Another group was given the same flavor but no treatment. A third group got chemotherapy but no ice cream. The group that received the chemotherapy after the ice cream were the children who most often refused the ice cream when it was given again. This situation is very much like the conditioned response that Pavlov elicited from his dogs, which learned to salivate at the sound of a bell because they associated it with being fed. One patient had a similar learning experience while on chemotherapy. "I couldn't keep anything down for a few days following the treatment, and my husband kept trying to give me foods like plain yogurt and soup. It took until months after I was off chemo to again start eating these things he gave me." Refusal of food becomes a conditioned response not related directly to the presence or absence of nausea; as a result, patients avoid certain foods or all foods throughout the therapy, not just during the time after therapy.

Another example of conditioning as a result of chemotherapy is called anticipatory nausea and vomiting. This occurs in about 25 percent of those taking chemotherapy and is characterized by the patient feeling the side effect before the drugs could possibly have taken effect, often before they are even administered. Some patients wake up nauseated on the day of treatment, or they begin to feel symptoms on the way to the doctor, or just as the needle is being inserted or nonemetic agents are being administered. Sometimes just seeing the physician, whether on a treatment day or not, passing the hospital, or being in the same neighborhood as the clinic can trigger nausea and vomiting. A patient remembers, "If I even smelled rubbing alcohol, I would start retching from the association." Anticipatory nausea and vomiting can make posttreatment nausea and vomiting even worse. Oncologists are giving some patients antianxiety medication or sedatives such as Ativan and Decadron before the treatment to help relieve anxiety and block anticipatory nausea.

In addition, relaxation therapies are being used to reverse this reaction, with very encouraging results. Matthew Loscalzo, who treats patients for this and other problems related to cancer and chemotherapy at Memorial Sloan-Kettering in New York, says:

"Anticipatory nausea and vomiting is a conditioned aversion. Usually by the third or fourth session, upon waking that day the patient may vomit, just at the thought of going in to the hospital. One thing I do with patients is to let them know that this is at first a physiological response to the drugs. The body becomes nauseated, and the patient learns to associate the entire environment of the hospital with the side effect. People tend to learn very quickly when they are under stress, or are emotionally depleted, or when their anxiety level is high.

"It is not simply a psychological process—there is nothing psychologically wrong with you. You simply have to relearn something. It's in part a physiological process like learning to play the piano. After a while, your fingers play the piano and you don't have to think about it. It's the same with this."

Relaxation techniques are also being used to reduce the postchemotherapy nausea and vomiting that result after a chemotherapy treatment has been given, though with not quite such dramatic results. Loscalzo continues:

"With postvomiting and nausea there's a good reason for people to be ill. Their bodies have been subjected to chemotherapy. It's very different from the conditioned aversion experienced before a chemo treatment. It can, however, also be exaggerated. We can help these people with their anxiety, but only up to a point. They are still going to feel ill—that is normal. But we can help them to reduce some of the distress that they're feeling because they can control their anxiety."

This patient underwent relaxation and hypnosis to relieve her anticipatory nausea and vomiting:

"I was getting sick even before I had the treatment. One of the nurses mentioned that a doctor was using hypnosis for chemo patients and it seemed to work well. In the beginning I had five sessions a week with the hypnotherapist. This was disturbing because he was in the same building as my chemotherapist, and the second time I went I got sick because of the association. My hypnotherapist assured me it would never happen again—and it didn't. I stopped having the anticipatory nausea and vomiting.

"He also tried to help me control the nausea after the chemo, but that he couldn't do completely. What did happen was that I was able to recover from the chemo faster. The nausea went away faster, and I could eat sooner. He just suggested it to me while I was in the trance. He told me what was going to happen, what I should expect to eat. Within twenty-four hours I could handle light food."

M. L. Frohling, who uses these techniques at Denver Presbyterian Hospital, illustrates another example of how these techniques are used to control side effects:

"There was one patient who had to be hospitalized for severe nausea and diarrhea. She was getting chemotherapy after surgery as a precaution. She didn't believe there was any cancer left in her body, and she perceived the chemo as coming in and killing off only healthy cells. Through visual imagery I was able to help her realign her belief system to be more oriented toward regaining her health instead of thinking the chemo was destructive. Once her conflict was resolved, she had her third round of chemo without a bit of nausea."

Nondrug Measures to Reduce Nausea and Vomiting

Cancer professionals have devised many hints to help their patients reduce nausea and vomiting. You might want to try them if your nausea and vomiting are mild, or you don't want to take antiemetics, or you want to do something on your own to help reduce this side effect instead of or in addition to taking antiemetics.

- Methods of consuming foods and beverages that have worked under other nausea-inducing conditions such as illness, stress, or pregnancy may work in this case. For example, nausea in the morning may respond to remedies recommended for morning sickness—eating melba toast, dry toast, or crackers upon awakening and before getting up.

- It is important to avoid dehydration—drink plenty of water and other liquids, especially before and as soon after a treatment as possible. Carbonated beverages such as ginger ale, 7-Up, and Coca-Cola can help curb nausea. Clear liquids such as fruit juices, clear soups, Popsicles, and gelatin desserts are usually tolerated.

- Bland, light foods—mashed potatoes, applesauce, sherbert, toast, yogurt, cottage cheese—stay down more easily.

- Avoid sweet, salty, greasy, and hot or spicy foods with strong odors.

- Eat foods cold or at room temperature to avoid releasing strong odors that can sometimes trigger nausea.

- Sometimes sour or tart foods—pickles, lemons, sour hard candy—or rinsing the mouth out with lemon juice and water can help curb nausea.

- Always sip liquids and eat foods slowly. Avoid drinking during meals. Eat in a still, relaxed, quiet environment.

- Experiment with the amount and timing of your meals. For some patients, avoiding any food or drink for one or two hours before and after a treatment helps. Sometimes eating a large meal three to four hours before the treatment and eating lightly the rest of the day does the trick. If neither of these helps, try eating several small, light meals during the day.

- If the smell of food nauseates you, let others do the cooking and avoid the cooking area. Stick with foods that do not have strong odors.

- Ask to have the timing of your treatment changed—some patients report a decrease in nausea when the treatment is given early, others when it is given late in the day. The method of administration can sometimes make a difference: The slower drip (infusion) method can cut down on nausea.

- Oral chemotherapy that makes you nauseous can be taken along with food or milk and/or an antacid. This sometimes reduces nausea, but check with your physician to make sure there is no compatibility between drugs.

- Distract yourself. Watch TV, go to the movies, or socialize to take your mind off nausea.

- Many patients report that exercise reduces nausea. As I mentioned in Chapter 9, this worked well for me, and swimming worked best of all. However, activity after meals can increase your discomfort and perhaps even trigger vomiting.

- Use relaxation techniques such as meditation, hypnosis, and visualization. Studies have shown that these therapies do help reduce nausea and vomiting in many patients (see Chapter 7) and are especially effective in anticipatory nausea and vomiting.

- Try acupressure or acupuncture, which some people have found to be successful in controlling nausea and vomiting. You might also try a device originally designed to stop motion sickness, seasickness, and morning sickness. The device (made by Marine Logic in West Palm Beach, Florida, and available in diving shops and pharmacies for around $15) is a pair of wristbands that exert gentle pressure on the p-6 acupuncture point. The manufacturer claims a success rate of 70 percent with morning sickness, and while results from physicians using the product for chemotherapy are not complete as of this writing, they show great promise—and no side effects.

Many patients find that one or a combination of these methods helps them handle nausea and vomiting. Often they come up with tricks of their own—some of them bizarre—to help them get through it:

"I tried to do something to occupy my mind, to talk myself out of feeling sick. I convinced myself that having a Coke and a doughnut before a treatment helped."

"I craved fruit juices. And I ate salty pretzels before a treatment—somehow they were not too unpleasant when I vomited, and they stayed pretty much the same on the way up as on the way down."

"Chicken soup and toast were the only things I tried. But after a while I didn't try anything. I'd wait until I came home from work, have a brandy, and get knocked out. I'd go to sleep immediately, and I guess that's why I thought it was the only thing I could tolerate."

"I smoked cigarettes while I was on chemo, though I don't anymore. They were my crutch. You'd think that they would have made me sicker, but every time I felt a wave of nausea, I'd light up and it went away. Maybe it was the deep breathing rather than the cigarette."

LOSS OF APPETITE, WEIGHT LOSS

Loss of appetite (anorexia) and the resulting weight loss are of primary concern during chemotherapy. Often it is complications caused by malnutrition that lead to other illnesses and possibly death, especially in advanced cancer patients. Losses of five, ten, fifteen, and even more pounds are common, but they should be minimized or prevented if possible because patients do better and feel healthier and stronger physically and psychologically if their normal weight is maintained.

Causes of Appetite Loss

Anorexia is one of the most difficult side effects to treat because it can have so many contributing causes. These include psychological and emotional factors, the disease itself, and its treatment. For example, depression, fear, and anxiety often cause people to lose their desire for food. These emotions can begin to take their toll early on: Patients who have been told that they might have cancer have been known to lose between five and ten pounds while waiting for a firm diagnosis! After diagnosis, emotions continue to affect the appetite, and they don't stop during the ups and downs of treatment or if the disease recurs.

Side effects of chemotherapy such as mouth sores, diarrhea, constipation, malabsorption, lethargy, sleep disturbances, and alterations in the ability to taste and/or smell food also play their parts. So do changes in life-style such as isolation from other people and reduced physical activity. In addition, conditioned responses from nausea or pain caused by the treatment make the idea of food less appealing. Physical problems related to the location of a tumor (in cancers of the head, neck, esophagus, stomach, bowels) can affect ability to eat; surgery and radiation to these parts can cause difficulty in swallowing, dry mouth, pain, and problems with digestion and taste perception. The tumor itself, rapidly dying cells, or toxicity to organs such as the hypothalamus or liver can release chemical messages that interfere with the appetite.

How to Increase Food Intake

Patients who are overweight at the start of their therapy often don't mind the expected weight loss. However, as explained in Chapter 8, it is important to keep well nourished. In addition, weight loss can set off harmful chemical reactions in the body or may be interpreted as a sign that the disease is advancing. Health professionals do not like to see their patients lose weight at this time. Lisa Logan, clinical dietitian at Denver Presbyterian Hospital, says, "The last thing I usually recommend for cancer patients is weight loss, no matter how much they weigh when I assess their conditions." Dr. Ronald Bash agrees: "Oncologists get scared when they see their patients losing weight. It's a bad sign in cancer. And you never know when a patient is going to need his or her weight."

There are many practices that can help increase or maintain your appetite and/or the amount of food you eat. Many are simple tips or tricks, some involve behavior modification, and others rely on special products or foods to boost nutrition.

- You may need to change the meaning of food in your life. Instead of eating to satisfy your taste buds or your hunger, you may need to eat foods that seem tasteless and eat at times when you are not really hungry. A good deal of pleasure may be missing, but eating good, nourishing food is an integral part of your treatment.

- If possible, consult with a dietitian and/or nutritionist who will explain what a balanced, nutritious diet contains and help you plan your daily menu. Take a few sample hospital menus home with you as examples when planning your own meals after you have been released. It may be advisable to add vitamin/mineral supplements to your diet to supply the nutrients that you are missing.

- Drink plenty of liquids and emphasize those with high nutritional content, such as milk, milk shakes, and juices. Fruit nectars are high in calories and are delicious.

- If appetite-depressing side effects such as pain, stress, tiredness, mouth sores, taste blindness, constipation, and diarrhea are present, try relieving them by using the methods recommended elsewhere in this book.

- Eat in a relaxing, pleasant atmosphere with soft music, good company, perhaps a glass of wine. It is helpful if friends and family members encourage you, but they should understand that it is unwise to try to force to you eat at this time.

- What you eat is as important as how much you eat. Although you should eat the foods you like, it may be wise to stay away from your favorite foods when you don't feel like eating. Patients often develop an aversion to foods eaten when ill and then find them undesirable even when they feel well. It's better to stick with nonaromatic cold foods about which you have neutral feelings, such as juices, Popsicles, and gelatin desserts.

- Try to include as many highly nutritious foods as possible, especially in between treatments, when your appetite is better. That's the time to indulge in your favorite foods, too. Patients often talk about making up for lost time by gorging on pizza or cheesecake after the nausea subsides. Donna Park thinks that "people are too strict with chemotherapy patients sometimes and insist that they eat something nutritious when they have no appetite for it. I'd rather they eat something that is maybe less nutritious but at least gets eaten. At least it has calories. So what if a patient eats ice cream three days a week?"

- Arrange to have your biggest meals whenever your appetite is at its best—this is usually in the morning, but it may be different for you.

- If you are too tired to shop and cook, ask friends and relatives to help out. During your "up" periods you can cook and freeze food portions that you can easily warm up and eat during your "down" times. Or rely on nutritious convenience foods such as creamed soups or "Lite" frozen dinners.

- Exercise before a meal can perk up a flagging appetite. Do simple range-of-motion exercises, walking, or anything you like and can manage for at least five or ten minutes a half hour before meals.

• Studies show that cancer patients can require up to hundreds
  of additional calories and twice as much protein as noncancer
  patients. However, many high-protein foods—meat particularly—are often repulsive to cancer patients; unfortunately,
  many high-protein foods are also high in fat, which chemotherapy patients may have trouble digesting and are of ques-
  tionable value healthwise. Many professionals nevertheless
  advise patients to try to add high-calorie, high-protein (and,
  often, coincidentally high-fat, high-sugar) foods and food
  supplements to their diets and usual recipes. These foods include butter, peanut butter, cheese, eggs, powdered milk or
  protein supplements (found in health food stores) added to
  milk, juice, shakes, other prepared dishes, instant breakfast
  or granola bars, or eggnogs and milk shakes. Other sources
  of low-fat protein can be found by combining plant proteins
  with each other and with small amounts of fish, poultry, milk
  products, or meat. Vegetable protein made from soybeans can
  be added to ground meat dishes—this lightens them by reducing the fat content without sacrificing the protein.

Supplementation

In cases of severe weight loss—5 percent or more of the total
body weight—patients become "candidates" for nutritional
supplements. There are commercially prepared high-protein,
high-calorie food supplements available in liquid or pudding
form. These "formulas" are available in drugstores and from
home health care suppliers and can be used as substitutes for
regular food or in addition to it. "These do tend to have an
unpleasant aftertaste," admits Lisa Logan. "So I try to make
them more palatable for the patient by adding ice cream, fruit,
milk products, and eggs, which mask the flavor and boost up
the nutrients." Other possible additions include flavoring ex-
tracts, fruit juice, and carbonated beverages. These preparations
are low-residue, however, and can lead to constipation. Sometimes freezing liquid supplements and eating them like ice cream
or blending them in a milk shake makes them more palatable.

In advanced cancer patients, when there is pronounced weight
loss, weakness, and malnutrition, hyperalimentation may be
used. The patient is fed with liquids containing vitamins, minerals, protein, fat, and other substances through tubes inserted
into the gastrointestinal tract or the veins. Up to 4,000 calories
can be taken in this way by patients who badly need them and

whose condition can improve remarkably because of this therapy.

Medications

We're learning how certain drugs can help fight cachexia (wasting-away syndrome) from studies done with AIDS patients. "Megace, a progesterone, is used in high doses to produce weight gain in patients who are losing too much weight from chemo, radiation, or the cancer process itself," says Dr. Richard Cohen. "This is useful weight gain—both fat and muscle."

Hydrazine sulfate, another compound, has been studied in the United States and the Soviet Union for fifteen years. In studies conducted in the Soviet Union it reduced wasting away and extended lives in half the people who received it. It also reduced tumor size in 40 percent of patients. In the United States clinical trials using hydrazine sulfate are under way, and the drug has not yet gotten FDA approval for this purpose. However, it is available from Great Lakes Metabolics in Rochester, Minnesota.

TASTE BLINDNESS

Many chemotherapy patients experience a loss of taste or a change in the way foods taste, which occurs because the lining of the tongue and the chemical receptors that detect taste are altered. Patients often find that food tastes "different" or "bad." High-protein foods such as meat—beef and pork in particular—usually lose their appeal; it is thought that this low tolerance for meat stems from a lower threshold for bitterness because chemical imbalances in the body react to amino acids in the food. Patients have said, "I found myself gagging on certain foods, like steak," or "I didn't like meat at all—I'd cook it for my family, but I wouldn't eat it myself."

Sweets can also seem less seductive than usual. Some researchers have found that patients have an elevated threshold for sweets up to a certain point. Once that point is reached, though, additional sweetness becomes intolerable. Many patients find in general that "nothing tastes right," and their appetites suffer. One patient remembers: "I didn't like anything sweet. My appetite wasn't normal; I usually just had one serving of what we were having, no seconds. I cooked still, that didn't bother me. Just the sweet stuff—cake, candy. I still baked for my husband,

and it didn't bother me to see him have it; I just didn't want any for myself.''

There are very few ways of getting around the alterations in taste that chemotherapy patients experience; the condition may be aggravated by a bad, metallic taste left in the mouth from certain drugs. But here are some suggestions that may help:

- Sometimes hypnotherapy and visualization help. (See Chapter 7.)
- Incorporate other, nonbitter high-protein foods if you find you have an aversion toward meat. Fish and poultry are usually still palatable, for instance, and dried beans, cheese and other milk products, eggs, and the complementary proteins found in beans, whole grains, and nuts can be made into many appetizing dishes.
- Protein supplements may be helpful. Those derived from soybeans supply complete protein, and there is no danger of lactose intolerance. Protein supplements are available in liquid and powder form and usually supply 28 grams of protein per two tablespoons—the same amount you get from a three-ounce steak.
- Add extra seasonings and spices to foods if you can tolerate them.
- Acidic foods such as oranges and grapefruits tend to stimulate the taste buds, so include some with your meals.
- As when dealing with loss of appetite, attractively served, well-prepared food served in a comfortable setting can be helpful in restoring (or ignoring) the way food tastes.
- A zinc deficiency can alter your ability to taste food; ask your physician about taking a zinc supplement.

WEIGHT GAIN/WATER RETENTION/ BLOATING

The popular picture of the chemotherapy patient is someone who is sick, vomiting, not eating, and losing weight to the point of emaciation. Many patients do lose weight, but many others, particularly women on adjuvant chemotherapy for breast cancer, instead find themselves tipping scales in the opposite direction. This can be aggravated by or partially caused by an increase in appetite, water retention, and abdominal bloating. Even though I lost weight on chemo, I developed a little potbelly during the time I was on prednisone; this bloating disappeared when the drug was withdrawn. Many women, however, find it a real problem to lose weight they gained while on chemo that is not due to water retention. Donna Park says this weight gain can be "devastating":

> "The women are often gaining tremendous amounts of weight, so they have an altered body image not only because of the mastectomy but because of the weight they gain. They put on fifteen, twenty, thirty pounds—it depends on how careful the patient is. We're not sure if it's only because of the prednisone. One of the theories we have is that patients are eating constantly to relieve their continuous nausea. Another theory is that they're feeling, 'Well, I don't know what next year will bring, so I'm going to eat to make myself feel better.' Or it might be because they are engaged in less activity, so they burn fewer calories."

Marylin Dodd, in *Managing the Side Effects of Chemotherapy and Radiation*, says that chemo drugs can change the way your body metabolizes fats contained in food, resulting in an increase in appetite and in fat deposits in the body.

Whatever the reasons, weight gain is a particularly common and frustrating side effect for women on chemo for breast cancer. The weight just keeps coming, especially when they are on chemo for a long time. They hate the weight gain, partly because of the change in appearance, self-image, and self-esteem, but some also worry about the possible connection between obesity and the progression or development of breast cancer. To be sure, these are legitimate concerns, but if you are in this situation, you may be able to take heart from the somewhat positive observations of several cancer patients and physicians. They have noticed that some patients seem to tolerate chemo better if they eat to the degree that they become overweight. I have personally known two women who deliberately ate more and gained weight during chemo, and they are informally called "our miracles"— both were on chemotherapy for over three years with minimal side effects and far outlived their prognoses. No one really knows why this should be so. Perhaps they were getting more protective micronutrients (such as vitamins and minerals) along with the calories, or perhaps fat itself has some as yet unknown protective effect. What we do know is that there may be some undiscovered process at work and that this information may help some patients find weight gain a bit easier to take.

Prednisone and dexamethasone are corticosteroids given as part of several chemotherapy plans. Their side effects include an increase in appetite and salt and water retention. A diet low in salt and refined carbohydrates and high in protein and potassium is usually recommended to help keep weight gain and water retention to a minimum. Here are some tips to help keep the scale's numbers down.

- Do not add salt to foods that are being cooked, and leave the saltshaker off the table when you eat.

- Watch out for hidden salt in prepared and convenience foods. Avoid anchovies, bouillon, soups, canned fish, bacon, cold cuts, corned beef, frankfurters, sausages, potato chips, corn chips, pretzels, salted nuts, soy sauce, catsup, and hard cheeses. Look for salt-reduced versions of these products.

- Look for cookbooks with salt-reduced recipes and tips that help you lower your salt intake without sacrificing too much flavor. Use herbs, spices, and lemon juice to perk up recipes.

- To reduce edema in the ankles and legs, avoid standing in one place for long periods of time and elevate your feet as much as possible. You may find special support hose or pressure stockings helpful.

- If the problem persists or is severe, your doctor may prescribe a diuretic (a pill that rids the body of excess water). Some foods are natural diuretics: citrus juices, parsley, some herbs, and water itself. Exercise (swimming in particular) seems to act as a diuretic, too.

- Eat foods high in potassium—bananas, apricots, cantaloupe, orange juice, potatoes—which cortisone depletes from the body or take a potassium supplement. Using diuretics also depletes potassium.

One contributor to overweight are the binges that go on between treatments when the patient feels well. For example, "I'd lose weight for the five days I was on chemo, but the moment I stopped, I ate like a pig. I hate pizza normally, but I'd bring home a big pizza and just gorge myself. Ice cream, anything. Just to get rid of the memory of the nausea."

As Ms. Park mentioned, constant nausea may drive you to a constant nibbling in an effort to mask the unpleasantness; a bad taste in your mouth, a common side effect of many drugs, can do the same. Perhaps low-calorie food items such as raw vegetables, fresh fruit, hard candy, fruit juices, ginger ale, and no-calorie herbal teas will serve this function as well as more fattening foods do.

According to Dr. Grace, some of his patients find that if they take their oral chemotherapy spaced out over the day instead of all at once, the slight nausea they get helps keep their appetite down. Some patients also take Dexatrim while on chemo—this not only curbs the appetite but counteracts some of the fatigue caused by the therapy. He suggests that if patients take a corticosteroid such as prednisone, they take it on alternate days instead of every day. "They don't get anywhere near the amount of bloating they usually get, even though they take the same total amount."

Eating to "make yourself feel better" because of anxiety about your prognosis or condition may be remedied by a talk with your oncologist or by the psychological/relaxation therapies described in Chapter 7. It's always preferable to prevent a weight gain than to have to lose it afterward, as this patient discovered:

> "One thing I was very down about was the way I ate—I put on thirty-five pounds while I was on chemo. I changed my eating habits and had a huge breakfast, lunch, and dinner. This was not me—but when I ate, I felt stronger. Now I'm fighting to take it off—even though I went back to my old eating habits, I've only managed to lose about twelve pounds."

Exercise is highly beneficial to chemotherapy patients, but you may not be getting as much as usual. Activity helps burn off calories, curb your appetite, improve your mood, and reduce nausea that you may be trying to alleviate with a steady stream of food. Exercise also takes up the time that you might otherwise fill by eating, as does any distraction. Only four things made me forget about the nausea: food, sleep, exercise, and the movies.

A bloated feeling and appearance can have many causes other than glucocorticoids. Some anticancer drugs can set off processes that render the stomach and intestines less capable of digesting food. Or the digestive process may slow down because of nervousness, tension, lack of exercise, or constipation. Eating gas-producing foods or swallowing air as you eat can contribute.

As a result, the lower abdomen bloats, and you look and feel too full too quickly. Small, frequent meals may help here, as may avoiding hard-to-digest fatty or high-protein foods. Eating slowly and eliminating foods, such as onions and cabbage, that cause gas may solve the problem. Hydrochloric acid tablets or other digestive aids taken with meals may help reduce the bloated feeling and appearance. Bloating may also be caused by lactose intolerance. (See pg. 198.)

CONSTIPATION

Overall, constipation occurs less frequently in chemotherapy patients than does diarrhea. This condition, which is characterized by infrequent bowel movements, hard, dark small stools, or straining, is uncomfortable and can be dangerous. The abdomen becomes distended, and there is cramping, a decrease in appetite, and possible fecal impaction. Oddly enough, constipation can lead to diarrhea when it increases the bacterial growth within the intestines. The result is explosive diarrhea occurring around the hard stool.

Constipation in chemotherapy patients may be due to a lack of fiber in the diet, the use of narcotics to control pain, antidepressants, diuretics, tranquillizers, a lack of exercise, and emotional stress. Often these are contributing factors to constipation caused by a group of drugs called the vinca alloys: vincristine and vinblastine. Vincristine, for example, has been reported to cause this side effect in 30 percent of those who get the drug. These drugs are toxic to the nerves. This leads to a sluggish or paralyzed bowel because the muscle contractions (peristalsis) that move food through the bowel do not occur.

Constipation from chemotherapy may occur within twenty-four hours of treatment, but it may not be obvious until several courses of treatment have been received. This side effect, when it is due to nerve damage, is usually accompanied by numb or tingling fingers and/or toes. It appears to be minor but is an early warning of neural drug toxicity, a potentially serious and nonreversible condition when allowed to progress.

Be sure to tell your physician if you are experiencing constipation. He or she may want to test you to see if there is nerve damage and adjust your drugs accordingly. Laxatives, suppositories, enemas, or stool softeners may also be prescribed as needed until the condition eases or reverses. Thereafter, or if the condition is slight, the following measures may help alone or be used in addition to occasional treatment with the harsher measures listed above. (The continual use of laxatives can be habit-forming. They irritate the digestive tract and make it difficult to have normal bowel movements without them.)

- Eat high-bulk foods: fresh fruit and vegetables—raw or cooked but still crisp—dried fruit such as prunes, whole grain breads and cereals, nuts, popcorn, and bran. Add bran to your diet gradually—start with two teaspoons a day and slowly work up to two tablespoons, then up to four or six. Too much fiber too soon can cause cramping, gas, and diarrhea.

- Avoid raw fruits and vegetables if your white cell count dips below 1,800.

- Drink plenty of fluids, which the fiber will absorb, keeping stools soft.

- Liquid or powdered acidophilus, available in health food stores, is another natural way to keep "regular."

- Coffee, tea, and alcohol tend to stimulate the intestines but should not be overindulged in.

- Get more exercise—walk, do isometrics.

- Set aside enough "bathroom time" to give sluggish bowels a chance to move.

- Take measures to alleviate depression or anxiety. A hot bath relaxes you all over, including the sphincter muscle.

- Avoid cheese, refined grain products (white flour), and chocolate because they can be constipating.

DIARRHEA

Diarrhea, to one degree or another, is a common complaint among chemotherapy patients. It occurs when bowel movements are more frequent, loose, and fluid than usual. There is often cramping, flatulence (gas), bloating, and sore, irritated skin around the rectum. Diarrhea is not merely uncomfortable and embarrassing; it can disrupt your life-style and lead to weakness, malnutrition, dehydration, and chemical imbalances because nutrients and water are not properly absorbed by the body.

The anticancer drugs that are prime culprits in this side effect are the antimetabolites and the antibiotics. These drugs kill the rapidly dividing cells that line the intestines. This causes a reduction in the production of the food-digesting enzymes normally present in the intestines, irritation, swelling, and an overproduction of mucus. Neither food nor water is absorbed, and since intestinal activity is stimulated, the food is passed along to the outside world before it is fully digested.

If you suffer from three or more loose bowel movements a day, consult your physician. He or she may suggest that you adopt an all-liquid diet for a few days to give the bowels a rest and then gradually add some low-bulk, "binding" foods. Your doctor may also prescribe antidiarrhea medication such as Kaopectate or Lomotil.

It is usually advised that the following foods be avoided because they tend to encourage diarrhea—they are high in fiber or irritate or stimulate the gastrointestinal tract in other ways.

• Whole grain bread and cereal

• Nuts, seeds, coconut, popcorn

• Fried, greasy, fatty foods; pastries, potato chips

• Fresh and dried fruits and fruit juices—exceptions are noted later

• Raw vegetables, cooked vegetables that are gas-producing, dried beans and peas

• Strong spices and spicy foods such as chili powder, pepper, curry, garlic, horseradish, olives, pickles, relishes

• Chocolate, alcoholic beverages, coffee, regular tea, tobacco, carbonated beverages (unless they have been allowed to go flat)

• Milk and milk products (also may cause diarrhea—see pg. 198)

The following "binding" foods are low in residue or fiber, are easily digestible, and tend to be soothing to the digestive tract:

• Soft high-protein foods such as cottage cheese, cream cheese, mild soft cheese, eggs, custards, creamy peanut butter

- Mild high-protein foods such as fish and poultry; low-fat meats such as veal, lamb, some cuts of beef—broiled or roasted rather than fried

- Cooked cereals such as cream of wheat, farina

- Some fruits such as bananas (high in potassium), applesauce, peeled apples (contain pectin, an antidiarrheal), apple juice, grape juice, avocados

- White bread or toast

- Macaroni, white rice, noodles; baked, broiled, or mashed potatoes

- Some cooked vegetables such as asparagus tips, green beans, carrots, peas, spinach, squash

- Nutmeg (added to dishes sometimes slows down the digestive tract)

In addition, you should

- Include rest periods during the day if you find you are very tired.

- Drink plenty of fluids to replace the water lost through diarrhea; sip slowly.

- Add foods high in potassium—bananas, apricot and peach nectars, potatoes, broccoli, halibut, asparagus—to replace the potassium depleted during fluid loss. If the problem is severe, your doctor may prescribe a potassium supplement.

- Eat small, frequent meals, slowly—this is easier on the digestive system. Foods served at room temperature or slightly warmer are advised, since very hot or very cold foods can stimulate contractions of the digestive tract.

- Cleanse the rectal area after each bowel movement if it becomes sore from frequent evacuation. Use warm water and a nondrying, nonirritating deodorant-free soap such as Dove, Basis, or Castile soap. A healing salve such as Desitine or A & D ointment, or a local anesthetic such as Tucks will give you comfort, as will frequent sitz baths or sitting in a tub of warm water.

MILK INTOLERANCE

Some people are born without the ability to digest milk; a chemotherapy patient, however, may develop this inability because the drugs destroy the cells in the intestine that produce the enzyme (lactase) that digests a milk sugar (lactose). Without lactase, the milk sugar will not be digested, and watery, fermentative diarrhea, flatulence, and cramping result. Since chemotherapy patients often rely heavily on dairy products and add milk-based nutritional supplements to stave off weight loss and malnutrition, this becomes an important symptom to diagnose and treat.

Though there are various laboratory tests to definitively diagnose lactase deficiency, they are not often done because of the time and expense involved. Therefore, the following clues are used: complaints of gas, indigestion, diarrhea, or vague abdominal pain thirty to sixty minutes after drinking milk or eating a milk product.

If you suspect a lactase deficiency, consult your doctor. He or she may recommend that you begin a lactose-free or lactose-reduced diet in addition to adopting the measures suggested in the section on diarrhea.

Patients should cut down on or avoid completely foods high in lactose: milk, cream, ice cream, most cheeses, and custard or pudding desserts. Many patients are able to tolerate milk and milk products in which the lactose has been totally or partially broken down: acidophilus milk, lactose-free cottage cheese, buttermilk, yogurt, fermented cheese such as cheddar, and sour cream. In addition, there is a product (Lact-aid) that can be added to milk, or taken orally, or sprinkled on dairy food to predigest the lactose.

Many other foods have milk or lactose in their ingredients; read labels carefully. Some of these include instant coffee, imitation dairy coffee creamers, cocoa and chocolate drinks, breads, party dips, commercial instant potatoes, cakes, cookies, pies, cordials and sherries, sherbert, creamed soups, and chewing gum. Lactose is a common ingredient in many oral medications and vitamin and mineral supplements, so if you are very sensitive to lactose, check labels carefully; you may need to find a substitute.

If milk and milk products usually are prominent in your diet as a source of protein, look for foods made with soybean milk. This milk can be bought plain or flavored, in containers just like those with cow's milk, as tofu (which can be substituted for cheese in recipes), and as various forms of "ice cream" desserts. Kosher pareve (milk-free) products can be another good source of protein.

SORE MOUTH, GUMS, AND THROAT

Chemotherapy drugs—particularly the antimetabolites and antibiotics—can produce sores in the mouth (stomatitis), sores in the throat and in the food pipe (esophagitis), and sore, bleeding gums. These side effects are caused by the destruction of fast-growing surface cells in these areas. As a result, minute raw or bleeding ulcerated patches or spots appear because the blood counts may be low. There may also be a bacterial or fungal infection present or spontaneous bleeding from the gums. Patients may experience dry mouth, difficulty in chewing and swallowing, an unpleasant taste or odor in the mouth, and alterations in the taste of foods; esophagitis causes mild to severe chest pain that can resemble heartburn.

These side effects can be very painful and distressing and can lead to other complications, such as loss of weight and malnutrition; gum trouble can lead to a loss of teeth. The soreness usually peaks one week after a treatment and clears up in a few days as the body repairs itself. However, the healing process may be slowed by malnutrition, and deficiencies in zinc, folic acid, riboflavin, and vitamins B_{12} and C can increase the severity.

There is relatively little that can specifically be done to prevent these side effects from occurring, but there are ways to alleviate them, minimize them, live with them, and prevent complications. They *can* be prevented from recurring by reducing the doses of the drugs that cause them.

Preventive Dentistry and Oral Hygiene

Starting chemotherapy with a clean, healthy mouth and maintaining good oral hygiene will go a long way toward minimizing and preventing later mouth problems and infections. Many oncologists—though not all—advise preventive dentistry for patients they feel might be at high-risk for oral problems as a result of chemotherapy. Dr. William Carl, a dentist at Rosewell Park Memorial Institute in New York state, wrote in an article in the February 1983 *American Family Physician*:

> "Oral care is very important in patients receiving chemotherapy, but it is often overlooked in the urgency of a patient's cancer treatment. Ideally, dental evaluation and preventive care should become a part of the workup preceding chemotherapy. These measures reduce potential complications that may be difficult to control later."

Always inform your dentist, preferably before you do it, that you are undergoing chemotherapy. Although many patients can safely undergo procedures such as simple fillings and tooth cleaning while on chemotherapy, it is never certain how any one patient will react, so it is best to take care of cavities and rough edges on your teeth before treatment begins. A thorough cleaning is also advisable because the inevitable minor bleeding that occurs during cleaning could be serious later on and because accumulated tartar can harbor bacteria that might infect mouth sores later on.

If you have gum problems or teeth that are so decayed that they might be abscessed, it is wise to make an appointment with a dentist and schedule as much work as possible before the treatment begins. Serious procedures such as periodontal surgery and tooth extraction generally should not be done while you are on chemotherapy, and the conditions that indicate these procedures can be worsened by your treatment.

Sometimes chemotherapy can be delayed a few weeks for this purpose if the likelihood of oral complications from the treatment is great. Your oncologist may be able to recommend a dentist who specializes in the rapid and sometimes radical procedures that are necessary.

If you wear full or partial dentures, it is recommended that you have the fit checked. Have them refitted if necessary to avoid irritation and possible infection. Poorly fitting dentures should not be worn; well-fitting ones may be worn after the worst of the side effects of each treatment have subsided. Orthodontic devices (braces) usually are too irritating and need to be removed during chemotherapy.

Floss daily and clean your mouth after each meal and at bedtime; use a soft-bristled brush and a minimal amount of dentifrice. Rinse afterward with warm saline water (one tablespoon of salt or one to two tablespoons of baking soda, which is milder, in one quart of water). This solution raises the pH of the mouth and helps prevent the growth of acid-loving microorganisms such as Candida, which causes yeast infection. Patients are usually advised not to use a commercial mouthwash unless it is alcohol-free, so check the label.

If your blood count is low and stomatitis is severe, avoid dental floss and Water Piks. Clean your teeth gently with a soft-bristled brush or cotton swab or with special sponge-tipped swabs (Toothetts) impregnated with a mild dentifrice. After each cleaning, use the following healing, bacteria-fighting rinse, which can also be used by itself to clean your teeth if brushing or swabbing is too painful. To make it, mix one part hydrogen peroxide with five parts saline water; add a few drops of alcohol-free mouthwash if desired. Prepare it fresh each time you use it; salt water can be made and kept ahead of time, but the peroxide will lose its effectiveness unless added immediately before using. Swish a mouthful around your mouth for a minute (it will bubble and foam) before spitting it out. Repeat once or twice. You may need to experiment using various proportions and combinations of water, soda, and hydrogen peroxide until you find a rinsing solution you can use frequently without it burning.

Medication and Other Measures

Some doctors paint individual mouth ulcers with an antacid such as milk of magnesia. To do this yourself, use a cotton-tipped swab. Allow the antacid to stand until the liquid rises to the top, pour off the liquid, and dip the swab in the thick white residue. This relieves pain and promotes healing. Antacid simply swished around the mouth will also stick to ulcerations and protect them. If the pain is severe, oncologists sometimes prescribe topical anesthetics such as Xylocaine to kill the pain. These come in spray, lozenge, and liquid forms. If you use such a preparation, be aware of extremely hot foods—you may burn your mouth without realizing it and create further damage.

Dr. William Grace uses viscous lidocaine, a kind of jelly, in his patients with mouth or throat ulcers:

"This is a kind of Solarcaine for your mouth and is quite good for keeping people's nutritional status up. You may have to swish and swallow a few times to get total anesthesia, and it works only for about twenty minutes to a half hour, but you can get a lot of food down in a half hour. The food doesn't taste like much because lidocaine also numbs the taste buds, but some people learn how to keep it off their tongues so that taste perception is maintained. The other thing with stomatitis is that people have a hard time coping with the pain, but painkillers can be given to relieve that."

If an infection is present, your oncologist will prescribe medication: an antibiotic for a bacterial infection or an antifungal for a yeast or fungus infection. Local medication is usually "swished and swallowed"—if the mouth is infected, it is assumed that the esophagus is also.

If your lips become dry and cracked, it will be difficult for you to open your mouth wide enough to clean or medicate it. Keep them moist with a soothing cream, drink plenty of liquids, and make sure there is no nutritional deficiency. If you have a history of herpes (cold sores/fever blisters) on the lips, be sure to tell your oncologist, who may prescribe an ointment to use to help prevent sores from forming while you are on chemotherapy. If your mouth is very dry, your doctor may prescribe an artificial saliva.

Eating Tips

- Avoid irritating foods: tart, acidy foods such as citrus fruits and juices, tomatoes, carbonated beverages; hot, spicy foods; and foods that are very dry, coarse, crunchy, or salty and require a lot of chewing and/or saliva to digest, such as chips and pretzels, raw vegetables, nuts, and whole grains.

- Avoid tobacco, alcohol, and extremes in temperature—these can injure delicate tissues.

- Nonirritating foods include bland, soft foods such as fruit nectars, creamed soups, soft cheese, eggs, milk shakes, cooked cereals, eggnog, pudding, applesauce, mashed potatoes, and macaroni and cheese. Yogurt may be particularly soothing.

- Try overcooking and pureeing foods such as vegetables and meats to make them easier to eat. Try using junior baby foods. Adding plenty of liquids such as sauces and gravies to foods or using moist heat in cooking (stewing and steaming) will make food easier to chew and swallow. Have casseroles and soups.

- Drink plenty of fluids. If you are eating less, make nutritious high-calorie, high-protein drinks. Liquid supplements may be needed to help keep up your nutrient intake. Sipping tepid tea may soothe your mouth and throat.

- Some people find cold foods such as ice cream, ice cubes, frozen yogurt, Popsicles, and sherbert soothing, but others find these things painful.

- If esophagitis is present, milk and milk products such as sour cream, yogurt, and cottage cheese tend to coat the throat and protect the cells. You can eat these every two to four hours.

Hair, Skin, and Nail Effects

The average normal scalp contains 100,000 hairs, 10 to 15 percent of which are in the resting stage at any given time. Most hairs are therefore in the growing stage, which makes them unwitting targets for the effects of many of the most commonly used chemotherapy drugs. In addition to the drugs, a faulty diet and severe stress—particularly from illness, surgery, and emotional trauma—can affect the health of your hair and scalp. The skin and nails can be sensitive to chemotherapy drugs, too, although the effects on these are generally more subtle, transitory, and less common than those on the hair.

HAIR LOSS

Chemotherapy patients may lose all or some of the hair on their heads, including the scalp, beard, mustache, eyebrows, and eyelashes. Body hair may eventually thin out or disappear completely from the arms, armpits, legs, and groin. Though far from dangerous medically, for the patient this loss of hair (alopecia) is often devastating psychologically.

Being bald on top of being sick is a terrible blow to our self-image; it can plunge some of us into the depths of depression or make those who are already depressed even more so. The anxiety about our appearance is a daily insult to our quality of life; it jeopardizes our health and casts doubt on the wisdom of continuing with chemotherapy. Our hair means so much that sometimes the mere prospect of losing it is enough to make patients refuse to begin a therapy that could save or extend their lives.

Patients' experiences with hair loss and their reactions to it vary greatly. Some say they feel naked, ugly, sexless, and vulnerable, that being bereft of hair is a constant reminder of their cancer. Most do eventually adjust, and a few actually manage to derive pleasure from or get a few laughs out of their nearly hairless state:

"I don't know . . . I had never thought I was vain about my hair. It never really mattered. I had sailed through the surgery and the diagnosis so well, relatively speaking. There I was, traveling through Europe and I had cancer, and I was going through chemotherapy, and I was on top of the world . . . and suddenly, *that* happened to me—and prehistoric feelings of *maleness* were coming out. It was devastating, it really was."

"Because the drugs took my hair—my scalp hair and mustache too—I became anonymous for two years. All those boring people I didn't have to talk to—I'd just walk right by them in the street. Nobody recognized me. *I* didn't even recognize me. I'd had my beard for ten years, and a face can change a lot in that time."

"You know what? It was a trip being bald. I used to run the pulsating shower over my head!"

I remember being in a yoga class where the teacher came over to me in order to correct my head position. As she touched my head and my wig shifted, she drew back in surprise and said, "Oh, your hair!" I looked up and with a devilish grin said, "It isn't mine!"

Edith Imre, the proprietor of Edith Imre Hair Fashions in New York City, who has designed wigs for nearly forty years and has recently devoted much of her own time to fitting cancer patients, thinks that "losing the hair is so devastating because cancer is so often not really visual, and it can be ignored or denied. But being bald is very visual, a tremendous psychological problem." She tells of a woman in her thirties who came into her salon. "She was completely beyond herself, saying, 'I want to die, I want to die.' " Another businesswoman client of hers found the hair loss a greater blow than the cancer; she quit her job and refused to talk to friends. An elderly gentleman felt like a freak; he became a recluse because he feared ridicule.

One oncology nurse supervisor remarked that "among side

effects, hair loss is the one that patients are the most disturbed about. That's what you present to the public; it's the first thing others see. I had had patients who refused chemotherapy because they didn't want to lose their hair."

It is important for chemotherapy patients to know that not all drugs cause hair loss. And those which are known for this side effect do not always cause it in every individual or to the same extent.

Fifteen percent of chemo patients do not lose their hair. Except in very rare cases, hair loss from chemotherapy is temporary. The hair does grow back after the chemotherapy is stopped and sometimes before that if the hair growth becomes resistant to the drugs. Although losing your hair is traumatic, embarrassing, and terribly inconvenient, there are psychological and practical ways to prepare yourself and to cope with the possibility or actuality.

Minimizing the Effects

Many patients want to know if there are ways they can make the possibility or reality of losing their hair less traumatic psychologically, whether they can make their hair look better if it becomes thinner from chemotherapy, if there is anything they can do to prevent, delay, or minimize their hair loss.

The first step in coping with this side effect is to get an idea of what you will be dealing with. Be sure to talk over your concerns with your doctor. Ask how likely it is that the drugs you will be taking will cause hair loss, how much you can expect to lose, and when. Although in most cases it is impossible to be very specific or sure, in others the track record is clear. At any rate, for many patients the experience of losing their hair is harder if the doctor downplays the possibility, extent, or importance. Mr. Nicholas, the wig stylist for the Kenneth Beauty Salon in New York, comments:

> "People who are unprepared take the bad road. I get asked a lot of questions about what I've seen or what they should expect because most of the doctors don't give their patients enough information. Some do care and understand that this is one of the major problems that people face when they go through chemotherapy. Some doctors are right up front—they tell patients they might lose their hair—either because that's the way they are or because with some types of therapies they can be more sure than with others."

Donna Park says:

"It's fine for doctors to say that chemotherapy causes hair loss. But you really need to get down to the nitty-gritty. Which drugs do; which drugs don't; which ones do to a certain degree. For instance, 90 percent of the patients who receive adriamycin do lose their hair. But you're not going to wake up the morning after your first treatment and find all your hair on your pillow. One patient I know had overheard other women talking about wigs. She became very frightened and asked, 'Where am I going to find a wig tonight?' I had to tell her that she wouldn't wake up bald the next morning but that she should start looking for a wig."

When my hair fell out, I was devastated. I can't deny that vanity played its part, but a good deal of the blame lies in my not being well enough prepared. My oncologist did warn me that it all might fall out but said it was possible that only some of it might. He observed that since I had a lot of hair to begin with, I could afford to lose some. He mentioned that a lot of people on chemo get wigs, but I said, "Not me! Even if some hair falls out, I'm not so vain that I can't live with hair that looks a little thin." I thought I'd wait and see if I needed one. I don't know if he was soft-pedaling hair loss in order to be kind and not to scare me off or if it just didn't sink in that I might become totally bald and what this would mean to me. As a result, I was totally unprepared—in psychological and practical terms—when it did fall out, all of it.

The incidence of scalp hair loss varies from individual to individual and depends in part on the drug dosage. Nevertheless, some drugs have a higher potential to cause this than others have. In "Alopecia and Chemotherapy," an article published in the May 1980 issue of *The American Journal of Nursing*, the drugs listed as being the most common causes of alopecia were cyclophosphamide (Cytoxan), doxorubicin (adriamycin), and vincristine (Oncovin); moderately common were Actinomycin D (Cosmegen), the bleomycins, daunorubicin, and methotrexate.

As a general rule, hair begins to fall out within three or four treatments. It may begin sooner and peak one or two months afterward. In some people, it falls out very gradually or the loss is so slight it is hardly noticeable. In others, it falls out in huge clumps or all at once. Some people wear caps or scarves to bed to catch the shedding hair. People can become completely bald except for a slight "peach fuzz" effect. If the hair doesn't all fall out but becomes thinner, it can continue to grow, but with a change in texture and appearance.

"I woke up one morning, lifted my head up, and my hair just stayed there, on the pillow."

"My hair had been falling out a little bit. I lathered up my head, began to massage my scalp, and with a sinking feeling I could almost feel the whole thing shift . . . with the water and the lather. . . . I got almost physically sick. I know I at least came close to tears; I don't think I actually cried. But I was paralyzed. I couldn't do anything. I just felt disgusting with all this hair all over the place. My wife came in and had to finish rinsing me off and cleaning out the tub while I got out and tried to not throw up. It was really devastating."

"I lost a lot of my hair—but not all of it. I'd say I've lost half of it. I don't need a wig; I've always had a lot of hair. Now it just looks sparse—people come up to me and say it looks gorgeous—I used to have too much hair. I wear it very close-cropped, and I trim it every three weeks. The texture has changed—I used to have very curly hair, and now it's straight. And it breaks. It still looks good, but it's not me."

The onset of my hair loss was much more difficult to deal with than it had to be because, as I said earlier, I was so ill-prepared; my being away from home when it happened made it even more of a nightmare. I had had three treatments, and I didn't feel too bad at all. No hair had fallen out, so I figured I was home free and would be spared the worst of the side effects. Full of relief and nonchalance, I went on a trip. In a glorious example of "perfect" timing, my hair began to shed slightly on the plane. Four days later I was barely presentable: You could see right through to my scalp. There I was stuck, away from home with no scarf, no wig, in unfamiliar surroundings with nowhere to hide. I finally found a few horrendous scarves to wear, which at least left me looking human. I cried a lot during that week; I never felt so down at any other time because finally toxicity had built up. Not only had my hair fallen out, I was beginning to feel physically ill because of the nausea and tiredness that had hit at the same time. Eventually I bought a wig that looked fine, but I still felt a sense of revulsion every time I saw myself without it. Losing my hair was the most dramatic, tangible side effect I experienced. Everything else was vague and invisible or purely medical. Then I not only felt sick, I looked sick.

I have come to believe that no one is fully prepared for hair loss because it requires you to know yourself so well that you can predict how you will react. So, in retrospect, I think what surprised me most about my hair falling out was the way I felt about this event. Before the hair loss I didn't think I was so vain that it would bother me. But it did fall out, and it did upset me— and then the fact that it bothered me upset me even further!

If your oncologist seems unable to help you cope, speaking with a counselor such as a nurse or social worker or with a patient who has had or is having chemotherapy may help you prepare yourself psychologically for hair loss. All the sources for emotional support discussed in Chapter 6 will help you adjust to both possible and actual loss of hair.

Most experienced professionals recommend that patients begin to look for a wig, and possibly buy one, before beginning chemotherapy and before the hair has started to fall out. Although many patients may not need or want a wig, many others will, and the peace of mind in knowing that an attractive hairpiece is handy is an important factor in how well people cope with hair loss. Donna Park says the advantage to looking for a wig early is so that "when you start to feel uncomfortable— either from the other side effects or because the hair loss is noticeable—you're not pressured to go out and buy something that you really can't afford or one that isn't right for you. You need time to shop around to find something that's right." Or some other kind of head covering should be on hand—turbans, scarves, hats, and caps are preferred by some instead of wigs or are used until they obtain a wig.

Because hair loss is one of the more distressing side effects, numerous attempts have been made to prevent it. Some patients have been able to prevent some scalp hair loss through the use of tourniquets or ice-filled caps. These devices are placed on the head during chemotherapy treatments in an effort to reduce the flow of blood there and thus expose the hair follicles in the scalp to lower concentrations of the drugs. Techniques vary, but generally when a tourniquet is used, it is worn during and immediately after the injection and is left on for up to twenty to forty-five minutes afterward. When ice is used, it is put on five minutes before and left on for about fifteen minutes after the injection.

This practice is not the answer to all chemotherapy patients' prayers, however. While it has met with some success, the effectiveness varies greatly and total prevention of hair loss is not yet possible. The ice and tourniquets are uncomfortable. People report headaches, chills, and dizziness from them. When drugs are given by slow infusion or when oral chemotherapy is taken several times a day, the devices have to be left on too long to be safe or comfortable for the patient.

Many physicians do not endorse the use of the tourniquets or caps except under certain conditions. They feel this practice should be avoided in patients for whom chemotherapy offers a chance for a cure, because there is the danger of creating a sanctuary for tumor cells circulating in the scalp. This is the case in adjuvant chemotherapy and in some metastatic diseases that can be cured as well as with leukemias and lymphomas, where the chemotherapeutic intent is to kill every single malignant cell.

Dr. William Grace, an oncologist in New York's St. Vincent's Hospital, says:

"The problem with chemo caps is the propensity to develop scalp relapses in people who are being treated for a cure. This is not theoretical—I've seen it and it has been confirmed several times in the literature. I had a patient whose disease went into remission everywhere but the scalp line—where it grew."

Patients are usually responsible for bringing their own tourniquets or caps and for obtaining and maintaining ice—no mean task when the wait for your treatment can stretch to hours. Donna Park says the patient has to get a written order from the physician and that the policy varies from physician to physician at Memorial:

"Because of the controversy, the decision is left up to the patient and the physician. If the patients want ice caps, they have to bring in their own. We'll put them in the refrigerator, but if something has to remain frozen, patients come in with ice chests."

Some oncologists and American Cancer Society chapters are telling chemotherapy patients about a product that may help minimize or prevent hair loss. It is called E. V. P 3 Chemaid and is available from JanBe Corporation in Chatsworth, California. The hair treatment is applied for ten minutes and is especially effective when used with ice caps or turbans. When it was tested, participating oncologists and patients both observed that it helped prevent hair loss normally associated with regimens that included adriamycin, Cytoxan, vincristine, and Oncovin. An oncologist who prescribes this product for his patients feels that the treatment may make a difference although there has been no controlled study that proves it stops hair loss. The product may also help slow hair loss that has already begun, speed hair regrowth, and strengthen the outer hair shaft, reducing breakage and dry, brittle hair. Tests have shown that the product is safe and nonirritating to the skin. E. V. P is not inexpensive, but it may be covered by your insurance company, so check with your doctor.

There are other promising leads that may be available in the future to stop hair loss. These include interleukins, proteins found naturally in the blood that are used as immunotherapy and can prevent hair loss in humans, and ImuVert, another biological substance, which is still experimental and has been found to reduce hair loss in rats.

Some people try to hold on to their hair once it starts falling out. Often they stop shampooing it or combing it because they have heard that this will keep it in longer. African-Americans, whose hair can be tightly braided and left untouched, have some success with this approach. The hairs that don't come loose from the scalp anchor the ones that do; this and the texture help maintain the illusion of a full head of hair. In a misguided attempt to make thinning hair look fuller, some patients get a permanent, but this usually backfires and instead accelerates the loss of hair.

For those with smooth-textured hair, the "don't touch" approach doesn't really work well. Mr. Nicholas has had clients who have tried it:

"Once it starts falling out, it's going to come out. But if you don't touch it—if you don't pull it, wash it, or comb it—it's going to stay in longer—if you can handle it. Some people do; some are nervous, frightened, and sensitive and don't want any of their hair to come out until their wig is ready. I've seen people who haven't touched their hair for four weeks. But their hair is uncomfortable and it doesn't look good—it is dirty, dull, matted. I will cut off the matted hair when they are ready for it. I do think it is much more comfortable for them if they get the shortest possible haircut that they will be comfortable with. It's a lot less dramatic or traumatic when it's short and close than when it's long and becoming matted. It's a lot easier to deal with thinning hair when it's short.''

Many others recommend that patients cut their hair short before it starts falling out. Joseph Rodriguez, general manager of the Vidal Sassoon Salon in New York, has had many clients who have undergone chemotherapy:

"Clients come in, they tell me that they are beginning chemotherapy and that their doctors recommend that they get a haircut. I always suggest that we cut the hair very short—as short as possible—as long as it suits them. It will be easier for them and make the hair last longer. When the hair is short, it looks thicker. Shorter hair keeps the hair strong because you don't pull it when you comb it, so it is easy to manage. And when it falls out, there will not be the additional problem of matting hair.''

I, for one, can vouch for the advisability of taking this step. My doctor recommended getting a haircut before my hair started falling out but didn't say how short. I just lopped four inches off my shoulder-length hair—why give up more than I had to? I thought maybe it wouldn't fall out after all. If I knew then what I know now! About half of it came loose during one shampooing. I could feel it matting as I lathered up. I ended up with instant dreadlocks that wouldn't budge. Losing so much hair at once was a bad enough shock, but now I had a gargantuan task ahead of me, and I thought I would never be able to untangle that rat's nest. Using an Afro pick, crying and feeling sick to my stomach, I pulled and tugged for an hour and cursed the fact that the pulling was making even more hair fall out. If I had gotten a much shorter haircut, it definitely wouldn't have been as bad an experience.

Often the hair growth is not completely halted, and some hair remains. Chemotherapy can sometimes just shrink the hair bulb, or root, which constricts the hair shaft as it grows. The hair—chemo hair—becomes thinner, sparser, weaker, with a brittle, finer texture, and takes on a dull appearance. Those with thick, strong, bouncy, curly hair find themselves with limp, straight hair. These people usually do not wear wigs and are still "presentable" but can be far from happy with their appearance:

"My hair didn't fall out completely, but it was a mess. It was very thin and fine; it was always shiny, and now it was drab. I looked like a nun who had just come out of the convent. I'd turn my head, and hair would fall out—there was hair over everything. I went to my hairdresser and he asked me, 'What have you done?' I burst into tears and told him I hadn't done anything, that I was on chemo. We tried henna, everything, to thicken and liven it up, but nothing worked."

"I never got a wig, though I played with the idea because my hair had gotten very thin; it was straight, with no life, and it just lay there. I'd show pictures of myself to people I had just met, who didn't know me before the chemo, and say, 'This isn't me—this picture is the real me.' I wore a lot of hats—I love them—I had different hats for different outfits."

To look its best, chemo hair should be treated gently, shampooed often, and styled to make the most of what's there. Avoid harsh hard-bristled brushes, sleeping with hair rollers, chemical treatments such as coloring or permanents, and hot hair dryers. The so-called hair thickeners are not recommended because they leave only a temporary coating along each hair shaft; they give the hair the appearance of thickness but leave a gummy deposit that dulls the hair further. As Mr. Rodriguez says:

"Thickeners do not work. If they did, I would use them on my hair, which is very fine and thin. Let's face it: There is not a whole lot you can do for a person whose hair is falling out. I think the best thing is to get a good short haircut and keep the scalp clean. If the hair falls out heavily, there is nothing you can do but wear a scarf, hat, or wig."

In our culture it is much more acceptable for men than for women to be bald. Generally women feel much more uncomfortable without their hair than do men. Hereditary baldness, far more common among men, has occurred in male role models—fathers, grandfathers, entertainment personalities, and great men of history. Also, stunning female "Star Trek" aliens and rock singers notwithstanding, bald men are considered normal, masculine, and sometimes even sexy. Many men on chemotherapy shave their heads rather than see their hair fall out before their very eyes, or walk around with a head of thinning hair, or suffer the expense, discomfort, and inconvenience of wearing a hairpiece. Bald is just their "new look." However, many others do cling to whatever is left and are deeply affected by hair loss.

Peggy Knight, president of the Peggy Knight Collection of quality hairpieces, has found that in her experience women have a hard time accepting the loss of scalp hair but men are more disturbed when they lose their body hair. Again, this reflects what we perceive as normal—in the United States it's common for women to remove body hair, but for men, only some types of athletes remove body hair without threatening their perceived masculinity or sex appeal.

Buying a Wig or Hairpiece

Having a wig in which you feel comfortable is an important factor in the difficult process of coping with hair loss. After having been fitted with wigs, Edith Imre's clients have told her that keeping their spirits up is an important part of the treatment; then they feel "hopeful, relieved, not like outcasts." "At least now I can leave the house without a hat or feeling that I'm going to scare the kiddies in the neighborhood," said one. "You don't know what a feeling of comfort and confidence this is to me," said another.

Mr. Nicholas says, "The better people look, the better they adjust to baldness. If you have a lousy wig on, you'll feel terrible. Many patients see others wearing bad wigs in the doctor's office, and they are turned off by them."

Wigs are available through barbers, hairdressers, beauty salons, and wig specialty shops; directly from wig suppliers; through the mail; and in department stores. They may be made of real or synthetic hair, prestyled, ready-made (the equivalent of "off the rack"), handmade, or custom-made. The kind of wig or hairpiece you get and where you buy it depend on your individual taste, how important it is for you to duplicate your own hair, how much money you can spend, where you live, what's available, and how much time you have.

For me, buying a wig was a relatively simple matter in which luck played a big part. I just looked up "Wigs" in the Yellow Pages and made a few phone calls: I knew I didn't want to spend much. I went to a wig supplier—real primitive conditions. I looked at the samples, picked out a couple, hid in the bathroom to try them on, and that was that. I was lucky—I paid only $40 for the one I ended up with, and it was a mass of natural-looking curls very close to my own hair color but very different from my usual style. So I didn't have to worry about a phony-looking part or hairline or explaining everything to people I only knew slightly. It was the right style, and perfect strangers would walk up to me on the street and ask where I got my perm. I'd send them to my hairdresser, of course.

You will do best, though, if you allow yourself as much time as possible for the selection, ordering, and preparation of your hairpiece. You can begin by asking your oncologist, nurse, or social worker to recommend a source for a good wig—they have probably seen many different hairpieces and are in a good position to judge. Or you can ask a fellow patient who is wearing one that you like.

To feel most comfortable and look most natural, wigs should be fitted and styled professionally. If you get the names of several sources, you can shop around and compare. Most of the preliminary scouting can be done over the phone—find out about the types of wigs available, the price range, the waiting time, the personality of the wig stylist, and the degree of privacy. Ask what their payment policy is. If you order a wig in advance, will they refund your money if your hair doesn't fall out and you don't need the wig, after all? What if you are not happy with the wig? Will they restyle it or offer you another at no or minimal extra cost?

In most cases it's best to buy a wig before your hair falls out. That way the wig specialist can see your natural hair color and hairstyle and then match it closely. Some will take a Polaroid photo of you or ask that you allow them to snip a sample of your hair for accurate color selection. (If you wait until your hair has fallen out, try to bring a photograph of yourself and save some of your hair to bring in.) Although wigs will fit differently after hair loss has begun, a good professional will be able to compensate for this as well as for hair regrowth.

If you delay buying a wig until after your hair has begun to fall out, the stylist's personality and the degree of privacy offered are even more important. As one patient said, "When you lose your hair, your spirits fall and you are ashamed to be seen. A regular salon is inappropriate for a chemo patient who is not buying a wig for fun and pleasure and who doesn't want to explain or show hair loss to a stranger."

More than enough has been said or written about the psychotherapeutic overtones in the client-hairdresser relationship. Suffice it to say that this aspect can assume even more importance when the client is a cancer patient who has lost his or her hair. One of Ms. Imre's patients told her, "You saw the pain inside

me and used patience and understanding to help tremendously.''
Out of a desire to help people who could not afford wigs, Ms.
Imre has established the Edith Imre Foundation for Loss of Hair
and has given away over six thousand wigs to hospitals and the
American Cancer Society. She says, "Nothing gives me more
pleasure than to see the feeling of joy in the faces of unfortunate
and suffering human beings."

Mr. Nicholas also stresses the importance of understanding
and patience for his special clients:

> "You develop a more personal relationship with clients that
> are going to have chemotherapy than you do with people who
> are just coming in for haircuts. They have to rely on you a
> little bit more, and you have to understand what they're going
> through and be able to deal with it. Because they are not
> always going to feel well, they're not always easy to get along
> with. They can get difficult, and it can be frustrating, but
> that's part of being in this business. When people are having
> problems, you have to be understanding."

In wigs synthetic hair is less expensive than human hair in
terms of both initial cost and upkeep. Synthetic wigs are easy
to maintain since they do not require "setting." Although
some of the less expensive synthetic wigs can still look un-
natural, 80 percent of today's wigs and hairpieces are made
using a new synthetic fiber called Kanekalon. This moda-
crylic fiber doesn't friz, droop, or lose its set and comes in
dozens of shades that can be blended to look and feel quite
natural. Even if you decide that you want a custom-made or
human hair wig, some people recommend that you buy a
cheaper, ready-made synthetic one before your hair falls out.
If you do lose your hair, at least you have something to tide
you over until your better wig is ready.

Still, human hair wigs generally look and feel more natural.
However, they are more expensive and require more care than
do synthetic wigs. Both kinds have a mesh or lace base that
varies in degree of give, comfort, appearance, and practicality.
Wig prices range from a forty dollar ready-made synthetic to a
fifteen-hundred- or three-thousand-dollar handmade human hair
wig that will match your own hair perfectly. Higher-quality synthetic wigs cost a few hundred dollars and up.

Most experts agree with Ms. Imre, who believes that

"It's very important that a wig be easy to handle. I wouldn't recommend human hair wigs—they're too expensive, too delicate, and require too much care. Especially if someone isn't feeling well most of the time, he or she doesn't want to be bothered with taking care of a wig. It should be comfortable, and the base should not be made of a very large mesh—this is okay for someone who still has some hair, but in a totally bald person, the bare scalp will show through."

Peggy Knight points out that machine-sewn ready-made synthetic wigs are made for people with hair. "Most not only allow scalp to show through the base when the wind blows, but they are scratchy and uncomfortable on a totally bare scalp." She recommends buying a soft cotton fabric close to your hair color and wrapping it around your head to form a liner to wear under the wig. A similar solution comes from a chemo patient who used the upper part of a pair of pantyhose for the same purpose.

"There are really two types of people," Ms. Imre says. "Those who want to look as much as possible like they did before, and those who go in the opposite direction." Most people still have at least some of their hair when they come to a salon for a wig. If they don't, the stylist asks them to bring in a photograph or has them describe how they looked.

Mr. Nicholas feels it can be difficult for people to find a natural-looking wig:

"Ready-made, prestyled synthetic wigs tend to look very artificial unless you are very lucky. This type of wig can be helped if your hairdresser styles it. Ready-made is the least expensive and faster to buy. When I start off with one of these, I take a sample of the person's hair and buy the wig that's closest in color and texture to it. I then fit, cut, and style it on the person's head. This I can do in a week or less, depending on the availability of a matching wig."

Handmade and custom-made wigs look better, are more comfortable and lighter on the head, and are less hot in the summer. They are much more expensive ($3,000 and up), and there's a longer wait (up to six weeks) for them to be ready. Nevertheless, people do order them and some come from all over the country and the world to have their wigs made at Kenneth. (Real hair wigs can be made from your own hair, provided that it is cut off early—once it falls out, it is too tangled to use.)

A new approach called hair integration may be an option for some people with thinning hair. These custom-made pieces consist of a spiderweblike base with human or synthetic hair attached. The hair is blended in with your own remaining scalp hair for a comfortable feel and a natural appearance.

Another recent improvement is the development of the vacuum-fit hairpiece. The base is made of a type of plastic that holds the wig on very securely even during activities such as tennis and swimming. Peggy Knight not only supplies these hairpieces but wears them because of a medical condition that caused her to lose all her hair. Her vacuum hairpieces are custom-made, and the base is made from a mold of your head. "They are for women with complete hair loss," she says, "and since they take longer [four months] to make than other wigs, they are not for most chemo patients." However, for a person who will be on chemo for a long time, this type of wig may still be an option.

If possible, you should buy the wig in person. Only then can you be assured of getting the best fit and the most flattering style. Some recommend bringing a friend along, but Ms. Imre feels differently:

> "Bring a spouse instead. A friend or sister comes in with a chemotherapy patient who doesn't have any hair, and it's very difficult. The friend starts in, 'Oh, she had such beautiful hair, you should have seen how thick it was.' I tell you, this only makes the woman feel worse. Don't people realize how damaging this is?"

With the proper care, a good wig can last for up to a year of moderate wear, so many recommend that you buy two wigs. You might want one that resembles your own hair and another that's very different, just for fun. Mr. Nicholas advises that "people have a good one that's comfortable and always looks good and a cheaper one that they can wear when their good wig is being serviced, or for every day, or for times like emptying the garbage. Usually two wigs will do it for a year."

Some people become so devastated and self-conscious about their appearance that they remove their wigs only for sleeping and showering. However, even the new lightweight wigs can be pretty uncomfortable, especially after weeks of daily wear. Many people, though shy at first, eventually loosen up, give way to comfort, and do not wear their hairpieces at all times. Most children and spouses quickly adjust to the appearance of the chemotherapy patient, and of course do not love them any less because they are temporarily bald. Families understand that at a time when you are not feeling well, every little bit of understanding helps. It is a show of trust and security to let those close to you see you as you really are. As one woman said to me, "I run around a lot without my hairpiece because it's so hot and uncomfortable. My kids are used to it; they don't care—I'm still Mom."

I liked the way my wig looked, but sometimes I hated the way it felt. As is the case with my shoes, it was a relief to be rid of the wig and I couldn't wait to take it off the minute I got home. I was very self-conscious about it, though Michael, God bless him, tried to convince me he actually preferred me bald. I felt so naked, so vulnerable, so ugly. We tried to make jokes about this and he gave me the nickname Baldielocks. At times he'd make me feel better about it by cradling my head in his hands and gently stroking my peach fuzz. Still, I often wore a scarf or knitted cap instead of the wig, although this was partly because my head got surprisingly cold without the protection of my usual mane of long blond hair.

Turbans, hats, scarves, and head wraps can alternately or completely take the place of a full wig. Turbans come in many colors and are stretchy, soft, and comfortable. A turban stays on easily and stands up to wear and tear, so it is especially useful on days when you feel really sick or during a treatment cycle if you are a hospital inpatient. The somewhat severe look of a turban can be softened with a small wiglet attached to the front so that some hair peeks out from underneath. This combination is more comfortable than a wig; it is less expensive and more practical and still gives the illusion of hair.

Hairpieces needed as a result of medical treatment are a tax-deductible expense, and some insurance policies cover them. Wigs can be obtained free—or their cost defrayed—through the social service departments of some hospitals and clinics, the American Cancer Society, and other agencies, organizations, and foundations. Wigs can also be obtained through public assistance programs.

Facial and Body Hair

Although most patients find the loss of scalp hair the most distressing, some find the loss of facial or body hair just as disturbing, if not more. Donna Park remarks that some patients say that losing the hair on their heads was more acceptable than losing the hair on other parts of their bodies. And people don't realize that they can lose their pubic hair. One woman remarked that she felt like "a plucked chicken." I found it weird but not unpleasant to be as hairless as a nine-year-old again, and not to have to shave my legs or underarms for months was a definite plus.

There is not much you can do about replacing or disguising the loss of facial or body hair. You can wear eyebrow and eyelash makeup or eyeglasses with large frames and tinted lenses. Mr. Nicholas says he suggests that if a woman's hairstyle can cover her brow line, she can leave it a little bit longer than usual. False eyebrows, eyelashes, mustaches, and beards do exist, but people rarely ask for them.

Health and beauty professionals have recognized what a difference it can make for some cancer patients when they feel better about the way they look. A program called Look Good . . . Feel Better has trained and organized volunteer cosmetologists and beauty advisers in communities all over the United States. The volunteers conduct group sessions where women receive complimentary makeup kits and learn tips about makeup, hair, wigs, turbans, and scarves; there may also be a personal consultation available. To find out about Look Good . . . Feel Better programs, call your local American Cancer Society or 1-800-395-LOOK.

When the Hair Grows Back

The loss of hair brought about by chemotherapy is almost always reversible. Regrowth often begins even before the treatment is over, as the hair grows resistant to the chemicals. This initial growth may appear to be abnormal: People with straight hair commonly grow curly hair—to the surprise of many patients. It may at first, however, be finer, or silkier or of a different color or texture. This chemo hair is a transient stage; the hair eventually becomes thicker—in many cases thicker than before the therapy—and usually eventually returns either completely back to normal or nearly so.

I spoke with this patient six months after he had completed his chemotherapy and was due for a second haircut; he said of his hair: "It feels a little softer and is curly. My barber says it feels like infant's hair. If I just step out of the shower and don't comb it, it's a mass of Byronic curls. In fact, I'm thinking of going as Byron to a costume party next month. It's definitely less gray than it was, but my beard is more gray."

Once the hair starts growing back, when and how to "come out" can be an agonizing decision; it can be a difficult transitional period. Some people are ecstatic when their hair regrows, and they discard their wigs at the earliest possible moment. I was elated when my hair began to grow back three months after it had fallen out—I felt the stubble or, as my oncologist called it, the "five o'clock shadow." I kept rubbing my head in glee and disbelief. Nevertheless, I had to wait another three months until I felt comfortable in public without a wig, my hair was so thin and fine. Still, it was only a half inch long when I began to seriously entertain thoughts of appearing au naturel. I did it in stages. First I took out the garbage, just to see how it felt to be outdoors. It felt okay! Then I mailed a letter in the mailbox across the street. No one stared; no one ran away screaming! Then, getting braver by the minute, I went to the grocery store and made actual contact with people. Still no reaction. That was it from then on. I hadn't trusted my friends who said: "Do it, do it," or Michael, who said, "Well, it *is* awfully short." I had to test it out myself.

Others are reluctant to give up their wigs because they prefer the way they look over their real hair. A social worker told me about a patient who began shaving her head when her hair started to grow back because it was uncomfortable under a wig, which she wanted to continue to wear. Mr. Nicholas says:

> "Half the people can't wait to throw out their wigs and stomp on them when their hair has grown back. The other half have learned to like their wigs, especially if they're expensive ones. They get compliments when they wear their wigs and use them when their hair isn't right. Usually they buy new hairpieces, though, because their chemotherapy wigs are usually pretty worn out by then."

He also tells of the problem faced by patients who have been coloring the hair blond before the chemotherapy and whose hair grows back gray mixed with brown and sticks out from under their blond wigs. "I tell these people to check with their doctors, and if it's okay, we'll lighten up just around the hairline so it can be combed in with the wig." Mr. Imre says patients often use water-soluble rinses to cover hair that is growing in gray because of the cancer scare with stronger dyes, which may also be too harsh for the new growth.

Some people can't wait to run out and get perms to make

their new hair look better. This, as is true with hair coloring, is usually not advisable unless the hair is strong and has a good texture—check with your doctor. What is advisable is a haircut as soon as there is hair to cut. "Once hair starts growing in and looking straggly," says Mr. Nicholas, "I like to have my clients come in and I'll trim it—clean it up. That makes people feel comfortable about themselves. They can look better with their own hair, and pretty soon they'll be wearing their wigs only for special occasions."

SKIN CHANGES

The skin can be affected by chemotherapy in many ways. Most effects are minor and disappear between treatments or after the course of therapy is over. Some patients experience dry, itchy, flaky, sensitive skin while on chemotherapy. The reason for this is that since the skin cells multiply rapidly, the skin sheds more than usual and becomes thin. The sweat glands may also be affected, which leaves the skin drier than usual, as one patient describes. A breast cancer patient recalls:

> "I was concerned that my skin was going to get old fast from the chemo. I didn't get wrinkles or creases, but my skin did get very dry. I looked like I had dandruff all over my body— not just my head. When I peeled off my stockings I'd shake them out and flakes of skin would fall. It was disgusting! I used *a lot* of Nivea. And when my scalp got dry I used mineral oil on it, and baby oil, but that just made my thin hair look limper and thinner."

Patients with problem skin should protect it from harsh, cold, dry weather and too much water. Long hot baths tend to dry skin even further; quick showers and sponge baths with super-fatted nondrying soaps are better. Daily use of emollient and moistening creams and lotions is recommended; used immediately after washing while the skin is still damp, they help seal in moisture. Raising the humidity in the house with a humidifier will also help.

If your scalp becomes itchy and flaky, a dandruff shampoo may help, as may oil rubbed into the scalp, although as mentioned above, this can make thinning hair look worse. Wearing a wig or head covering has not been shown to affect hair growth, but it can increase perspiration, dandruff, and itching and can irritate a sensitive, newly bared scalp. Frequent cleansing with a mild shampoo and keeping the head uncovered whenever possible will help here.

The skin may be prone to more bacterial and fungal infections than usual because of its increased sensitivity and a person's lowered resistance to disease in general. These local infections should be treated with local medication; refer to Chapter 10 for information about protecting the immune system and avoiding infections.

Some drugs cause changes in skin color, and these changes may be triggered or worsened by exposure to sunlight. Many patients are advised to avoid the sun, although others are permitted to sunbathe in moderation. Check with your doctor to see if your drugs can cause photosensitivity; if they do, wear protective clothing, hats, and a sun block while in the sun. The areas usually affected by the drug-sun combination are the backs of the hands, bodily creases, nails and nail beds, the face, and the elbows. Rarely, the skin over the whole body can be affected.

Some drugs can cause a local irritation or red rash around the injection site. This is not serious and should disappear within an hour or two after the treatment. Some drugs may also cause the veins to darken. This is not serious either, and the vein is not damaged; the darkness should disappear within a week or two. Patients may also experience mild discomfort during an injection, both from the needle and from the drugs themselves. This should not be confused with *extravasation*, a potentially serious complication that occurs at the site of the injection when some of the drug escapes into the surrounding tissue rather than into the vein where it belongs. This is a slight, though real, danger with intravenous therapy.

There are varying degrees of extravasation; even though my oncologist was very careful, I had a minor brush with it myself. I usually avoided looking at the injection site during a treatment, but I couldn't help but take a peek the time I felt more pain than usual. I saw a mound of purple swelling in the crook of my arm, but I wasn't really worried—yet. My oncologist told me the mound was blood mixed with vincristin. I made some jokes about whether this was how people got those special effects in the movies; he patched me up and continued the injection in another vein. The pain became so bad, I hardly slept that night, and when I called him, he prescribed a very strong cortisone cream. In a few hours, it felt much better and the swelling went way down. I put ice on it all week, and when the time for my next shot rolled around two weeks later, it was almost completely healed.

Most but not all drugs cause problems if they leak into the surrounding tissue. Methotrexate, for example, is harmless—it can be injected into the muscle. But extra precautions should always be taken with a drug such as adriamycin, which is perhaps the most caustic anticancer drug. Dangerous drugs that can cause *necrosis* (tissue death) should not be the first or the last substances to enter the vein; they should be safely sandwiched between either harmless drugs or a saline solution. After the treatment is over and the needle is withdrawn, rather than applying pressure with the arm in the usual lowered bent elbow position, some doctors have their patients raise their arms up over their heads as they apply pressure to the injection site. This collapses the vein nicely and prevents any remains of the drugs from backing up out of the vein and causing problems.

The sooner extravasation is caught, the better. Always tell the doctor or nurse about any pain or burning sensation during the injection so they can check whether the reaction is normal or if something is amiss. Try to keep movement to a minimum during treatment and complain like hell if you are being treated by a clumsy technician.

Another danger with intravenous chemotherapy is "blown" veins. Preferred veins, those used again and again during blood tests and chemotherapy, get a real workout. Eventually, they may say "enough" by shutting down in protest, becoming hard, and no longer allowing the blood to flow through. This is not particuarly dangerous since other blood vessels will learn to take over, but it may make treatment gradually more and more difficult as more and more "good veins" get used up. These problems are becoming rarer with the increased use of indwelling catheters and ports, which protect the veins from chemotherapy drugs.

Occasionally, phlebitis may occur. This is a painful inflammation of the vein that is somewhat common in patients taking drugs they are sensitive to. Treatment for phlebitis includes the application of heat and oral painkillers. This condition takes several weeks to subside.

NAIL PROBLEMS

Discolored and disfigured nails are a rare complication of chemotherapy. Nails can become brittle, cracked, and ridged; they may tear, flake, and break off painfully near the quick. Remedies for hardening and strengthening brittle nails have not been proved, but they are generally harmless and, unless you experience a reaction to the ingredients, may help. Nail polish—especially the kinds containing nylon fibers—can support and protect the nail; use as many coats as necessary to form a thick enough shield. You can minimize the dangers and damage to your nails by wearing rubber gloves and protective gloves when performing chores; using rich hand creams may also help if you massage around the nail beds with them.

Effects on Sexuality

Many patients are eager to know about how chemotherapy affects people's sex lives. As Grace Christ, formerly of New York's Memorial Sloan-Kettering says, "Sexuality is a product of many things. Chemotherapies do impact on sexuality—but we're not sure as to how." Some patients report an increase in sexual activity; others say there is no difference. Many, however, do report a decrease to varying degrees:

"I would say there's moderate sex on chemo. We weren't exactly swinging from the chandeliers . . . but I did feel like 'doing it.' I did feel somewhat asexual because of the combination of a lost breast and the lost hair. I couldn't imagine how anybody would want me."

"Sex? There is no sex on chemo. My husband and I sat down and talked about it, and he really understood. We always had a really nice sexual relationship, and suddenly I had no interest whatsoever. It wasn't because of the mastectomy; it had nothing to do with my feeling less desirable. I was just indifferent. Fortunately, we learned to live with it; we knew it was temporary."

Obviously side effects caused by chemo such as tiredness, infection, nausea, weight fluctuations, hair loss, depression, low self-esteem, and fear of losing a partner can lower our libidos and inhibit us sexually. Chemotherapy may also affect hormone levels and otherwise throw our reproductive systems off course, as when young women are thrown into premature menopause.

As with other side effects, there are no hard and fast rules. Science has taught us that the brain is the most potent sexual organ there is: The mind is the true source of our sexuality. Our mental attitude can be a surprisingly powerful force both in overcoming any obstacles chemo has placed in our path and in adapting to those it cannot override. Though sexual intercourse may be put on the back burner, many people have found that sexual expression is not. Sex during chemotherapy may not be quite the same as before, but it can still be enjoyable and satisfying for both partners.

If sexuality is important to you (and to many people it is not, at least at this time) and you find yours is being adversely affected, help can be found through many channels. As one of the patients just quoted has shown us, having honest, open discussions with your partner is an excellent place to start and may be all you need. In addition, you might seek out medical solutions to physical side effects that affect sexuality, look for outside psychological support, or brush up on your sex education and learn about alternatives to previous sexual habits and preferences. Remember, it is natural to have some concerns and questions about sexuality in relation to cancer treatment, although this issue is not often discussed openly with patients and very little information is volunteered. You may even find that your questions are being avoided, but don't allow this to convince you that your fears and thoughts are imaginary or foolish. Don't give up if sexual satisfaction and expression rank high in your needs and their absence or diminishment poses a threat to your quality of life.

YOU AND YOUR PARTNER

The keys to enjoyable sexual activity for anyone are the ability to communicate openly, relax, and be flexible. This is no less true for people who are having chemotherapy. The quality of the relationship, the sexual skills, and the affection between partners that existed previously also help determine the level of sexual enjoyment during chemo.

If chemo does impose changes on the way you're feeling emotionally and physically, you must make your new needs and limitations known. For example, you may be ready to resume sexual activity but your partner may not realize it, or sex may be the furthest thing from your mind but not your partner's. You might want to be sociable or affectionate at this time, but not sexual.

Psychological and emotional factors may cause us to withdraw from the whole experience as a way of protecting ourselves from possible failure or rejection. Whether we try to express our sexuality or we withdraw depends also, to a large extent, on our sexual partners, be they permanent (a spouse or steady lover) or randomly available. Although rejection is a real possibility—partners may find chemo patients unattractive, or fear catching the disease, or be afraid of hurting them, or be reluctant to bother them "after all they've been through"—these anxieties are often not grounded in reality.

Often, whatever differences happen because of chemo are fortunately short-lived. If you had a good relationship and enjoyed sexual activity before your illness, chances are that these things will reassert themselves eventually of their own accord. Sometimes the increased closeness that a serious illness can bring between two people not only will change their sexual relationship, it will ultimately change it for the better.

There's more to sex, love, and affection than intercourse and/or orgasms. Even when you are too ill or tired or when surgery is too recent for you to indulge in the athletics of the whole sexual gamut, you and your partner can express yourselves sexually—and have a very good time doing it. As adults, we have come to think of kissing, cuddling, and caressing as preludes, but they are quite nice all by themselves.

In my household sex wasn't exactly a thing of the past, but it sure wasn't what it used to be. We often found ourselves content with the less vigorous forms of affection and appreciation. That was what I needed most at the time, not more excitement! The simple fact of having a warm, caring body next to mine was immensely reassuring, comforting, therapeutic, and meaningful. Gentle, heartfelt, loving stroking and hugging were good for my body and soul; they helped heal me emotionally and increased my sense of physical well-being, too.

And just as you can have intercourse without orgasm, you can have orgasms without intercourse. As Kinsey and Masters and Johnson have shown, the parameters of healthy sexual behavior are broader than we thought; patience and a willingness to experiment may open up whole new vistas of sexual pleasure. Many chemotherapy patients turn to self-stimulation and find it a reasonable solution to needs that might otherwise go completely unfulfilled at this time.

Starting up new relationships is difficult for anyone but can pose a special challenge for people on chemotherapy. You may feel reluctant and awkward about bringing up the subject of your cancer and its therapy at first. But once the discussion has begun, communicating your feelings can help strip away superficialities and cultivate a closeness that might not otherwise have occurred or might have taken forever to develop. Cancer patients have the ultimate satisfaction of knowing that they are loved for themselves, not just for the way they look or for their ability to become parents.

OUTSIDE HELP

Sometimes the chemo-related sexual changes are such that they can't be dealt with between partners. At times, referral to a sex clinic or therapist may be in order. But often just talking things over with a sympathetic person can be a help. A nurse, a social worker, other patients, support groups, or your gynecologist or urologist will help you find some answers. A sensitive oncologist may be able to answer your needs for sex counseling or information; he or she may also be able to suggest material for home reading. However, many patients find it difficult to bring up the subject with their oncologists, who rarely bring it up themselves.

Lari Wenzel, a medical psychologist, says:

"I think the problem is much greater than people will admit. The problem starts when the physician doesn't ask, and most patients aren't going to bring it up. It's not a routine part of your physical exam. And unless you have a very close relationship with the doctor and you are very assertive, it's just a problem that's not acknowledged the way it should be."

Both patient and doctor may feel awkward and uncomfortable discussing intimate sexual details. Physicians often are not equipped or eager to do sex counseling, or they don't realize that sexuality can be a concern at this time. Dr. William Grace, an oncologist at St. Vincent's Hospital in New York, says: "A lot of people just resign themselves and say, 'Well, I'm not going to be sexually active at this time.' A lot of people don't want to talk about it; it's very hush-hush. I'd say only about 10 percent of my patients bring it up, and when they do, it's usually with a nurse, who then tells me."

Wenzel emphasizes that "as cancer care becomes more sophisticated, it's incumbent on all health professionals to recognize multiple needs in their patients—not just the medical needs.'' To that end, she feels strongly that ''any cancer treatment program should have the built-in opportunity to acknowledge the possibility of sexual problems. This could be part of an overall emotional assessment—a brief questionnaire or interview that asks whether they are suffering from depression or anxiety. How is this interfering with their functioning at home, on the job, or with their sexual functioning?''

Although sexuality may get brought up during a support group, Mary Hughes, psychiatric clinical nurse specialist, thinks that individual therapy is a more comfortable setting. Timing also enters into it in terms of being ready to look at long-term living. ''In groups, you're still focusing on survival,'' she says.

According to Wenzel, preliminary research shows that in many cases psychosocial intervention can help. In a study of women with gynecologic cancer, a substantial proportion of those who received counseling said they had returned to their predisease frequency of intercourse compared with the women who received no counseling.

Fortunately, many problems have simple solutions. ''A lot of patients' sexual problems are related to the physical side effects of chemotherapy,'' continues Dr. Grace, and here the oncologist's medical skills can surely help. ''They may have painful intercourse due to vaginal dryness. If there is an infection present—infections like trichomona and candida have an increased risk at this time—we treat that.'' If there is fatigue, nausea, constipation, or diarrhea, you can take medications and measures that reduce them, too.

STERILITY AND MENOPAUSE

For many chemotherapy patients, the drugs' impact on their reproductive system is a discrete, though important, issue closely related to their ability to express themselves sexually and to their feelings about themselves as complete human beings. Some chemotherapy drugs—primarily the alkylating agents such as chlorambucil and Cytoxan—are well known for their ability to reduce sperm counts or sperm vitality in men. These drugs plus two others—busulfan and vinblastine—are also known to suppress ovarian function and menstruation in women.

As a result, the chemotherapy patient runs the risk of becoming infertile or subfertile during therapy. This condition may be temporary and disappear after treatment is over. But it can take a long time to reverse itself, and it sometimes never does or does so incompletely.

The total amount of these drugs and the length of time you take them play key roles in the incidence and reversibility of early menopause and fertility problems. Permanent sterility is most common in patients who receive high-dose long-term chemotherapy, such as for Hodgkin's disease, and less common in low-dose short-term chemo plans such as adjuvant treatment for breast cancer.

Another variable is your age. The younger you are, the more resistant you are likely to be and the better your chances are for reversing infertility or menopause caused by chemo. For example, in women undergoing adjuvant chemo for breast cancer, the cutoff age seems to be about thirty. Women under thirty tend to resume menstruation, and women over thirty tend not to.

Sterility is more of a long-term problem than an immediate one because conception is inadvisable during chemotherapy. This is primarily because anticancer drugs have the potential to cause birth defects (teratogenesis) and mutations in offspring that are exposed to the drugs while in the womb and as sperm or eggs even before conception. However, there is no firm proof that the danger occurs with every drug, and so, as Drs. Holland and Frei point out in Cancer Medicine, this problem is hard to assess. There are patients who while on chemotherapy have produced apparently healthy offspring, but some warn that even in seemingly healthy babies chromosomal damage may be latent and may not show up until some future generation. Most of the danger appears to be in the first trimester of pregnancy, and the overall risk in later trimesters appears to be the same as under normal conditions. Nevertheless, many physicians feel that the risk is high enough to recommend that their patients use contraception during chemotherapy. Dr. Grace says, "Chemotherapy is not a form of birth control. It is difficult to get pregnant while on chemo but not impossible."

If a woman is pregnant at the time of diagnosis, she is usually not given chemotherapy unless her life is in immediate danger from the disease and chemotherapy has a chance to produce a cure or remission. Breast-feeding may be hazardous to the baby if the mother is on chemo. Sometimes an abortion is advised if a pregnancy is already established, but again, the decision is not clear-cut. Patients should discuss the possible risks with their doctors. Women patients who are sexually active and who miss a period should have a pregnancy test as soon as possible.

In the past there was a special concern when the patient had cancer of a reproductive organ such as the breast, which is sensitive to the levels of hormones in the body. Since pregnancy changes these levels, it was theorized that a pregnancy could stimulate the growth of cancer and precipitate a recurrence. However, recent studies show that pregnancy does not significantly raise the rate of recurrence.

Sterility, or the possibility of it, is more of an issue for some patients and their spouses than for others. Age, former plans, and the presence of previous children affect its importance:

"I don't like it at all. My wife's reaction isn't good, either. The old affection isn't there now that we can't have children together. Sure we have sex, but it isn't like it used to be. The little things—like stroking—are left out. My wife is going to a psychiatrist. I go out a few nights a week—not for a one-night stand but to get attention and affection and to boost my ego a little. I'm a very sensual, romantic guy at heart, and that part of me is not being expressed while my wife isn't interested."

The possibility of being sterile was not a major problem for me, since I had no overwhelming desire to have children. But it does seem odd—extending your own life in exchange for a potential child. At the time it didn't bother me—except that I do like to have options, whether I intend to exercise them or not, and this may have removed one of them. Now that I'm 44, and having my own child is out of the question, I sometimes feel a pang of regret. But who knows? I probably never would have had a child anyway.

If you are still of childbearing age, you should talk over family planning and contraception with your physician, nurse, or social worker. (The pill and IUD are usually not recommended for chemotherapy patients.) This should be done *before* you begin chemotherapy. Although sterility or subfertility may be reversible, it may not be. Therefore, male chemotherapy patients are often advised to visit a sperm bank while they still have viable sperm. Should the chemotherapy leave them permanently sterile, they may still be able to father children via artificial, or in vitro, insemination. Women about to undergo chemotherapy unfortunately do not have an equivalent option at this time and are usually counseled about the possibility of adoption. (Several reports discuss some possible ways of preventing ovarian failure in women; these include the use of oral contraceptives in humans and of other types of hormone manipulation in mice and rats. However, the results of these efforts have by and large been inconclusive.) Still, these alternatives leave much to be desired, especially for young single adults who want children and for couples whose families are not yet complete. Anxiety and regret over this loss can spill into many aspects of their lives, and sometimes professional counseling helps people adapt.

For men, cytotoxic agents kill the rapidly producing sperm and damage the testes. This reduction in the production of sperm is not of itself directly responsible for reducing either the desire or the ability to have sex from a physiological point of view. Theoretically, unless "feminizing" hormone therapy is also being given, a man's testosterone levels are not affected and he can still achieve and maintain an erection and ejaculation. An infertile man can still enjoy sex, and so can his partner. However, no one is sure about this, and in reality, some men do find that their libidos are lessened during chemotherapy. (It is uncertain whether this is due to physical or emotional factors.)

It's quite different for a woman, whose reproductive system, with its delicately balanced menstrual cycle, is much more complex than a man's. A woman is born with her total supply of ova, or eggs; unlike a man's sperm, they are not manufactured constantly in the body—they mature, one at a time per cycle, during ovulation. A woman on chemo undergoes estrogen withdrawal and possibly other hormonal changes. These changes prevent the egg from maturing and cause menstrual irregularities, and women can undergo real, verifiable physical and emotional changes. Aside from the discomfort and embarrassment of hot flashes, women experience profuse sweating, vaginal infections, dry or sore vaginas, uncomfortable intercourse, dizziness, difficulty in breathing, mood swings, and a greater than usual uncertainty about the possibility of pregnancy. If hormonal therapy is administered simultaneously with or sequentially to chemotherapy, these problems are compounded and women may experience signs of masculinization such as excess facial and bodily hair and a lowered voice.

These effects may be almost immediate or take several months to become evident; other changes in the vagina, cervix, skin, and bones can occur eventually if the menopause becomes permanent. All these sex- and hormone-related side effects can reduce the quality of sex and the quality of life for women during and after chemotherapy. Even if their periods do not stop completely, some women miss the rhythm of a physical phenomenon that has occurred so regularly up to then.

Women may be thrust into artificial menopause, often at a very young age. Doctors don't often warn women about this eventuality and often fail to realize, believe, or accept the amount of distress this can cause. Here are two women's experiences:

> "I had lost my period completely about six months after beginning the chemo; it got irregular, and very light, and then stopped. I'm on tamoxifen now, which suppresses the hormone production in the body. When I get a hot flash, my body temperature goes sky-high and my face gets beet red. Sometimes my emotions will set it off. The sweat pours down, and I feel like I can't breathe—like I'm having an anxiety attack. Then there's the erratic behavior. . . . I hope this is temporary, as my doctor says. I'm a young woman yet."

> "When I went into chemical menopause, my doctor told me it was my imagination. Right! There in the middle of winter I was sitting in church, fanning myself like crazy, turning bright red. My periods never came back, even though my doctor said there was enough estrogen so they might. I have no symptoms now; I'm not uncomfortable with it."

Health professionals sometimes dismiss the symptoms of menopause as "psychosomatic" or tell patients to grin and bear it. Physicians have generally been hesitant to prescribe hormone replacement therapy (HRT), which is widely used to ease symptoms in women without cancer. This is especially so in women with reproductive cancers because the hormones can stimulate cancer cells to grow. However, there is some evidence that the short-term use of low-dose estrogen/progestogen is safe and may actually protect against the growth of breast cancer. If vaginal dryness is the main problem, ask your doctor about prescribing a testosterone-containing cream. Or you may find that lubricants such as K-Y Jelly and the spectacular Astro-Glide provide what chemo has taken away. There are other ways that you can deal with the physical and emotional changes brought about by this side effect. You can contact women's support groups whose members have gone through menopause themselves. You can refer to the books on this subject listed in the Resources section. One of them, *Coping with a Hysterectomy* by Susanne Morgan, explains how to make "home-brew estrogen." This involves a general change in life habits that encourages overall health and the body's own production of estrogen. The plan includes exercise, stress reduction, nutrition, and diet. Experience has shown, for instance, that symptoms are reduced when women cut down on sugar, coffee, and salt consumption and take supplements such as calcium, and vitamins B, E, and C. Ms. Morgan also discusses the importance of remaining sexually active—it is a common misconception that sexual desire diminishes after menopause. But this may be in part a self-fulfilling prophecy (use it or lose it).

Other Side Effects

BLADDER AND KIDNEY PROBLEMS

Cyclophosphamide (Cytoxan) can cause acute noninfectious (hemorrhagic) cystitis. Since 70 percent of this drug is excreted by the kidneys, the bladder is given plenty of exposure, and it is thought that the cystitis results from the drug acting directly on the mucosa that lines the bladder. Chronic bladder irritation can cause scar tissue to form, and as a result the bladder is able to hold less and there is a need for more frequent urination. In this rare complication of therapy, the symptoms are painful: frequent urination, urgency of urination, low back pain, and blood in the urine.

Cystitis seems to appear to be more of a danger in those who receive large doses of this drug intravenously, who are on prolonged therapy, or who do not drink enough fluids. It is recommended, therefore, that anyone who is receiving this drug should drink as much liquid as possible—at least two quarts a day, which may be in the form of water or other beverages such as soda, and juices or in the form of Popsicles or Jell-O.

The onset of the symptoms may occur as early as twenty-four hours after the first drug dose or be delayed until several weeks after the end of the treatment. Acute symptoms usually go away when the drug is stopped, but slight bleeding may persist for months. Treatment for noninfectious cystitis that is not severe consists of medication; when it is more serious, surgery may be be necessary. The same symptoms of noninfectious cystitis may indicate infectious cystitis, which may be treated with antibiotics.

Other drugs given to treat cancer can act on the kidneys (renal toxicity). These include cisplatin, dacarbazine, daunorubicin, doxorubicin, lomustine, methotrexate, the mitomycins, and mithramycin. Kidney damage can be serious and sometimes is severe and leads to fatal kidney failure. However, it may be reversible if caught early enough. Symptoms include headache, swelling of the body, and flank pain. As is beneficial against bladder toxicity, drinking large quantities of liquids can prevent these problems from occurring or at least minimize them. In some cases and with some drugs, large doses of vitamin C, mannitol, or sodium bicarbonate have been used in an attempt to further minimize the risks. (Doxorubicin in the system creates red-colored urine, which lasts only one or two days and is not serious.) Renal function may also be affected by the remnants of dead cancer cells that pass through the kidneys. Drinking plenty of liquids usually forestalls any problems, but allopurinol may also be prescribed to prevent problems in patients with leukemia and lymphomas, where large numbers of cancer cells are destroyed.

FLULIKE SYMPTOMS

While on chemotherapy, patients sometimes feel like they have the flu—an all-over achiness in their muscles and/or bones, possibly a fever and chills, fatigue, nausea, or a feeling of general malaise. They may indeed have caught an infectious virus, since their immune systems are likely to be compromised. However, some drugs used in chemotherapy can themselves cause these symptoms to appear when no infection is actually present. Any of the antibiotics can give you flulike symptoms, as can cytarabine, dacarbazine, thio-TEPA, and VP-16-213. Vincristine and vinblastine can give you an all-over achy feeling. These symptoms are temporary and pass within days of treatment. They should respond to the usual nostrums prescribed for the flu: Tylenol, fluids, rest.

HEART PROBLEMS

Heart damage (cardiotoxicity) is the principal dose-limiting side effect of two antibiotics: daunorubicin and doxorubicin (adriamycin). Prednisone may also damage the heart. When cardiotoxicity occurs, the drugs' effects are usually cumulative; they can lead to chronic congestive heart failure, which may be progressive and eventually fatal. The onset of the symptoms (swelling of the body, shortness of breath, dizziness, loss of appetite, fluttering of the heartbeat) may not occur until long after the drug has been begun—usually two weeks to six months after therapy has been completed. Cumulative congestive heart failure may be irreversible, but it may respond to drug therapy with digitalis and diuretics.

In the rarer acute form of cardiotoxicity, the effects on the heart occur during or shortly after the drug is administered. The effects usually reverse quickly without serious complications and are usually not considered a reason to stop the drug. At one time 75 percent of those who experienced cardiotoxicity died, but it is being recognized earlier and treated more successfully. Studies are under way to improve early diagnosis even more and perhaps prevent cardiotoxicity's occurrence through blocking chemicals. Vitamin E, for example, has been found to protect the heart from adriamycin in animals and may prove to do the same in humans.

In some cases a drug called Novantrone may be used instead of adriamycin; it can be just as effective but can be given for longer periods without endangering the heart. In addition, heart-toxic drugs can be given by slow infusion, which, for example, reduces the heart toxicity of adriamycin by 50 to 75 percent.

LIVER PROBLEMS

Many of the drugs used in cancer chemotherapy produce some degree of liver impairment (hepatotoxicity); most are difficult to measure and unnoticeable because of the liver's ability to withstand a tremendous amount of abuse. And abuse is what it gets during chemotherapy because the liver works overtime to detoxify harmful substances before they are excreted from the body.

Methotrexate and 6-mercaptopurine are the two drugs usually associated with cirrhosis and fibrosis (scarring) of the liver, especially during long-term use. Other drugs, such as L-asparaginase, carmustine, Cytoxan, dacarbazine, doxorubicin (adriamycin), mithramycin, streptozocin, and thioguanine, have also been implicated in liver dysfunction. Combination chemotherapy, preexisting liver dysfunction, and alcohol intake can compound these drugs' effects on the liver, which may become evident within one or two months after treatment or as late as two years afterward. Symptoms include jaundice, nausea, fatigue, and pain on the right side of the body.

LUNG PROBLEMS

Lung damage (pulmonary toxicity) is a rare side effect, although many drugs have the potential to cause it. Busulfan, carmustine, chlorambucil, Cytoxan, the bleomycins, and methotrexate have been known to cause lung damage in a small percentage of patients. The damage, which is a kind of scarring (fibrosis), is characterized by a dry cough, shortness of breath, high pulse, and a low-grade fever. Pulmonary damage may be reversible with time when the drug is stopped early and corticosteroids are administered. However, there is irreversible damage in some people, and as a result, they are chronically short of breath and must change their life-styles accordingly.

Pulmonary toxicity may occur after the first treatment; this is usually due to a hypersensitivity to the drug and is helped by corticosteroids. However, it may not become evident until long after chemotherapy, even years after the therapy has ended.

Because this reaction is so rare and the early symptoms are subtle or unreported, lung damage may be undetected until quite late. Dr. William Grace, an oncologist at St. Vincent's Hospital in New York, says:

> "Early diagnosis is the key. If it goes too far, there may be no coming back. If a patient has symptoms and an X ray shows nothing, you go on to test for pulmonary functions. I think that what you often see is a busy oncologist who keeps giving the drug because toxicity is not detected soon enough. Subclinical or early forms of toxicity are often not recognized."

To prevent or minimize the possibility of lung damage, reduce the amount of tobacco (or anything else) you smoke; quitting is even better. You might also try taking deep breaths several times a day; this will expand your lung tissue and may prevent fibrosis.

NERVOUS SYSTEM PROBLEMS

There are several chemotherapy drugs that are known for their effects on the nervous system.

As a result of taking vincristine or vinblastine, patients may experience peripheral neuropathy (nerve damage in the hands and feet), the symptoms of which are a tingling or a numbness in the fingertips and/or toes. You may feel clumsy and have trouble opening jars or tying your shoelaces. There may be damage to the nerves that control the action of the intestines, which results in constipation, sluggish bowels, or a coliclike pain. Sometimes the facial nerve is affected and there is a deep aching pain in the jaw or throat. A loss of deep tendon reflexes or increased motor weakness causes foot or wrist drop, difficulty walking or rising from a chair, clumsiness, or a loss of coordination. In addition, the impotence of which some men complain is possibly a result of nerve damage.

Vincristine was part of my chemo protocol, and I did experience some tingling and numbness in my fingers and toes. It came on so gradually, I barely noticed it. It was winter, so I thought maybe the cold had something to do with it. I never would have said anything if my oncologist hadn't eventually asked me about it. I got quite constipated for a while, but we don't know whether that was from the drugs or from my different diet and decrease in exercise. I noticed one foot would sort of lag behind when I walked, but I thought I was just tired.

In addition to these fairly concrete, measurable signs of neurotoxicity, there is a whole constellation of others that are vague and much harder to put a finger on. They can result in a mental muzziness or cloudiness, a feeling of being doped up, off balance, and not "with it." Some people on chemo, myself included, just feel slower, duller, and clumsier mentally and physically. Though it is difficult to distinguish the emotional and physical contributors from the direct pharmacological culprits, certain drugs are associated with these effects.

Vincristine and vinblastine, for example, can cause muscle weakness; vincristine also can cause muscle cramps. Both drugs have been known to cause mental depression. L-asparaginase may affect the nervous system by causing mental depression, hallucinations, confusion, lethargy, and nervousness. Procarbazine's effects include depression, tiredness, agitation, dizziness, hallucinations, confusion, weakness, and unsteadiness. Floxuridine can cause depression and lethargy; mitotane, depression, drowsiness, and tremors; thio-TEPA, dizziness; 5-fluorouracil can also cause clumsiness and a little bit of slowness. Dr. Grace says, "Since neurological damage is not a well-known effect, it is often not recognized or looked for. Some people say they become complete klutzes—they just fall down. People also can't do serial sevens—subtracting seven from one hundred, then seven from that result, then seven from that, and

so on. They can't balance their checkbooks, or themselves."
Three patients relate their neurological side effects:

"I lost my balance a few times, and I actually fell. My legs
got so wobbly, like butter. My doctor called it 'sea legs'—he
said that many patients get it. It's been nearly two years since
my last treatment, and I still feel like my legs haven't gotten
their strength back. I still feel like they could buckle under
me any time. I'm a forty-four-year-old person! Sometimes I
walk like an old person—with little tiny steps. My doctor says
they should get stronger; he's heard of this."

"While on chemo, I lost my equilibrium. I tripped and broke
my leg two months after chemo began; that healed well. Several months after that I lost my balance and broke my shoulder and arm. And then I fell in my kitchen—I fractured my
ribs and tore a muscle in my arm. Then I punctured my ear-
drum with a Q-Tip because I again lost my balance and felt
uncoordinated. I lost my hearing in that ear. People said they
used to cry when they saw me."

"I used to flounder for words, have trouble finishing sen-
tences. I also found I was forgetting things—I'm not talking
about forgetting keys—I would forget entire conversations."

Thus far, we know more about short-term and long-term neurological effects in children who have had chemo than we do
about adults. But adult patients do notice difficulties that doctors
have trouble explaining or pinning down. Peter Silverfarb, a
prominent researcher in this area, reports that almost all commonly used chemotherapeutic drugs affect cognitive abilities
(memory, attention, concentration) and that if you look for
subtle and mild symptoms, they will be found in many chemo
patients. But thus far there is very little concrete proof.

Part of the problem lies in differentiating cognitive impairment caused by the drugs from the signs of mental depression.
They may exist simultaneously and make each other worse, and
both may be due to chemicals. Another problem is the generally
held belief that the blood-brain barrier protects the brain from
harmful chemicals circulating in the blood.

Although the research documenting this type of neurological
damage is still inconclusive, patients like my friend who complained, "I'm slow, I'm confused, I'm stupid, I don't feel like

me at all. Am I going crazy?'' need to be reassured that they are not crazy, that what they are going through is probably related to the chemicals in their system, and that they are not imagining it.

With cisplatin, another side effect on the nervous system occurs. This takes the form of ototoxicity, where there is a hearing loss and/or tinnitus (ringing in the ears). When there is a loss of hearing, it's usually only in the high frequencies. Ototoxicity occurs in approximately 30 percent of the patients who receive cisplatin. It may also occur in patients receiving mechlorethamine. A testicular cancer patient who experienced both hearing loss and tinnitus says:

> "I had a dramatic hearing loss for a while, which worried me because so much of my job entails telephone contact. I've gotten some hearing back, but telephone conversations are still very difficult. The doctors aren't sure whether it will ever come back, and they say if not, maybe a hearing aid will help later on.

> "I sit at my desk in the dead of winter, in a high-rise building in the middle of the city; there is construction going on outside, and I could swear there's a nest full of blue jays fighting right outside my window. Every once in a while in the evening I'll be sitting listening to records or reading the paper and I'll turn to my wife, just to be sure about this, and ask her, 'There is not a nest of birds fighting outside the window, is there?' She'll say, 'No—it's back again, isn't it?' "

Stool softeners, laxatives, enemas, and an increase in dietary fiber are used to counteract sluggish bowels caused by neurotoxicity. The risk of ototoxicity from cisplatin may be minimized by using forced diuresis—massive doses of fluid given intravenously before and after the drug—and if the drug is given very slowly. Hearing tests can be administered regularly to prevent severe, irreversible hearing loss. Exercise may reduce the risk of other forms of neurotoxicity because when you exercise, you're using the nervous system. "I don't know of any hard data," says Dr. Grace, "but I will tell you this: I see less neurotoxicity in active people. Those who are most inactive have more problems with clumsiness and confusion. Practice makes perfect—you get more coordinated by being physically active. I do tell them, though, to avoid sports that require skills or are dangerous. I recommend vigorous walking, for instance, and advise them to stay off bikes and be careful when walking down stairs.'' Other than that, he says, ''There is not much you can do for neurotoxicity other than reduce the drugs. The doctor has to be very careful in addressing this toxicity.''

Neurotoxicity is for the most part temporary and reversible. (Those who undergo therapy with vincristine or vinblastine in high doses or over a long period of time are at a higher risk to develop neurotoxicity that is less reversible.) Its symptoms may peak a few days after a treatment and then gradually subside. They usually disappear completely after treatment has been concluded. But this may take up to two years, and in some patients they may never go away completely.

Neurotoxicity can be dangerous. Patients should tell their doctors if any of the above symptoms occur. Though tingling toes may seem like ''nothing,'' they could indicate more serious nerve damage that should be caught early.

SLEEP DISTURBANCES

Nighttime is often a difficult time for a chemo patient, and for many reasons. Some drugs are directly blamed for causing nervousness or agitation. The corticosteroids, such as prednisone, are notorious for their stimulating effects, which may be advantageous during the day but disastrous at night. Many people have trouble falling asleep while taking these drugs, but they are unaware that there may be pharmacological reasons and blame their sleeplessness on everything else. Another drug, procarbazine, is known to cause insomnia and nightmares.

Pain and discomfort seem to grow and fears and problems loom larger in the still of the night, when daytime activities are not around to distract you. Surgical pain, emotional stress, and sleeplessness can feed on each other in a vicious cycle. It may be even more difficult to sleep if you are being treated in the hospital and sleeping in a strange bed, with nurses and staff buzzing around, your roommate groaning or snoring, and machines whirring or clanking.

Any sleeping problems should be discussed with your nurse or doctor so he or she can begin to help you do something about them. If you are taking a corticosteroid like prednisone, your oncologist might suggest that you take the drug early in the day in order to give the stimulating effects time to wear off before bedtime. Taking measures to relieve any emotional anxieties that are coming between you and a good night's sleep is another good initial step. Establishing a ritual usually helps lull people to sleep. Reading, listening to soft music, watching TV, taking a hot bath or shower, having a soothing massage, doing some deep breathing or stretching or relaxation exercises, and even drinking the proverbial glass of warm milk are several conservative, nondrug methods you can use to help you get to sleep. Drinking fewer caffeinated beverages such as colas, coffee, and tea also may help. You may have not needed these techniques in the past, but that's no reason not to explore them now and to use them for as long as you need them. Nor should you hesitate to ask for or use some kind of sleeping pill to get you through a particularly tough time. Sometimes a single good night's sleep can make all the difference in your outlook and general well-being. Sleep is especially important for the chemo patient because it enables you to better face the next day's challenges.

PAIN

Most people associate cancer with pain, sometimes great pain. Yet the amount of pain and the way you respond to it vary tremendously from person to person. It depends on the type of cancer and its location, the stage of the disease, the type of treatment, your past experience with pain, and your cultural background and psychology.

Pain is rarely caused by chemotherapy; one of the goals of chemotherapy is to reduce pain by shrinking the tumor. But other side effects, both physical and emotional, can cause pain to seem worse and vice versa. "Prolonged pain destroys the quality of life. It can erode the will to live," writes Ronald Melzack, who has been studying pain for thirty-five years. "Severe, persistent pain can impair sleep and appetite, thereby producing fatigue and reducing the availability of nutrients to organs."

It is estimated that 60 to 90 percent of cancer patients have enough pain that they require pain medication. Fortunately, pain can be controlled today, if it is properly recognized and treated. There are all manner of drug and nondrug therapies for pain relief. Still, one-fourth of cancer patients suffer needlessly because of misinformation or a reluctance to use narcotics the way they should be used.

Gabriel Hortobagyi, a breast cancer specialist at the M.D. Anderson Cancer Center, says,

"The common mistake made by physicians and patients alike is to be too conservative about pain control. Pain is an extremely destructive symptom. With the tools we have available today, there is very little reason why a person should not be able to have virtually complete control of pain their whole lives."

Diane Blum, director of Cancer Care, Inc., a social services and psychosocial support agency, describes part of the problem:

"People with pain don't want to ask for medication. People believe pain is inevitable or that it builds character. They say they are going to concentrate on the chemo or nutrition— they're not going to bother their doctor about pain. It's sad because it takes so much energy to cope with pain, and you need that energy to cope with the disease."

Another issue is fear of addiction. Hortobagyi says that people have got to realize that "people who have real pain do not become addicted to narcotics. They need to have as much as it takes for them to have pain control." A related and serious stumbling block is that many of us were raised to believe that taking narcotics is "wrong." But Hortobagyi argues, "They are applying this principle to their own situation, and it's totally out of context. In their situation, narcotics is the drug of choice, and there's nothing wrong with taking it."

Hortobagyi feels that both patient and doctor need to be savvy about pain control: "People wait until their pain gets real bad before they ask for or take pain medication. It's much easier to control pain when you start, when there is very little pain. You can control it well and get virtually uninterrupted pain relief." As a patient, you need to talk to your doctor about any pain you are experiencing. Cancer Care advises patients to

- Keep a record of what makes pain better or worse and what triggers the pain or relief.
- Describe the pain. Is it shooting, sharp, dull, burning, aching, numbing, tingling?
- Rate your pain on a scale of zero to ten.
- Rate the effectiveness of medication the same way.

Pain Medication

Pain medications (analgesics) range from mild pain relievers such as aspirin and Tylenol, to stronger ones such as Darvon, to weak narcotics such as codeine and Percodan, to strong narcotics such as morphine, Demerol, and Dilaudid. Some drugs that are not painkillers per se (coanalgesics) can reinforce the effect of painkilling drugs. Tricyclic antidepressants are especially effective for pain arising from malfunctioning nerves, such as shingles. Cortisone-type drugs are also sometimes prescribed. Combining drugs of different types, such as Tylenol and codeine, makes them more effective. Treatment should be carefully individualized as to drug, dosage, and timing so that you don't feel pain but the trade-off in terms of side effects from pain medication is acceptable to you.

For severe, persistent pain, morphine is the drug of choice. Enlightened practitioners know that when morphine is given or taken at fixed intervals around the clock, pain is much better controlled, smaller doses are required, and so side effects are fewer than when it is dispensed "as needed," that is, when pain has returned. This preventive approach is easier to achieve, and patients have more control over their medication now that morphine no longer needs to be injected. Morphine is available in oral forms including slow-release capsules, in skin patches that last for three days, and in suppositories. Portable pumps can also deliver a slow, steady infusion of injectable morphine within or outside the hospital.

These advances reduce but do not eliminate entirely the side effects of narcotics, including sedation, confusion, and disorientation. Another notorious effect is constipation, which, Blum insists, "needs to be talked about up front." This type of constipation usually cannot be prevented by the usual dietary measures or by stool softeners or mild laxatives. You will probably need stronger laxatives on a regular basis to counteract this universal side effect of narcotics.

Nondrug Measures

In addition, there are nondrug measures that are effective for some people. These measures are generally used to enhance the effects of medication so doses can be lowered. They include acupuncture, biofeedback, relaxation techniques, hypnosis, and visualization and are best begun when the pain is still mild or moderate.

Emotional Impact

Because you are a cancer chemotherapy patient, your emotional balance receives a terrific one-two punch: one, the diagnosis of a disease that is highly symbolic and threatens your very life; two, a long-lasting toxic treatment that threatens the quality of your life but whose effectiveness is uncertain. Cancer patients face both their own reactions and those of others to their disease and its treatment. They are called on to adjust to new environments and new people; they must find ways of dealing with big and little stresses and responsibilities. It is no surprise that for many patients the emotional stress of the disease and its treatment is far more devastating than the physical stress.

Just as no two patients will have the exact same physical response to chemotherapy, so people's emotional reactions and resulting behavior are as individual as fingerprints. Unlike the physical side effects, which are concrete, measurable, and observable by others, the emotional consequences of cancer and chemotherapy are not tangible, easily measurable, seen, or felt by anyone else. This does not mean, however, that they are not real or that they have to be endured. As Karen Ritchie, chief of psychiatry at M.D. Anderson Cancer Center, says, "To call the nonphysical problems a lower priority is a mistake. They should be treated, just as nausea is treated."

The emotional reactions of cancer patients vary:

"I can't really describe how I felt. I think I just didn't want to believe it. I just felt so deserted that day."

"I had adjusted pretty well to the mastectomy—I was glad I still had my eyes, my arms, my legs—you know, I didn't really miss having a breast, and the rehabilitation wouldn't be too involved. But the chemo really blew my mind. I had a fatalistic attitude at first.''

"I was an ultramarathon runner and found myself barely able to do a ten-minute mile. When my doctor told me the final diagnosis, I had an out-of-body experience. I felt like I was viewing the situation as if it were someone else being told. After about ten minutes I came back to earth and started talking to people about my options. Soon after that I started poring through the medical literature. I went straight to the acceptance stage; I became galvanized into action.''

"A lot of people look at you and say, 'God, I'm so sorry.' And deep down inside they're thinking, 'Thank God it isn't me.' I would, too—I'll be honest about it. If there were some way I could have given it to someone else, I would have.''

MAKING SENSE OF IT ALL

Dr. Judith Bukberg, a psychiatrist who specializes in treating cancer patients, says:

"I think there's too much stoicism in the world. People seem to have the idea that because this is real—because something real and bad is happening to them—that all kinds of emotional reactions are to be tolerated. That's ridiculous. Sure, you have a reason to be depressed, but that doesn't mean you can't do something about it.

"People also don't want to upset other people—either their families, friends, or doctors—and so they put on a great face to the world, and meanwhile God knows what's going on inside of them. People want to protect each other, but it isn't always helpful in the long run—either to themselves or their relationships.''

That cancer patients do suffer a lot of stress and emotional turmoil was shown in a study done by the Psychosocial Collaborative Oncology Group. The investigators found that 47 percent of the patients who were interviewed and tested showed serious emotional turmoil, mostly depression or anxiety, in trying to adjust to their illness.

The emotional effects of cancer and its treatment—how it influences your behavior, work, social interaction, and overall quality of life—are called *psychosocial effects*. The study of the psychosocial impact of cancer and chemotherapy is still young. Its importance has only recently been recognized. Nevertheless, some basic patterns have emerged as to what emotions patients are likely to feel, when they are most likely to feel them, and what can be done to help patients cope with their emotions. By becoming familiar with the way others have seen things, you may develop a framework that makes some sense out of your own experience. By becoming acquainted with various probabilities and possibilities you can begin to get a handle on your emotions and thus be in a better position to cope. You will be aware of the availability of others who can help.

Emotional Stages

One concept of the impact of cancer and chemotherapy involves thinking in terms of the emotional stages that many people go through when faced with death or any stressful, unpleasant situation. You will probably recognize this pattern in yourself or in your family.

- *Denial.* No not me! It's all a mistake. I don't believe it; this can't be happening. I don't want to think about it.

- *Anger.* Why me? What did I do to deserve this? Why not somebody else?

- *Bargaining or guilt.* I promise I'll do anything to be cured— I'll change my life, my personality, I'll be "good."

- *Depression.* I feel so low and discouraged. Nothing matters, nothing will help, what's the use?

- *Acceptance.* Okay, this is the way it is. Now let's get the show on the road and do something about it.

The five-stage cycle begins around the time of diagnosis; it continues into the therapy and persists long afterward. With each subsequent stressful event such as surgery, the beginning of chemotherapy, or the failure of chemotherapy, the cycle is repeated. Some people may need to skip stages or remain in one stage longer than others. Denial, for instance (which can masquerade as healthy optimism and vice versa), was once thought best gotten over quickly. Now mental health experts think it may be an appropriate, helpful stage that should not be rushed. Richard S. Lazarus writes in Paul Ahmed's book *Living and Dying with Cancer* that denial or self-deception is "often a valuable initial form of coping, occurring at a time when the person is confused and weakened and therefore unable to act constructively and realistically." Denial is a way to buy time, to recover from the shock so we can digest the news and gradually come to deal with the threat. When our reasoning powers return, we will be able to act rationally. Some people just need more time.

In the hospital after my surgery, people were amazed at my good spirits. An army of friends practically never went home, and the jokes were flying fast and furiously. "The Perle Mesta of the cancer ward" is what they called me, but I realize now it was good old denial doing its job and helping me survive.

Living with surgical scars, pain, and loss of functioning, going for chemotherapy treatments and suffering the side effects—all can be more distressing because they remind us of our situation and so make denial harder. Every time I went to the oncologist for treatment, I was reminded that I had cancer. It wasn't only the side effects I knew the drugs would bring that made me not want to go. It was that gut-wrenching kick to my psyche: I'm going here because I have cancer and may die.

Confronting The Basic Emotional Issues

Another approach to making sense out of emotional turmoil centers on the four general issues of alienation, mutilation, mortality, and vulnerability. As is explained in *Coping with Cancer*, a handbook published by the National Cancer Institute and geared toward health care professionals, most cancer patients at some point are confronted by these basic issues, from which spring a host of emotional reactions.

Alienation. Patients who feel alienated have fears of abandonment, unacceptability, and isolation—they feel alone in the world, unconnected, apart, and unable to relate to other human beings. Patients' feelings may originate within themselves or be based on real situations and the very real reactions of others. Cancer is a disease with many negative connotations. Many of these feelings are unfounded or exaggerated, but this does not diminish their impact. Chemo patients may feel sorry for themselves and shut out the rest of the world. They may think their diagnosis is a punishment for past wrongdoings or personality traits or an automatic death sentence, and they may break off contact from loved ones as a preparation for the final separation.

(A chemotherapy patient may indeed be *physically* alone and apart because of time spent in hospitals or undergoing treatment or being away from work or being sick and unable to socialize.) People may withdraw emotionally from chemotherapy patients for various reasons, including fear that the patient may die; feelings of guilt, anger, and resentment; and fear that the disease is contagious.

Patients and others may fall prey to the nonsensical myths and superstitions that surround cancer—that it is something of which to be ashamed, that it is a form of punishment for being "a bad person," that it is contagious. They may be embarrassed by a change in bodily functions and reluctant to expose them to others. For example:

> "We call it 'the big C.' Amazing how you put cute little nicknames on everything. Cancer is a very difficult word to say. And when you tell people you have it, they can't look you in the face."

> "While I was on chemo, I would not permit anyone to kiss me or to come too close to me. I just felt—and they also helped me feel—like a leper. I would never permit anyone to eat from my food, even my husband. Except when we went out to a restaurant once a week with other people, he would offer me food, and I would take it from his fork. I would subject him to something that I thought was contagious because I wanted them to see that he was not afraid."

Mutilation.   Many aspects of cancer and its treatments are disfiguring and invasive; patients may feel mutilated as a result of surgery, for example, and mourn the loss of parts of their bodies, their attractiveness, and their abilities to function. They may not feel "whole" and may suffer from changes in body image. And chemotherapy does change body images when large amounts of weight are lost and gained, when hair is lost, or when people feel they just don't look like themselves. These changes are even more devastating when they are visible to others and when treatment of cancer of the reproductive organs leave patients feeling that they are less than a woman or not quite a man. I, for example, would avoid looking in the mirror, although there was a strange attraction to do it, a fascination—like rubbernecking at an accident. I couldn't believe the scar, the bald head, the lack of eyelashes and eyebrows, the circles under the eyes, the pallor.

I'd feel where my breast had been—gone. Touch where my hair had been—gone. Who was this person? I felt like such a phony. I had to wear a wig and a prosthesis just to be "normal," to be accepted.

Mortality. Cancer patients become more aware of the inevitability of death—their own, whether from their cancer or another cause. Death is no longer the abstract philosophical concept it is for most other people—it is a reality. Mortality is an unavoidable issue regardless of the prognosis and goal of the therapy—be it cure, remission, or palliation.

Most days I'd chug along just fine, even though it was in the back of my mind. But every once in a while it would get to me: *This disease could kill me.* I'd flip out and scream and cry from fear and remorse. I'd imagine my own death and rage against the unfairness of it all. I wonder what the neighbors thought. I didn't want to die!

Vulnerability. Many cancer patients become distressed by the loss of control over their lives and their health. They hate feeling dependent, helpless—at the mercy of their disease and other people. They feel a loss of self-esteem and self-confidence, which is worsened by the fatigue, debility, weakness, and consequent inability to perform their usual functions. Feelings of worthlessness may surface. The uncertainty of treatment, the duration of the disease, and the steady stream of side effects create an atmosphere of unending sickness. For some people the fact that the cancer itself is defined as a disease of uncontrolled growth reinforces feelings of the loss of control.

"Every time another side effect appeared, it was another blow. I kept feeling worse and worse; I worried what could go wrong next and where it would all end."

"I'm not afraid of pain or of death. I'm afraid of being disabled . . . of being stuck in bed, not even able to wash myself."

Every patient will not necessarily go through the full spectrum of possible emotions; nor will he or she feel them all at once. At various times some feelings will recede and others will come into the foreground. Studies of cancer patients have found that people (except for those with lung cancer) are usually most vulnerable psychologically three to four months after diagnosis. As a result of her experience in social work, Grace Christ finds it useful to think in terms of a series of potential crisis points. Chemotherapy patients and their families are under the most stress during these times and must perform adaptive tasks at each of them if and when they occur: (1) the time of diagnosis, (2) the beginning of treatment, (3) negative physical reactions to treatment (side effects), (4) failure of conventional treatment, (5) the end of a treatment protocol, (6) the recurrence or metastasis of the disease, (7) the beginning of investigational treatment, (8) the end of active treatment, and (9) terminal illness.

HOW YOU COPE

Chances are that if you cope well generally, you will manage to cope with chemo, too. People who cope best tend to be flexible and have the ability to shift their perspectives and see situations in new ways that allow problems to be solved. Other useful characteristics include independence but a willingness to lean on others when necessary, cooperativeness without complete passivity, and a positive attitude. People who cope poorly are often already in emotional turmoil from personal problems and disrupted family background, have a pessimistic attitude, expect no help from others, have poor self-esteem, and rely on tension-reducing devices rather than activity to change the source of tension.

Dr. Bukberg points out that what is especially stressful for one person may be less so for another and that how—and how well—you cope with cancer and chemotherapy depends on three basic factors: how much stress you are actually under, how you perceive the stress, and your own unique coping style, abilities, and support system. Age, sex, personality, intelligence, values and beliefs, the type and extent of the cancer and treatment, what they mean to you, and the quality of your relationships with others will enter into the coping process.

How Much Stress?

Some therapies are indeed more stressful than others. There may be more toxic effects and more physical and thus more emotional stress. A patient's life may be quite disrupted by physical symptoms or the location and timing of the treatment. Some cancers are more malignant than others, and some prognoses are worse. There may be other stresses outside of the treatment or caused by the treatment (such as financial problems or family troubles) that are already straining the patient's coping abilities.

How Do You Perceive Stress?

A situation such as chemotherapy treatment may be perceived as a threat, a source of pain, a challenge, or an attempt to help. Some people are much more able to contain anxiety, or they just don't get anxious easily. Others become fearful and nervous very readily. Also, your past medical history can influence the way you feel about medical treatment; if you've already had a bad experience with a certain procedure, you will be more anxious about it than will someone who hasn't. "People who come from loving, trusting families," says Dr. Bukberg, "have more trust in health professionals and are more able to put their lives in their hands."

How Do You Handle Stress?

Dr. Bukberg defines coping as "something that an individual does—either as an automatic response or as a thought-out, planned response to a stress—that is designed to decrease the amount of emotional upheaval and/or in some way to affect the environment to reduce the stress." Each person has certain coping mechanisms—a certain way to deal with things—as a part of his or her personality. People have tendencies to respond one way or another, based on what else has happened to them in the past and what has worked under previous conditions. Broadly speaking, people cope actively or passively. As Dr. Bukberg observes, referring to a concept introduced by Dr. Lipowski, some people tend to avoid all kinds of stress—they deny or minimize a problem. They may disregard the facts, the true meaning of a piece of information, or their emotional state. At the other end of the spectrum, some people become "hypervigilant." They are anxiety-prone, intellectualizing, and somewhat obsessive—they loathe ambiguity and uncertainty, and they want to know as much as they can and become totally involved in their treatment.

Some people rely on their religious convictions. Others become stoical or rationalize their cancer by saying there are people who are worse off. Some merely defer thinking about it until they are strong enough to cope. Some, accepting every blow, attempt to treat their problems lightly and try to shrug everything off with jokes. Others are problem solvers. There are many,

many ways of coping, and usually a person will need to combine several of these ways to get the best effect.

All these mechanisms do help us relieve stress. But they may not work as well as they have in different circumstances in the past. They may work temporarily or partially but not enough to reduce our fears, anxieties, or depression to a bearable level. If your usual ways of coping are not working now or are not working as well as you'd like them to, perhaps this is the time to expand your coping repertoire.

For any given stressful situation, there are usually several options, some or all of which you may not be aware of. Here, for example, is a stressful situation experienced by many chemo patients: You are not happy with your oncologist—he is abrupt and cool, he doesn't treat you like a human being or ever tell you anything. This is making you anxious, and you are tired of feeling like a pincushion with a checkbook instead of a patient. Your usual passive, accepting, or minimizing attitude is no longer working. What do you do? Dr. Bukberg says:

"There are three options. You can do something behaviorally such as talking to your doctor about it or changing to another doctor. Or you could do something cognitive, which would be to try to understand, for example, that he may be upset at having to cause discomfort to people or at having so many people to see that he can't get more involved—in some way redefine the situation so it is more manageable to you. Or you could do something that is directly tension-reducing such as relaxation techniques or hypnosis, where you are primarily reducing the tension that is aroused by the situation."

No coping mechanism is intrinsically "good" or "bad," "right" or "wrong." A mechanism may, however, not be *useful* in a particular situation. When your usual style of coping is not working well enough—when it does not solve a problem or at least bring stress down to a tolerable level—it is time for a change. Change doesn't mean admitting that you were "wrong." Your favorite sneakers may serve you well in weather when you can wear them; they may be comfortable and familiar. But comes a snowstorm and they do not work well. Learning how to cope better may take practice. It may take work. It may be painful and slow in spite of your immediate need for it: Trading in your old ways of thinking and acting for new patterns is not easy. But coping can be learned just like any other skill.

In addition, the changes that chemotherapy puts you through may not seem pleasant at the time, but many people find it is ultimately a positive experience and feel it changes them for the better. Patients say it can be a tremendous personal growth experience. Dealing with their troubles in a time of crisis makes them more mature, more tolerant, more understanding of others, and they feel more—not less—in command of their lives. Their relationships with others can improve, too, as loved ones grow along with and become closer to the patient.

IMPROVING YOUR COPING SKILLS

There are four basic, interrelated areas for you to explore if you want to expand your coping repertoire—attitude, communication, education, and support services. Chapters 5 through 9 will also give you some ideas for supporting your mind, body, and spirit through the tough times.

Attitude

We hear these all the time: Accentuate the positive, eliminate the negative. The power of positive thinking. Look at the bright side.

How, someone might ask, can anyone remain cheerful and optimistic when he or she has cancer and is going through a debilitating therapy? Obviously, this is an unenviable situation for which no one would wish. But there *are* two sides to everything. Is the glass half-empty or half-full? Of course it is both, but which side you choose to emphasize makes a big difference in how well you tolerate chemo.

Many patients and many health care workers have found that a positive attitude—toward chemotherapy, their chemotherapists, and life in general—helps people cope better. Those who are highly motivated and do not let chemo get them down, who strive to assume as normal a life as possible, who remain actively involved and live their lives to the fullest, who work and play and cultivate hope instead of passivity, inactivity, and despair—these are the people who do best during their time on chemotherapy. This patient's good attitude helped her cope well: "I told my mom, 'It's cancer,' and we both started crying. We cried for about five minutes and then I said, 'Okay, that's enough.' I then went on an errand. That's how you have to handle it. You cannot let it monopolize your life. I've seen too many who died because they gave up. And you can't give up."

Rena Blumberg wrote of her experiences during an intensive course of chemotherapy for metastasized breast cancer during which she remained energetic and able to "celebrate" each day. She calls her book *Headstrong*, a word meaning "to have your own way," but she means it in a very positive sense. She writes:

> "For me, 'having my own way' meant I was going to *survive*. To live—and live fully. This took willfulness, to be sure. And at certain moments, particularly during chemo, yes, it took downright obstinacy. But more than any other attitude, I feel this 'headstrong' approach to coping with cancer was the quality that allowed me to survive and to get on with the business of living and living joyously."

However, blind, unquestioning faith or a complete Pollyanna stance may be harmful. You can't always ignore the negative—doing so is unhealthy if it prevents you from taking any corrective action. But by allowing the positive to take precedence you become free and have more energy to take care of the negative.

It certainly helps if you are sure that you want the treatment and remember that the purpose of chemotherapy is a longer, better life. As Dr. Michael Van Scoy-Mosher, an oncologist at Cedars-Sinai Medical Center in Los Angeles, says, "Patients need to realize that chemotherapy is not the enemy—the cancer is."

The Wellness Community, which provides psychosocial support to people with cancer, believes that attitude is a crucial component of a comprehensive treatment plan. They have coined the term "Patient-Active" to describe a person who is part of the team fighting for his or her recovery. Their philosophy is based on the new field called psychoneuroimmunology (PNI), which is beginning to show us just how large a role patients can play in their recovery and how this will probably improve their quality of life and perhaps even affect the outcome of their illness. PNI studies suggest that we can strengthen the body's innate ability to fight illness by psychological and psychosocial means.

In his book *From Victim to Victor*, Harold Benjamin, the founder of the Wellness Community, suggests that you consider eleven ways to become Patient-Active. Briefly, these include making plans for the future, not allowing people to abandon you, not becoming a recluse, pursuing happiness, being with other cancer patients, becoming a partner with your physician, keeping up hope, maintaining intimacy and affection, and maintaining as much control over your life as possible.

Communication

The value of telling others about your hopes, fears, needs, and wants is a recurrent theme in discussions with patients and health care workers and in the literature on coping with cancer. Just talking about your feelings, admitting you have them, can be therapeutic even if you don't find the exact words to describe them. An open, communicative relationship with your doctor or nurse can be a real advantage and play a central part in how well you do with chemo. But a lack of communication with friends and family is one of the most common and troublesome scenarios of cancer patients. This is often the fault of both the patients and their families and friends to one degree or another and is a shame because they all can be the most valuable source of emotional support for each other. It is ironic, then, that poor communication often results from each's concern and desire to protect the feelings of the other. Although people who are close to each other may be more sensitive to unspoken feelings, they are not clairvoyant. People cannot begin to grasp what you are going through unless you tell them. And you cannot expect people to understand and act on your wishes if you do not give them any clues.

Of course, it is difficult for some people to talk with each other under normal circumstances, and the stresses of cancer can accentuate the problem. Lari Wenzel observes:

> "There are certain patients who have difficulty addressing their emotions or fears. They may have lived their entire lives in this fashion. Having the diagnosis of cancer will not necessarily lead them toward self-disclosure. For example, men tend to verbally acknowledge their feelings less than women do, probably due to the socialization process. Generally, people who are well educated about their disease tend to be more acutely aware of their feelings and can discuss them at length."

Dr. Bukberg says she has had people come to her for therapy because they believed their families couldn't tolerate hearing about their situations. "They really needed to sit down with somebody and talk," she says, "before they could get it together and do the talking that needed to be done with their families."

The severe stress of cancer and chemotherapy can aggravate or accentuate one's style of coping, exacerbate present problems, or bring up old ones. In couples, observes a social worker who has treated many cancer patients, this can create a problem: "Typically, a man may want to cope through action, by doing an activity. The female may want to cope by talking. If that becomes exaggerated—the male wants to distance himself more, the female wants to talk, they may find they have a problem." She continues:

> "Sometimes this takes the form of what I call dissynchronization. An example is the forty-year-old man with acute leukemia. He and his wife would sometimes have trouble communicating and used fighting as a way of reengaging with each other; that was their style. When he went back into remission, they were both very relieved, but the rhythm and pacing of their relationship had been thrown off. They found that they were both very distant from each other, very uncomfortable, and unhappy. She was afraid to face the possibility of his death, of fighting with him and being angry with him, and of being open and valid with him because she was so afraid what she might do to him. But also she was fearful of getting reengaged with him and going through the same pain again. But she was able to look at what she was doing and work out another mode of relating. It made marvelous changes in their relationship."

Education

Often mental states such as fear, anxiety, anger, confusion, and repression are due to a lack of information. Fear of the unknown and an inaccurate picture of reality are two circumstances the chemo patient should guard against. The reality of your situation is tough enough to deal with—why add to it unnecessarily? A well-informed patient usually does better in many ways than an uninformed patient. You can feel you are in control and make wise decisions only if you have the facts and can compare the options. The better you understand your therapy—what its goals are, what the side effects may be, and what can be done about them—the better you will tolerate it and the less ominous it will seem. It may help to have a clear picture of your prognosis and to realize that a diagnosis of cancer is not an automatic death sentence: Heart attack victims generally have a much worse prognosis than we do.

Posing questions to your doctor or nurse is the best way to start getting whatever information you need and want. Write down your questions as you think of them so you don't forget them; take notes or bring a cassette tape recorder. Many patients find that bringing along a clear-thinking friend or relative is a great help—when you're under the kind of stress cancer imposes, it's usually difficult to retain everything you hear.

Dr. William Grace, chief of oncology at New York's St. Vincent's Hospital, notes that "things go in one ear and out the other. I insist that my patients have notepads. They write everything that I tell them. And then they write down their questions to me, while leaving enough space between them to write the answers. This is a stressful environment, and otherwise, they forget."

Remember: Physicians may sometimes seem to be magicians, but they are never mind readers. They are trained to tell you only the basics and to depend on you to cue them as to how much further detail to supply. Patients vary greatly in their need to know and in their ability to absorb information. So if you want more than you have gotten, you must come out and ask. Don't be shy or feel guilty for taking up your doctor's time. On the other hand, if you want less information—if you can do without the technical details—let the doctor know that, too. Too much information, especially when given in a small time span, can be overwhelming and thus just as harmful psychologically as too little information.

Sometimes an outside person such as a social worker can help. Patients sometimes have inner conflicts about the amount of information they want and what it means to them, as this case illustrates:

"A classic problem is 'The doctor isn't telling me anything.' Well, that may be, but it could also be that the doctor is telling the patients more than they can process. Or maybe they haven't asked the questions.

"I once saw a patient, a young man with advanced cancer who was very sick. He complained that the doctor wasn't telling him how the chemo was working, and he didn't know whether he should keep fighting. I said, 'Have you asked him?' He said, 'Well, no.' I gave him some ideas about questions to ask the doctor, such as 'What would happen if I stopped? What would happen if I stay on the drugs? Would you still take care of me?' He asked me to write them down.

He ended up not asking the doctor. In fact, he already knew the answers but was struggling with the conflict inside himself.''

If you want to learn more about your cancer and its treatment, you can go beyond your health care providers and turn to booklets, medical journals, and pamphlets. If you are unable to go to the bookstores and libraries, you can ask a friend or relative to do the legwork. This is one concrete way people can help you, and they are usually more than happy to do so, as was the case with this patient:

"My doctor was very vague about everything—especially my prognosis and the other treatments available. And I wanted to *know* before he began pumping that stuff into me. My friends were very supportive and photocopied articles from medical journals for me to read while I was still in the hospital. It made me feel a lot better knowing what the whole story was.''

You may have trouble deciphering some of the medical terms and concepts in the technical or scholarly publications, so perhaps your physician, oncologist, or other doctor will help explain whatever you don't understand. Other sources for information are cancer agencies and societies, and large cancer centers listed in the Resources section.

Support Services: Asking For Help

Many chemotherapy patients and their families are very good at coping and can bounce back easily—or they become experts quickly. However, many other patients and their families can use some outside help. This does not mean that they are weak or helpless. It simply means that outside help can make them cope better during a time of extraordinary stress. Diane Blum, director of Cancer Care, Inc., says, "Ups and downs are to be expected. Cancer is a crisis, no matter how good the prognosis, no matter how mild the treatment. You can't get through it without some kind of strong emotional response.''

It is logical to turn to friends, family members, and perhaps coworkers for emotional support, and we may be more comfortable expressing our innermost thoughts to those who are close to us. However, this may not always work out or be enough. We may, for one reason or another, get negative reactions. Those people may withdraw: Sometimes the very people to whom we would like to turn are having trouble coping themselves. We may, in fact, feel less comfortable baring our souls to people we know than to people who will be less judgmental and more objective and who are experienced listeners, counselors, or therapists. Fortunately, there are many alternative sources for emotional support, both for ourselves and for our families. We may turn to our doctors or nurses, certainly, but they are often not trained to give emotional support. Social workers, the clergy, support or self-help groups, and patient volunteers are better targets for our outpourings. Or a psychotherapist, a family therapist, or a stress management technique may be what we need.

Of the huge variety of forms of psychosocial support, one or more is bound to be right for you. You might require help for extended periods—all through chemotherapy and possibly thereafter. More commonly, though, patients and their families find that they need a "leg up" only periodically, when some new twist in the situation makes them feel too overwhelmed to cope on their own. (These "twists" may coincide with the crisis points mentioned earlier.)

Dr. Bukberg says that the appropriate help depends on what the problem is and who the person is:

> "A group is a very, very good place to start. If the problem is that you're feeling kind of alone and going through a rough situation, and other people obviously do not understand in the same way that another person going through it can, if you're feeling very different from other people—and these kinds of things can make you feel so awful—for a lot of people a group is probably the best thing."

Sister Rosemary Moynihan would like to see a range of options but acknowledges that "groups are good for some people. The main advantage is they help normalize the experience, lessen isolation, give people a better sense of how others deal with this, to learn different ways of coping."

Blum agrees: "There's a wonderful moment in support groups when a person says, 'I didn't know other people felt that way.' " But for people who don't get to support groups, she recommends education programs: "A lot more people are willing to sit and listen . . . they get the information they need, and the acknowledgment that the way they're feeling is not unique.

Often someone will come up to the staff afterward and talk about feelings that they didn't want to talk about in front of the group.''

Grace Christ thinks that ''talking with a patient volunteer—someone who has gone through the experience—is also valuable.'' And Jimmie Holland, M.D., chief of psychiatry at Memorial Sloan-Kettering, extols the virtues of working over the telephone: ''I think the telephone is underused and underappreciated for its value. Here at Memorial we do a lot of work with people who live too far away or who can't come in for face-to-face contact.''

Dr. Bukberg points out that ''the behavioral approach may also be a good first step for people who are having a lot of tension, anxiety, and/or those who are having difficulty with anticipatory nausea. Progressive relaxation, hypnosis, and imaging techniques are appropriate.'' She continues:

> ''But if, after people have tried something like that, anxiety is still really high or depression is still really bad—if it's interfering with their functioning, if people can't concentrate on work, if their relationships with others around them seem to be disrupted—then it's worth taking a look and trying to see what else may be going on, what else could help. Sometimes counseling that's meant to explore an individual's particular situation can just help clarify things.''

Occasionally psychotherapy can help, according to Dr. Bukberg. ''Psychological meanings that a person may not be so much aware of also affect how they are experiencing a stress, and people sometimes find themselves reacting in surprising ways. Psychotherapy can uncover what some of these additional meanings are, and sometimes that helps.'' She gives the example of people whose self-esteem is very tied up in particular parts of their bodies—their breasts or their hair. ''The loss of these is obviously much more devastating than it is for people who have other things in their lives that are more important for their self-esteem.''

Holland is seeing a more appropriate use of medication to diminish anxiety. ''Although patients are still afraid of becoming addicted, if we can persuade them to take antianxiety medication during a crisis, they do much better. Getting sleep at night again is especially helpful. They have less anxiety, fear, and distress and have no trouble stopping the medication when the crisis is over. You also reduce post- and pretreatment side effects such as nausea and vomiting if they come to a treatment feeling relaxed, rather than tense and worried.''

THE CHEMO BLUES

Depression is perhaps the most common and debilitating emotional reaction in chemotherapy patients. At some time or other almost everyone—even the staunchest optimist—feels pessimistic, down, sad, weepy, blah, and blue:

"I'm a very lively person. I'm not a depressed person. But I do get depressed over my illness. I wish I were healthy like everyone else.''

"I would be depressed many times. I kind of spaced out, just withdrew. I would cry very easily. I felt so different from the person I had been, the person I knew. I felt like an observer of life because I was so debilitated, so out of it most of the time. And I was so used to being a participant.''

As the patients and cancer professionals who speak on the next few pages show, depression is quite common. They also show that the coping techniques just discussed can help a great deal to lift you out of your depression and prevent it from becoming incapacitating or unbearable.

Depression in chemo patients can happen at any time, but it doesn't usually settle in until after some earlier reactive stages have been experienced. Many patients are well into their treatments and have been through all the terrifying (and in a sense exciting) and demanding parts before the pressing weight of depression becomes noticeable or intolerable. One oncology nurse finds that, for instance, with people on a two-year protocol, "Once they get through the first year and into the second, it's really just awful. But at any midway point patients tend to have a downward feeling—'Are we ever going to get this over with?' ''

In my case, the tensions and insults accumulated gradually until one final event provided the crucial jolt. I seemed to be coping just fine until the side effects really kicked in. My oncologist said that the toxicity had finally built up, and I started to feel really sick about one month into the treatment, and really down. And then my hair fell out, which made it even worse. A little while later John Lennon was killed, and that really did it.

Between that and the cancer, I felt as if a part of my past had died, was gone forever, and nothing would ever be as carefree, as good, as it had been before.

Grace Christ explains that depression in chemotherapy patients is usually a "reactive" depression. "Chemo patients are depressed for a good reason," she says, in that they are feeling sad and down as reactions to a specific external event.

Lari Wenzel points out:

"The conditions surrounding the treatment could promote feelings of depression. If you are feeling physically ill all the time or a good deal of the time, you are not looking your best, your life has been disrupted, and you know your life is also being threatened, which is why you are undergoing the treatment . . . it's quite easy to understand why people become depressed."

Matthew Loscalzo says:

"There are many different theories on depression. Some propose it's due to a learned helplessness. We often see this in our patients at Memorial, and I think it's one of the key issues. Another theory is sensory deprivation: People who are not stimulated amply get depressed and tend to withdraw. Cancer patients are physically depleted, with chemical changes taking place because of the cancer and chemotherapy; their personal space is violated by everyone from the cleaning lady to the doctors, and by everybody else in between. They don't understand what the doctors are saying half the time. And they're not up to snuff—their thinking processes may not be too clear because of the cancer or treatment or both. Patients need to be actively involved in their own care."

In addition, there is some evidence, and some professionals believe, that the drugs themselves cause chemical changes that lead to depression. Mood changes are not unusual when the hormone-producing endocrine system gets thrown out of order. For example:

"After the second treatment I got a depressed feeling after I got home; I felt very down. The next treatment I got a depressed feeling on the way home. Then I felt it as I got to my car and became weepy as I drove home. Then it was when I got to the front steps of my doctor's office. By the time of the ninth or tenth treatment I really went berserk. At the end I couldn't make it out of his office. What upset me was that I always felt I had been a together person.''

"I had terrible mood swings. If you looked at me, I cried. I never knew if it was the surgery or the drugs, but I was in chemical menopause at that time. And I remember my mother going through menopause and having some tremendous mood swings. She was a real bitch at times; I became a bitch at times. Even I didn't like me. I remember one day I came home from work; I was off the next day. I just locked the door and didn't answer the phone, didn't do anything. I just sat. God, I didn't like myself for a long time! I didn't put on lipstick or take care of my hair. I didn't care what I looked like. Hell, I didn't like me, so why should anyone else?''

Depression is bound to go hand in hand with not feeling well for a prolonged period of time. As one patient said, "It just wears you down.'' So some aspects of depression can be alleviated when physical side effects are taken care of. This book gives many suggestions for relief; perhaps a support group or your oncologist will be able to guide you further or suggest more.

Patients often find that mental or physical activity is an antidote for the blues—sitting around doing nothing but feeling sorry for yourself not only is boring, it encourages you to dwell on your problems. Time could be so much better spent on enjoyable, esteem-building distractions such as hobbies, friends, social functions, work, and support groups. Exercise has many advantages and has gotten many a chemo patient out of the dumps. The fact that they don't feel like themselves does not stop them from doing whatever makes them happy. Some people have let—or have learned how to let—others help keep them cheerful and maintain their perspective.

I was at the very bottom of my depression—the pits—when a girlfriend of mine called with some horrifying news. A young man we knew—in his twenties and about to be married—was in an accident and was paralyzed from the neck down. Awful as it was, it really shook me out of my own depression. What the hell was I so upset about compared to his bad luck? At least I could walk, work, do things.

Mental health professionals are careful to point out that there's a difference between what most patients call depression and a medical diagnosis of clinical depression. This distinction changes treatment options. Loscalzo explains:

"Depression is to be expected in about 25 percent of patients. However, recent data show that cancer patients are no more depressed than other equally ill patients. There's no question that chemo patients get the blues and get sad. They may feel 'depressed.' But we have to separate out fatigue and those sad feelings in someone who is chronically ill or is receiving certain drugs from clinical depression. That's a very specific diagnosis with specific ways of measuring it. With true depression, you are depressed about yourself. But chemo patients are depressed about something outside themselves."

As Bukberg says, "There are depressed people who just don't get better." The signs include being in a depressed mood, losing interest or pleasure, sleeping too much or too little, poor appetite, constant fatigue, feelings of worthlessness or excessive or inappropriate guilt, diminished ability to think or concentrate, and recurrent thoughts of suicide. "If depression is persistent, a trial of antidepressant medication should be considered," Bukberg says. She points out that a variety of studies show that psychotherapy works for depression in some people, medication works in others, and a combination might be best of all.

The Aftermath

According to the National Cancer Institute, there are 6 million Americans who are living with cancer; of these, 3 million have survived for five years or more. Some are cured, some are in remission, and some have active disease.

The lives of those survivors who are in the first two groups and are off treatment will be different from the lives of those who continue to battle active disease and need treatment either intermittently or perhaps for the rest of their lives. But all cancer patients share similar issues and concerns once the acute phase of diagnosis and treatment is over. Living with cancer, in the words of one research team, "is not trouble-free." It can, in fact, be the most challenging period of time you will face in your life.

Even those who are in remission or are probably cured face permanent life changes. As cancer survivor Susan Nessim writes, "Although I was cancer-free, I certainly wasn't free of cancer . . . there was more to overcoming this disease than surviving the hardships of treatment. Instead, the end of treatment marked the beginning of a new and unexpected challenge: adapting to life after cancer."

Adapting for me began with the end of chemo.

As with most chemo patients, it would be an understatement to say I looked forward to my last treatment. Although chemotherapy wasn't as bad as I thought it would be, I was very glad it was over. After giving me my last injection, my oncologist smiled, shook my hand, and said, "Congratulations. You made it. Now you can go out and play." In spite of the side effects and the misgivings, I had managed to see it through to the end. I felt a real sense of accomplishment. I was free at last! No more nausea; no more fatigue; no more jabbing needles. I *did* go out and play: Michael and I left on a celebratory vacation. I felt high for weeks as I started to look and feel good again; I ate and ate, putting back all the weight I had lost and then some.

After the first delirious weeks, however, I noticed a strange new feeling creeping in, a vague uneasiness. Playtime was, after all, over. It was time to return to real life. But I had changed; my life had changed. Somehow the old familiar pieces didn't quite fit together the way they used to. I began to realize I couldn't go back to life exactly the way it was. I wondered: What do I do now?

Though certainly happy to be off chemotherapy, many patients experience a similarly bumpy transitional period. This process of "normalization" can be made more difficult by residual side effects, the need for follow-up care, and fear of recurrence. Our old "normal" lives may be beyond our grasp, but we can try to create new "normal" lives for ourselves. To varying degrees, life after chemo will be different, but in certain ways it can be better than life was before. Just as life on chemo is in part what you make it, how you handle the aftermath is up to you.

Dr. Michael Van Scoy-Mosher, an oncologist at Cedars-Sinai Medical Center in Los Angeles, believes that life after chemo is a matter of adaptation: "There's a difference between coping and adapting. Coping, I think, is what you do in an acute situation. Adapting is what you do with a permanent change. In the long run you have to adapt to what has happened to you; it becomes a part of you, it gets incorporated for better or for worse."

Ingrid Bergman, who played two of her most demanding roles (in *Autumn Sonata* and *A Woman Called Golda*) during her eight-year battle with breast cancer, said in an interview that she was determined not to let her illness prevent her from enjoying the remainder of her life. "Cancer victims who don't learn to live with it," she said, "will only destroy what time they have left."

MAKING THE TRANSITION

Once the therapy is over, patients are exhilarated to see side effects subside. Who wouldn't be elated by the return of appetite, strength, and energy, hair growing back, the entire body gradually resuming its normal functions? One patient happily attests: "I was amazed at how quickly I bounced back. About two months after my last treatment, I was running two miles a day again. Unfortunately, I was also expected to cook and take care of the house just like in the old days. But I really didn't mind. It felt good to be me again."

Although this period of normalization is for the most part suffused with relief and joy, it is sometimes tempered by the fact that like any time of transition, it is full of stresses of adaptation for the cancer patient and the family. As side effects diminish, everyone needs to stop thinking of the patient as being sick, to resume former roles and responsibilities, and to start thinking about and planning for the future, however uncertain that might be.

The former director of social services at New York's Memorial Sloan-Kettering enumerates some of the psychological and practical difficulties inherent in moving back into the community and normal life:

"There are all kinds of problems and resistances. There may be job problems, insurance problems, problems with confronting an ongoing life or having to change your goals. Sometimes during treatment you have to constrict your time perspective: You learn to think day-to-day, which is a very useful way to manage a difficult experience. But then you learn to plan ahead, expand your time perspective, make long-range plans, and think more about the future."

After all that activity—treatments, blood tests, side effects, surprises—my life seemed somehow dull, a touch ordinary. So much time and energy had been focused on fighting the cancer, it felt strange to suddenly be doing nothing. I felt like a soldier coming home from active combat: battle-weary but let down by the unexpected absence of danger and excitement.

Sometimes such mixed feelings surface because stopping chemotherapy is anxiety-provoking. Much to everyone's—including the patients'—surprise, patients dread or regret the end of therapy because it means leaving the constant surveillance of the hospital, no longer being so closely monitored, and being out on their own. After the patient has been seeing a doctor every week or two, the security of knowing that if anything develops it will be picked up immediately is suddenly taken away. Some patients do not, in fact, want to go off their chemotherapy and ask their doctors to continue even though it is medically appropriate for them to be taken off it. As one health professional says, patients become so accustomed to doing something to control the illness, that "being without [chemo] is often really a downer for some people."

"Some people are so relieved that this is not an issue at all," comments Dr. Michael Van Scoy-Mosher. However, he is well aware that patients can have ambivalent feelings about ending the therapy:

> "I usually bring up the issue toward the end of the therapy. I'll mention the way some others have felt and try to get my patients to talk about it. Most of the time they have begun to feel that way themselves—I reassure them that they will still be seeing me, not as often perhaps—and discuss the fear of recurrence and why more therapy is not given. I give them a game plan for follow-up, so although they may not be getting more therapy, they will be closely observed. Beyond that, they just have to cope with it. First they have to cope with getting the therapy, then they have to cope with not getting it.
>
> "I have a patient whose adjuvant therapy I wanted to stop after six months. But she's fought with me to continue it for as long as I can. She's terrified of stopping. It's not as if she doesn't have any side effects, but she's more afraid of the cancer than she is of the side effects. But there are good reasons not to go on with the therapy."

As time goes on, so does the challenge. Cancer survivors continue their journey along a path that is strewn with physical, psychological, social, and economic changes, issues, and hurdles.

LONG-TERM AND DELAYED EFFECTS

Most side effects subside rapidly after treatment is stopped; however, a few may take longer—months or years—and some never disappear completely. There are a few that may even crop up later on. Although these long-term side effects are usually just annoying or uncomfortable, a few may be debilitating or life threatening. Researchers have begun to document the impact of cancer and its treatment on long-term survivors. The physiological fallout can occur in any organ system, causing problems such as infertility; menstrual irregularities and menopause symptoms; impotency; decreased lung capacity; transient heart attacks or strokes; bladder, kidney, and blood disorders;

hearing loss; lowered ability to exercise; chronic fatigue; increased infections; dry skin; constipation; development of second or third cancers; and pain. In addition, patients may need to live with changes caused by surgery or radiation. Patients often become very body- or symptom-conscious; so little is known about these long-range side effects that almost anything can be blamed on chemotherapy.

Dr. Charles Vogel, director of the Comprehensive Cancer Center of Miami, admits that "the long-term sequelae of cancer and its treatments have only begun to be noted and understood." Yet they are important pieces of information for patient and doctor alike. The possibility of long-term effects needs to become part of the decisions made early on, when assessing risk versus benefit and treatment is being done. Knowledge of residual and late side effects also increases the likelihood that they will be recognized and treated when they occur and possibly prevented from occurring in the first place or at least minimized. For example, the MOPP regimen for Hodgkin's disease is being replaced by another, ABVD, which has fewer short- and long-term effects. Young women who are thrown into early menopause because of chemo are also likely to encounter osteoporosis earlier in life. As a breast cancer specialist reminds us, "The best remedy for that is estrogen, but we are still very uncomfortable about giving that to breast cancer patients." Instead, he says, "There are a number of drugs that seem to preserve calcium content of bones, which are being tested in women who have had chemo."

It may be difficult to determine where psychological trauma ends and physical damage begins and whether a symptom is in fact due to chemotherapy or is a condition that might have developed anyway. One patient remarks:

"I still have some nausea now and then, but I've gained back all the weight I lost anyway. People tell me how great I look. I almost feel guilty that I still feel tired all the time. People tend to judge too much how you are by how you look. It makes me feel strange because I don't feel as good as they think I look. People may really wonder if you really have been through all this."

Although basically I'm well and functioning, it bothers me that no one can say for sure to what extent I've been permanently affected by chemotherapy. The nausea is gone, my hair is thicker than ever, my blood levels are fine, except for my white blood cell count, which has remained below normal. My menstrual cycle has reasserted itself, though with exasperating irregularity. The foot and leg cramps I suffered during vincristine withdrawal gradually became less frequent, no doubt helped by the advice I got from a physical therapist and an addiction to aerobic exercise. These lingering effects, though tangible, are merely annoying, like gnats I can swat away. The one thing the experience has left me with that I find not so easy to handle is a lingering muzziness, a blunting of my physical and mental powers. I often—but not always—feel slightly slowed down, held back. My mind isn't quite as sharp as it used to be, and my energy tends to fade earlier than before. It is subtle, but it is there. Sometimes I think this could be an imagined change: Maybe I wasn't really as smart and energetic as I like to think I was; maybe I'm getting older like everybody else; maybe I'm looking for an excuse for real or imagined shortcomings. Or my symptoms may be due to something other than the chemo. Although chemo's effect on mental function during treatment has been acknowledged, there is very little scientific research on chemo's long-term effects on the brain. Until recently talking with other chemo patients has been the only way I could validate my own observations. We commiserate about having chemo brain, mush brain, or no brain. We make jokes about our memory problems and affectionately refer to this syndrome as CRS (can't remember shit). We share those magical moments during a conversation when, in the middle of a sentence, both talker and listener realize that the talker has lost all recollection of purpose ("Now, why am I telling this story?").

In 1992 Mary Wieneke, a doctoral candidate in clinical psychology at the California School of Professional Psychology, completed an exploratory study on the effects of chemotherapy in breast cancer patients. The subjects were twenty-eight women, twenty-eight to fifty-four years old, who had undergone three to eighteen months of chemotherapy. When Wieneke assessed their neurocognitive status from one month to one year after completing therapy, she found "statistically significant impairments in their mental flexibility, speed of processing, memory, and motor function." Depression was not found to have an impact on these findings, nor did the length of time the women had been off chemo. She says, "The only variable related to level of impairment was the amount of chemo"—those who had a longer course or greater amount of chemo were more affected.

Susan Nessim in her much-needed book *Cancervive: The Challenge of Life after Cancer,* writes that instead of patients regaining energy after treatment ends, "months or even years later, they may find that they're still feeling run down, mustering all their reserves just to get through the day." According to a social worker and breast cancer survivor Nessim interviewed, chronic fatigue is just beginning to be recognized as a potentially debilitating long-term effect of cancer treatment. While chronic fatigue used to be dismissed as a sign of mental depression, the likelihood of an organic origin is finally being acknowledged. The causes are still unknown, but some theorize that they include permanent bone marrow suppression of the red cells, which causes anemia, or of the white cells, which means the body needs to expend more energy to repair itself and fend off infections.

As my oncologist told me, the experience does make a dent in you. I still feel "dented" and probably always will to some extent. Although I may never be "good as new," time and effort continue to help straighten things out, and perhaps I'll ultimately end up better than new in some ways.

PSYCHOLOGICAL EFFECTS

Cancer survivors also face a myriad of possible psychological effects. These include fear and anxiety about a cancer recurrence, death, depression, changes in body image, decreased interest in sex, and concern about the treatment's side effects (and feeling like a hypochondriac). Some people have lowered self-esteem, but others emerge with improved self-esteem. As with the physiological effects, these changes and issues have just begun to be studied.

An intriguing overview of the postchemo patient's plight comes from Ellen L. Maher of the Department of Sociology at Indiana University. Interviews with cancer survivors revealed that although they were in remission or possibly cured, all were not completely at ease with their good fortune. Ms. Maher describes their unease as *anomia,* a mental state characterized by confusion and anxiety, uncertainty, loss of purpose, and a sense of alienation.

Ms. Maher discusses the many factors that contribute to this strange, vague, unexpected discomfort that can occur when chemotherapy is stopped: the patient's initial perception of a poor prognosis and hence an unanticipated cure or remission; a sense of loss of purpose if a great deal of time and energy has gone into the treatment; uncertainty about the advisability of stopping treatment; the possibility of recurrence and its attendant insecurity and anxiety; the inability to make the switch from "living one day at a time" to thinking about future-oriented activities; ambivalent feelings toward the imperfect system to which patients nevertheless owe their lives; and the withdrawal of support from health care givers and families who are convinced that "the healthiest thing is to put it all behind," even though the patient is not quite ready to do so.

Some of us may have doubts about whether we chose the "right" treatment. A year after surgery and six months after her last chemo treatment, a friend of mine who was recently diagnosed with breast cancer continued to regret her decision to have a mastectomy rather than a lumpectomy. The fact that there were good medical reasons for a mastectomy, as confirmed by a second surgical opinion, didn't matter. She felt that she was rushed, that her surgeon pressured her into deciding, that he made the decision. She was beating herself up psychologically for allowing her breast to be removed: "How could I have done that to myself—to my beautiful, wonderful breast?"

Sister Rosemary discusses the other side of the coin:

"Women who have lumpectomies and then the disease recurs sometimes think, 'I didn't value my life enough to suffer through extensive surgery.' If they have a mastectomy and survive, they might feel later, 'I wanted too much to live, and I could have done so—with less suffering and disfigurement.' The technology isn't perfect, so you're constantly struggling with how to deal with what happened to you."

Adjuvant chemotherapy, the type I had, poses other dilemmas. As I write this, twelve years after my diagnosis, I have no evidence of disease. Two medical oncologists have told me that since my disease-free survival is longer than chemo was expected to give me, it was probably the surgery that was responsible. In other words, there's a good chance I had chemo unnecessarily. On the other hand, I may be among the ten percent of premenopausal women who do show an improvement in the ten-year survival rate if given adjuvant chemotherapy.

How does anyone really know how well he or she would have done with another form of therapy? Or with no therapy? How do you find answers where there are no answers? How do you give up wanting certainty when there is only uncertainty? We can never know if we made the "right decision"—we can only make the *best decision*, given the circumstances at the time.

SURVIVOR'S SYNDROME

Perhaps the biggest, most frustrating obstacle to enjoying a full, happy postchemo life is the possibility of having a recurrence. Naturally, anyone who has been treated for cancer is concerned about a recurrence, and when chemotherapy was less effective than it is now, many people did indeed have recurrences, some quite soon after therapy. Some of course, still do, but now that long-term remissions and cures have become more common, a new medical phenomenon has been born: the survivor's syndrome. This anxious state of mind has also aptly been dubbed the Damocles syndrome, after the character in Greek mythology who sat at a banquet under a sword that was precariously suspended by a single hair. We, like Damocles, see that a sword hangs over us and never know how long we have until the hair breaks and the sword drops. A former mastectomy patient expresses this: "Sometimes I'm afraid to look at my other breast. I do self-examination, but I'm afraid I'll find something. I'll cover it up, or I'll take showers in the dark. It's not that I'm ashamed of the mastectomy—I'm afraid of something showing up in the other breast."

The necessity of follow-up care, with its frequent medical checkups and tests, places an additional stress on postchemo patients, with each serving as a reminder of a time in the past and of a possible future that most patients would prefer not to think about. Sometimes a physical crisis—any new symptom, no matter how minor—sets off an inner alarm:

"Every time I go to the doctor for a follow-up, I am forced to remember why I am going and I think, 'Oh God, will he find anything this time?' "

"My surgeon is very, very thorough when I go for exams. It scares me he's so thorough—you want him to find it if it's there, but you're hoping he doesn't."

"Now I've turned into a very paranoid person. When any little thing goes wrong . . . One night I turned over on my stomach, and I felt a soreness in my rib. I kept pushing it and pushing it to see if it still hurt, and of course the more I poked at it, the more it did hurt. It was only a month away from my regular time for a bone scan, mammogram, and chest X ray, so my doctor suggested we do it then, just in case, rather than wait.

"My husband came with me, and I waited around inside while they looked at the results quickly to see if they had to be done over. The nurse and a doctor came in, and I couldn't wait to ask them how they looked. They said, 'Oh, fine, there's nothing abnormal.' I can't tell you how relieved I was . . . I heaved a huge sigh and went out to see my husband, who looked at me and didn't know what to do—I broke out into this big smile and all I could say was 'They're okay.' He broke out in such a smile and began to cry. I never realized how frightened he was too. We both sat there—he was hugging me—just crying like a couple of idiots.''

Ms. Christ has noticed that people may have strong reactive feelings on their "anniversaries"—the day of surgery, the day of diagnosis, the start or end of treatment. Approaching benchmarks of one, two, five, or ten years can also cause considerable anxiety. In addition, Ms. Christ notes:

"Sometimes normal life phases such as getting married or having children can be difficult for people because they're markers in their lives. They can remind someone who's had cancer of the whole traumatic experience.

"Young people who have had Hodgkin's disease—when do they tell the people that they're dating? What do they say? If they're going to get married, then they have to confront the question of how long their lives will be. Are they going to be able to have children? There are a lot of uncertainties about that. What kind of sexual partners are they going to make? And if they are going to be able to have children, what impact will this have on their children?''

In addition to a recurrence, patients may be concerned about developing a second cancer in the years to come. Although the percentages vary, patients who have had one cancer are statistically at a higher risk of developing additional cancers than is the average person of getting an initial cancer. There are several theories as to why this may be so.

Possibly factors that led to the first malignancy are also responsible for allowing a second to arise and flourish. Regardless of the form of treatment, people who have had certain types of cancers seem to be more prone later to development of other specific types of cancers: Breast cancer is associated with colon cancer, colon cancer with cancer of the endometrium, and uterine cancer with rectal cancer; cancers of the female reproductive system in general tend to occur together with cancers of the digestive and respiratory systems. Those who have had cancer of the breast, ovary, skin, head and neck, bladder, colon, or rectum are at a higher risk of getting another cancer in the same or a paired organ. Finally, since heredity seems to play a role in the development of some cancers, there may be worries about other members of the family getting cancer. This issue is especially prominent when a woman with breast cancer has a daughter who it is feared might also get it.

Another group of statistics shows that people who have been treated with chemotherapy and/or radiation are more likely to develop cancer—usually leukemia—later on. This is usually associated with Hodgkin's disease patients and specific drugs that belong to the alkylating group. Whether this is because the treatment has suppressed the immune system or is itself carcinogenic or both is not certain.

In general, people tend to either minimize the possibility of a relapse or exaggerate it. Some people think about it almost all the time, others almost never. Although they run the risk of ignoring real problems that could be successfully treated if they were acknowledged early, true minimizers are lucky. They seem to be able to absorb the shock and go on to live full, happy lives. The others, the worriers, seem to be unable to forget their cancer even for a moment. They are obsessed by their disease and their health; they anticipate the worst to such an extent that it taints the remainder of their lives by overshadowing and taking time away from the more pleasurable and positive pursuits that life has to offer. Dr. Richard Gralla, an oncologist, says about this:

"Part of coping with chemotherapy is being well, being free of disease, doing the normal things, but still having that sword hang over you. Of course it's more real for the postchemo patient, but that same sword hangs over me. As a human being living in modern society I can get cancer, and I have to deal with it, too. I can ignore it—as can you—but that's probably not too healthy. I think it's better to come to grips with it rather than totally ignore the issue."

Dr. Van Scoy-Mosher points out that fears of a recurrence generally recede as time goes by: "I find that although this concern never goes away completely, it does get better and patients are able to tolerate it. It depends on their capacity for denial: Some people are defenseless and don't have a capacity for denial—they can't push things back, and those are the people for whom it is worse."

Natalie Springarn, a journalist, had been living with cancer for many years when she wrote *Hanging in There*. In her book she eloquently and unflinchingly describes what it is like to be "hanging in there," to live the different life of the subculture of the "not well." It is tough for her to keep going, but keep going she does, helping herself lose her fear by keeping alive her hope in the future. She writes:

> "Unlike most 'normal' people, we subculture members have to live with the persistent knowledge of our own mortality. 'Background music' Stewart Alsop called that knowledge, and it is true that when I am occupied the fearful dark tones stay in the background. But they can blare forth, affecting my attitude and ability to get on with the business of living. I have found no skill more important (no matter how it's gained) than the ability to believe in my own survival."

The reasons for someone's uncertain health remaining subdued "background music" or becoming a full brass band may vary. Psychiatrist Judith Bukberg thinks that "people have certain styles of coping based on who they are. If you've had a life of bad things happening to you, then obviously you're going to have more of those thoughts than somebody who hasn't; similarly, some people are pessimistic by nature."

SOCIAL AND ECONOMIC ISSUES

Being concerned about the cost of initial treatment and continuing care is stressful enough, but survivors also may have problems with continuing or getting medical insurance coverage or increasing life insurance coverage. Benefits may change, or you may be concerned about changing jobs because you may lose insurance coverage. Eighty percent of people with cancer return to work, but one of four cancer survivors experiences some form of employment discrimination because of his or her history of cancer. Some are unable to work or need to change their type of work or reduce their work load because of the aftereffects of treatment. Some people get right back into the swing of things with or without the support of their employers and coworkers. Others may take a while longer to get up to speed or run into misconceptions at the workplace that cause problems on the job.

Studies show that cancer survivors notice changes in their personal relationships—sometimes for the better, sometimes for the worse. Relationships may get better as the crisis of cancer brings people closer. Sometimes families and friends become overly protective, or you may feel they are uncomfortable about your cancer or feel pity for you.

You can contact the National Cancer Institute and the American Cancer Society (see Appendices) for booklets to help you overcome insurance and employment problems.

SUPPORT FOR SURVIVORS

As the number of cancer survivors increases, clearly more studies and support resources are needed if we are going to be able to live our hard-won time more fully rather than just "survive." And we need to recognize our own needs and have better access to the support that already exists. Dr. Bukberg says:

"It's useful for people to know that the survivor's syndrome exists, even though it's difficult to give specific solutions. I do think that continuing support groups are very important. So are hypnosis and other kinds of relaxation techniques. If you tend to be anxious about things, and you want to change that tendency, I'd say the best chance to do that is psychotherapy. Sometimes just by decreasing anxiety, obsessional thinking will stop. Sometimes cognitive approaches can help. It's a shame that more people don't enter psychotherapy if these techniques don't work."

Lois Loescher's work also shows that the need for counseling and support doesn't end when treatment does. In addition, she found that cancer survivors feel it is helpful to hear about other survivors' experiences, talk about their own experiences, and participate in survivor programs. Fortunately, there are survivor programs cropping up, such as Cancervive (with chapters in several states) and Memorial Sloan-Kettering's Post-Treatment

Resource Program in New York, which offers four-week workshops to help patients improve their quality of life.

If you think a survivors group would be right for you, ask your doctor, nurse, social worker, or local cancer support organization to help you locate one.

I had had some dark moments while on chemo, but it seemed easy to dismiss them then—it seemed natural to feel anxious about so many things. I buried my feelings because I was sure that I could handle them for the duration and that things would be fine once I was off the therapy and I could put some time between me and the experience. But about two and a half years after I finished chemo I found it was still hard for me to live with intruding thoughts about my disease and worries about my prognosis. I'd be in the middle of something perfectly ordinary—grocery shopping, for instance—and find myself overcome with sadness. I would think, "What if the chemo didn't work?" I'd have to fight to keep back the tears as I fantasized the bleakest scenario: in pain, unable to work or take care of myself, completely miserable. That I was working on this book, immersed in cancer facts and reliving my experiences daily, no doubt heightened my awareness and made my anxiety more acute. In a way, I am grateful for that: If my anxiety had stayed at a low level, I might never have decided that enough was enough and sought help from a psychotherapist. She incorporated hypnotherapy into the sessions, and I was able to resolve a lot of unfinished business. I must say the therapy allowed me to feel much better, much more relaxed about having had cancer.

The Cancer Support Community (CSC) in San Francisco has an ongoing after-treatment group for women with breast cancer that has been meeting for two years. The women meet once a month and have developed very close relationships. I'm not a participant in the group, but I do have my own free-floating group of friends who have or have had cancer, including the director of CSC. Although I enjoy close relationships with other friends who are not cancer patients, as one cancer veteran put it, "It's different when you're talking to someone to whom you don't have to explain certain things."

FOLLOW-UP CARE

Even though chemical therapy is finished, as cancer patients we will be getting follow-up medical care for the rest of our lives. Checkups and tests will be regularly scheduled, frequently at first and less frequently over the years as we remain well. Though the last thing we may want to do is spend more time in a hospital or waiting room, follow-up care is a useful and necessary part of postchemo life. It may be anxiety-provoking, but it is also reassuring.

For one thing, follow-up care may be able to address any problems with the residual effects of the therapy. Although our minds and bodies have remarkable resiliency and recuperative powers, sometimes medical support can strengthen us and hasten the recuperative process. Your doctors or other health practitioners may also be able to help you with any practical or psychological hurdles you face in living with cancer. If, for instance, you are preoccupied with your body and any symptoms—at one point I thought every cough might mean lung cancer, every bump or pimple was melanoma, every little ache was a metastasis to the bone, every little bit of constipation was bowel obstruction, every headache was cancer spreading to the brain—talking your fears over with your oncologist and getting some facts and assurances may help. You can ask what the likelihood of spread is, where the metastases usually occur in your cancer, and what the symptoms might be.

Additionally, many people, especially women who have undergone mastectomies, have found that acquiring a good prosthesis or having reconstructive surgery to improve their functioning and appearance after surgery is an invaluable coping device. This can be particularly important to psychological well-being, and reconstruction can finally allow people to feel "whole" or "normal" again. Mine has certainly improved the quality of my life from both an emotional and practical point of view.

But regular contact with your oncologist is perhaps most advisable because as with primary cancer, the earlier recurrent cancer is detected and treated, the better. As we have seen, cancer is not an automatic death sentence; neither is a recurrence. If you suspect your cancer has spread, do not delay going to your oncologist. Make sure it *is* a recurrence. Get a physical confirmation—blood tests, X rays, and scans. Consider a second opinion. Diagnosis can be inaccurate at any stage of this disease.

There are many cases where a patient was presumed to have a metastasis and treated as if he or she were terminal but was in fact found to be metastasis-free later on.

If there's a recurrence, it may make even more sense than before to turn to psychological support to help deal with feelings of shock, anger, and disbelief; with fears of pain, disability and death; and with physical and psychological inadequacies. Patients may find themselves blaming themselves or their families or feeling betrayed by their bodies and their doctors. Bitterness and a mistrust of the medical system are not unusual. A mental health worker speaks about her awareness of the devastating impact recurrence can have on patients: "This is a very big crisis for people who kind of thought they were going to do all right, and they *were* all right for a while, and then suddenly . . . it's a very big crisis for the staff, too."

As before, be aware of your treatment options. There is usually some form of treatment available, be it standard or investigational. Radiation is often used effectively at this point to reduce pain from metastases; in some cases surgical removal of metastases is successful. It is important for patients to have realistic expectations: Usually no more than a temporary halt to the progression of cancer and/or the palliation of symptoms can be expected when chemo is being used for a second or third time. However, even though additional treatment usually does not offer the chance for a cure, it still may prolong life significantly and can make it more comfortable.

Dr. William Grace at New York's St. Vincent's Hospital, for example, says:

"Sometimes oncologists just run out of therapeutic options and don't have access to newer drugs and methodologies. So it may be fruitful to explore investigational drugs, treatments, and combinations at larger cancer care facilities. Even old drugs may be administered so they are effective. I had a patient with breast cancer who had been through all the medications. We finally decided to give her a drug that had no longer worked for her, and we used it in a new way, called continuous infusion. She had a marvelous response.

"So there are always things to do, although we don't always know exactly what to do in every case. The problem is the combinations and permutations of different cancers, their different sensitivities, the different types of agents—the variables are astronomical. You just do the best you can. If you're lucky, you'll pull the ace out of the deck.''

You especially need to weigh the cost versus the benefits of treatment for recurrent cancer because the primary goal is to keep patients free of pain and as productive and able to enjoy life as possible. If the side effects are too severe, the quality of life is not being improved. Some people feel that once is enough; having been there, they feel they know what is in store and are reluctant to go through it again.

It is especially important for a patient with progressive disease to have a good relationship with an oncologist capable of seeing patients through the tough times that lie ahead. As always, patients have the right to get a second opinion or to refuse or stop toxic treatment altogether.

For some patients, unorthodox treatments may seem more attractive at this point than at the time of original diagnosis and therapy. Many feel that if conventional medical treatment has little or nothing to offer, it may be better to pursue an alternative therapy because it keeps their hopes and sense of control alive. Although some alternative therapies are very rigorous and the cost-benefit ratio may be high, many do opt to have them. The Appendices have sources of information about alternative cancer therapies.

Even if all therapies fail or become inappropriate and the end draws near, patients should be aware that they can still try to maintain a degree of control over their lives. There is still reason to hope that the rest of our lives will be as full of dignity and comfort as possible for us and our loved ones. Within the last decade or so, real strides have been made in understanding and coping with this final phase of life. The works of Elisabeth Kübler-Ross and the hospice movements may prove enlightening and comforting, and they are listed in the Appendices. Also listed are resources for information about making plans for the future and putting your affairs in order. This includes writing a will, a living will, and a durable power of attorney. These steps may be unpleasant to think about, but they are necessary and will help relieve your loved ones of an extra burden.

A BETTER LIFE

Whatever time we have left—be it months, years, or a full lifetime—it can be high-quality time if we let it. There's a growing survivorship movement, with individuals, treatment centers, professional societies, and groups such as the National Coalition for Cancer Survivorship working to develop resources to support people living in the aftermath of cancer. And there are enough research studies for the National Cancer Institute to publish a seventy-eight-page annotated bibliography of articles on survivorship issues.

Many patients have discovered that just because life is different, that doesn't mean it has to be worse. Life after chemo can be an improvement over life before. Although shaken, they emerge from the cancer/chemotherapy experience strengthened, with a fresh perspective and a heightened appreciation for the big and little things in life that they used to take for granted and that others still do. Although the experience may have imposed its share of difficulties, they find it has made them learn about themselves, about others, and about how precious life is. They have learned that the extent to which they can take control over their lives and the way they feel is greater than they ever imagined. Although they may look back wistfully at a more innocent time, they realize one can't go back, one can go only forward, toward a life that may not be normal but may be better than normal in many ways. Ask them their philosophy and they might tell you, "When life hands you a lemon, make lemonade."

In fact, it seems that these people—those who are able to pull something positive out of having had cancer and chemotherapy—*are* able to cope better. It is important for them to feel that it wasn't all for nothing, that it wasn't all bad. Dr. Van Scoy-Mosher has found this to be true in his practice:

> "I've noticed again and again from personal observation that people who seem to cope better than others are able to extract something positive from their experiences. It may be a change in their value systems, their motivations, their family structures, their interests. It may be writing a book about chemotherapy. Often levels of intimacy in a family that were good before are intensified. Even the motivation to adopt a healthier life-style—to stop smoking, to be more careful about your diet—is a good thing."

Dr. Gralla has witnessed this same phenomenon:

"A young patient of mine was on chemo for Hodgkin's. He said, 'You know, as much as I hated the whole horrible experience, it's been about the most important and maturing experience in my life, and it's made a better person of me.' In almost every aspect, from athletics, which were important to this fellow, to his life with his wife, to his career, it's made a not very mature adult into a quite mature, quite introspective, and thinking young adult."

Barbara Carter, a San Francisco nurse, published a study in 1989 of the long-term psychosocial adjustments of a group of women who survived breast cancer beyond five years. Carter feels that the study highlights the importance of understanding that survivors go through a process involving many phases of recovery that persists for many years after recovery. During this time, her subjects felt that they had moved "from something to something"—and emerged from the experience with a clearer sense of self, a gratitude for life, and strength and confidence in their ability to manage life crises.

The ways people find to express this change are varied. Many choose, for example, to make changes in their diets and lifestyles. Some postchemo patients react by plunging into a kind of live-for-today hedonism and deny themselves no pleasure; others swing in the other direction and adopt stringent dietary regimens in the hope that this will increase their chance for a cure. Still others make no changes. Most, however, probably fall somewhere in the middle.

Making constructive, health-building changes can be a very useful, positive step: Becoming involved in creating better health has many benefits, some directly related to cancer. It improves the quality of your life because you feel better, have more energy, and are able to fight illness of all kinds. When you are a participant in positive health building, you help reduce some of the anxiety and letdown about stopping chemotherapy or any active medical treatment. Optimizing the strength of your immune system and all your organ systems may inhibit the growth of any residual cancer or secondary cancer. This is a very important possible benefit, given the fact that we are at such high risk. Additionally, the healthier you are, the better you will be able to cope with a relapse should one occur.

My oncologist believes that "what one does after chemotherapy needs to be individualized," just as is the case with what one does while on chemo. He stresses common sense and moderation:

"Obviously one doesn't get into the situation where one is going to be tantalizing the system any more than is necessary. Does a person go out and smoke cigarettes because now he or she is as free as a bird? No, that would be foolish—nicotine is an immune suppressant. Does one go out and drink barrels of coffee? I don't think so; coffee is a growth stimulant. But does one say that one will never drink a cup of coffee? No, that's not human.

"I think it makes sense to do the things that are the least likely to create second malignancies, since the incidence of second malignancies is high in people who have had one. For instance, it's important to have a fairly high fiber diet that's going to include plenty of good things. Modest intake of vitamins is a good idea. Being involved with things that are life-building is a good idea, and getting back into the mainstream is terribly important."

Dr. Michael Schachter, who treats cancer patients who are receiving chemotherapy from their oncologists, feels strongly about postchemo care. He bases his recommendations on "years of long-term observation, which have made it pretty clear that nutritional and life-style changes are crucial over the long haul in terms of quality of life and survival time during and after chemo."

Because the evidence linking diet, stress, and exercise with overall health (and cancer) is building every day, I have made several changes in the way I live. I have reduced my intake of fats and refined carbohydrates and have increased my intake of fiber. I keep potentially harmful chemicals to a minimum and continue to take the vitamin/mineral supplements recommended to me while I was on chemo. I make a continual effort to improve the way I handle stress, and I exercise almost daily. I don't smoke, and because of the dangers of side-stream smoke, I try to avoid smoke-filled places (although with a musician for a husband, this is admittedly hard to do). I recently added a monthly acupuncture treatment to my health habits. It has proved to be marvelously relaxing and has miraculously straightened out my menstrual cycle, which had been totally unpredictable ever since chemo.

There are no guarantees, but these practices don't compromise my quality of life; they enhance it. Not only do they support good general health (how ironic it would be to beat cancer and succumb early to some other disease I could have easily prevented), they may have a direct bearing on my chances of avoiding a recurrence or another cancer. I can't be on chemo all my life, but I can continue in a life-style that may affect any cancer cells the chemo left behind as well as any new ones that might be produced.

Patients notice and cultivate spiritual and intellectual differences in the postchemo life, too. Natalie Springarn found that having cancer can be a challenge that forces people to grow and search for personal meaning, to set priorities, to view life more critically and intensively, to sort out the things they really want to do and do their best to do them. The prospect of death, she says, can teach you what life is all about. These patients agree:

"I don't think my life will ever be the same. But that's not a bad thing. It's not even the cancer at this point. It's just the idea—this brush with death—I look at life now and I see how tenuous it is, how very short it is. You have only your moment. Not just me, but all of life. Most of the time you don't recognize how insignificant your life is, or how short. After something like this you realize that nothing is forever."

"A couple of good things came out of this whole mess. My relationship with my husband is even better than it had been. People are more important. Relationships are more important. Things that people do that would bother me before don't bother me anymore. I think about something, 'Is this worth the time and energy?' Things get put in their proper perspective when you're faced with something like cancer."

Since my diagnosis and treatment, the quality of my life and the way I look at things have changed in many ways. I have learned to be more assertive, to ask questions. I have learned to be less accepting of the way some things are and more accepting of others. A former perfectionist, I've become more tolerant of my failings, and therefore of other people's too. Reaching out and helping others has given meaning to my experience—that's why I wrote this book and speak to cancer groups and individual patients. I have learned how to sit still—every moment, though precious, does not have to be jam-packed with activity; some moments it's okay just to "be," to merely enjoy the fact of existence. Michael has changed and matured, too; I am happy to report that our relationship has deepened to the point where we decided to get married six months after my chemotherapy was over.

Many cancer patients find meaning and purpose in their experience by voluntarily sharing it with other cancer patients by becoming peer counselors:

> "People ask me, 'How can you be doing this? Doesn't it bother you to be constantly reminded of old memories?' I say it doesn't really, that I was in their position once—I didn't have anybody to talk to. If I can pass something on, I feel good inside; talking to them is soothing to me, too. Out of the nineteen years I've been nursing, the three that I've been counseling cancer patients have been the most rewarding. I was looking for a reason why this happened to me—now I kind of have an idea why it did. If you can just get to somebody—if I can just reach one in five—if they're happy and can adjust to their lives, it can make it all worthwhile."

There are many opportunities to volunteer your knowledge and insights to people who are going through cancer and chemotherapy. Your local hospital, chapters of the American Cancer Society, and the other support groups listed in the back of this book will be able to guide you in finding a situation that is satisfying and helpful to both you and the uninformed patients who need you. You can let your oncologist and friends know that you are available to talk with newly diagnosed cancer patients. Some people prefer to make financial contributions to cancer foundations or help raise funds for cancer care and research. One woman with malignant melanoma started a newsletter; many others have started local self-help groups. Others find meaning and purpose by becoming cancer activists, either starting grass-roots organizations or joining them. The National Coalition of Cancer Survivors, Breast Cancer Action, and Cancervive are just a few of the advocacy organizations founded by cancer patients. Cancervive's Susan Nessim writes, "While the camaraderie of other survivors may be our greatest source of comfort and support, education and advocacy are our greatest weapons against fear and discrimination. We need to band together to make a difference."

Admittedly, this type of activism isn't for everyone. Although exhilarating, it is hard work and takes a certain personality and commitment that not everyone will be able to offer. Some of us are simply not suited for it and never will be. Others need a certain amount of time to heal themselves and come to terms with cancer before reaching the point where they are ready to assume an activist role. Some prefer to do their part as an individual, to educate themselves about cancer prevention and pass that knowledge on to others. Many people find it liberating and therapeutic to talk openly with friends or in front of small groups or to write an article for the local newspaper or club newsletter. The more people we reach, the easier the path will be for everyone.

On the other hand, some choose to contribute in other ways not so directly related to cancer. In addition to joining cancer organizations, I have become an active member of one environmental organization and donate money to others. I simply couldn't ignore the connections between the fragility of the health of the earth and my own health and that of other living things. And what is life worth if there's only a battered world to enjoy? A Hodgkin's disease survivor once wrote about how he labored to establish an income source for charitable organizations that provide food, clothing, or shelter for the poor. What drove him to such an undertaking? He wanted to make his life count, but he also felt "survivor's debt"—the need to somehow repay for being cured.

No matter how it is expressed, the positive changes that many postchemo patients have made signify an affirmation of life and a commitment toward improving and maintaining their health and happiness. Death has tapped them on the shoulder, and they have said "Not yet," first by taking chemotherapy, and then by continuing to do everything in their power to continue to improve their prognosis and quality of life. They want to give themselves every chance there is by making positive changes in their life-styles, attitudes, and priorities. These may include improving their diets, avoiding known harmful substances such as tobacco, getting more exercise, reducing and managing stress, dealing openly and honestly with their emotions, relaxing and enjoying hobbies and friends, having fun, getting rest and sleep, helping others, being productive, and enjoying sexual expression. Rather than wasting time and energy worrying about things they can't control, they prefer to deal with the things they *can* control.

Many cancer patients are able to make some of these moves

toward living better lives while they are on chemotherapy. (See Chapters 6–9.) For those for whom it was too difficult to initiate and maintain such changes: It is not too late now to turn over a new leaf! Whether you have chemotherapy only once or it becomes an intermittent part of your continuing care, you can still live life to the fullest while continuing a multifaceted program to stay in the best possible health.

Dr. Michael Van Scoy-Mosher ended my interview with him with these encouraging words we can all live by:

> "There are two components of health. One consists of the aspects that we have some control over; the other of things we don't, like genetics or things that just happen. And I think we have a certain responsibility to at least control what we can. It's not going to answer it all, but I, for one, don't want to lie on my deathbed and say that I could have delayed death or avoided it but I didn't because of certain things I did or didn't do. With chemotherapy, you have to resolve the conflict of the intellectual side—understanding the need for treatment—and the emotional aversion to it in favor of rational thought. You just have to know in your heart of hearts that you did what you could. And you should see that as a source of pride, that you were able to understand it, cope with it, tolerate it, and get it done with. Even though we know it's no guarantee, at least you know you did all you could do."

It took some time and the writing of this book to realize it fully, but I *am* proud I underwent chemotherapy. Though I have mixed feelings about it, I have no regrets. Chemotherapy is not an easy undertaking no matter how you look at it. It has its ups and downs, its imperfections and uncertainties. But it is too often thought of in solely negative terms. Chemotherapy, when given well, can do a lot of good; this often goes unrecognized or is lost sight of. Yes, I experienced side effects while on chemotherapy, and some have yet to subside completely. But chemo was worth it, and this is true whether it ultimately has given me only a few extra years or a normal life span. Because of chemo, I at least have a better chance of survival; I'm also a different person, a better person, a more knowledgeable person. I walk around during the day and go to sleep at night knowing I gave cancer my best shot. I hope I have helped you to give it your best shot, too, and to make your best even better. And that is all anyone can ask.

Appendices

Guide to Anticancer Drugs

There are three categories of drugs or substances used against cancer: cytotoxic drugs, hormones, and biologicals. This section contains specific information about how they work and their known side effects. The cytotoxic drugs listed here are all approved by the Food and Drug Administration (FDA) for commercial use (sometimes referred to as "standard" drugs); other drugs are available on an experimental basis but have not yet been approved, and they are not included here. The drugs used in hormone therapy that are listed here are also FDA-approved. Although very few biological therapies have been approved for use outside of a clinical trial as of this writing, I have included the ones that are most commonly used and show the most promise thus far.

TYPES OF CYTOTOXIC DRUGS

As we have seen, cytotoxic anticancer drugs (or antineoplastic drugs) kill cancer cells by interfering with their ability to grow and reproduce. They do this either by blocking the cells' supply of essential building blocks for growth or by interrupting the reproductive cycle. These anticancer drugs fall into four main groups, depending on the way in which they work.

Alkylating agents. These are the oldest chemotherapeutic chemicals we have. These compounds cross-link with DNA—they grab the strands of DNA, which then cannot pull apart during cell division. When the cell tries to divide, it self-destructs.

293

Antimetabolites. These work because they resemble substances that the cell needs in order to grow. The cell mistakes an antimetabolite for the needed substance, absorbs it, and tries to use it during division and growth. Because antimetabolites are not really usable, the cell dies. Drugs belonging to this group were the first to be designed specifically to combat cancer.

Vinca alkaloids. This is a very small, specialized category of drugs that are derived from plant sources. They destroy cells by halting a particular mechanism (mitosis) necessary for the physical process of division.

Antibiotics. Similar to the antibiotics used against bacterial infections, these are derived from naturally occurring soil fungi. They are believed to act by blocking cell growth by slipping between the strands of DNA and thus preventing it from copying itself.

Miscellaneous drugs. These include a few drugs, such as L-asparaginase, dacarbazine, and cisplatin, that act in a variety of ways against cancer and don't fit into any of the above categories.

Experience with these drugs has shown that some cancers respond well to a single drug (single-agent chemotherapy); these include some chronic leukemias and some lymphomas. Most cancers, however, respond much better when several drugs are used (combination chemotherapy). From the approximately one hundred standard and investigational drugs available, oncologists choose two, three, four, five, or six drugs—and sometimes as many as a total of twelve—to be given concurrently or in a certain sequence. Most protocols consist of at least three drugs, which can triple or even quadruple single-agent response rates while minimizing toxicity. This is possible because

• The drugs used have different mechanisms of action, so various phases of growth are affected.
• Using several drugs reduces the likelihood of drug resistance.
• The drugs are chosen to work synergistically, with one enhancing the effect of the other.
• The drugs are chosen to produce different kinds of toxicity at different times, so the harm to the tumor remains high without increasing the harm to the cells in any one organ or system.

• The doses are timed far enough apart, so the normal cells have time to recover but the cancer cells don't.

STANDARD DRUGS AND THEIR SIDE EFFECTS

In addition to their desired effects, chemotherapy drugs have unwanted side effects. The list that follows gives the standard (i.e., not experimental) anticancer drugs along with their known possible side effects. As you look up the drugs in your treatment plan, remember that these are the side effects that *might* happen—not the ones that necessarily *will* happen. It is highly unlikely that you will experience all or even most of them. A few side effects are not listed because they are so unusual that they occur in only a handful of the people taking the drug. (It is also possible for a drug taken in combination with others to produce side effects different from the ones that occur when it is taken alone.) In most drugs, the rare side effects far outnumber the common side effects. Whatever the potential side effects of the drugs you are taking, a skillful, caring oncologist will be able to avert or minimize the risks. There are many measures that both you and your doctor can take to prevent most side effects and make others more tolerable.

If you want more information about your drugs and their side effects, ask your doctor, nurse, or pharmacist. Many hospitals make available to their patients individual drug information cards which list the major common side effects and ways to alleviate them. The package insert that comes with the drug is daunting but very informative; your oncologist or pharmacist will supply these upon request. In addition, there are several reference books with detailed information on anticancer and other drugs. The *Physician's Desk Reference* (*PDR*) has been a standard source for drug information, but its text can be hard for the average person to decipher. Alternatively there is the *United States Pharmacopeial Dispensing Information* (*USP DI*), published by the United States Pharmacopeial Convention, or its *Physicians' and Pharmacists' Guide to Your Medicines*, which is written for a general audience. *Professional Guide to Drugs* is another readable source. Your doctor, pharmacy, library, and bookstore are possible sources for these materials. If you are taking investigational drugs, the known side effects will be listed on the informed consent form that you sign before beginning therapy.

Name of Drug	More Common Side Effects	Less Common or Rare Side Effects
Actinomycin D *see* Dactinomycin		
Adriamycin *see* Doxorubicin		
Adrucil *see* 5-Fluorouracil		
Alkeran *see* Melphalan		
Aminoglutethimide (Cytadren)	drowsiness skin rash nausea and loss of appetite dizziness	headaches low blood pressure
Amsacrine (*m*-AMSA)	nausea, vomiting diarrhea pain at injection site allergic reaction low blood counts	hair loss liver problems heart problems nerve problems
Ara-C *see* Cytarabine		
Asparaginase (Elspar)	abdominal pain nausea, vomiting skin rash, itching difficulty breathing joint pain light-headedness slow blood clotting liver problems headache irritability loss of appetite weight loss	diabetes risk of infection shaky body movements mouth sores mental depression drowsiness, confusion hallucinations nervousness tiredness
5-Azacitidine (5-AC)	nausea, vomiting low blood counts liver damage	lethargy, weakness confusion skin rash

Name of Drug	More Common Side Effects	Less Common or Rare Side Effects
	diarrhea	mouth sores fever
BCNU see Carmustine		
Blenoxane see Bleomycin		
Bleomycin	fever, chills cough breathing problems	nausea, vomiting fainting, weakness hair loss mental confusion loss of appetite change in taste perception skin rash, discoloration swollen, painful legs or fingers headache changes in fingernails
Busulfan	slow blood clotting risk of infection tiredness	lung problems, cough skin darkening, acne loss of appetite hair loss dizziness, fatigue impotence nausea, vomiting menstrual irregularities mental confusion breast enlargement (men) stomach pain joint pain, swollen feet

Name of Drug	More Common Side Effects	Less Common or Rare Side Effects
Carboplatin (paraplatin)	low blood counts risk of infection anemia nausea, vomiting pain	hearing problems neuropathy central nervous system problems liver abnormalities heart problems breathing problems allergic reactions hair loss
Carmustine (nitrosourea) (BCNU)	nausea, vomiting risk of infection slow blood clotting	lung problems, cough liver problems loss of appetite pain at infusion site mouth sores tiredness, weakness diarrhea hair loss skin rash, itching
CCNU see Lomustine		
CDDP see Cisplatin		
Chlorambucil (nitrogen mustard) (Leukeran)	slow blood clotting risk of infection tiredness	hair loss nausea, vomiting stomach pains skin rash, itching lung problems, cough menstrual irregularities joint pain, swollen feet mouth sores
Cisplatin (Platinol)	nausea, vomiting hearing problems sore throat	tiredness kidney problems loss of appetite

Name of Drug	More Common Side Effects	Less Common or Rare Side Effects
	diarrhea stomach pains risk of infection joint pain, swollen feet slow blood clotting	loss of taste perception numbness/tingling in fingers or toes tremors rapid heartbeat
Cisplatinum *see* Cisplatin		
Cosmegen *see* Dactinomycin		
Cyclophosphamide (Cytoxan)	nausea, vomiting loss of appetite menstrual irregularities risk of infection hair loss	tiredness cough painful urination bloody urine liver problems joint pain, swollen feet rapid heartbeat slow blood clotting dizziness, confusion stomach pain skin darkening, flushing headache mouth sores sterility
Cytarabine (Ara-C)	nausea, vomiting tiredness, weakness risk of infection slow blood clotting fainting headache irregular heartbeat	stomach pain liver problems mouth sores joint pain, swollen feet diarrhea skin rash
Cytosar-U *see* Cytarabine		

Name of Drug	More Common Side Effects	Less Common or Rare Side Effects
Cytoxan *see* Cyclophosphamide		
Dacarbazine (DTIC)	nausea, vomiting loss of appetite redness, pain at injection site risk of infection slow blood clotting	blurred vision confusion, uneasiness headache hair loss joint/muscle pain
Dactinomycin (Cosmegen)	nausea, vomiting tiredness vein inflammation at IV site risk of infection slow blood clotting	hair loss stomach pain mouth sores skin rash, discoloration, acnelike condition loss of appetite
Daunomycin *see* Daunorubicin		
Daunorubicin (Cerubidine)	nausea, vomiting hair loss risk of infection shortness of breath	stomach pain heart problems mouth and throat sores diarrhea loss of appetite skin darkening joint pain pain at injection site red urine (not bloody) slow blood clotting
Doxorubicin (adriamycin)	nausea, vomiting risk of infection mouth sores shortness of breath hair loss slow blood clotting	stomach pain diarrhea swollen feet, joint pain red urine (not bloody) pain at injection site

Name of Drug	More Common Side Effects	Less Common or Rare Side Effects
		skin and nail darkening
		liver problems
		heart problems
DTIC *see* Dacarbazine		
Elspar *see* Asparaginase		
Endoxan *see* Cyclophosphamide		
Epipodophyllotoxin *see* VP-16-213		
Etoposide *see* VP-16-213		
Floxuridine (FUDR)	nausea, vomiting diarrhea stomach cramps, pain mouth sores	risk of infection vertigo slow blood clotting skin rash, sores depression, lethargy
5-Fluorouracil	nausea and vomiting diarrhea	risk of infection hair loss mouth sores skin darkening skin rash nail problems weakness and clumsiness
5-FU *see* 5-Fluorouracil		
Hydrea *see* Hydroxyurea		
Hydroxyurea (Hydrea)	nausea, vomiting risk of infection slow blood clotting	diarrhea mouth sores skin rash skin darkening

Name of Drug	More Common Side Effects	Less Common or Rare Side Effects
		drowsiness, dizziness loss of appetite constipation
Ifosfamide (IFEX)	bladder problems (irritation, loss of control, blood in urine) hair loss nausea, vomiting low blood counts slow wound healing slow blood clotting	central nervous system problems drowsiness confusion hallucinations depression dizziness forgetfulness kidney problems liver abnormalities fever heart problems mouth sores
L-asparaginase *see* Asparaginase		
Leukeran *see* Chlorambucil		
Lomustine (nitrosourea)	nausea, vomiting risk of infection slow blood clotting loss of appetite	tiredness, weakness hair loss mouth sores kidney problems confusion skin darkening skin rash
L-PAM *see* Melphalan		
Matulane *see* Procarbazine		
Mechlorethamine (Mustargen)	nausea and vomiting risk of infection	loss of appetite hair loss hearing problems

Name of Drug	More Common Side Effects	Less Common or Rare Side Effects
	slow blood clotting menstrual irregularities metallic taste	pain/redness at injection site dizziness, drowsiness headache weakness
Melphalan (nitrogen mustard) (L-PAM)	nausea and vomiting risk of infection slow blood clotting	loss of appetite stomach pain joint pain mouth sores hair loss
6-Mercaptopurine (6-MP)	nausea and vomiting risk of infection slow blood clotting	stomach pain loss of appetite mouth sores weakness skin rash liver problems headache dizziness, drowsiness
Methotrexate	nausea, vomiting diarrhea loss of appetite mouth sores stomach pain risk of infection slow blood clotting	hair loss headache liver problems joint pain acne skin rash or darkening shortness of breath, cough tiredness, weakness bloody or dark urine blurred vision
Mithracin see Mithramycin		
Mithramycin (Plicamycin)	nausea and vomiting diarrhea	drowsiness fever headache

Name of Drug	More Common Side Effects	Less Common or Rare Side Effects
	mouth sores loss of appetite slow blood clotting risk of infection	tiredness, weakness depression
Mitomycin (Mutamycin)	nausea and vomiting pain at IV site risk of infection slow blood clotting	blood in urine loss of appetite mouth sores hair loss skin rash tingling skin, fingers, and/or toes
Mitotane	nausea and vomiting diarrhea mental depression drowsiness, dizziness tiredness aching or twitching muscles	loss of appetite skin rash or darkening fever visual problems
Mitoxantrone (Novantrone)	low blood counts skin bruises fatigue nausea, vomiting diarrhea heart problems mouth sores risk of infection fever lung problems central nervous system problems (seizures, headache) hair loss	gastrointestinal bleeding mucositis heart failure abdominal pain liver abnormalities kidney failure blue discoloration of nails and urine

6-MP
   see 6-Mercaptopurine

Name of Drug	More Common Side Effects	Less Common or Rare Side Effects
Mustargen see Mechlorethamine		
Mutamycin see Mitomycin		
Myleran see Busulfan		
Novantrone (see Mitoxantronc)		
Oncovin see Vincristine		
Paclitaxel see Taxol		
Paraplatin (see Carboplatin)		
Platinol see Cisplatin		
Procarbazine (Matulane)	nausea and vomiting diarrhea slow blood clotting risk of infection loss of appetite low sperm counts tiredness, weakness cough, shortness of breath drowsiness muscle or joint pain	mental depression, agitation muscle twitching mouth sores skin rash, itching, darkening nervousness, insomnia nightmares hallucinations confusion, clumsiness headache hair loss constipation tingling or numbness in fingers or toes
Purinethol see 6-Mercaptopurine		

Name of Drug	More Common Side Effects	Less Common or Rare Side Effects
Rubidomycin see Daunorubicin		
Streptozocin (Zanosar)	nausea and vomiting pain at IV site	kidney, liver, and blood problems
Taxol*	low blood counts hair loss mucositis (sores in mouth and esophagus) muscle and joint pain nerve problems (numbness, difficulty moving) allergic reactions (low blood pressure, breathing difficulties, skin rash)	fever anemia nausea, vomiting diarrhea fatigue headache increase in blood triglycerides heartbeat irregularities
6-TG see 6-Thioguanine		
6-Thioguanine (6-TG)	nausea and vomiting diarrhea risk of infection slow blood clotting	stomach pain skin rash liver problems loss of appetite mouth sores joint pain
Thio-TEPA	nausea and vomiting pain at IV site risk of infection slow blood clotting	stomach pain loss of appetite menstrual irregularities low sperm counts

*This drug was still in Phase III trials but close to FDA approval as of publication; side effects listed are those known thus far.

Name of Drug	More Common Side Effects	Less Common or Rare Side Effects
		skin rash
		headache
		hair loss
		dizziness
		tightness of throat
Triethylenethiophosphoramide *see* Thio-TEPA		
TSPA *see* Thio-TEPA		
Velban *see* Vinblastine		
Vinblastine (Velban)	nausea and vomiting pain at IV site if drug leaks risk of infection hair loss	headache jaw pain mouth sores constipation mental depression tingling and numbness of fingers and toes muscle pain, weakness loss of reflexes loss of appetite stomach pain low sperm counts skin rash
Vincristine (Oncovin)	pain at IV site if drug leaks constipation difficulty walking hair loss headache jaw pain joint pain tingling and numbness in fingers and toes weakness	confusion, agitation dizziness hallucinations depression, insomnia loss of reflexes bloating diarrhea skin rash loss of appetite mouth sores

Name of Drug	More Common Side Effects	Less Common or Rare Side Effects
VP-16-213 (Etoposide)	nausea and vomiting loss of appetite diarrhea mouth sores	low blood count hair loss headache, fever

Zanosar
   see Streptozocin

HORMONES AND ANTIHORMONES

Hormone treatment is used mostly in cancers of the reproductive system such as breast and prostate cancer. In many cancers the adrenocorticoids are widely used in addition to anticancer drugs because of their ability to help patients tolerate the therapy better.

Name of Medication	Side Effects
Adrenocorticoids (cortisonelike) Prednisone Decadron (Hexadrol) Medrol	increased appetite and sense of well-being sleeplessness and agitation fluid retention and weight gain diabetes high blood pressure increased risk of infection acnelike skin condition stomach and intestinal ulcers loss of potassium muscle weakness, cramps, or pain hirsutism (abnormal hairiness) decreased or blurry vision frequent urination mood changes menstrual problems, sterility irregular heartbeat headache osteoporosis (weakening of bones)

Name of Medication	Side Effects
Estrogens	nausea, vomiting
("female hormones")	fluid retention and weight gain
	swollen, tender breasts
DES (diethylstilbestrol)	headache, dizziness, depression, lethargy
Stilphostrol	lowered blood calcium
Tace	heart and circulation problems
Estradiol	worsening of nearsightedness or astigmatism, difficulty wearing contact lenses
	abdominal cramps, diarrhea, constipation
	changes in menstruation, sterility
	loss of potassium
	vaginal infections, cervical secretions
	skin changes
	excess body hair
	in males: impotence, enlarged breasts
Antiestrogens	transient nausea and vomiting
Tamoxifen	hot flashes
(Nolvadex)	loss of appetite
Nafoxide	vaginal discharge, itching, bleeding
	headache
	blurred vision
	confusion
	weakness
	sleepiness
	increased fertility
	bone pain
	pain or swelling in legs
	skin rash
	weight gain
	shortness of breath
Androgens	nausea, vomiting
("male hormones")	liver problems
	lowering of voice, skin changes
Halotestin	water retention and weight gain
Depo-testosterone	changes in libido
Deca-Durabolin	constipation, diarrhea
Flutamide	bladder problems, liver problems
(Eulexin)	in women: changes in menstruation

Name of Medication	Side Effects
	hot flashes
	itchy, burning vagina
	in males: impotence, enlarged breasts, low sperm counts
Estramucine	breast enlargement and tenderness
	heart problems, heart failure
	leg cramps
	nausea, vomiting, diarrhea, loss of appetite
	lethargy
	insomnia
	low white cell count
	liver abnormalities
	water retention
	trouble breathing
	blood clots, stroke
Leuprolide (Lupron)	heart abnormalities
	high blood pressure
	water retention
	blood clots
	loss of appetite
	constipation
	nausea, vomiting
	hot flashes
	impotence
	anemia
	enlarged, tender breasts
	pain, achy muscles
	headache
	insomnia
Progestogens Delalutin Depo-Provera Medroxypro- gesterone	fluid retention, weight gain
	nausea, vomiting, abdominal cramps
	dizziness, headache, lethargy, depression
	heart and circulatory problems
	changes in menstruation
	cervical secretions, vaginal infections
	decreased libido
	skin rash
	breast enlargement or tenderness

Name of Medication	Side Effects
Megace (Megestrol- acetate)	fluid retention, weight gain increased fat deposits hair loss or thinning liver damage fatigue nausea, vomiting carpal tunnel syndrome

BIOLOGICAL RESPONSE MODIFIERS

Most of the biological agents are available only experimentally. They generally work by stimulating the immune system, although some work in other ways, such as by directly affecting tumor cells. Side effects differ among these substances, but most of them cause fever, fatigue, chills, and skin rash; other effects are malaise, flulike symptoms, kidney problems, severe allergic reactions, severe breathing problems, and possibly death. Some research shows that stimulating one part of the immune system may result in an overall imbalance that may be harmful and actually may lead to the growth of cancer.

Interferon (IFN)   There are several interferons that seem to work together in ways that are not yet understood. Alpha-interferon first became known for its antiviral abilities but soon was hailed for its anticancer properties. Although it is not the miracle cure it was once thought to be, interferon has shown some effectiveness and continues to be tested.

Interleukin   Interleukin (IL) transmits signals between leukocytes (white blood cells). Some interleukins have shown promise in fighting cancer. For example, patients are treated with cells that have been stimulated by IL-2 outside the body, called lymphokine-activated killer cells (LAK cells), and are given additional doses of IL-2 as well.

Tumor Necrosis Factor (TNF)   Tumor necrosis factor acts as a chemical messenger between cells, triggering immune defenses that destroy tumors. Animal testing has shown that animals with cancer can no longer produce their own TNF. It is hoped that artificially produced (by genetic engineering) TNF can be administered to destroy tumor cells.

Colony-Stimulating Factor (CSF)   Colony-stimulating factors are substances that are normally produced by the body to help the bone marrow cells develop. They are also being manufactured in laboratories and are used after chemotherapy to restore the bone marrow more quickly. This way, higher doses of chemotherapy may be given more safely and theoretically with more effectiveness.

Monoclonal Antibodies (MAbs)   Monoclonal antibodies are bits of protein that can locate and bind to tumor cells in the body. They can be used alone to detect or eliminate tumors, or they may be linked to drugs, toxins, or radioactive material, which they carry directly to cancer cells, avoiding healthy cells.

BONE MARROW TRANSPLANTS (BMTs)

Bone marrow transplants are generally not used to treat cancer themselves. Rather, they are used to allow higher and presumably more effective doses of cancer-killing chemotherapy (and radiation). After high-dose therapy, the bone marrow is used to "rescue" the patient.

Bone marrow is the soft, spongelike material in the cavities of bones. The chief function of bone marrow is to produce blood cells: red blood cells (RBCs, or erythrocytes), white blood cells (WBCs, or leukocytes), and platelets (thrombocytes). Blood cells normally do not enter the bloodstream until they are fully developed, so the marrow contains cells in all stages of development.

Although chemotherapy affects many organs, the bone marrow is usually the most sensitive. Toxicity to the bone marrow therefore limits the doses that can be given because damaged bone marrow leaves the patient susceptible to infections, which could be fatal. However, the more chemo you give, the more cancer cells are killed and the higher the likelihood of a remission or cure. Bone marrow transplantation was developed to allow physicians to use doses of chemotherapy or radiation therapy so high that they severely damage and destroy the patient's marrow. When the wiped-out bone marrow is replaced, the immune system cells have a chance to regenerate, and the patient is "rescued" from the very high risk of a potentially fatal infection.

Today transplantation is recognized as an effective treatment for some cancers, among them leukemia and lymphoma. BMT is also being studied for other types of cancer, including brain tumors, cancers of the bone and connective tissue (sarcomas), melanoma, and breast and lung cancer.

Types of Transplants

A patient's marrow may be replaced with healthy marrow from a donor such as a sibling, a parent, or an unrelated person (allogeneic transplant). This is the type most often used for leukemia. The success of an allogeneic transplant depends on how closely the donor's marrow "matches" the recipient's marrow. The closer the match, the less likely that the transplanted bone marrow will react against the patient's body, a condition called graft-versus-host disease (GVHD), or that the patient's body will reject the marrow.

A transplant also may consist of marrow that has been taken previously from the patient (autologous transplant). Because the patient serves as his or her own donor, matching is not necessary. The marrow is usually removed, or harvested, when the cancer patient is in remission or when cancer cells cannot be detected microscopically. To be sure that any undetected cancer cells in the patient's marrow are destroyed, it may be treated in a process called purging.

For autologous transplants, researchers are exploring the possibility of harvesting stem cells that are circulating in the blood. These immature, peripheral stem cells eventually turn into RBCs, WBCs, and platelets. The advantages to this procedure are that the donor requires no hospitalization or general anesthesia for the harvesting and that there is less likelihood of harvesting cancer cells along with the stem cells.

After a period of chemotherapy to see if the tumor responds to the particular drugs being used, the patient receives high-dose chemotherapy for several days with or without radiotherapy. During the vulnerable "window" resulting from high-dose chemo, the patient usually is placed in a hospital room where it is easier to prevent exposure to infectious agents; this is called protective isolation. The patient is also given antibiotics to prevent and/or treat infections and may need periodic transfusions.

Shortly after high-dose chemotherapy is completed, the marrow or stem cells are administered just like a blood transfusion. The cells travel through the bloodstream and find their way to the bone marrow, where they eventually begin to manufacture new WBCs, RBCs, and platelets, a process called engraftment.

BMT causes tremendous stress for patients and their families,

who must struggle physically, emotionally, and financially with
the therapy and the disruption of their lives. Bone marrow transplantation is very expensive, and is not always covered by insurance plans (see The Cost of BMT, below). Families often
must travel a long distance to a specialized treatment center and
live away from home for an extended period.

In addition, it is a dangerous and uncomfortable process, with
more intense side effects, particularly the risk of infection, than
conventional chemo. As with all therapies, there are no guarantees of a cure or long-term remission; autologous transplants
always run the risk that the marrow being replaced contains
undetected cancer cells. However, researchers are making rapid
progress in improving autologous grafts by refining the methods
used to cleanse the marrow of cancer cells. In addition, colony-
stimulating growth factors show promise in speeding the growth
of the transplanted marrow, reducing the risk of infection during
the most vulnerable period. This cuts down on the time spent
in isolation.

Still, the decision to undergo high-dose chemo and BMT is
not an easy one. Usually it is the only chance for cure or long-
term remission, so more and more people are deciding that the
risks are worth the possible benefits. In addition, for many people with advanced disease, the shorter duration of intense chemotherapy is a preferable alternative to the months and years
they would spend on conventional chemo.

The Cost of BMT

Bone marrow transplants are highly technical and expensive;
they usually cost over $150,000. Most transplant centers require
a guarantee of funds in advance to cover these costs. Health
insurance plans generally will reimburse the costs of BMT for
leukemia and lymphoma but not for other diseases in which this
approach is considered experimental. As a result, some patients
are not able to have this treatment. Others have sued their insurance carriers—and won—or have been able to come up with
the money in some other way.

In addition, although the actual hospital time is about one to
two months, the patient may need to stay near the treatment
center for an additional two to three months for follow-up care.
This costs more money, including for some people the income
lost from time off the job. The recovery process at home takes
a significant amount of additional time and may require home

helpers or visiting nurses to assist with the care of the patient. This is another potential expense.

The National Cancer Institute has some suggestions for relieving the financial burden: Patients and their families may set up a tax-deductible contribution fund through the Internal Revenue Service or use an existing fund from a church or service group (Kiwanis, Lions, Rotary, Masons). Families can also contact the Leukemia Society of America and the American Cancer Society for help with costs of transportation and other expenses. Income tax deductions can be claimed for some BMT expenses. Families should check with an accountant or attorney regarding such deductions. Other suggestions for dealing with the costs of chemotherapy are found elsewhere in this book.

HOW NEW ANTICANCER DRUGS ARE DEVELOPED

The Food and Drug Administration (FDA) and its sister organization, the National Cancer Institute (NCI), are jointly responsible for overseeing the testing of new cancer drugs and other treatments. Since 1955 the NCI has supported a program to identify, evaluate, and make available to the public effective anticancer drugs.

There are over thirteen hundred different investigational protocols in the NCI drug development program.

Preclinical Screening and Testing

A new drug may be truly brand-new and just discovered, or it may be an analog—a modified version of a drug that has been found effective. Many of these drugs, or compounds, are submitted to the NCI by industry or universities. All new drugs must eventually be tested on humans (clinical trials). But in order to make this testing as justifiable as possible from a humane and economic point of view, scientists try to learn all they can about the drugs by testing them first in the laboratory. It costs about $600,000 just to screen one drug.

Every year thousands of chemical compounds are screened. Most of them are not effective against cancer; some, however, are effective but are too toxic to be useful. And every once in a while a drug is found that is effective without being too harmful to consider using in humans. It has been estimated that of every forty thousand compounds screened, only one is found useful in human cancers.

The screening process begins by testing the drugs on cancer cells to see if they kill them in vitro (in a test tube). If the drugs are found to be active, they are then tested for toxicity in mice. The results of these animal trials give researchers some idea of the side effects as well as the range of safe dosage for humans. This is accomplished by determining the lethal dose in 10 percent of the mice; the equivalent dose is calculated, and the drug is ready to go into phase I human trials. At this point the sponsor of the drug—usually the NCI—files a New Drug Investigational (IND) application with the FDA. The application provides information about the drug, the results of the animal trials, and a protocol or detailed outline explaining the plan for testing the drug. The IND is a license to use the drug on humans experimentally. Human studies generally proceed through three phases.

Phase I All drugs in this phase are investigational and are being given to humans for the first time. This phase usually involves fifty to two hundred patients with a wide variety of tumors. These are advanced cancer patients who are dying and who usually know it; they have failed to respond to earlier standard therapies, or they have a type and stage of cancer for which no effective standard treatment exists.

Phase I studies are *toxicity* studies. The primary purposes of this phase are to determine the maximum dose a person can tolerate before severe, unacceptable side effects occur (toxicity); what the side effects are; whether toxicity is reversible; how to schedule treatments; and how the drug is absorbed, used, and excreted by the body. If possible, the therapeutic effects of the drug are observed and recorded. The plan of treatment, or protocol, is arrived at after studying the results of animal trials; in subsequent phase I trials, the results of earlier phase I tests are also considered in designing new protocols. Tests begin with a low dose of the drug; this is increased according to a logical plan as the testing progresses. The initial dosage is administered to a small group of patients. If no toxicity is observed in the first group, the dose may be doubled in the next group; thereafter, doses are increased by specific percentages in subsequent groups of patients until dose-limiting but tolerable toxicity occurs or until clear signs of therapeutic activity occur. Increasing the dose in the same patient is discouraged because delayed toxic effects of the first dose could be mistaken for early toxic effects of subsequent doses. Such a practice could both obscure the results of the study and result in irreversible damage to the patient. Also to protect the patient against delayed toxicity, relatively long intervals between cycles of treatment are recommended—usually at least four weeks. Sometimes pilot studies are conducted much like phase I studies, in which a new drug is added to an established combination of drugs to see if there are any drug interactions.

At the end of phase I investigators have enough information to decide whether to carry the drug over into phase II studies. It is felt that a lack of antitumor activity at this level is no reason not to test the drug further; the only reason a drug may be dropped is because of severe toxicity. For example, cisplatin and streptozocin, two drugs that are highly effective in specific tumors, showed early negative testing results. A small number of patients with a variety of cancers were used, and the doses were below those required to elicit a response. These drugs would have been lost if they had been discarded from the testing program prematurely. Even under ideal conditions, if only one or two out of fourteen patients with the same tumor respond to a drug, it could indicate a possible 20 percent response rate, which is cause for no little excitement in chemotherapy.

Phase II Drugs that show promise in phase I go on to be tested in phase II. All the drugs being tested in phase II are investigational, and some may be only two to five years old. By and large, patients in phase II studies are those who have advanced cancer and for whom conventional chemotherapy and/or phase III studies did not work. Phase II may not be their only option for treatment: There may be an alternative conventional chemotherapy or an alternative phase III study.

Phase II trials are *efficacy* studies for therapeutic effect. The primary purpose is to determine the drug's activity against specific cancers and to eliminate drugs that are inactive for a specific cancer, so a variety of cancers must be entered into these trials. There may be up to six hundred patients participating in a phase II study.

The protocols for early phase II studies are based on phase I results and ongoing animal studies. Investigators know some of the side effects and know what dose range is safe. This phase is complex in design: The relationships among the dose of the drug, the timing of the drug, the response, and the toxicity are all studied. Therefore, phase II protocols include a wide variety of plans—different doses and schedules—and each permutation must be tested on each tumor type entered in the study for a fair and accurate comparison.

When the phase II trial is completed, the drug may be discarded because of lack of efficacy or excessive or intolerable side effects in relation to the therapeutic effects. If the drug approaches or betters the data for standard drugs, the new drug is entered into phase III studies.

Phase III   Most patients receiving investigational drugs are in phase III studies. Patients who are offered this treatment are those for whom effective standard treatment exists but for whom phase III drugs might be better. Only patients with the same type of cancer that responded to the drug in phase II studies participate in phase III. And only drugs that are reasonably certain to be either superior to or in the same range of effectiveness as an established therapy, either alone or in combination, are entered into phase III.

Phase III is a *comparison* study. The treatment usually is compared head-to-head with the standard treatment in use for the same cancers. The new treatment may be a single new drug that is being tested alone or a new drug that is being incorporated into an established drug combination to determine whether it increases the effectiveness and/or tolerability of the established regimen. A patient who chooses to participate may be randomized to receive one of several treatment options. One is the conventional treatment—the best established treatment medicine has to offer at that time. The others are the investigational arms of the study. Randomization is a process that occurs at a central office, a method by which it is left to chance to choose whether a patient is slated for one arm or the other. It exists to eliminate any possible bias from the doctor. Not all drugs in phase III studies are investigational; only the ones in the investigational arm of the study may be. The protocols for phase III trials are based on the findings from phase II. The dosages and schedules that proved most effective are adopted. After the researchers have accrued and treated hundreds of patients with the same type of cancer, various statistical tools are applied to compare the data to see if there is a significant difference in the effectiveness of the drugs.

If a new drug compares favorably with the standard treatment and has been tested to the satisfaction of the FDA, then a new drug application is filed, which gives permission to market the drug.

Changes in Drug Approval, Availability, and Development In most instances, promising new drugs require ten to twelve years of research and $200 million before they become available outside clinical trials. Thanks to the efforts of AIDS and other activists, FDA procedures are undergoing reform in an effort to streamline the approval process and increase access to investigational drugs, or drugs available outside the United States.

In some cases, patients working with their doctors have been able to obtain promising drugs that are not yet generally available. For example, some patients qualify for Group C drugs, compassionate use of unapproved drugs outside a clinical trial, or drugs distributed through a parallel track system. These drugs must be applied for through the FDA.

In addition, the National Cancer Institute is intensifying its search for drugs from natural substances. Natural products are resources with enormous potential, having been the major source of effective drugs for many diseases, including cancer. Natural substances contain chemical structures that, according to the NCI, "would not have been conceived by medicinal chemists and are frequently too complex for synthetic reproduction." That is why the NCI has developed a program to collect plants, fungi, marine animals, and blue-green algae.

As part of this program, the NCI is rushing to collect tropical plants from rain forests before the forests disappear and the plants become extinct, taking their undiscovered virtues with them. Another type of vanishing ecosystem, the ancient forest of the northwestern United States, is the primary source for the Pacific yew tree. This tree is the source of taxol, a new drug that offers new hope to people with ovarian and breast cancer. Thus far the natural form of the drug is in very short supply because yew trees have been nearly wiped out by indiscriminate logging practices, and no one has been able to synthesize the complex taxol molecule. The vanishing tropical rain forests and ancient northwest forests are but two examples of the wide-ranging effects on us all of destroying irreplaceable ecosystems.

Resources

INFORMATION AND SUPPORT SERVICES

Your local hospital is the best place to start looking for support services in your community. Looking in the telephone directory under "Cancer" (in the White Pages) or "Social Service Organizations" (in the Yellow Pages) will also help you find what you need.

This listing includes the national and regional organizations that are the largest and that will be able to refer you to their chapters near you or to other similar local resources.

American Cancer Society (ACS)
1599 Clifton Road NE
Atlanta, GA 30329
(800) ACS-2345
(Check telephone directory for your local office)

Local units offer patient education and information, counseling information on home health care, community services, psychological support, physical rehabilitation, transportation to and from treatment, financial counseling, employment assistance, equipment, loans, and wigs and prostheses. ACS has a variety of programs for cancer patients and their families. *I Can Cope* is a hospital-based program that provides education and psychological support for patient and family. *CanSurmount* is a short-term visitor program that provides patient and family education and information. *Reach to Recovery*'s trained volunteers have had breast cancer themselves and provide practical information and support to women with breast cancer. The *Look Good . . . Feel Better* program provides education and consultation with volunteer salons to evaluate skin and hair needs and help deal with the appearance-related side effects of cancer treatments. Call (800) 395-LOOK.

American Association of Marriage and Family Counselors
225 Yale Avenue
Claremont, CA 91711

American Association of Sex Educators, Counselors, and Therapists
5010 Wisconsin Avenue NW
Washington, DC 20016

Cancer Care, Inc.
National Cancer Foundation
1180 Avenue of the Americas
New York, NY 10036
(212) 221-3300

A social service agency that provides professional counseling and planning for patients and families. Consultation, education, nursing care, home health care, homemakers and housekeepers, and financial assistance are provided. They will refer you to appropriate resources in your geographic area if you live outside the New York area.

Cancer Consultation Service
237 Thompson Street
New York, NY 10012
(212) 254-5031

A regional resource for emotional/supportive counseling to help people think through treatment options as well as deal with the emotional, spiritual, and psychological issues of those options.

Cancer Hopefuls United for Mutual Support (CHUMS)
3310 Rochambeau Avenue
New York, NY 10467
(212) 655-7566

A national self-help organization that includes crisis intervention, information, self-help rap sessions, educational meetings, and a newsletter. Founded by a psychologist.

Cancer Hotline (Kansas City, MO)
(816) 932-8453

A service that provides "phone mates" for cancer patients.

Cancer Information Service (CIS)
1-800-4-CANCER
Hawaii: 524–1234; Washington, D.C.: 636-5700; Alaska: 800-638-6070

A toll-free telephone inquiry system. Supplies information about local and regional resources and programs for those interested in psychological, emotional, medical, physical, financial, and employment assistance, support, and education. Publishes printed educational material. Most chapters are affiliated with a Comprehensive Cancer Center. This will also get you access to PDQ (Physicians' Data Query), a computerized listing for patients and health professionals that provides the latest treatment information, including clinical trials of promising new cancer treatments.

Cancervive, Inc.
6500 Wilshire Boulevard, #500
Los Angeles, CA 90048
(213) 203-9232

Support groups that deal with issues involving cancer survivors and the disease itself. Face-to-face counseling is offered; you can be referred to local resources if you live out of their region.

Candlelighters
2025 I Street NW, Suite 1011
Washington, DC 20006
(202) 659-5136

Over a hundred chapters for parents of children with cancer; provides emotional support and education. Publishes newsletter.

Center for Attitudinal Healing
19 Main Street
Tiburon, CA 94920
(415) 435-5022

Helps patients with life-threatening illnesses cope by changing their perceptions about illness and its related problems. Groups, programs, books, and tapes are available.

Commonweal
P.O. Box 316
Bolinas, CA 94924
(415) 868-0970

Offers weeklong retreats at two locations: at Bolinas, north of San Francisco, California, and near Buckingham, Virginia, south of Charlottesville. The program is designed to help you reduce the stress of cancer, explore better health habits, be in the company of others in similar situations, and consider information about mainstream and complementary therapies.

Exceptional Cancer Patients (ECaP)
1302 Chapel Street
New Haven, CT 06511
(203) 865-8392

Provides individual and group counseling for patients, families, and cancer survivors.

The Health Resource
209 Katherine Drive
Conway, AK 72032
(501) 329-5272

Founded by a cancer patient who provides individualized, indepth research reports on specific health problems; includes both traditional and alternative treatments, new treatments, self-help measures, and physicians who specialize in the specific disease.

Leukemia Society of America, Inc.
733 Third Avenue
New York, NY 10017
(212) 573-8484

Provides referral to local support services. Gives financial assistance for drugs, transportation, and other treatment-related costs. (Check with your local chapter.)

Make Today Count
P.O. Box 22
Osage Beach, MO 65065

Local chapters offer patients and family members peer support groups, lectures, and speakers.

M.D. Anderson Network
(800) 345-6324 (Texas): (713) 792-2558

Matches callers with Anderson patients who have had a similar cancer or treatment.

National Alliance of Breast Cancer Organizations (NABCO)
1180 Avenue of the Americas
New York, NY 10036
(212) 719-0154

A central breast cancer information network and publisher of a newsletter and resource list.

National Association of Oncology Social Workers
1233 York Avenue, Suite 4P
New York, NY 10021
(212) 734-8891

A national organization whose members are trained to deal with the emotional issues and concerns of cancer patients.

National Coalition for Cancer Survivorship (NCCS)
1010 Wayne Avenue, 5th Floor
Silver Spring, MD 20910
(301) 585-2616

A network of groups and individuals concerned with survivorship and support of cancer survivors; acts as a clearinghouse for information, advocates for the rights of cancer survivors, and publishes a newsletter.

National Lymphedema Network
2215 Post Street
San Francisco, CA 94115
(800) 541-3259

Provides information and treatment for people suffering from lymphedema, a common but underrecognized complication from lymph node surgery and radiation therapy.

National Self-Help Clearinghouse
(800) 555-1212

Helps people locate self-help groups in their region.

National Women's Health Network
1325 G Street NW
Washington, DC 20005
(202) 347-1140

A national consumer rights group concerned with women's health needs, including those related to cancer. Publishes brochures and an informative newsletter.

Office of Cancer Communications
National Cancer Institute
Building 31, Room 1018A
Bethesda, MD 20205
(301) 496-9000

Provides current, accurate information on standard and investigational treatment; offers nutritional and emotional support.

Planetree Health Resource Center
2040 Webster Street
San Francisco, CA 94115
(415) 923-3680

Offers research packets by mail tailored to specific medical problems. Researchers draw on medical texts and computer data bases as well as on printed material geared toward the general public; both traditional and alternative approaches are covered.

Second Opinion Hotline
(800) 638-6833

Provides physician referrals for patients who would like a second opinion.

United Cancer Council, Inc.
1803 N. Meridian Street
Indianapolis, IN 46202
(317) 923-6490

Provides education programs, therapy groups, nursing, homemaking, and medication and prostheses.

United Ostomy Association
2001 Beverly Boulevard
Los Angeles, CA 90057
(213) 413-5510

Has five hundred nationwide chapters. Offers information, peer support, and new techniques and equipment; has an insurance plan for members.

Vital Options
4419 Coldwater Canyon Avenue, Suite A
Studio City, CA 91604
(818) 508-5657

Offers support to young adults with cancer.

Wellness Community
2190 Colorado Ave.
Santa Monica, CA 90404
(310) 453-2300
A program that promotes active participation by patients in their treatment and quality of life.

Y-Me Breast Cancer Support Program
18220 Harwood Avenue
Homewood, IL 60430
(800) 221-2141 (9 A.M. to 5 P.M. CST)
(312) 799-8228 (24 hours)

Provides support and counseling through its telephone hot line. Publishes a newsletter.

COMPLEMENTARY AND UNCONVENTIONAL CANCER THERAPIES

If you are interested in studying treatments offered outside of mainstream medicine, these three publications offer a wealth of information.

Unconventional Cancer Treatments. U.S. Congress, Office of Technology Assessment. Washington D.C.: U.S. Government Printing Office, 1990. A landmark government investigation of alternative cancer treatments that is considered to be a remarkably fair assessment of the major alternative therapies, although the report is not without its detractors.

Third Opinion: An International Directory to Alternative Therapy Centers for the Treatment and Prevention of Cancer. John Fink. Garden City Park, N.Y.: Avery Publishing Group, 1992, revised edition. For people who want to make informed decisions about alternative cancer care programs, support groups, and informational services.

Choice in Cancer. by Michael Lener, is a compendium covering choices in healing mainstream therapies, complementary therapies, pain control, and dying. The main focus is on complementary therapies, with major sections on spiritual, psychological, nutritional, and various specific unconventional treatments. Available from Commonweal, P.O. Box 316, Bolinas, California 94924; 415-868-0970.

You can also contact these research services:

Can Help
3111 Paradise Bay Road
Port Ludlow, WA 98365-9771
(206) 437-2291

Patrick McGrady, Jr., the founder, will send a personal computer printout of up-to-date information regarding alternative therapies, tailored to your specific case. (Requires that medical records be sent.) Send SASE for information and fees.

The Health Resource (see earlier listing)

FOR TERMINALLY ILL PATIENTS

National Hospice Organization
1901 North Moore Street, #901
Arlington, VA 22209
(703) 243-5900 for professionals; (800) 658-8898 for patients and families.

Provides general information on the hospice concept, philosophy, and services and referral to local hospice programs. Publishes an informative booklet.

Choice in Dying
250 W. 57th Street
New York, NY 10019
(212) 246-6962

A nonprofit organization that distributes information about and forms for the living will, which records the patient's wishes concerning treatment, and durable power of attorney for health care.

If you would like more information about hospices, refer to *The Hospice Movement: A Better Way of Caring for the Dying* by Sandol Stoddard (Briarcliff Manor, N.Y.: Stein & Day, 1977); *Hospice* by Parker Rossman (New York: Fawcett Columbine, 1979); *A Consumer Guide to Hospice Care* by Barbara Coleman, National Consumers League, 815 15th Street, NW, #516, Washington, DC (1985); *On Death and Dying* by Elisabeth Kübler-Ross (New York: Macmillan, 1978).

For those who wish to die at home, read *Coming Home: A Guide to Dying at Home with Dignity* by Deborah Duda, Aurora Press, Santa Fe, NM (1987).

HELP WITH THE COST OF CHEMOTHERAPY

The cost of chemo varies tremendously—from a few thousand dollars to hundreds of thousands of dollars. The drugs themselves account for a good portion of the cost: Some are inherently more expensive than others, but the dosages, the frequency and length of treatment, and the facility at which you receive them can also influence the cost. In addition to the drugs, you will be charged for the administration of the drugs, the doctor's time and examination fees, and frequent tests used to monitor your condition. Add to this any hospital charges if you are admitted for chemotherapy or any serious side effects caused by chemotherapy—plus any support services that you will require, such as additional drugs, nutritional supplements, hairpieces, psychosocial counseling, and home care personnel. Transportation and accommodations for you and/or your companions may also be a part of the total bill.

Some medical insurance policies cover chemotherapy, and some don't. Some cover chemotherapy only when administered in a hospital, not in a private doctor's office. Some cover only a percentage, some cover 100 percent, and others cover only up to a certain amount. Insurance policies do not cover transportation or accommodations, and some may not cover all the support services you need.

In some cases the reactions to chemotherapy are so severe that the patients cannot work or cannot work well while having treatment. Some must follow a reduced work schedule or work performance suffers, or prejudice and fear may cause the loss of a job. Even with medical insurance and sometimes even in spite of disability insurance, chemotherapy can be a very heavy financial burden to bear.

You can begin to cope with your financial concerns by discussing them openly with your doctor, nurse, social worker, or health insurance representative. Find out exactly what your insurance covers and how to get maximum coverage. Reading the fine print may reveal that your policy covers chemotherapy only when administered in a hospital, not in your doctor's office, and you may want to adjust your treatment plan. Make sure to keep a careful record of all your expenses and claims. Chemo can leave you exhausted and confused. If you need to, enlist the aid of your family, friends, or a social worker in filing claims and keeping records. If any claim is refused, ask why. You may need to ask your doctor to talk or write to the representative to explain why your claim meets their requirements. Discuss with your doctor the way the office submits the paperwork; sometimes the way your treatment is described influences the degree of coverage.

10-Step Plan for Submitting and Collecting Claims

Diana Bryan has generously allowed me to reproduce her system for keeping track of bills and making sure she gets reimbursed properly.

1. Make and label a folder for each quarter year of the insurance claims you have submitted. On the outside of the folder list all bills submitted, including the date submitted and the amount and date of the invoice. Put all bills (duplicates) inside the folder; each submission should be stapled together with a file card on top showing the date of submission.
2. Make and label another folder for insurance claims that have been processed and put all the paperwork accompanying the checks inside.

3. Compare submitted claims with processed claims to make sure all bills were received.

4. Try to find out what the codes on processed bills stand for. Check all rejected bills for code numbers to see if they exceed the deductible.

5. As checks come in, cross off the paid bills or bills applied to the deductible on the outside of the folder containing submitted claims.

6. Make a third folder for out-of-pocket expenses.

7. Make a fourth folder for all correspondence and notes taken during phone calls to the insurance company and your doctor. Put dates on everything; try to get the names of everyone you speak to on the phone.

8. Write or call the insurance company about uncovered bills or other discrepancies.

9. Resubmit the claim, if necessary.

10. As checks for resubmitted claims come in, cross them off the folder.

It pays to ask questions and get what you deserve. For example, you may have problems with reimbursement if your doctor has prescribed a treatment that is "off label," in other words, a use that is not specifically approved by the Food and Drug Administration and so not listed on the label for that purpose. Your doctor can help you by documenting that the labeled uses of a drug are not all-inclusive and that the usage of the claimed drug is appropriate. Another example of procedures and drugs that your insurance carrier may be unwilling to cover is the use of high-dose chemo with autologous bone marrow transplant (see p. 311).

If you are having trouble with reimbursement, you can contact the Association of Community Cancer Centers (301-984-9496) to find out if there is an association chapter in your state that is involved in solving these problems. As a last resort, some cancer patients are suing insurance companies to pay for treatments, and in many cases they are winning.

Consult with an accountant, if necessary, to receive all the federal income tax deductions allowed, including gas mileage for transportation to and from medical treatment and insurance deductibles and out-of-pocket expenses not covered by your policy.

Make every effort to continue to work. You may want to

discuss the possibility of modifying your therapy so you are less debilitated. Thoroughly utilize any support services or therapies you need to keep you physically and emotionally as strong as possible.

If you have no insurance or inadequate insurance, there are several ways to get help. For instance, you can ask a social worker about obtaining Medicare or Medicaid or some other form of public assistance to help pay your bills and about Social Security disability. The American Cancer Society, the Leukemia Society of America, and Cancer Care, Inc., are examples of sources of financial help with drugs, home care expenses such as housekeepers and nurses, transportation, equipment, and blood transfusions. Other sources of free transportation include local volunteer ambulance and fire departments, the American Red Cross, and local religious organizations. The Corporate Angels Network (914-328-6962) provides free air transportation on corporate planes to and from treatment centers when flights are available.

If you cannot afford chemotherapy, there are many ways to reduce or at least begin to whittle down the cost. One patient I spoke to had had several operations, had been misdiagnosed, and was emotionally and financially depleted. She found an oncologist who finally got her diagnosis right, and for her inoperable tumor she was put on maintenance chemotherapy that will last the rest of her life. She says: "I wrote to the company who makes my drug and pleaded my case. I said I could no longer afford my cancer. They now send me the drug for free." Her oncologist allowed his fees to accumulate and let her pay him off (very) gradually. Many pharmaceutical companies have patient assistant programs for indigent patients. Ask your doctor to contact the Pharmaceutical Manufacturer's Association (800-PMA-INFO) for their directory of Prescription Drug Indigent Program, or a representative of the company or companies that supply your drug(s). Those with known programs include Adria Laboratories, Bristol Meyers, ICI Pharmaceuticals, Lederle Laboratories, Eli Lilly, Merck, Sharpe & Dohme, Miles Inc., and Roche Laboratories.

Chemotherapy is available at some institutions for free. Veterans Administration hospitals give free treatments to veterans; Public Health Service hospitals give free treatments to former Merchant Marines and to Native Americans. The National Cancer Institute and some other cancer centers give treatments that are wholly or partly paid for by the institution. Sometimes, but not always, the treatment is experimental. Even if you have financial problems, you will rest easier if you do your homework: Investigate the treatment, the doctor, and the institution to find out if this is a situation in which you feel comfortable.

WELLNESS COMMUNITY STATEMENT

The effective treatment of serious illness requires a considerable effort by both the patient and the physician. A clear understanding by both of us as to what each of us can realistically and reasonably expect of the other will do much to enhance the outlook. I am giving this "statement" to you as one step in making our relationship as effective and productive as possible. It might be helpful if you would read this statement and, if you think it appropriate, discuss it with me.

As your physician I will make every effort to:

1. Provide you with the care most likely to be beneficial to you.
2. Inform and educate you about your situation, and the various treatment alternatives. How detailed an explanation is given will be dependent upon your specific desires.
3. Encourage you to ask questions about your illness and its treatment and to answer your questions as clearly as possible. I will also attempt to answer the questions asked by your family; however, my primary responsibility is to you, and I will discuss your medical situation only with those people authorized by you.
4. Remain aware that all major decisions about the course of your care shall be made by you. However, I will accept the responsibility for making certain decisions if you want me to.
5. Assist you to obtain other professional opinions if you desire, or if I believe it to be in your best interests.
6. Relate to you as one competent adult to another, always attempting to consider your emotional, social and psychological needs as well as your physical needs.
7. Spend a reasonable amount of time with you on each return visit unless required by something urgent to do otherwise, and give you my undivided attention during that time.
8. Honor all appointment times unless required by something urgent to do otherwise.
9. Return phone calls as promptly as possible, especially those you indicate are urgent.
10. Make available test results promptly if you desire such reports.
11. Provide you with any information you request concerning my professional training, experience, philosophy and fees.
12. Respect your desire to try treatment that might not be con-

ventionally accepted. However, I will give you my honest opinion about such unconventional treatments.

13. Maintain my active support and attention throughout the course of the illness.

I hope that you as the patient will make every effort to:

1. Comply with our agreed-upon treatment plan.
2. Be as candid as possible with me about what you need and expect from me.
3. Inform me if you desire another professional opinion.
4. Inform me of all forms of therapy you are involved with.
5. Honor all appointment times unless required by something urgent to do otherwise.
6. Be as considerate as possible of my need to adhere to a schedule to see other patients.
7. Attempt to make all phone calls to me during the working hours. Call on nights and weekends only when absolutely necessary.
8. Attempt to coordinate the requests of your family and confidantes, so that I do not have to answer the same questions about you to several different persons.

Glossary

Acute: Occurring suddenly or over a short period of time.

Adenocarcinoma: Cancer that originates in glandular tissues such as the breast, lung, thyroid, colon, and pancreas.

Adjuvant chemotherapy: Anticancer drugs used in combination with either surgery or radiation as part of the initial treatment of cancer, before detectable spread, in order to prevent or delay a recurrence. Neoadjuvant chemotherapy is given before surgery.

Allogeneic transplant: Transfer of a tissue, usually bone marrow, from one person to another.

Alopecia (al-o-pee'shah): Hair loss, a common side effect of chemotherapy drugs.

Amenorrhea (a-men-o-ree'ah): Abnormal absence or stoppage of menstruation, a side effect of chemotherapy.

Anorexia: Loss of appetite, a common side effect of chemotherapy.

Antiemetic: A drug used to reduce nausea and vomiting.

Aspiration: Removal of fluid or tissue with a hollow needle or tube.

Autologous transplant: Removal of a patient's own tissue, usually bone marrow, which is returned to the patient after chemotherapy.

Benign: Not cancerous.

Biopsy: Removal and microscopic examination of tissue from the body for purpose of diagnosis. An *exisional* biopsy removes the entire suspicious tissue; an *incisional* biopsy removes only a small portion.

Bone marrow: The spongy inner core of the bone that produces blood cells, usually affected by chemotherapy.

Bone scan: A picture of the bones taken after a radioactive dye has been injected; causes abnormalities to show up as "hot spots." Helps determine if cancer has spread to the bones.

337

Cachexia (ka-keck'see-ah): The wasting away of the body often seen in advanced cancer.

Cancer: A general term used for over a hundred different diseases characterized by abnormal, uncontrolled cell growth.

Carcinogen: A cancer-causing agent. Carcinogenesis is the cause of cancer.

Carcinoma: Cancer that originates in the epithelial tissue (glands, skin, and lining of the internal organs) of the body. Most cancers are carcinomas (80 to 90 percent).

Catheter: A rubber or plastic tube that is inserted into the body to drain fluids or deliver fluids or medication such as chemotherapy.

CEA (carcinoembryonic antigen): A tumor marker that may indicate the presence or growth of certain cancers.

Chemoprevention: Attempt to prevent cancer by giving drugs, vitamins, or minerals, or other chemicals.

Chronobiology: The study of body cycles that govern our susceptibility to disease and our response to medications.

Chemotherapy: The treatment of disease, especially cancer, with chemicals or drugs.

Chronic: Lasting a long time (as opposed to acute); said of a condition.

Clinical: Pertaining to direct observation and care of patients, as opposed to research.

Clinical trials: Studies of new cancer drugs in humans; done after studies in animals.

Combination chemotherapy: Use of two or more anticancer drugs together or sequentially.

Complete blood count (CBC): A laboratory procedure that determines the number of red cells, white cells, and platelets in a sample of blood.

Cooperative group: A group of physicians and hospitals that together take part in clinical trials, increasing the number of patients enrolled.

CT scan (computerized tomography): A type of X ray that creates cross-sectional images of the body and may show metastases better than other methods.

Cytology (sy-tol'a-jee): Scientific study of the origin, structure, and functions of cells. Cytotoxic drugs are drugs that inhibit or kill cells in the body, such as anticancer drugs.

Differentiation: Characteristic of a cancer cell; the more differentiated the cell, the more it resembles a normal cell.

Dose limiting: When the amount of some drugs that can safely be given is limited by certain risks or side effects, such as heart damage with adriamycin.

Edema (e-dee'mah): An abnormal accumulation of fluid in tissues of the body that causes swelling; a side effect of hormone therapy.

Emesis: Vomiting; an emetic is a substance that causes vomiting; an antiemetic blocks or minimizes this reaction.

Epidemiology: The study of factors that influence the frequency and distribution of diseases, such as cancer, in an effort to find the causes and therefore prevent them.

Extravasation: Leakage of an intravenous drug into the surrounding tissue.

Flow cytometry: A test done on cancer cells to determine the aggressiveness of the tumor; used to decide whether chemotherapy should be considered.

Hematologist: A physician who specializes in blood diseases and may also specialize in cancer.

Hematoma: A lump of clotted blood under the skin.

Hormonal therapy: The manipulation of hormone levels in the body; can cause a tumor to stabilize or shrink.

Immunotherapy: An experimental therapy used to stimulate the body's own defense mechanism to control cancer.

Informed consent: A legal standard (put in writing for experimental therapies) that states how much a patient must know about the potential risks and benefits of a therapy before being able to undergo it knowledgeably.

Infusion: Administration of drugs or fluids into a vein or artery over a period of time. Infusion pumps are sometimes used to infuse intravenous chemotherapy for a specific amount of time.

Intraarterial: Administered into an artery through a catheter.

Intramuscular: Injected into a muscle.

Intraperitoneal: Administered into the abdominal cavity.

Intrapleural: Administered into the space around the lungs.

Intrathecal: Administered into the spinal fluid.

Intravenous: Administered into a vein.

Investigational new drug: A drug that has been licensed by the Food and Drug Administration (FDA) for use in clinical trials but not yet approved by the FDA for commercial marketing.

Lesion (lee'zhun): A change in the structure of part of an organ or tissue as a result of disease or injury; a tumor is often referred to as a lesion.

Leukopenia: A decrease in the number of white blood cells in the blood.

Lymph nodes: Small, bean-shaped structures in the body that act as filters, collecting bacteria and cancer cells that may travel through the lymphatic system, a part of the immune system. When infection or cancer is present, lymph nodes may become enlarged and are commonly called ''swollen glands.'' Nodal involvement in cancer means that cancer cells have spread from the primary tumor site to nearby nodes.

Lymphedema: Swelling of an arm or leg as a result of damage to lymphatic vessels that connect to lymph nodes; caused by surgery or radiation.

Malaise: A state of feeling tired, with no ''oomph.''

Malignant: Life-threatening. In medical terminology it usually means cancerous as opposed to benign.

Metastasis (me-tas'ta-sis): The migration of cancer cells from the primary tumor site to other parts of the body, producing cancer spread. Metastatic cancer occurs when cancer has spread from its original site to one or more distant sites.

Modality: A method of treatment, such as surgery, radiation, chemotherapy, or immunotherapy.

Monoclonal antibodies: Substances that react with a specific type of cancer and are currently being researched to deliver drugs exclusively to tumor cells.

MRI (magnetic resonance imaging): Creates images of the body using a magnetic field and radio waves, rather than X rays, from the top, bottom, and side.

Mucositis: Inflammation and soreness of the mucous membranes of the mouth.

Myelosuppression: A decrease in the bone marrow's production of blood cells.

Nadir: The lowest point of the white cell or platelet count after chemo.

Neoplasm: A new, abnormal growth of cells, also called a tumor, which may be benign or malignant.

Oncologist (on-kol'o-jist): A physician who specializes in cancer. Oncology is the study of tumors, especially cancerous ones.

Palliation (pal'ee-ay-shun): The act of relieving or soothing a symptom, such as pain, without actually curing the cause. Chemotherapy is sometimes used for this purpose.

Pathologist: A doctor who is specially trained to interpret and diagnose the changes in body tissues caused by disease.

Prognosis: The expected or probable outcome of an illness or disease.

Prophylactic: A treatment to prevent a disease or complication that has not yet occurred but is likely to occur, such as antibiotics to prevent a bacterial infection.

Protocol: The outline or plan for a cancer treatment.

Recurrence: The return of cancer after its apparently complete disappearance.

Regression: The shrinkage or disappearance of a cancer.

Remission: The decrease or disappearance of detectable disease.

Scans: Procedures that help detect cancer or metastases of internal organs such as liver, brain, and bone.

Side effect: A second, unintentional, and usually undesirable effect from a drug or other treatment, besides the primary therapeutic effect. The primary effect of chemotherapy is to control or kill cancer cells; side effects may be hair loss or nausea.

Single-agent chemotherapy: Treatment of cancer using one drug rather than a combination of several drugs.

Staging: System for classifying cancer as to how far it has spread; helps determine the prognosis and treatment.

Stomatitis: Inflammation and sores in the mouth; a common side effect of chemotherapy.

Thrombocytopenia: A decrease in the number of platelets in the blood.

Titration: A method used to determine the smallest amount of a drug that is required to bring about a desired effect. In chemotherapy, this balancing keeps the toxicity and side effects to a minimum and the anti-tumor activity to a maximum.

Toxic: Poisonous.

Tumor: An abnormal mass of tissue that results from excessive cell division and performs no useful function; may be benign or malignant.

Bibliography and Suggested Reading

GENERAL BOOKS

Ahmed, Paul, ed. *Living and Dying with Cancer.* New York: Elsevier North Holland, 1981.

American Cancer Society. *Cancer Facts and Figures 1992.* New York: American Cancer Society (updated annually).

Beattie, Edward J., Jr. *Toward the Conquest of Cancer.* New York: Crown, 1980.

Benjamin, Harold H. *From Victim to Victor: The Wellness Community Guide to Fighting for Recovery.* Los Angeles: J. P. Tarcher, 1987.

Benson, Herbert. *The Relaxation Response.* New York: William Morrow, 1975.

Brody, Jane. *You Can Fight Cancer and Win.* New York: Quadrangle/Times Books, 1977.

Bursztajn, Harold, et al. *Medical Choices, Medical Chances.* New York: Delta Books/Dell, 1981.

Cornacchia, Harold J., ed. *Shopping for Health Care.* New York: New American Library, 1982.

Dodd, Marylin. *Managing the Side Effects of Chemotherapy and Radiation.* New York: Prentice Hall, 1987 (a consumer's guide written by an oncology nurse).

Dollinger, Malin, Ernest Rosenbaum, and Greg Cable. *Everyone's Guide to Cancer Therapy.* Kansas City: Andrews and McMeel, 1991 (comprehensive, clearly written by cancer experts).

Epstein, Samuel S. *The Politics of Cancer.* San Francisco: Sierra Club Books, 1978 (environmental carcinogens).

Fiore, Neil A. *The Road Back to Health—Coping with the Emotional Side of Cancer.* Berkeley: Celestial Arts, 1990 (based on a psychologist's personal and professional experiences).

Glassman, Judith. *The Cancer Survivors—and How They Did It.* New York: Dial Press, 1983 (inner and outer resources: alternative therapies).

Greenberg, Mimi. *Invisible Scars: A Guide to Coping with the Emotional Impact of Breast Cancer.* New York: Walker and Co., 1987.

Inlander, Charles. *Take This Book to the Hospital with You.* New York:

343

Pantheon, 1991 (revised edition) (by the president of the People's Medical Society).

Johnson, Judi, and Linda Klein. *I Can Cope: Staying Healthy with Cancer.* Minneapolis: DCI, 1988 (by one of the founders of ACS's I Can Cope program and a professional writer).

Kahane, Deborah. *No Less a Woman: Ten Women Shatter the Myths about Breast Cancer.* New York: Prentice Hall, 1990 (an educational and inspirational account of ten women with breast cancer, written by an educator and breast cancer survivor).

Kauffman, Danette. *Surviving Cancer: A Practical Guide for Those Fighting to Win!* Washington, D.C.: Acropolis Books, 1989 (resources for managing the medical, emotional, and financial aspects of cancer).

Kleinman, Arthur. *The Illness Narratives.* New York: Basic Books, 1988.

Kushner, Rose. *Alternatives—New Developments in the War on Breast Cancer.* New York: Warner Books, 1985.

LeShan, Lawrence. *You Can Fight for Your Life: Emotional Factors in the Causation of Cancer.* New York: M. Evans and Company, 1977.

———. *Cancer as a Turning Point.* New York: Penguin Books, 1990.

Levine, Stephen. *Healing into Life and Death.* Garden City, N.Y.: Doubleday, 1987.

———. *Meetings at the Edge: Dialogues with the Grieving and the Dying, the Healing and the Healed.* Garden City, N.Y.: Anchor Press, 1984.

Locke, Stephen. *The Healer Within.* New York: New American Library, 1987 (the new science of psychoneuroimmunology and the ways emotions can affect your health).

Love, Susan M., with Karen Lindsey. *Dr. Susan Love's Breast Book.* Reading, Mass.: Addison-Wesley, 1990 (good general reference for breast cancer patients by a well-respected breast surgeon and feminist).

MacDonald, John A. *When Cancer Strikes: A Book for Patients, Family, and Friends.* Englewood Cliffs, NJ: Prentice Hall, 1981.

Matthews-Simonton, Stephanie. *The Healing Family: The Simonton Approach for Families Facing Illness.* New York: Bantam Books, 1984.

Morra, Marion, and Eve Potts. *Choices: Realistic Alternatives in Cancer Treatment.* New York: Avon Books, 1987 (revised edition).

———. *Triumph—Getting Back to Normal When You Have Cancer.* New York: Avon, 1990.

Moss, Ralph W. *The Cancer Industry.* New York: Paragon House, 1991. (revised edition of *The Cancer Syndrome*).

Mullan, Fitzhugh, and Barbara Hoffman. *Charting the Journey: An Almanac of Practical Resources for Cancer Survivors.* Mount Vernon, N.Y.: Consumer Reports Books, 1990.

Nessin, Susan, and Judith Ellis. *Cancervive: The Challenge of Life after Cancer.* Boston: Houghton Mifflin, 1991.

Noyes, Diane Doan, and Peggy Mellody. *Beauty and Cancer.* A. C. Press, 1988 (how to look better while on chemotherapy or radiation or after surgery).

Reich, Paul R., M.D. *The Facts about Chemotherapy: The Essential Guide for Cancer Patients and Their Families.* Consumer Reports Books, 1991.

Rosenbaum, Ernest. *Living with Cancer.* St. Louis: C V Mosby Medical Library, 1982.

Rosenbaum, Ernest H., and Isadora R. Rosenbaum. *A Comprehensive Guide for Cancer Patients and Their Families.* Palo Alto: Bull Publishing, 1980.

Rosenfeld, Isadore. *Second Opinion: Your Medical Alternatives.* New York: Simon & Schuster, 1981.

Roth, J. S. *All about Cancer.* Philadelphia: George F. Stickley, 1985.

Rothman, Roger A. *Using Marijuana in the Reduction of Nausea Associated with Chemotherapy.* Seattle: Murray Publishing Company.

Salsbury, Kathryn H., and Eleanor L. Johnson. *The Indispensable Cancer Handbook.* New York: Seaview, 1981.

Siegel, Bernie S. *Love, Medicine and Miracles.* New York: Harper & Row, 1986.

Siegel, Mary-Ellen. *The Cancer Patient's Handbook.* New York: Walker and Co., 1986 (by an oncology social worker).

Silffer, Bill. *Life in the Shadow: Living with Cancer.* San Francisco: Chronicle Books, 1991.

Simonton, Carl O., and Stephanie Matthews-Simonton. *Getting Well Again: A Step-by-Step Guide to Overcoming Cancer.* Los Angeles: J. P. Tarcher, 1978 (visualization).

Sontag, Susan. *Illness as Metaphor.* New York: Farrar, Straus & Giroux, 1977.

Stoddard, Standol. *The Hospice Movement: A Better Way of Caring for the Dying.* New York: Vintage/Random House, 1978.

Tache, Jean, Hans Selye, and Stacey B. Dan, eds. *Cancer, Stress, and Death.* New York: Plenum, 1979.

"Guidelines for the Clinical Evaluation of Antineoplastic Drugs." U.S. Department of Health and Human Services Publication No. 81-3112. Rockville, Md.: Bureau of Drugs, Food and Drug Administration, 1981.

National Cancer Institute. *Coping with Cancer: A Resource for the Health Professional.* National Institutes of Health Publication No. 80-2080. Bethesda, Md.: National Institutes of Health, 1980.

U.S. Congress. Senate. Subcommittee on Investigations and General Oversight of the Committee on Labor and Human Resources. *Examination of Deficiencies in the Use of Experimental Drugs on Cancer Patients.* 97th Cong., 1st Sess., 1981, and 2nd Sess., 1982.

NUTRITION AND GENERAL HEALTH

Bohannon, R., et al. *Food for Life: The Cancer Prevention Cookbook.* Chicago: Contemporary Books, 1987.

Borsenko, Joan. *Minding the Body, Mending the Mind.* New York: Bantam

Books, 1988 (practical exercises to promote physical and emotional well-being and an active role in healing).

Brody, Jane. *Good Food Book: Living the High Carbohydrate Way.* New York: Bantam Books, 1987.

Cousins, Norman. *Anatomy of an Illness.* New York: W W Norton, 1979.

Dadd, Debra Lynn. *Nontoxic, Natural and Earthwise.* Los Angeles: Jeremy P. Tarcher, 1990 (how to select products that are safe for you and the environment).

Downing, George. *Massage Book.* New York: Random House, 1972 (a classic how-to).

Fishman, Joan, and Barbara Anrod. *Something's Got to Taste Good: The Cancer Patient's Cookbook.* New York: New American Library, 1981.

Goodhart, Robert S., and Maurice E. Shils. *Modern Nutrition in Health and Disease.* Philadelphia: Lea & Febiger, 1980, sixth edition.

Hofer, Jack. *Total Massage.* New York: Grosset & Dunlap, 1976.

Lieberman, Shari, and Nancy Bruning. *The Real Vitamin and Mineral Book.* Garden City Park: Avery Publishing, 1990 (how to create your own vitamin and mineral program to supplement a wholesome diet).

Ornstein, Robert and David Sobel. *The Healing Brain: Breakthrough Discoveries about How the Brain Keeps Us Healthy.* New York: Simon & Schuster, 1987.

———. *Healthy Pleasures.* Reading, Mass.: Addison-Wesley, 1989.

Ramstack, Janet L., and Ernest H. Rosenbaum. *Nutrition for the Chemotherapy Patient.* Palo Alto: Bull Publishing, 1990.

Reingold, Carmel Berman. *The Lifelong Anti-Cancer Diet.* New York: New American Library, 1982.

Weil, Andrew. *Natural Health, Natural Medicine.* Boston: Houghton Mifflin, 1990.

Self-Care Catalog and Journal. 349 Healdsburg Avenue, Healdsburg, CA 94558 (products and articles about health and fitness, including massage, exercise, stress reduction).

The American Cancer Society and the National Cancer Institute also publish material on diet and cancer.

PERSONAL ACCOUNTS

Reading other people's personal accounts gives you a reassuring glimpse at what other individuals have gone through, although these experiences may or may not resemble your own. Many of these stories also contain medical and practical information and can give you a sense of not being alone, which you may find helpful.

Blumberg, Rena. *Headstrong.* New York: Crown, 1982.

Brady, Judy, ed. *1 in 3: Women with Cancer Confront an Epidemic.* Pittsburgh: Cleis Press, 1991 (the social, interpersonal, environmental, and political dimensions of cancer).

Brinker, Nancy, with Catherine McEvily Harris. *The Race Is Run One Step at a Time: My Personal Struggle—and Everywoman's Guide—to Taking Charge of Breast Cancer.* New York: Simon & Schuster, 1990.

Frank, Arthur. *At the Will of the Body: Reflections on Illness.* Boston: Houghton Mifflin, 1991.

Gunther, John. *Death Be Not Proud.* New York: Harper & Row, 1949.

Hargrove, Ann. *Getting Better.* Irvine, Calif.: CompCare, 1988.

Howe, Herbert M. *Do Not Go Gentle.* New York: W W Norton, 1981.

Ireland, Jill. *Lifewish.* New York: June, 1988.

Kelly, Orville E. *Until Tomorrow Comes.* New York: Everest House, 1979.

Mullan, Fitzhugh. *Vital Signs: A Young Doctor's Struggle with Cancer.* New York: Farrar, Straus & Giroux, 1983.

Murcia, Andy, and Bob Stewart. *Man to Man: When the Woman You Love Has Breast Cancer.* New York: St. Martin's Press, 1988 (by men who are married to women with breast cancer).

Photopulos, Georgia. *Of Tears and Triumph.* New York: Cogden & Weed, 1988.

Radner, Gilda. *It's Always Something.* New York: Simon & Schuster, 1989 (comedienne Gilda Radner tells about her experience with ovarian cancer).

Rollin, Betty. *First, You Cry.* New York: Signet, 1978.

Ryan, Cornelius, and Kathryn Morgan Ryan. *A Private Battle.* New York: Simon & Schuster, 1979.

Sattilaro, Anthony J., with Tom Monte. *Recalled by Life.* Boston: Houghton Mifflin, 1982 (personal account of cancer treatment with a macrobiotic diet).

Spingarn, Natalie Davis. *Hanging in There: Living Well on Borrowed Time.* Briarcliff Manor, N.Y.: Stein & Day, 1982.

ARTICLES IN GENERAL AUDIENCE PUBLICATIONS

Boffy, Philip. "Cancer Progress: Are the Statistics Telling the Truth?" *New York Times*, Sept. 18, 1984, page C-1.

"Cancer Survivor Advocacy." *Health Facts*, newsletter of the Center for Medical Consumers. February 1991, page 1 (includes criticisms of the "war on cancer").

"Chemotherapy: A Dull Weapon." *Innovation*, health letter of the Foundation for the Advancement of Innovative Medicine. Spring/Summer 1991, page 26 (translation of an article in the German magazine *Der Spiegel* about Ulrich Abel's findings).

Poppy, John. "Last Rights." *Longevity.* (Dec. 1991): 38–58 (on living wills).

ARTICLES IN PROFESSIONAL JOURNALS

Averette, H. E., et al. "Effects of Cancer Chemotherapy on Gonadal Function and Reproductive Capacity." *CA* 40 (4): 199–209 (1990).

Bailar, John C. III. "Rethinking the War on Cancer" *Issues in Science and Technology*: 16–21 (Fall 1987).

Bailar, John C. III, and Elaine Smith. "Progress Against Cancer?" *New England Journal of Medicine* 314:1226–1232 (May 8, 1986).

Begg, Colin B., et al. "Participation of Community Hospitals in Clinical Trials." *New England Journal of Medicine* 1076–80 (May 6, 1982).

Blair, Steven. "Low Fitness Levels Associated with Increased Mortality." *Journal of the American Medical Association* 263: Nov. 3, 1989.

Cairns, John, and Peter Boyle. "Cancer Chemotherapy." *Science* 220:254–256 (1983) (criticisms of cancer mortality statistics, with a reply).

Carl, William. "Oral Complications in Cancer Patients." *American Family Physician* 27 (2): 161–170 (Feb. 1983).

Carter, Barbara J. "Going Through: A Critical Theme in Surviving Breast Cancer." *Innovations in Oncology Nursing* 1989; 5(4):2–4.

Christ, Grace H. "A Psychosocial Assessment Framework for Cancer Patients and their Families." *Health and Social Work* 8(1): 57–64 (Winter 1983).

Dreizen, Samuel. "Nutritional Deficiencies in Patients Receiving Cancer Chemotherapy." *Postgraduate Medicine*. 87(1): 163–170 (Jan. 1990).

Gold, Joseph. "Hydrazine Sulfate: A Current Perspective" (review article). *Nutrition and Cancer* 9: 59–66 (1987) (interrupts the wasting away of advanced cancer cachexia).

Hanson, P. G., and D. K. Flaherty. "Immunologic Responses to Training in Conditioned Runners." *Clinical Science* 60(2): 225–228 (Feb. 1981).

Hegsted, D. M. "Optional Nutrition." *Cancer* 43(5): 1996–2003 (May 1979).

Hrushesky, W. M. J. "Circadian Timing of Cancer Chemotherapy." *Science* 228: 73–75 (April 5, 1985).

Loescher, Lois, et al. "The Impact of the Cancer Experience on Long-Term Survivors." *Oncology Nursing Forum* 17(2): 223–229 (1990).

———. "Surviving Adult Cancers (part I): Physiological effects." *Annals of Internal Medicine*. III(5): 411–432 (1989).

Lokich, Jacob. "Improved Cancer Chemotherapy: Benefits of Delivery by Infusion." *Postgraduate Medicine* 87(2): 239–246 (Feb. 1, 1990).

Mahler, Ellen L. "Anomic Aspects of Recovery from Cancer." *Social Science Medicine* 16: 907–912 (1982).

Maule, W. F., and M. C. Perry. "Management of Chemotherapy-Induced Nausea and Emesis." *American Family Physician* 27 (1): 226–234 (January 1983).

Maxwell, Mary B. "Scalp Tourniquets for Chemotherapy-Induced Alopecia." *American Journal of Nursing* 80 (5): 900–903 (May 1980).

Melzak, Ronald. "The Tragedy of Needless Pain." *Scientific American*. 262(2): 27–33 (Feb. 1990).

Morrow, Gary R., and Christine Morrel. "Behavioral Treatment for the Anticipatory Nausea and Vomiting Induced by Cancer Chemotherapy." *New England Journal of Medicine* 307(24): 1476–1480 (Dec. 1982).

Renshaw, Domeena. "How Cancer Patients and Their Families Cope with Cancer." *Medical Opinion* 73: 843–848 (August 1975).

Scott, Diane W., et al. "The Antiemetic Effect of Clinical Relaxation: Report of an Exploratory Pilot Study." *Journal of Psychosocial Oncology* 1(1): 71–84 (Spring 1983).

Silverfarb, Peter, et al. "Chemotherapy and Cognitive Defects in Cancer Patients." *Annual Review of Medicine* 34: 35–46 (1983) (review article).

Speigel, David, et al. "Effect of Psychosocial Treatment on Survival of Patients with Metastatic Breast Cancer." *The Lancet* ii: 888–891 (1989).

Stoll, B. A., and Santilal Parbhoo. "Treatment of Menopausal Symptoms in Breast Cancer Patients" (letter). *The Lancet*: June 4, 1988.

Trounce, J. R. "Antiemetics and Cytotoxic Drugs." *British Medical Journal* 286(6362): 327–329 (Jan. 1983).

Welch, Deborah, and Keith Lewis. "Alopecia and Chemotherapy." *American Journal of Nursing* 80(5): 903–905 (May 1980).

Welch-McCaffrey, D. W., et al. "Surviving Adult Cancers (part II): Psychosocial implications." *Annals of Internal Medicine* III(6): 517–524 (1989).

Winningham, M. L. "Walking Program for People with Cancer: Getting Started." *Cancer Nursing* 14(5):270–276 (1991).

Winningham, M. L., et al. "Effect of Aerobic Exercise on Body Weight and Composition in Women with Breast Cancer on Adjuvant Chemotherapy." *Oncology Nursing Forum* 16(5): 683–689 (1989).

Anticancer Research 3: 59–62 (1983). Vitamin E was found to reduce free-radical damage in experimental animals that were given anticancer chemotherapy. The authors conclude that this provides strong evidence for the protective use of vitamin E in cancer-free animals. They further suggest that its use during anticancer therapy is theoretically advisable because it may reduce the toxicity of some drugs without reducing their effectiveness. The authors cite several other studies that report the benefits of large doses of vitamin E and other antioxidant vitamins to cancer patients.

Journal of Nutrition, Science, and Vitaminology 31: 129–137 (March–April 1985). The antioxidants alpha-tocopherol and coenzyme Q inhibited lipid peroxidation caused by the chemotherapy drug adriamycin but did not interfere with the suppression of DNA synthesis in cancer cells.

Medical Tribune. 23: 23 (March 1983). Breast cancer patients with higher blood levels of vitamin A responded twice as well to chemotherapy as did women with lower levels. The authors also cite research reporting an association between improved chemotherapy response and higher vitamin A levels for patients with cancer of the breast and bowel and for melanoma.

Wieneke, Mary H. (1992–in process). Neuropsychological sequelae of cancer chemotherapy in adult breast cancer patients. Doctoral dissertation, California School of Professional Psychology, Berkeley/Alameda.

MEDICAL TEXTS

DeVita, Vincent, Jr., et al. *Cancer: Principles and Practice of Oncology.* Philadelphia: J B Lippincott, 1990 (third edition).

Frie, Emil III, and James Holland, eds. *Cancer Medicine.* Philadelphia: Lea & Febiger, 1982.

Greenspan, Ezra M., ed. *Clinical Interpretation and Practice of Cancer Chemotherapy.* New York: Raven Press, 1982.

Holland, Jimmie C., and Julia Rowland, eds. *Handbook of Psychooncology: Psychological Care of the Patient with Cancer.* New York: Oxford University Press, 1989.

Johnson, B. L., and J. Gross. *Handbook of Oncology Nursing.* New York: John Wiley, 1985.

Zhang, Dai-zhao. *The Treatment of Cancer by Integrated Chinese-Western Medicine.* Boulder: Blue Poppy Press, 1989. Zhang is a specialist in the treatment of cancer in Beijing. Since the mid-1970s he has been working with integrated Chinese-Western medicine. "Since neither modern Western nor traditional Chinese medicines in themselves treat cancer totally satisfactorily, attempting to combine the two approaches offers the possibility of capitalizing on the strengths of each system as well as using one system to neutralize or ameliorate the shortcomings of the other" (from editor's preface).

Up-to-date information about specific forms of cancer and treatments may be found in the journals geared toward health professionals and indexed in the *Index Medicus*. This index and a selection of professional publications may be found in large public libraries and in medical libraries. Some MEDLARS centers, available at medical libraries and hospitals, will provide computer data base searches for nonprofessionals. If you have trouble getting access to any of these sources, ask a physician or other health professional to help or contact the National Cancer Institute and ask about Physician's Data Query, a computerized data base.

BOOKLETS

The National Cancer Institute, the American Cancer Society, and many cancer centers provide booklets on chemotherapy and its side effects and other aspects of cancer upon request. Especially useful NCI publications include *Chemotherapy and You, Eating Hints—Tips and Recipes for Better Nutrition During Cancer Treatment, Taking Time: Support for People with Cancer and People Who Care about Them, Facing Forward: A Guide for*

Cancer Survivors, When Someone in Your Family Has Cancer, and *Cancer Survivorship: An Annotated Bibliography.*

Coping: Living with Cancer is a quarterly magazine published for cancer patients and their families. P.O. Box 1700, Franklin, TN 37065.

Index

About the Author

Nancy Bruning has counseled cancer patients informally and was a volunteer at the Memorial Sloan-Kettering Cancer Center in New York. A writer with a particular interest in health and medicine, her other books include *Swimming for Total Fitness* (with Dr. Jane Katz) *The Real Vitamin & Mineral Books* (with Shari Lieberman) and *Breast Implants; Everything You Need to Know.* She is a board member of Breast Cancer Action, an education and advocacy group based in San Franciso, where she now makes her home.